MUNTU WA NZAMBI
PORTRAIT OF HUMAN AS GOD'S SPECIAL CREATION

FROM AFRICAN CREATION STORIES,
RELIGIOUS BELIEFS, AND
CULTURAL PRACTICES

Tshilemalema Mukenge, PhD
with the collaboration of Muadi Mukenge, Editor

MUNTU WA NZAMBI
PORTRAIT OF HUMAN AS GOD'S SPECIAL CREATION

FROM AFRICAN CREATION STORIES,
RELIGIOUS BELIEFS, AND
CULTURAL PRACTICES

TSHILEMALEMA MUKENGE, PhD
WITH THE COLLABORATION OF MUADI MUKENGE, EDITOR

ABOUT THE AUTHOR

Tshilemalema Mukenge (formerly Léonard Mukenge), is a retired Professor, and Professor Emeritus from Morris Brown College, in Atlanta, Georgia, USA. While at Morris Brown, he founded the Africana Studies Department and served as its Chair. His research interests to the present have expanded from family and religion among the Luba of Congo (1967), to culture and customs of the Congo (2002), and now to the portrait of Human from the African universe of creation stories and religious beliefs. In recent years, he has developed a strong interest in reformulating written academic knowledge from Luba ethnography into a language that the general public can understand and appreciate. Among his publications, he is the author of *Culture and Customs of the Congo*, by Greenwood Press. Born in the Democratic Republic of the Congo, Dr. Mukenge is the founder and leader of *Coins of Hope*, a charitable ministry in Congo that provides education to the youth and functional literacy to adults in preventive health and sustainable farming. Dr. Mukenge holds a PhD in Social Anthropology from McGill University, Montreal, Canada. He is married to Dr. Ida Rousseau Mukenge, Professor of Sociology, Morehouse College, in Atlanta. They have four children Ndaya (deceased), Muadi, Tshimpo (wife Jewett), and Malongo; and three grandchildren: Mfumu Ngoyi, Mulaya kudi Maweja, and Kazadi Mukumbaji.

A Madu-Ndela Press Book
Philadelphia, PA
www.madundelapress.com

Cover Art: David Chukwuka
                                              (at GLOWLOGO-2020)

Interior and Composition: Madu-Ndela Press
                                              www.madundelapress.com

Copyright © 2021 by Tshilemalema Mukenge, with the collaboration of Muadi Mukenge, MA.

All rights reserved. This book, or parts thereof, may not be reproduced in whole or in part, or transmitted in any form, or by any means electronic, mechanical, photocopying, recording or otherwise without permission from the publisher, except by a reviewer who may quote brief passages in review.

ISBN-13: 978-1-7368586-0-8

TO
THE GLORY OF GOD
CREATOR, INSPIRER
WHO MAKES ALL THINGS POSSIBLE.

TABLE OF CONTENTS

Acknowledgments	I
Introduction	3
PART ONE: THE HUMAN SELF IN SELF	15
Chapter 1. A Spiritual Being in a Physical Body	17
Chapter 2. A Moving Body Full of Vitality	51
Chapter 3. A Speech Master	69
Chapter 4. A Creative Mind	95
PART TWO: THE HUMAN SELF IN INTERACTION WITH THE SPIRITS	119
Chapter 5. A Firm Believer in God	121
Chapter 6. A Fervent Devotee of the Spirits	143
PART THREE: THE HUMAN SELF IN INTERACTION WITH FELLOW HUMANS	163
Chapter 7. An Ethic-bound Community Member	165
Chapter 8. A Family-Kinship Community Builder	181
Chapter 9. A Compassionate Caretaker of Fellow Humans	205
Chapter 10. A Freedom Seeker and Nation Builder	233
PART FOUR: THE HUMAN SELF IN INTERACTION WITH THE NATURAL ENVIRONMENT	253
Chapter 11. A Steward of Community's Natural Resources	255
Chapter 12. An Explorer and Transformer of Spaces and Civilization Builder	283
CONCLUSION	315
Cited Academic Bibliography	321
Index	331

LIST OF TABLES

Table 1: Similar Manga Practices (Luba-Dagbamba)	30
Table 2a: Repartees between Non-human Characters about their Imperfections	76
Table 2b: Repartees between Non-human Characters about their Imperfections (Continued)	77
Table 2c: Repartees between Non-human Characters about their Imperfections	77
Table 3a: Single Digits in the Yoruba and the Luba Number Systems	82
Table 4b: Base Numbers in the Yoruba and the Luba Number Systems	82
Table 3c: Ten Plus in the Yoruba and the Luba Number Systems	83
Table 4: Sample of God's Names and Exclusive Attributes	123
Table 5: Palm Tree Uses in Luba Society	136
Table 6: Sample Minerals per African Country	138
Table 7: Statements of Innocence and Corresponding Natural Rights	168
Table 8a: Appropriate Kinship Terminology by Generation	197
Table 8b: Appropriate Kinship Terminology by Generation (Continued)	197
Table 9a: Elaborate Cow Naming System of the Hema People of the Congo and Uganda	267
Table 9b: Elaborate Cow Naming System of the Hema People of the Congo and Uganda (Continued)	268
Table 10: Somalia's International Trading Partners across the Centuries	307

ACKNOWLEDGMENTS

To an extent, this book is an elaboration on selected episodes from my life history. It starts with experiences from my youth in *Luba* villages in *Eastern Kasai, Democratic Republic of the Congo, DRC*. For that, I am grateful to my parents and other adults who introduced me to Luba culture, including the aspects discussed in the book. My first research project consisted of ethnographic interviews conducted in Luba villages in the 1960s to produce a publishable academic work required for graduating from college. Here, my gratitude goes to the men and women I interviewed, to my professors at Lovanium University, Kinshasa, Congo, who trained me and directed my work, and to the *Institut de Recherches Economiques et Sociales de L'Université Lovanium* that published my research, which immediately became a landmark in *Luba* studies and has remained so to date. My interest in other Congolese cultural studies came about in the 1970s when Abbé Vincent Mulago, then Professor in the Department of Religion at Lovanium University, published a compilation of extracts from studies on Bantu traditional religions, including one from my above mentioned study. Some of the extracts are among the major sources used in writing this book. To Abbé Mulago, and to the authors of those sources, I am indebted. In the 1980s, I expanded my research zone to include Africa outside the Congo in response to a demand by students at Morris Brown College, in Atlanta, Georgia, for an academic program in Africana Studies. To implement the new curriculum, I developed a course in ancient African civilizations which I taught for several years to college students. I also once used it in a workshop for Fulton County's elementary and high school teachers. My wife, Dr. Ida Rousseau Mukenge, Professor of Sociology at Morehouse College, Atlanta, Georgia, helped me with editing the course. Twice in the 1990s, she and I translated the course into Portuguese for educators in Salvador, Bahia, Brazil. She did the typing and we hired a native Portuguese speaker for editing. Without Ida, this particular experience, the many study trips we have made to Brazil and all I have learned about Afro-Brazilians, including the topics included in this book, would not have been possible. To her I am deeply obliged. Following the experiences in Brazil my interest in creation stories, belief systems and related cultural practices expanded far beyond the Luba and other Congolese ethnicities, to include ethnic groups from all over Africa. This book is a project in synthesizing findings from the works of many academic writers I have drawn from, some extensively. I have also supplemented academic sources with digital media sources where appropriate and needed. I am very grateful to all the authors whose works I have drawn from in writing this book. My deep gratitude also to Mr. Asar Imhotep, founder and owner of Madu-Ndela Press, for publication of this book; and to a sister and friend, Dr. Musau WaKabongo, former faculty member at Des Moines University Medical Center and former Director of the Placer County Public Health Laboratory, in California, for stepping in to help secure a meaningful picture for the

Acknowledgements

book front cover. Finally, I would like to express my deep gratitude to my daughter *Muadi Mukenge* for exhorting me to put a closure to the writing of this book and get it published, for editing the entire manuscript, and for spearheading the negotiations, conversations, and exchanges with the publisher. She also played a pivotal role in checking the book proof copy.

—Tshilemalema Mukenge, PhD
Coins of Hope
Atlanta, GA
July 2021

Introduction

Muntu wa Nzambi, this book's title, is in *Ciluba,* or *Tshiluba,* a language spoken by the Luba people of Eastern and Western Kasai provinces in the *Democratic Republic of the Congo, DRC. Muntu wa Nzambi*, pronounced *Moontoo wa Nzâmbe,* means *Human of God, Human belonging to God. Muntu* is God's special creation, Human in God's ideal form – at its best. *Human* as a noun stands for human being, man or woman, young or old. It is accepted as indisputable truth that the human being is God's special creation and steward of God's other creations on Earth. This book addresses a puzzle I had: "What concretely characterizes this special being?" For an answer, I turned to creation stories, religious beliefs, and cultural practices from Africa beginning with my life experiences and ethnographic research I conducted among the Luba of the Congo DRC. Then, I moved to monographs, comprehensive books, anthologies, and articles about ethnic worldviews and customs from the Congo and across Africa. This investigation led me to identifying dominant themes common to various African ethnic groups. Finally, an intensive study of the themes and the topics discussed therein enabled me to draw a portrait of the African as a multi-faceted character in multiple concurrent networks of interaction.

The book is written to the attention, not of the scholars and experts in the field, but of newcomers who would like to increase their understanding of African religious and related cultural practices from the angle of African believers and practitioners. Many individuals from different parts of Africa who grew up at the time when African religion was disparaged by Christian missionaries and agents of the colonial administration as paganism and superstition, grew up with little exposure to this religion. Some developed attitudes of condescendence toward African people's religious practices. Not knowing nor valuing these practices, they could not pass them over to their children. There thus came to exist at least a generation of parents and a generation of children who lack the exposure. However, with the decolonization of Africa and increase in efforts to revalue ancestral traditions, a growing number of people today, out of nostalgia, seek to know more about their ethnic traditions, or African traditions in general. Also, many African Americans who want to reconnect with Africa culturally find some meaningful connections in worldviews and religious practices. Afro-centric intellectuals, clergy and lay people alike, and seminary students are some of the social circles this book is intended to reach and who, we believe, will benefit from it.

1. CREATION PROCESSES AND THE MAKING OF HUMAN

The core of the book consists of recurrent themes taken from religious traditions across Africa, first from my personal family life experiences, and then personal ethnographic interviews I conducted in Luba villages, in Eastern Kasai, Congo DRC. Most themes were derived from the works of researchers on beliefs and customs of ethnic groups in the Congo and other countries of Africa. The most fundamental theme and starting point is the existence of only one God who is the eternal Supreme Being and omnipotent Creator of the universe and all that exists in it, visible and invisible. Africans across the continent share this view. The narratives of how creation unfolded differ from group to group. Students of African religions, belief systems, and worldviews have identified several modes of creation. These include creation by self-emanation, by the word, by manual action, by breathing, and by gesture (Morlighem et Fourche 1973, Kalanda 1992, Mudimbe 1991, and Zahan, in Olupona 2000). Zahan (in Olupona 2000) reports a single case of creation by vomiting found in the creation story of the Kuba of the Congo. The self-emanation mode of creation is creation by divine thought, that is, emergence of a being or a thing that has never existed before and that is brought into existence by the mere fact of God conceiving the existence of that being or thing. This mode of creation is also called metamorphosis (Mudimbe 1991, Morlighem et Fourche 1973, Kalanda 1992). Creation by the word—thingification of God's word—found in the creation story of the Dogon of Mali, for instance, is also known as creation by divine speech or creation by naming (Carruthers 1995, in Beatty 2001), or summoning. In some cases summoning was accompanied with gesture. Creation by a manual action involves manipulation of some already existing, God-created matter. *Olódùmarè*, God of the Yorùbá, sent *Arch-Divinity Orìshà-nlá* with a bucket of dry soil, along with the pigeon and the hen to help him dry a pre-existing, God-created, marsh. As the divinity dropped the soil from the bucket, the pigeon and the hen spread it over the marsh until it became a dry land. Thus, was created Planet Earth (Idowu 1994). The Luba creation story combines the metamorphosis and naming modes and adds creation by the gesture and creation by exhaling the breath of life. *Maweja Nangila*, God, first metamorphosed Self into three Lord Spirits notably: *Maweja Nangila* (Creator), *Maweja wa Cyama* (Firstborn Son), and *Maweja Cyama* (First Lady). Thereafter, by the same process, *Maweja Nangila* brought *Mulopo Maweja,* the Emissary, fourth lord spirit, into existence (Kalanda, 1992). Thus there came to be four Lord Spirits:

Maweja Nangila:	the Creator Spirit,
Maweja wa Cyama:	the Firstborn Son Spirit,
Maweja Cyama:	the First Lady Spirit, and
Mulopo Maweja:	the Emissary Spirit.

Maweja Nangila resorted to three specific powers inherent in Him: the word, the gesture, and the breath of life. He created things that do not blink, such as the rain, stones, grass, and trees by the power of His word alone. For example, He created rain simply by saying: "Let there be rain." And rain there was. "Let there be trees." And trees there were. "Let there be grass." And grass there was. And so on. As to creatures other than humans that have eyes and can see, *Maweja Nangila* created them by way of a gesture followed by the naming word. He created insects by slowly moving and extending His lips forward while holding his breath and, finally, saying: "Let such insect species appear." And the insect species instantly appeared. He created animals by pointing his index finger forward and saying; "Let such animal species be." And the animal species appeared. The most distinctive feature about the creation of the human being is that, regardless of the actual processes in particular cases, God infused essential elements of God's divine nature into the physical structure that became the human body. In the Yorùbá story, *Olódùmarè,* God, commissioned *Arch-Divinity Orìshà-nlá* to build the physical structure into which *the Creator Himself* blew the divine breath of life to create the human being. In the Luba story, *Maweja Nangila* created the human being by the combined power of His divine breath and divine word. He filled His lungs with his breath and forcefully exhaled on the Earth saying: "Let there be *Gentleman*" (*Mukalenga Muluma*). And the *Gentleman* appeared. *Maweja Nangila* filled His lungs with His breath again and forcefully exhaled on man, saying: "Let there be *Gentle Lady*" (*Mukalenga Mukaji*). And the *Gentle Lady* appeared (Kalanda, 1992: 95-98). As a product of these creation processes, humans possess qualities of being that are similar to God's qualities, with the difference that God's qualities are more perfected and constitute the ideal African believers strive for in their religious endeavors. Qualitative similarities with the Creator distinguish human from God's other terrestrial creations. Not only does sharing the divine essence from creation make the human being a resemblance of God, but also of other beings who share God's spiritual nature, notably: divinities and ancestors (Idowu 1994, Kalanda 1992, Carruthers 1995, in Beatty 2001, Zahan, in Olupona 2000, Atal 1997).

2. THE HUMAN SELF IN SELF

The human in self means human as an entity considered from the standpoint of its make-up and characteristics. The most significant constitutive element is the divine breath of life incarnated in the human body, known in African religious thought studies as life force or vital force. The vital force keeps the body alive. Its departure from the physical body brings about death. The vital force does not exist nor does it operate in isolation. It is always a member of a cluster of inner forces which condition human destiny on earth. All ethnic groups have their own names and descriptions of the vital force and its cognate inner forces. For example, The Akan of Ghana identify four major aspects to the human being: *okra, sunsum, ntoro,* and *mogya*. **Okra** is the guiding spirit, bearer and instrument of a person's destiny. At a person's death his *okra* returns to God to justify his earthly existence. Only human beings have *okra* and it is the crucial factor in a person's identity. **Sunsum** is the spiritual substance that is responsible for character, genius, temper and quality. It may leave the human body during sleep and is susceptible to attack by witchcraft. **Ntoro** represents the total sum of a person's inherited characteristics. It is transmitted from man to children. **Mogya** represents reason in a person, which is a major necessary characteristic of a human being. After the person's death the *mogya* becomes *saman*, ghost, and is the one which is invoked in ancestral veneration (Abraham, 1974). The Zulu, the Yorùbá, the Kongo, the Luba, and other African ethnic groups, all have their own knowledge and understanding of the inner spirit and its innate, life-sustaining cognate forces.

Also inherent in African religious thought is the widespread belief that, at creation, God endowed humans with extraordinary mystical powers. For instance, the Azande believe that their art of magic and knowledge of making medicines are gifts from God.

Introduction

Likewise the Ewe believe that God created the first man and magic simultaneously (Mbiti, 1970). In the Luba creation story, *Maweja Nangila* created human beings with twelve orifices on their bodies: (1) the *mouth*, (2&3) the *two nostrils*, (4&5) the *two eyes*, (6&7) the *two ears*, (8) the *urethra*, (9) the *anus*, (10) the *fontanel pit*, (11) the *occipital pit*, and (12) the *epigastric pit*. He also endowed them with considerable mystical powers, along with the ability to release these powers through the twelve orifices. At the time of creation, Earth was part of the *Sky of the Summit* where *Creator Maweja Nangila* and great spirits live, which is located beyond the sky that we see. At the time, Earth and Sky were close to each other. Later, *Mulopo Maweja, Emissary Spirit*, last of the four lord spirits, rebelled against the *Creator Maweja Nangila* (the other two lord spirits were: *Firstborn Son, Maweja wa Cyama* and *First Lady Spirit, Maweja Cyama*). *Maweja Nangila* expelled *Mulopo Maweja* from the Sky of the Summit along with Earth and all its inhabitants. As a consequence of this punishment, human lost three important power-releasing orifices: *the fontanel, the occipital pit*, and *the epigastric pit*, along with the ability to release powers through them. To date, however, here and there, individuals, men or women, are being born with supernatural powers above ordinary people's powers. Witches and sorcerers use their powers to harm individuals they hate for some reason. Diviners, medicine-men or women, and seers use theirs to do good, including counteracting the malevolent actions of the evildoers (Kalanda, 1992).

The belief in threats to life by witches prompts and justifies the use of charms and medicines to stunt evildoers' malevolent plans, protect the individual or the community from other harms, or enhance one's chances of success in profitable undertakings. Along with mystical powers, at creation, God endowed the human being with the gifts of immortality or the power of resurrection after dying. This belief is found among the Khoikhoi, the Meru, the Akamba and the Zulu, for instance (Mbiti, 1970). Also widespread across Africa is the belief in the reincarnation of the spirits of the dead. According to this belief, newborn babies are returning spirits and arc to be welcomed with special rituals commensurate with their respective spiritual identities. The immortality of the body inherited from divine creation terminated with the breaking of the initial relationship with God whereas the human spirit remains immortal forever. Because of the limitations of the physical body, the human spirit is less powerful than pure spirits such as the spirits of ancestors or cultural heroes. But from creation, humans were endowed with the potential for spiritualization as mediums through trance or priests through consecration. Spiritualization through trance or consecration to priesthood is practiced throughout Africa.

Creation was an act of empowerment, a divine project for human enablement, not only for the spirit, but also the body and the mind. Enablement of the body can be seen in the story of the Fon of Benin. *Gu*, the firstborn son of the first created couple, *Mawu* and *Lisa*, had a head in the form of a tool that his parents used to shape the human form. After establishing humans on earth, *Gu*'s parents - *Mawu* and *Lisa* - changed his shape to that of a metal blade embedded in a rock. They then sent him to Earth to teach human beings how to make and use tools, thus enabling them to grow food and build shelters. That divine creation was an act of enablement is also portrayed in the story of the Dogon of Mali. The first human species *Amma*, God, brought into being were seven *skilled* professionals including the weaver, the blacksmith and the tanner. It is reported that in the post-creation era life was at its best. Sickness and death did not exist. Human and animal species were climbing up and down between Earth and Heaven. This is to say that physically, the human being, product of divine creation, is meant to be an apt body full of vitality, including the ability to move and to perform various manual tasks. The legendary Dogon professionals included a speech master who also assumed the function of teacher. Also, Creator *Amma* developed the faculty of speech and the ability to communicate meanings in all seven professions (Carruthers, 1995). Thus, the African human is called to master the art of articulate language. In one *Bambara* and Fulani story, life originated in a nine-division egg that gave birth to twenty marvelous beings representing all the forces and types of knowledge existing in the universe. To create the human being, *Maa Ngala* took a bit of each of the creatures from the egg and mixed all the bits and then blew a spark of his own name on the mixture. From this emerged *Maa*, the original ancestor of the humankind. Through his name, *Maa*, which is part of *Maa Ngala*'s own name, and through the divine spark infused into it by *Maa Ngala*, the new being contained something of *Maa Ngala* himself. Part of it was the mind. Another part was *Kuma*, the divine word that enabled *Maa* to activate his great potential (Caruthers, 1995). Human beings' mental faculties of insights, discernment, judgment, and creative imagination can be seen as outgrowth of this development.

The above observations—and many others by scholars of African worldviews, religion, and customs—have led us to visualize the human character, the special product of divine creation, as existing both structurally and qualitatively; that is, by his constitutional make-up and defining attributes, a spiritual being in a physical body full of vitality. The spiritual dimension is manifested in the presence and operations, in the human body, of the divine life principle and its cognate innate life-sustaining forces; mystical powers from divine creation, including personal magical protections; and the potential for spiritualization through trance or consecration while still on earth and reincarnation after death. The post-creation era appears to have been one of abundant living and exuberant life vitality: the Creator had provided for all material needs; sickness and death did not exist. Also, in some stories, the first legendary inhabitants of the Earth were versatile professional handymen equipped with productive tools. In addition to physical vitality, the human being has the ability to emit sounds and express ideas in articulate language. Articulate speech is a major definitional characteristic of humans. One of the professionals in the Dogon creation myth was speech master and teacher. A sound creative mind is another determinant characteristic of humanity. *Maa Ngala,* Creator of the Bambara and Fulani, through speech and the blowing of a spark from His mouth, transferred to the first human being part of His own name, *Maa*, and something of himself consisting of the mind and of *Kuma*, the divine word that enabled *Maa* to activate his great potential (Carruthers, 1995). In summary, structurally and qualitatively, the human self, product of divine creation, is a spiritual being in a physical body, an apt body full of vitality, a speech master, and a creative mind.

3. THE HUMAN SELF IN NETWORKS OF INTERACTION

The Human Self in Interaction with the Spirits. The human character, product of divine creation, does not exist, nor does it operate in isolation. He is always an active participant in networks of relationships with spirits, other humans, and living forces of the natural environment. The world of the spirits includes the Creator, divinities, ancestors, and nature spirits. The Creator is acknowledged and revered as the omnipotent Most High whose nature and magnitude the human mind cannot understand. He is the loving father who made Earth habitable and provided for humans even before creating them. For instance, *Olódùmarè* first sent *Divinity Orìshà-nlá* to earth to dry out the pre-existing marsh and turn it into a habitable dry land with the help of the hen and the pigeon. Afterwards, he sent him again with the hen and pigeon, but this time to be raised for meat and the palm tree for food, oil, and drink. He made lagoons for drinking water and sent the rain to fertilize the land and allow it to produce crops (Idowu, 1994). Another example, Creator *Ngai,* having provided the land of the Gikuyu with abundant natural diversity, took *Gikuyu* to the top of Mount Kenya and from there showed him the vast plain surrounding it. The plain was beautiful, populated with diverse and countless species of trees and animals. Ngai informed Gikuyu he had made them for him and his descendants (Jefferson and Skinner, 1990).

Divinities are the highest ranking spirits second only to the Creator. As God's mediators to the humans, some divinities participated in the creation process. Thus among the Luba, as *Maweja Nangila* created things, *Maweja wa Cyama* ordered them in his capacity of Firstborn Son, and *Maweja Cyama* conserved and fructified them as is expected of the *First Lady*. Other divinities serve as ministers in God's government among the living. For instance, among the Igbo, *Chi-Ukwu* is the Supreme God, Creator; river goddess *Nne Mmiri/Uhammiri* and dry-land goddess *Onabuluwa*, contribute to the making of human destiny by challenging the individual during the crossroad between conception and birth to make a choice between the destiny given them by *Chi-Ukwu* and a hidden one that may turn out to be better or worse. Water Goddess *Ogbuide* of Lake *Oguta* and deities of adjoining rivers regulate and protect activities that depend on water availability and fluctuations such as farming, fishing and water transportation. Trade is an important source of livelihood in Igboland. Igbo villages are connected through networks of markets held on different days to allow for inter-village circulation of traders, trade goods, and farm produce. Each market day is dedicated to a particular goddess (Jell-Bahlsen, in Olupona 2000).

Of all spiritual interventions, sacrifices to ancestral spirits are the most conspicuous. For instance, Luba people made sacrifices of chicken to ancestors in circumstances such as when one's enterprising activities, such as farming and trade enable one to acquire chickens for raising; when a man's family grows with the marriage to his first wife or the birth of a child from any of his legitimate wives; at the harvest of the first corn of the major rainy season; upon moving into a new residence; to reinstitute a wife that one has repudiated by conspicuously throwing out her personal belongings and cooking utensils; and at the fulfillment of a vow for which a sacrifice of chicken was promised. They sacrificed goats for major causes or circumstances, such as:

1. When, through his work, a man realizes great things, such as raising goats or procuring a wife for himself or for a relative.
2. Each time one receives the bridewealth from the marriage of a daughter.
3. When a request for which one had promised a sacrifice of goat has been fulfilled.

Introduction

For example: A man can promise his ancestors a sacrifice of goat if they give him a child or if they help a relative get out of prison. Then, if a new baby is born into his family, or if the relative in question is released from prison, everyone will see in this event the ancestors' response to his request. Consequently, he will feel obligated to honor his promise.[6]

4. In payment of fines for major offenses, such as insulting and beating an elder
5. When a man places his wives and children under the protection of the guardian spirit *Nkambwa*. This sacrifice is called *mbuji wa cikongo*, unity goat (Mukenge, 1967).

God's mediator spirits to humans include nature spirits. The Mongo of the Congo honored nature spirits called *Bilima*. The most generous *Bilima* favored human beings with abundant progeny: they were addressed as grandmothers. It is quite a widespread African custom for a person who is a source of generosity to be affectionately referred to as mother even if that person is a male. Grandmothers here is used in the sense of those who have provided for their offspring unceasingly and for a long time (Hulstaert 1961, in Mulago 1973). In brief, the African human in interaction with the spirits can be characterized as a firm believer in God's eternal existence and omnipotence, in divine creation, and in divine providence; and a fervent devotee of the spirits, including God, divinities, ancestors, and nature spirits.

The Human Self in Interaction with Fellow Humans: From creation stories, the human being is predestined to live in community and build communities of the likes. The first human inhabitants of earth in the Yorùbá story were a group of heavenly hosts brought over by Divinity *Orèlúéré* on *Olódùmarè's* request. The original ancestors of humans among the Dogon were a group of seven professionals with complementary skills: a blacksmith, a weaver, a tanner, a speech maker, and others. God endowed them, in addition, with the potential for developing articulate speech and communicating meanings. He also provided them with a set of rules to live by as a community.

Building human communities on Earth began with the divine institution of marriage. In the Mande story, marriage on Earth was preceded by differentiation, on the mythical plan, of seeds of life into pairs of male seeds and female seeds placed by Creator *Mongala* in the Egg of the World. Everywhere throughout Africa, the first couple was invested with the mission to procreate and multiply. Human multiplication gave birth to two phenomena: formation of kinship communities and migration to distant places. Kinship-based communities exist all over Africa as rural villages, such as the case among the Luba and the Kongo; urban towns, as in the case of the Songye of the *Congo*; or else as wards in a larger urban settlement, as found among the Yorùbá. Distant migration was implied in the creation story of the Luba when Creator *Maweja Nangila* brought together man-*Ngoyi* and woman-*Pemba*, and entrusted them with the mission to procreate and send their progeny away along the rivers where they would multiply. It is also reported that the descendants of *Odùdúwà*, the founding father of the Yorùbá people, left the birth city of Ile Ife and founded new communities throughout Yorùbáland (Idowu, 1994).

Human being's innate forces associated with the principle of life include consciousness of right and wrong in relationships with fellow humans and other of

Introduction

God's creations. The human being is born into a community of the living regulated by moral precepts which are protective of both the individual and the community. Moral precepts are evoked in plea of innocence and in pronouncement of conviction for wrong doing. A Luba man who experiences an unexplainable misfortune would declare his innocence saying, for example: "I have not killed anyone; I have not taken another man's wife; nor have I stolen anyone's property..." In pronouncing punishment, the judge or the lightning controller would tell the perpetrator: "Because you have taken another person's property or because you have molested a minor, you have brought upon yourself such or such punishment."

Every man or woman is called to contribute to the expansion of the community through marriage, procreation, and socialization of children into adult roles. All creation stories involve the bringing together of man and woman and the mandate to procreate or an anticipation of future progeny. In Africa, the nuclear family of father, mother, and children is only a constitutive segment of the true family, the extended family, a cluster of families from the closest known common ancestor. In turn, the extended family is a segment of a more comprehensive kinship-based community, the clan or a higher-level lineage. Often, communal ownership of land and other resources of the immediate environment characterizes the human community at this level. Community membership confers one free access to community's resources. All African societies have mechanisms regulating access to community's resources by both members and non-members. Most of mutual support and care among the members takes place at the extended family and clan levels. Here is where care for the household and the guests, the children, and the sick and the dying is most intensive and most emotionally felt.

At a higher level of human involvement, in networks of interaction with fellow humans, stands the national community, an amalgamation of kinship communities of diverse descents distributed over a larger geographic territory under common authority. Creation stories also suggest that in the making of communities the Creator wanted some individuals to assume leadership functions. *Olódùmarè* appointed Arch-Divinity *Orìshà-nlá* to lead the missions to create Earth and Divinity Orèlúéré to preside over the crew of heavenly hosts who became the first inhabitants of Earth. Among the Mande of Mali, when the time came to send human seeds to Earth, Mongala, God, transformed the original placenta of the world into an arc and placed *Faro*, a resurrected male seed, on top of the arc along with eight original male ancestors of humans from the same placenta as *Faro*, accompanied by animals and plants. The arc became the new Earth. *Faro* became distributor of *Mongala*'s divine blessings to other divinities. To *Simboumba Tangnagati* he gave the first 30 words and the 8 females seeds from Go's clavicles, making him responsible for the seeds, the rain, and speech. In turn, Simboumba Tanganagati gave some of the seeds to Kanisimbo who transformed part of Earth into a field and planted the seeds as petals in the form of cardinal points on the four sides of the field – east, west, north, and south (Dieterlen, 1955).[1]

In general, national communities are hierarchical, in that some of the member communities exercise power and authority over others whereas one oversees them all. A natural penchant is for the communities at a particular level to strive to maintain autonomy from each other while some challenge the authority of the one above. These two tendencies often force the national community to be on alert against both internal rebellions and external encroachments. In view of the above observations about human's involvement in networks of interaction with fellow humans, the human self can be characterized as an ethic-bound community member, a family-kinship builder, a compassionate caretaker, and a freedom seeker and nation builder.

The Human Self in Interaction with the Natural Environment: From creation, humans and other living species are called to live together and to cooperate to make life better for all. *Divinity Orìshà-nlá* built Planet Earth with the cooperation of the hen and the pigeon. As he was dropping loose soil on the pre-existing marshy land, the hen and the pigeon spread the soil until dry land was formed. *Chameleon* inspected the land twice to make sure it was firm enough for permanent occupation by multitudes of living species. On *Orìshà-nlá*'s second Earth-building trip, the hen, the pigeon and the palm tree traveled along to become permanent sources of food for humans. In the post-creation era, humans and animal species are reported to have lived in harmony and mutual support, debating issues of common interest, including sending delegations to God to inquire whether there should be death or not. Today, human-nature solidarity and mutual support are manifest in totemic relations between humans and certain animal or plant species, in attitudes of reverence toward medicinal plants, and in emotional care for some domesticated animals and plants. The Gikuyu people's totemic relations of mutual support with the sycamore tree and the Ethiopian farmers' life-long dedication to caring for the life-sustaining teff grass are some relevant living examples. Well-known also is the pan-African admiration for the legendary baobab tree. It is revered for its varied nutritional, medicinal and spiritual functions.

A related inclination of animal and human species is exploration of the unknown from the immediate environment outward into far distant places. To a large extent, divine creation stories are adventures into the unknown. For instance, Creator *Olódùmarè* sent *Divinity Òrìshà-nlá* to dry a pre-existing marsh that would become Earth. There is no indication *Òrìshà-nlá* had any previous knowledge of the location of the marsh. His flying there was an adventure into the unknown. After *Òrìshà-nlá* completed his mission satisfactorily, *Olódùmarè* appointed Divinity *Orelúerè to lead a* crew of heavenly hosts who become the first humans on Earth. The crew landed on a location until then unknown to them, which became Ile Ife, *Yorùbá* people's city of origin. A version of the Egyptian creation story has it that *Atum-Re* sent *Shu* and *Tefnut* on a mission to establish the world. It took them too long before returning. In the meantime, *Atum-Re* became very concerned about their safety. Believing they were lost, he removed his eye and sent it searching for them. The eye found them and brought them back to *Benben, Atum-Re's* residence. Evidently *Shu* and *Tefnut* did not know where they would establish the world. Neither did the eye know where to search for them. They all ventured into the unknown like if by faith (Mark, 2016).[2] The history of Africa is actually a history of explorations of near and distant unknown spaces by agents such as *the hominids, the first peoples, the Nubians, the Ethiopians, the Bantu migrants,* and the *Nilote conquerors*. These explorers became settlers where they went. Others, such as the Phoenicians and the Somalis, established trading networks between distant countries and across continents. Observed in relation to its interactions with the natural environment, the human-being qualifies to be classified as a steward of the community's natural resources and explorer and transformer of spaces.

4. PERSPECTIVES

Researchers have sought to characterize African traditional religion by its similarities or differences with other religions. Cheik Anta Diop (1991) and Jacob Hudson Carruthers (1995), for example, were concerned about establishing similarities between today's African religious traditions and the religion of Ancient Egyptians. Father Placide Temples (1965) and Abbé Vincent Mulago (in Olupona 1991), Gerhardus Cornelis Oosthuizen (in Olupona 2000) and many others have compared African religion to Christianity. In more recent years, new emphasis has been placed on the resurgence of African religious expressions that had been suppressed during colonization (Awolalu, in Olupona 1991). Some of these resurgences have given a more African face to Christianity (Obeng, in Olupona 2000). Such comparative approaches are legitimate. They ought to be applied with caution, however, to avoid the bias of trying to force African religion into a definition based on foreign standards of what a religion should be (Olupona 2000, xvi). Instead, Olupona recommends a phenomenological approach that attempts to apprehend the essence of religious phenomena through African people's own subjective definitions and behavioral expressions inherent in various cultural creations such as myths, proverbs, stories of origin, healing rituals, funerary rites, divination séances, public festivals, or witchcraft and sorcery practices (Olupona, in Olupona, Editor, 1991). From phenomenological data, one could also extract qualitative meanings that are reflective of the particular situation in which the phenomenon takes place (Olupona, Op. Cit.). A similar approach used in anthropology of religion focuses on symbolic meanings and functions of the phenomenon under observation. To give an example, in Ancient Egyptian religion, *Sun* was praised as the Creator when emphasis was placed on his life-giving powers; whereas every morning's rising sun, which indicated victory of light over darkness and life over death, symbolized the resurrected sun god. For its part, the sun's unchanging course through the sky was a symbol of justice (Frankfort, 2000).

Two related theoretical assumptions have served as guiding principles for interpreting the phenomena under consideration throughout this study:

1. Cultural behaviors and products are symbolic (carriers of meanings shared by the members of the community), holistic (made up of many interrelated parts forming units), and subject to change over time in adaptation to natural and social environments.
2. Cultural behaviors are better understood when studied in their natural milieu, intensively, holistically and diachronically.

Theoretically, the phenomenological approach dominates throughout this book as an attempt "to apprehend the essence of religious (and other cultural) phenomena through African people's own subjective definitions and behavioral expressions present in creation stories, proverbs, legends, funeral rituals, baby welcoming rituals and adolescent initiation ceremonies, chiefly and royal rituals, and other common cultural practices. Also evident all throughout the book is the comparative approach, particularly the search for similarities of meanings inherent in distant phenomena and practices. Linguistically, emphasis has been placed on the *emic* view (understanding the meanings

Introduction

and values that native speakers attach to their concepts and corresponding behavioral expectations) versus the *etic* view (the researcher's objective criteria for classifying meanings and values) (Goodenough, 1956). Where appropriate, I have also applied *holistic functional analysis*: looking at elements as integrated mutually-influencing parts of a whole (Parsons, 1951); *ethnomethodology*: using kinship terminology to map out and categorize patterns of interaction among relatives (Sturtevant, 1964); and *linguitico-ecological perspective*: explaining concepts that have ecological connotation in terms of spatial orientation, such as the position and direction of the rivers in the area (Crapo, 1987). On occasion, I have explained situations in terms of acculturative change, that is, change imposed by a dominant culture on a dominated culture (Ferraro 1992, Kapalan 1960), such as in a colonial context.

5. PORTRAIT OF HUMAN AND ORGANIZATION OF THE BOOK

When put together, the characteristics of Muntu identified in previous sections of this chapter constitute the portrait of human this book discusses. The book discusses twelve attributes (each in a separate chapter) divided into four parts. ***Part One*** analyses four constitutional attributes of the human self and its respective structural and operational characteristics. These are: (1) a spiritual being in a physical body comprised of the divine spirit in a cluster of cognate innate vital forces; mystical powers, from divine creation, to perform extraordinary acts; incorporated spirits as mediums or ordained priests; and reincarnated spirits of newborn babies. (2) a moving body full of vitality: endowed with flexible vibrant moving limbs, optimal bodily performance aptitudes, and agile versatile productive hands; (3) a speech master: gifted in expressing ideas in varied types of articulate speech; and (4) a creative mind: possessing the faculties of insights, discernment, and judgment fostering personal behavioral adjustments to some shared community standards; and creative imagination, that is, the ability to conceive ideas and turn them into symbolic representations as concrete actions or objects. ***Part Two*** highlights two attributes of the human self in networks of interactions with the spirits as (5) a firm believer in God's eternal existence and omnipotence, in divine creation, and in divine providence; and (6) a fervent devotee of the spirits, notably: God, divinities, ancestors, and natural spirits. ***Part Three*** describes in four chapters the characteristics of the human self in networks of interaction with fellow humans as: (7) an ethic-bound community member endowed with sacred natural rights, subject to moral restraints, and accountable for moral transgressions; (8) a family-kinship community builder through marriage, procreation, and socialization of children into adult roles; tracing biological links to common ancestors; and participating in collective sacred rituals, blood pacts, or kinship-based community politics; (9) a compassionate caretaker of fellow humans: care for the household and hospitality for guests, care for children, and care for the sick and the dying; and (10) a freedom seeker and nation builder: an agent in pursuit of free access to the community's natural resources, territorial autonomy, and national unity. Lastly, ***Part Four*** investigates, in two chapters, the attributes of the human self in interaction with the natural environment as: (11) a steward of community's natural resources: stewardship of land and connected natural resources, animal raising and care, and care for domesticated plants; and (12) an explorer and transformer of spaces and civilization builder: personified in *African* history by the *hominids*, *the first peoples*, the *Nubians*, the *Ethiopians*, the builders of the civilization of the *Western Sudan*, the *Bantu* migrants, the *Nilote* conquerors, and long-distance traders such as the *Phoenicians* and the *Somalis*, the *Twaregs* and the *Dyula*.

Through these multiple attributes of the human being derived from creation stories, religious beliefs, and cultural practices, the book articulates the theological foundations of African religion. In its totality, the book offers a comprehensive view of the human being from an original African-centered perspective.

(Endnotes)

1   Dieterlene, G. 1955. "Mythe et organisation sociale au Soudan français." *Journal des Africanistes/ Année 1955/25/pp 39-76* https://www.persee.fr/doc/jafr_0037-9166 1955_num_25_1_1873. Retrieved 4/30/2018

2   Mark, Joshua J. 2016. "Gods & Goddesses of Ancient Egypt – A Brief History." *Ancient History Encyclopedia.* https://www.ancient.eu/article/884/gods--goddesses-of-ancient-egypt---a-brief-history/ Retrieved 1-16-2020.

PART ONE

HUMAN IN SELF

Chapter 1: A Spiritual Being in a Physical Body
Chapter 2: An Apt Body Full of Vitality
Chapter 3: A Speech Master
Chapter 4: A Creative Mind

Chapter 1

A Spiritual Being in a Physical Body

> 1. Innate Divine Life Forces
> 2. Special Mystical Powers from Divine Creation
> 3. Call to Spiritualization while on Earth
> 4. The Gifts of Immortality and Reincarnation

African creation stories portray the human being as God's special creation on Earth: above all a spiritual being in a physical body. There are many more aspects to the human being than the organs and the fleshy and bony physical apparatus. The spiritual aspects outweigh the physical ones in resemblance to God. First, there is the breath of life infused through divine creation and a complex of cognate vital forces. Next come special mystical powers which have also originated from divine creation. Third, there exist all across Africa, sacred practices whereby human beings are elevated to higher spiritual statuses. Finally, there are the gifts of the immortality and reincarnation of the spirit through birth.

1. INNATE DIVINE LIFE FORCES

The Inner Divine Spirit

In all African creation stories, the making of the human being occurs at the very end of the process, suggesting that God wanted to make the human being the finishing touch of divine creation. "It is as if God exists for the sake of man" (Mbiti 1970, 119). There exists a common belief among Africans that God infused essential elements of God's-self into the structure that became the human being. The processes of infusion vary. According to the Yorùbá, *Olódùmarè*, the Creator, gave Arch-Divinity *Orìshà-nlá,* the mandate to make the physical structure of the first human being, but *Olódùmarè* Himself gave life to the structure by exhaling the divine breath of life into it. In the Luba story, *Maweja Nangila* first filled His lungs with his breath and forcefully exhaled on the earth saying: "Let there be Gentleman" (*Mukalenga Muluma*). And Gentleman there was. *Maweja Nangila* filled His lungs with His breath again and forcefully exhaled onto man, saying: Let there be Gentle Lady" (*Mukalenga Mukaji*). And Gentle Lady there was. In the creation story of the Bambara and Fulani of West Africa, *Maa Ngala*, God, first created a wondrous egg with nine divisions, each representing a particular state of existence. The egg gave birth to twenty marvelous beings representing all the forces and types of knowledge existing in the universe. To create the human being, *Maa Ngala* took a bit of each of the creatures from the egg and mixed all the bits and then blew a spark of his own name on the mixture. From this emerged *Maa,* the original ancestor of humankind. Through his name, *Maa*, which is part of *Maa Ngala*'s own name, and through the divine spark infused into it by *Maa Ngala*, the new being contained something of *Maa Ngala* himself. Part of it was the mind. Another part was *Kuma*, the divine word that enabled *Maa* to activate his great potential. Through the divine word, *Maa Ngala* initiated *Maa* into the secrets of the universe. Conceived in this manner, the human being is above all a spiritual essence in a physical body. As a product of this process, humans possess qualities of being that are similar to God's qualities, with the difference that God's qualities are more perfected and constitute the ideal African believers strive for in their religious endeavors. Qualitative similarities with the Creator distinguish human from other God's terrestrial creations. Not only does sharing the divine essence from creation make the human being a resemblance of God, but also of other beings who share God's spiritual nature, notably: divinities and ancestors (Idowu 1994, Kalanda 1992; Caruthers 1995, in Beatty 2001; Zahan, in Olupona 2000; Atal 1997).

The Inner Divine Spirit and Cognate Life-Sustaining Forces

God's spirit infused through the creation process is the greatest divine presence in the human body. It is the principle of life or life sustaining power generally referred to in African religious parlance as life force, or vital force. The vital force keeps the body alive. Its departure from the physical body brings about death. The vital force does not exist nor does it operate in isolation. It is always a member of a cluster of inner forces which condition human destiny on earth. All ethnic groups have their own names and descriptions of the vital force and its cognate inner forces. The illustrations below are drawn from the *Zulu* of South Africa, the *Akan* of Ghana, the *Yorùbá* of Nigeria, the *Kongo* and the *Luba* of the Congo, DRC; and the ancient Egyptians.

The Cosmology of Zulu of South Africa: In the cosmology of the *Zulu* of South Africa, the human being is an individualized portion of the Cosmic Ocean, of which he represents all the attributes. Human action is influenced by seven principles: (1) *itongo* – ray, (2) *utiwetongo* – spiritual mind, (3) *utiwomuntu* – human mind, (4) utwesilo – animal mind, (5) *amandhla* – lower mind, (6) *isitunzi* – etheric body, and (7) *umzimba* – physical body. *Umuzimba* alone refers to the physical body. The other principles represent different elements of the mind which permeate the body and influence human action. Below, the seven principles are presented in decreasing order of their respective powers (Bowen 1993).

Zulu Seven Principles that Influence Human Action

>*Itongo*/Ray: This is the highest level of spiritual power in the human body. It exists in the form of ray emanating from the Universal Spirit (Almighty God) and informs all lower manifestations of the Universal Spirit.

>*Utiwetongo*/Spiritual Mind: Represents spiritual Consciousness, which is a higher level than human Consciousness.

>*Utiwomuntu*/Human Mind: Its manifestations are human Consciousness, intellect, and human emotions, from among others.

Utiwesilo/Animal Mind: At this level, Mind takes the form of passions, emotions, and instincts.

Amandhla/Lower Mind: The portion of Mind that includes the life force and other forms of energy that animate the human body.

Isitunzi/Etheric Body: This is the human body as the medium through which Amandhla, Lower Mind, operates.

Umzimba/Physical Body: The human body as flesh and blood. (Adapted from P.G. Bowen 1993).

Spiritual Elements of the Human Being in Akan Worldview

The Akan identify four major aspects to the human being: *okra, sunsum, ntoro,* and *mogya*. Their respective roles are explained below:

Okra: The guiding spirit, bearer and instrument of a person's destiny. At a person's death his *okra* returns to God to justify his earthly existence. Only human beings have *okra* and it is the crucial factor in a person's identity.

Sunsum: The spiritual substance that is responsible for character, genius, temper and quality. It may leave the human body during sleep and is susceptible to attack by witchcraft.

Ntoro: Represents the total sum of a person's inherited characteristics. It is transmitted from man to children.

Mogya: Represents the reason in a person, a major necessary characteristic for making one a human being. After the person's death the *mogya* becomes *saman*, ghost and is the one which is invoked in ancestral veneration (Abraham 1974).

The Human Structure in the Belief System of the Yorùbá of Nigeria

That the human structure is complex can also be seen in the Yorùbá thought. The major components are *ara-ẹda , émi, okàn, orí,* and *orí-inú*.

Ara: Body—The human being's visible physical structure, first built by Divinity Orìshà-nlá during the Creation process.

Èmi: Spirit, invisible part of the human being, infused in the human structure by Creator Olódùmarè personally. It is the source of the breath that manifests the presence of life in the body. Its departure from the body coincides with death.

Okàn: Heart as the seat of emotions and psychic energy.

Orí: The physical head, also used in the sense of Orí-inú, the inner person, the personality-soul.

Orí-inú: The internal head, of which the physical head is the symbol; the inner-person, essence of personality. The Orí-inú rules, controls, and guides the life and activities of the person. Orí-inú, essence of being, comes directly, and is different from its source, Orisè, Olódùmarè, the Creator (Idowu 1994).

The Human Self in the Cosmology of the Kongo of the Congo, DRC

The Kongo of Congo identify six essential components of the human being and two extensions.

Moyo: Principle of life, divine life-sustaining force, survives death and journeys to the water, *ku masa*, also called *ku bazingila*, living space, home.

Nitu: The human body as sacred, that is, as permeated by the principle of life. It is the part of the human being that has the capacity to leave the flesh and the bodily envelop and operate independently.

Nsuni: This is the human body as flesh similar to an animal's flesh.

Mfumu Kutu: Kind of double soul, principle of sensible perception; resides in the ear; is the human essence that is projected in the shadow; disappears at the person's death.

Vuvulu: The human body as a physical structure

Menga: Blood; through the blood, the life-sustaining principle, *moyo*, permeates the entire human body and makes it sacred. Menga houses the person's supernatural force (Adapted from Van Wing 1959, quoted in Mulago 1973).

The Kongo recognize two extensions to human essence located outside the individual. These are the *shadow* and the *name*. Human essence persists in body reflections. The shadow and the name are such reflections. Wherever the individual is, there is also his/her shadow. The name is part of a person's essence. That is why it changes with status change (Adapted from Van Wing 1959, quoted in Mulago 1973).

The Human Self in Luba Conception

In Luba thought, the human being is comprised of three abstract components: the principle of life, the inner voice, and the soul; and the physical body. Two elements of the physical body, the heart and the blood, have an identity and significance of their own as relates to life. There is also the belief that severed body parts continue to carry the essence of the person to whom they belong. Even body reflections like the shadow and the voice can be mystically manipulated to produce some effects in the person who projects them. Three physical vital components of self and four metaphysical components are briefly explained below in that order.

Components of Human Self in Luba Conception

Physical Vital Components of Self:

Mubidi	*Moyo*	*Mashi*
Body	Heart	Blood

Metaphysical Aspects of Self:

Moyo	*Moyo*	*Moyo*	*Muvu*
Principle of Life	Conscience, Inner Voice	Soul	Double

Mubidi*, *Body, is the physical apparatus made of flesh and bones, includes both the external parts and the internal organs.

Moyo*, *Heart, is an internal organ located inside the chest. It functions as an engine, as a massive pump whose beats send *Mashi*, *Blood*, to different parts of the body thereby keeping the being alive.

Moyo*, *Principle of Life and Organ of Life. The power that keeps a living creature alive is *moyo*, principle of life. The term *moyo* also designates the organ of life, the heart. A beating heart indicates the presence of the principle of life in one's body. The Luba phrase for being alive is *kwikala ne moyo*, to have life (literally, to be with life). The antithesis is *kukuula moyo* (to breathe one's last). The end of heart beat signifies the separation of the principle of life from the body, a phenomenon named *lufu* (death).

Mashi*, *Blood, is physiologically connected to both *moyo* principle of life and *moyo* organ of life. *Moyo*, the life-sustaining principle, enables the *moyo* organ of life to beat, which in turn enables *mashi*, blood, to circulate, carrying the *moyo* principle of life across different parts of the body. As carrier of the principle of life, *mashi* is sacred. Each part of the body in which it circulates becomes permeated with the principle of life also, therefore sacred as well.

Moyo*, *Greeting Formula. Additionally, *moyo* is the greeting formula in Ciluba, the language of Luba peoples of Kasai: Luba Lubilanji, Luba Luntu, and Luba Luluwa. To greet a single individual, one says: "*Moyo webe aau*," or preferably, "*Moyo Maamu*" (Greetings Madame), or "*Moyo Taatu*" or "*Moyo Mukalenga*" (Greeting Sir). Both greeting formulas mean: "Life be with you". The response is "*Moyo weebe peebe aau*," when addressing a single individual; or "*Moyo weenu peenu aau*," when addressing many. Either greeting formula means: "Life be also with you".

Moyo*, *The Inner Voice. Moyo also designates the inner voice, *moyo wa munda*, that is, conscience. For instance, someone who has resisted the temptation to take someone else's property would say: "*Meema ne ngangata, moyo ubenga,*" "As I was to take it my heart (conscience) said no." Similarly, the Luba translation for double conscience is *myoyo yibidi*, literally, two hearts. *Myoyo* is plural of *moyo*.

Moyo, Soul. Finally, *Moyo* is also used as the location of internal states, good (*moyo mulenga*) and bad (*moyo mubi*), associated with the soul, thus a swarm of emotions, such as:

Exhilaration, joy: *moyo wa disanka*
Dyalukila dya tuutwenda dyakamupesha disanka dya bungi ku moyo:
His big brother's return brought exhilaration to his heart.

Grief, sorrow: *moyo wa dibungama*
Mvwa mumvwa dibungama dyabungi mu moyo wanyi:
I felt deep sorrow in my heart (soul).

Lufu lwa mulunda wenda lwakamutwa ku moyo bikola:
His friend's death deeply broke his heart.

Nostalgia: *dyangamwa*
Mwana udi ne moyo wa mamwenda:
The child misses its mother.

Love: *moyo wa dinanga*
Moyo wa buledi wa bu maamu wakapandisha mwanenda ku lufu.
Motherly love saved her child from death.

Jealousy: *moyo wa lubaabu*
Wakanyema lubaabu lwa baana baabo bwa byuma bivwaye nabi.
He ran away from his relatives' jealousy for his wealth.

Envy: *moyo wa lukuka*
Moyo wa lukuka lwa byuma bya bakwenda wakamusaka ku dibanyoka.
Envy for his fellows' wealth led him to hitting them.

Extensions of the Human Essence to Severed Body Parts and Body Reflections

Moyo principle of life permeates the entire human body and remains inherent in a person's body parts such as the hair and the nails even after they have been severed from the body. Individuals with mystical powers are capable of causing harm to a person they dislike by perpetrating acts of aggression on that person's lost body parts. Likewise, a person's clothes, especially those that have been in close contact with that person's body, continue to carry his or her essence, his or her personhood. So does the dirt from the baby's body that remains in the bath water. Footprints also are a person's extension outside the body. Only a living person can walk and leave footprints in the sand. An evil-hearted individual possessing some supernatural power can manipulate any of these elements to hurt the person whose essence they continue to carry.

Detached Body Parts Still Permeated with Self:

nsuki	*nzadi*	*tumvi twa mwana*
hair	nails	newborn baby's feces

Objects that Have Been in Close Contact with the Body:

bilamba:	*mâyi a mu cizaba cya mwana*:
clothes	dirt from the baby's bath water

buloba bwa mu dikasa
soil from the footprint

The Voice: *Moyo* principle of life extends beyond the body in some other ways. The voice is one. An ill-intended action by a person controlling some supernatural power can cause similar damage to that person as if the action were actually directed at the person's body physically. To prevent that from happening, adults in Luba villages did not instantly respond vocally to an identifiable live caller. To protect themselves when called from outside the house by an unidentified voice, they would listen carefully first. Then, they could ask: "*Nganyi weetu aau*?" "Which of our own is that one?" At night, they would first answer by clapping hands. Only after the caller had identified himself or herself, could the person being called respond verbally by naming the caller saying: "So and So, is that you?"

    The Shadow. The shadow is a person's other extension outside the body. Only a living person can stand and have his body featured outside of him or her in the form of shadow. A controller of supernatural powers smashing the head of a person's shadow or beating it with a stick can cause the same effect on that individual as if these evil acts were perpetrated on the person's body proper. Likewise, a mystically empowered individual can harm a person by appealing to maleficent powers while piercing with a knife the reflection of that person's head in a mirror, a basin containing water, or a river. He or she can produce similar effects in a person's life by evoking the same powers while plunging a knife into that person's picture at the location of the heart.

The Human Self in Ancient Egyptian Thought

Like the Kongo and the Luba, the ancient Egyptians identified both the essential components of the human personality and extensions. The elements are: the *ka*, the *ba* and the *akh*; the extensions are the *name* and the *shadow*.

> **Ka**: The most essential constitutive element was the *ka*, the life force spirit, inherited from the creator through the process of creation and transmitted through the parents' generation after generation. The *ka* incorporates an individual's unique personality qualities and characteristics, and also represents the person's double.

Ba: A second personality element called *ba,* was associated with the body of a person after death. The *ba* could travel independently outside the tomb, visiting the places the person enjoyed frequenting while on Earth, and periodically unite with the body.

Akh: A third constitutive non-physical element was the *akh*, a spirit known for bridging the terrestrial world and the afterlife, interceding on behalf of the living or the dead (Diop 1991).

The Name and the Shadow: According to the ancient Egyptians two elements still carried the essence of a person after his or her death, notably: the *name* (*ren*) and the shadow (*k^{h}ayebet* or *shu*). The *name* expressed the person's true nature and was inscribed on his mummy wrappings or statue to identify him. A person's *shadow* was believed to emanate from that person's god, representing the divine power, and symbolizing the god's presence within the person (David ND, Diop 1991).

2. SPECIAL MYSTICAL POWERS FROM DIVINE CREATION

A Widespread Belief across Africa

A widespread belief across Africa is that, at creation, God endowed humans with special spiritual gifts, not only the power to do extraordinary things, but also rejuvenation and immortality of the human body. In other words, the humans were meant to live eternally. If they died of old age or accidentally, they would resurrect reinvigorated and continue to live again in permanent harmony and happiness (Mbiti ND). In the post-creation time, Heaven, God's abode, and Earth, humans' abode, were contiguous. God and the humans lived in close proximity of each other. The humans and the animal kingdom lived in conviviality and harmony. But some incident occurred that trickled change in the God-humans relationship. In some mythical stories, a creature such as the jackal or the serpent was responsible. In others, humans were the perpetrators of whatever happened. In any case, heaven and earth separated as a consequence. Humans lost their original supernatural powers. Nevertheless, until this day, now and then, here and there, individuals are being born with extraordinary powers that most people do not have. Some receivers of such powers use them to harm the people they disliked for some reason; others, in contrast, use their powers to do good, including counteracting the malevolent acts of the former.

Twelve Power-Releasing Human Body-Orifices

In the *Luba* creation story, *Maweja Nangila* created human beings with twelve orifices on their bodies: (1) the *mouth*, (2&3) the *two nostrils*, (4&5) the *two eyes,* (6&7) the *two ears*, (8) the urethra, (9) the *anus,* (10) *the fontanel pit,* (11), the *occipital pit,* and (12) the *epigastric pit*. He also endowed them with considerable supernatural powers, along with the ability to release these powers through the twelve orifices. At the time of creation, Earth was part of the Sky of the Summit where Creator *Maweja Nangila* and great spirits live. The two were close to each other. Later, *Mulopo Maweja*, the Emissary Spirit, rebelled against the Creator. *Maweja Nangila* expelled him from the Sky of the Summit along with Earth and all its inhabitants. As a consequence of this punishment, humans lost three important power-releasing orifices: *the fontanel*, *the occipital pit*, and *the epigastric pit*, along with the ability to release powers through them. To date, however, here and there, individuals, men and women, are being born with supernatural powers. Witches and sorcerers use theirs to harm individuals they hate for some reason. Diviners, medicine-men or-women, and seers use theirs to counteract the malevolent actions of the evil doers. An elaboration on the uses of each type of powers follows (Kalanda, 1992).

Mystical Agents of Evil

Africans across the continent acknowledge that sickness and death can be caused by germs, poison, beatings, attack by a wild animal, lack of nutrients in the system, or any other natural factor. However, they believe that the incidence of such a factor to a particular individual, at a particular time and space, has its own cause, generally supernatural as illustrated below.

Witches as Agents of Illness and Death — Example from the Badyaranké of Senegal: Witches, *ngontunné*, are the cause of most sicknesses, accidents and deaths. They capture and eat their preys' souls mystically. The killer invites his/her colleagues to the feast. In most cases the invitees live in the same village. They may be from different clans or ethnicities. Each participant becomes a debtor to the host for an in-kind payback at the latter's request. The more the participants, the more people will be killed in succession. When in his estimate the time comes, the previous host, now creditor, travels to the location of the debtor in the form of an owl-sounding bird identified as *comidyidyi*. The killer bird can camouflage itself by putting on the head of an innocent bird, a chicken for instance, in order to be able to move closer to the target without raising any suspicion of malice. The debtor who fails to meet his obligation will be forced to pay with his or her own life. The witch can transform herself into various other forms than a bird, such as monkey, breeze, or snake. Sometimes, the witch moves in the darkness of the night with a red light that beams on and off from his or her anus (Simmons, 1971).

Witches among the Luba: The most common Luba term for mystically-empowered evildoers is *baloji* (singular: *muloji*). The *baloji* utilize different strategies for consuming their human targets. They may extract the vital force of a person by manipulating objects with which he or she has been in close physical contact, such as clothes or the soil from their footprints. The victim, generally a rich, intelligent, and generous person, cannot survive. The hero appropriates for himself the desired virtues and lucks of the victim. The *baloji* may also victimize the persons they detest by first debilitating them and then keeping them in a permanent state of feebleness. Sometimes, rather than eroding the victim's health, they may instead gradually stupefy him psychologically until such time they can finish him up without jeopardizing themselves. Lastly, the *baloji* may empower objects belonging to them, such as a walking stick, a bracelet or a necklace, and send them on a killing mission. They may metamorphose themselves into ferocious animals, which they send to devour their human cattle targets. In carrying out such a mission, the *baloji* generally take the form of a bird in order to fly closer to the targets and identify them unmistakably. Once at the reach of the targeted victim, the hero metamorphoses himself into a crocodile, a lion, or a deadly poisonous snake and then kills the person. Sometimes the *baloji* strike their victims by taking the form of lightning. The *baloji* can also mystically cause the person to lose their job, become sterile or ruin their wealth (Kalanda 1992, Kanyinda-Lusanga 1974).

Fetishes as Causes of Sickness — The Yansi: Experience: Fetishes are spiritually- or mystically-empowered objects. As objects, fetishes thus have a material basis and can be acquired through inheritance, purchase, or other action such as having killed a powerful animal, being invested with that animal's powers, and wearing insignia incorporating that animal's powers. Some *nkisi* (fetishes) are directed toward depriving the victims of their possessions, health, or even life. The perpetrator appropriates the victim's vital force, lucks, or wealth. The victim can be an innocent relative or non-related individual. Killing for one's own benefit, not in the interest of the community, is reproved. Some *nkisi* are associated with priesthood in certain rituals or cults. Priest *NgalLébui*, for instance, is the mediator of *Lébui*, the spirit responsible for the fertility of the land and success in hunting and fishing. He also punishes those who violate his restrictions with sterility, sickness, or bad luck. In such cases, the *NgalLébui* priest intervenes on behalf of the violator with prayers and offerings to the Fetish representing *Lébui* for clemency. Another example is that of priest *Ngalkudh*, who intervenes on behalf of women implicated in cases of incest or particular types of premarital intimacy (De Plaen, 1968).

Mystical Agents of Good

Diviners — Pa Diviners in the Jos Plateau of Nigeria: Umar Habila Dadem Danfulani (in Olupona 2000) provides an extensive inventory of *Pa* divination and related rites practiced by the *Ngas*, the *Mupun,* and the *Mwaghavul* of the Jos Plateau, Nigeria. Practiced with pebbles, *Pa* divination, like divinations elsewhere, is designed to uncover hidden knowledge or truth about causes of and solutions to illnesses, other misfortunes, and surrounding events. Normal life is characterized and sustained by a balance in the relationship between nature, humans, and spirits, particularly ancestors. Central to understanding *Pa* divination are daily, monthly, seasonal, and annual cyclical changes associated with the movement of the sun, the moon, and the stars. The movements of these celestial objects affect natural phenomena, plants, and animal and human conditions. These changes cause imbalance to life. *Pa* divination is followed by rites designed to bring about harmony and a new balance. Some events and related *Pa* divination and ritual performances are community-centered, whereas others are individual-centered. Major among community-centered *Pa* divination rites are those designed to redress national disasters, such as famine, drought, and small pox. Divination reveals the cause of the disaster and the appropriate rites for addressing the cause and re-establishing the lost balance. The incriminated party can be a whole village, particular clans or extended families, or individuals. In any case, the responsibility is collective, binding the whole entity, including the innocents. Clan and family heads of incriminated entities apologize to God, to deities, and to ancestors for their members' wrongdoings and ask for mercies. In a libation ritual, priests offer samples of the sacrificial blood, meat, and meal to God, deities and ancestors, imploring them to restore the broken harmony. Individual-centered *Pa* Divination and rituals are performed to address personal afflictions attributed to God, a few to free spirits, and most to deities and ancestors. Generally attributed to God are those cases where no other agent is involved. In such cases, diviners declare themselves unable to do anything. It is left up to the family head to make sacrifices to ancestors begging them to implore God to remove the afflicting condition. Afflictions attributed to free spirits are removed by performing rites of exorcism and or appeasement (Danfulani, in Olupona 2000).

Divination by the Basket: A form of divination practiced in Luba village when was growing up was called *lubuku lwa kanyingu*, clay-pot divination, or *lubuku lwa cibata*, divination by the basket. A *kanyingu* is a small clay pot. *Cibata* is a round close-knit basket generally used to sift corn or cassava flour in. To perform this form of *lubuku*, the practitioner puts a basket on the ground resting on its edge, that is, in a covered position. He then places a clay pot on top of it, sitting on a creeper crown liana crown. The pot is usually filled with some substances believed to possess some supernatural power. To proceed, the performer asks leading questions. After each question, he picks up the pot with one hand trying to lift it up from the basket. If the response is positive, he succeeds in lifting the pot. If it is negative, the pot sticks to the basket and the latter is lifted up along. To proceed from here, the performer slightly hits the basket with a finger, lifts the pot up, and then sits it back on the basket.

Divination, Prescriptions and Remedies: Divination for discovering the cause or causes of an illness generally ends with a prescription of some course of action to stop the illness. The prescribed action may be sacrifices to the ancestral spirits, reconciliation with an upset elder, or forcing an identified *muloji* (mystical man eater) to release his victim, her victim in most cases. It usually includes medicinal treatment of some sort. More often than not the healing process is believed to be activated both by the natural powers of the plants infused in the medicine and by the mystical powers of the healer. This double belief explains why the use of herbs, roots, or barks is often accompanied with the carrying of some charm. In general, the same healer prescribes the medicine and the charm. In many cases the healer is the very person who discovered the cause of the illness.

Operating as separate individuals or combined in the same person, the diviner and the medicine man (or woman) in Luba villages are always paid for their professional services. At least part of the fees must be paid up front. This portion of the payment is called *kupawula* (to unleash the healing power). The Luba believe that unless some payment is made to the satisfaction of the officiant, the divination will not show the real cause of the sickness, or else the healing powers of the medicine will not be released. Another reason for requiring a pre-payment is that the payment may become problematic if the sick person does not recover. On the other hand, when the healing occurs indisputably, the *dilonga*, as the fee for professional services is called, can be very substantial in case of severe illnesses. If a given illness has been attributed to the malevolent work of a *muloji*, and the latter has been identified, the family council will decide on the most effective course of action to follow. The members may pressure the accused right away to release his victim. This is usually the case when the accused is a woman and pressure is generally exerted through severe beatings. If there is still some doubt about whether the accused is the right person or not, the family will seek confirmation by consulting a *mwena bwanga*, medicine man or woman. The latter may be brought to the family or the accused and other suspects may be taken to his or her place. The accused person and other suspects will be subjected to some tests of guilt or innocence.

In the past, the proof of guilt or innocence was given by submitting the accused to a test of poison. The one who swallows the poison without showing any sign of fear, especially without any side effects, is innocent. The one who refuses to take the poison by fear of death, or who becomes troubled and vomits after taking it, is guilty. The doctor seeks the proof of *buloji* (the man-eating power) in the vomits. Generally, the proofs found in the vomits consist of objects such as a ring and a piece of old meat. The ring is the chain used by the *muloji* to keep his victim in captivity until the time will be ripe for him and his accomplices to eat him up without jeopardizing their own lives. The piece of meat is the part of the victim's body that the *muloji* has already started eating. In the sight of the family and other members of the community, these substances are irrefutable proofs that the person who allegedly vomited them is a *muloji*. The victim may still have some chances of survival if too much of his body has not been eaten yet. To maximize his chances of survival, the family will threaten the *muloji* of death if his victim died. Women accused are generally subjected to severe beatings in the meantime. The individuals who are related to the group by marriage are the most commonly accused. Very often, running away or being rescued by a relative is their only chance of surviving the ordeal. As a result of pressures exerted by the colonial administration, humans are much less used in the test of poison today than they were in the past. Instead, chickens represent the accused or suspects. There are other tests too. One test consists in pulling a bracelet from boiling oil. The hand of the guilty one will be burned, that of the innocent will not.

Medicine Men (Women)

Individuals of all ages and genders can be called to the practice of medicine, both herbal treatment of sicknesses and mystical powers. Some medicine practitioners have inherited their craft and the authority to practice from a parent: father, mother, or other older relative. Some have been called to the profession by an ancestral spirit. In addition to being acknowledged as knowledgeable and successful practitioners, medicine men and women are expected to be persons of good character and moral integrity, and trustworthy, as illustrated in the *Azande* case below.

Azande Traditional Medicine: The Azande live in South Sudan and Northeast Congo DRC. The *Azande* medicine-man (or woman) is a well-rounded professional, called to the profession by the spirits, and trained in a long system of apprenticeship. He is knowledgeable in many health-related aspects of life and socially expected to be a person of integrity, friendly, and willing to serve. His initiation into the profession included, from among other things, taking some medicine designed to strengthen his soul and give him the power of prophesy, undergoing public burial, and swallowing some witchcraft liquid. He was led to visiting a running water source and to be familiarized with a plethora of medicinal plants. He had to observe certain food and celibacy taboos during the initiation period and learn how to obtain, fabricate, and administer medicines from various plants, insects, and animal parts. He had to familiarize himself with the causes, cures, and prevention of various diseases; with ways of fighting witchcraft and sorcery; and of handling the spirits, including the ancestral spirits. Training and practice culminated in induction into the medicine men's association. As a practitioner, the *Azande* medicine-man was called to cure the sick and to prevent failures in many domains. He often also assessed cases in court or in homes, served as diviner, and exorcised victims of witchcraft (Mbiti, 1970).

Personal Magical Powers

The belief in witchcraft is widespread across Black Africa. This belief is almost inseparable from the practice of charms, medicines used to counteract the malevolent plans of the evildoer, or to protect the individual or the community from other harms, or else to enhance one's chances of success in enterprising endeavors.

Preventive Manga among the Luba: Witchcraft is called *bulogy* among the Luba. Medicines, herbal or mystical, to combat witchcraft are called *manga*, singular *bwanga*. Preventive *manga* were used for various purposes such as causing a weapon—spear, machete, or arrow—directed at a person to miss the target (*bwanga bwa myepu*). Preventive *manga* could keep the weapon from penetrating the target's body when it reached him or her (*bwanga bwa ntuji*). Some *manga* had the power to enable a person who is being tracked to get lost from the sight of the enemy (*bwanga bwa njiminyi*) or to instantly fly from a dangerous place to a safer one (*bwanga bwa nsamu*). Still, other medicines had the power to neutralize poison (*bwanga bwa mulungu*) or to protect a traveler from danger (*bwanga bwa lwendu*). Pregnant women used to wear amulets around their waists to prevent miscarriages (*manga a kukanga nawu difu*). During the colonial regime, men had *manga* to protect themselves against the exactions of the white man (Weydert 1938).

A Bwanga bwa Njiminyi Story. I have a personal story to tell about the *bwanga bwa njiminyi*. This is the charm that keeps a runaway person from being caught. The story occurred during my childhood in the village of *Tshamba*. It involves a woman named *Malu wa Kabuya*. She was living with *Pontien Nsunzu*. They were not married. I never knew where her parents lived. All we knew about her origins was that she was *a Luluwa* from the *Lower Country* (*ku Cibanda*), past *Mwene Ditu*. One day, around mid-morning, I was by myself in my parents' courtyard, in front of my mother's house. *Malu* came by holding some powder in her hands. She ordered me to step forward in front of her. I did without questioning why. Then, behind me, in a side-to-side movement of her head, she blew away the powder. Then she asked me to step aside. I did and she walked away. It was until late afternoon by sunset, when the adults began to wonder where *Malu* was that I told them the story. *Nsunzu* tried to track where *Malu* had gone but unsuccessfully. *Malu* was never found. My parents reprimanded me for not telling the story when *Malu* could still be found. They were afraid that she might have sold me to some mystical forces as a payment for her safe escape.

Chapter 1

Manga to Produce Desired Outcomes: Let us mention, in addition to *manga* designed to protect one from harmful situations, those which facilitate the occurrence of desirable situations. Pregnant women drink infusions or rub their abdomen with hot water and slippery herbs in order to have an easy delivery. Barren men and women seek *manga* to have children (*manga a lulelu*). Young men had *manga* to attract even married women they desired (*manga a kutomboja nawu bakaji*). Single women had *manga* to be attractive to and keep their preferred lovers (*manga a mpala wa baluma*). Achieving success in business is another noble motive for one to seek *manga*. A *bwanga* used for this particular purpose is called *bwanga bwa cisalu*. *Cisalu* is the Luba term for marketplace. Figuratively, it means business. Some *manga* were designed to help one find a job (*bwanga bwa dikasa dya mudimu*). There were also *manga* for general good luck (*bwanga bwa mwabi*). During colonization, some chiefs had *manga* to attract strangers to their lands. With larger populations under their control, their status in society and importance for the colonial administration would be enhanced.

Similar Manga between the Luba and the Dagbamba: Similar practices and beliefs are found to have existed in other parts of Africa. The following were found among the *Luba* and the Dagbamba of Ghana:

Table 1: Similar Manga Practices (Luba-Dagbamba)

Luba Magical Power	**Dagbamba** Magical Power	**Function**
Njiminyi	*Liliga*	Enables one to disappear from the sight of an enemy
Ntuji	*Sutili*	Keeps a weapon from penetrating the target person's body.
Mulungu	*Muhili*	Neutralizes poison.
Císálú	*Lukuri*	Enables one to prosper in business.
Mpala	*Vua*	Attracts lovers (Luba). Attracts game (Dagbamba).

(The information about the *Dagbamba* is adapted from John M. Chernoff in Olupona 2000).

3. CALL TO SPIRITUALIZATION WHILE ON EARTH

Human beings are given opportunities to ascend into spiritual states while on Earth. Mediums through trance, seers by revelation, ordination into priesthood, and consecration to certain high-ranking social statuses are the most known forms of spiritualization.

Spiritualization through Trance

Mediums: Mediums are persons who become possessed by spirits during religious ceremonies involving singing, dancing and drumming. Not everyone is amenable to spiritual possession. Those who are shake vibrantly, fall to the ground or Jump uncontrollably, whereas some candidate may remain completely unshaken and be declared hard-headed. It is believed that in last analysis the spirit chooses the medium it wants to get into and communicate through. Mediums can be men, but they are women most of the time. They can be trained for their duties or untrained. The spirit invades and speaks through the medium relaying messages. The possessed individual loses his or her own personality and manifests the personality of the possessing spirit instead. For instance, they can speak in an entirely different voice. During trance, not only do mediums relay messages from the possessing spirit, they also gain knowledge of things or occurrences, present, past, or future, that are imperceptible to the ordinary mind or eye. For instance, they may find lost articles or identify the thief without having had any experiential knowledge of them prior to the trance. They may have seen them in vision, not in person. During trance the medium acquires extraordinary power. They can throw themselves violently to the ground without getting injured or walk on fire without getting burned (Mbiti, 1970).

Spiritual Seers-Healers: Group Trance: Spiritual seers-healers are individuals who have the gift of seeing events—past, present, or future—while in a state of trance and interpret them. Like diviners, spiritual seers-healers are consulted about causes and treatments of diseases and handling of other misfortunes. Trance rituals are generally held in the evening before an audience seated around a fire. The trance medium can be one individual or several. Individual trance can be spontaneous or externally induced. Group trance is generally externally induced through intensive singing and dancing. Spiritual possession through group trance is called *dituuka mikishi* among the Luba of Kasai, Congo DRC, or *lubuku lwa bilumbu,* divination by spiritual possession. The story related here occurred in the 1950s. The scene was the evening family fire. Candidates to possession were women, married women more specifically. Mukenga Mudiabuloba and his two brothers—Ngoyi Tantamika and Kapiamba Binunu—had a common traditional medicine man**.** His family name was Kayembe. A stanza of one of the songs sung during the ceremony went like this:

> *Tatu Kayembe, kwanji kufwa**,** udi nsanga mweyemena, kwanji kufwa*; meaning:
> Father Kayembe, do not die yet, you are the oak tree against which many people are leaning, don't.

At the time, Mukenge Mudiabuloba had three wives: Muadi, Kapinga, and Nyemba. Ngoyi Tantamika had three wives as well: Meta, Kamwanya, and Shimatu. Their common younger brother, Kapiamba Binunu, had two wives: Masengu and Mulaja. From the beginning, seven of these women were candidates for spiritual possession. Kamwanya was not among them for a reason unknown to me. After a number of unsuccessful trials, Muadi and Kapinga were pulled out. They were pronounced hardheaded (*ba mutu mukole*). They did not shake at all.

To call the spirits in, people would gather in the evening around a big fire. The audience would sit on one side, the candidates for spiritual possession on the opposite side, with the musicians behind them. All the parties would be facing the fire. The space between the candidates and the fire was always well swept. Each candidate would kneel down, leaning forward and holding a fetish in the form of a horn or a wooden statue down to the ground. The musicians would beat drums and shake maracas, and sing song after song with the participation of the crowd. Then, one after another, the candidates to possession would begin to shake on their knees in all their bodies. One after another, they would fall on their backs uttering loud sounds. Some, especially the one possessed by the spirit called *Kasongo*, would jump up and down with considerable power, speaking in tongues and walking on the fire without getting burned. Some of the things they said during spiritual possession were supposed to reveal some hidden truth about a particular mysterious situation they were called to clarify.

Makenga: A Sole Seer-Healer: Father François Lufuluabo Mizeka, a Catholic priest, in his book, *L'Anti-Sorcier* (1977), reports several personal experiences of what he calls paranormal acts by a seer-healer called *Makenga wa Nzambi* (God's Sufferer One). Father Lufuluabo describes her as a woman endowed with many moral virtues, including purity, integrity, honesty, proverbial simplicity, and exemplary modesty. In a state of trance, however, *Makenga* is vivacious and quick at repartee. She confronts her challengers and is very proud when she brings in irrefutable factual authentications of her mystical revelations. Her exploits during trance include mystical fights against witches to liberate some of their prisoners, namely individuals who are victims of their malevolent secret deeds. In this respect, she recognizes that some of such fights are very dangerous for her own survival (Lufuluabo, 1977).

Makenga's Acquisition of Supernatural Powers. Makenga was named Nzeba at birth. She married normally but experienced numerous cases of sickness and loss of children to death. She and her husband Musampa sought help from a man who had undergone a similar fate but had succeeded reversing it. His name was Mikalayi. He treated *Nzeba* successfully with the same plants that someone had helped solve his own problems. The man had predicted that one from among the persons that he would treat will receive the gift of seeing hidden things and distant events. That is what happened to Nzeba. After receiving treatment from Mikalayi, she was healed of her sicknesses and her children began to survive. She had four children when Father Lufuluabo consulted with her. She was in her 30s then. Upon discovering her supernatural gift, Nzeba changed her name to *Makenga wa Nzambi,* God's Sufferer One, or *The Sufferer One Rescued by God*. She did this in remembrance both of her suffering and of the fact that God brought her out of it (Lufuluabo, 1977).

Makenga's Supernatural Gifts and Requirements. Makenga maintains that her supernatural gift is very difficult to keep. It could turn against her if she deviated from the moral requirements attached to it: never hate anyone, never wish evil to any one, never commit injustice by stealing or calumnies, never engage in sexual misconduct, and never seek to know the plants that stimulate in witches the knowledge and power to cause harm to people they dislike. Makenga's supernatural abilities reported by Father Lufuluabo include seeing individuals who prepare to come see her and communicate their unannounced visit before their arrival. She informs her collaborators of forthcoming visits even before the persons start the trip. She discovers the motive of her clients' visits without ever asking them (Lufuluabo, 1977).

Makenga's Consultations. She prepares for consultation by wearing a robe with her name sewn on it over her regular wrapping clothes. She carries a Roman Catholic rosary, an ordinary women's powdered perfume, and a towel with which she covers her face while drinking. When ready for consultations, Makenga places the rosary on a short small table, sprays some powder in the air, and collects herself profoundly. She ceases being of this world, a period during which she hears nothing and responds to no question. Then, in a brusque movement, she wakes up transformed. Not looking at the consultants, concentrating on and manipulating her rosaries instead, she asks questions and gives responses, including probing questions and responses. Then she speaks to consultants both about the things she sees clearly and about those she sees imperfectly. She describes the consultant's family, revealing hidden details no one has told her about, sometimes including details unknown to them that they will be able to verify later. When the consultant declares a detail incorrect, she searches again and generally comes up with undeniable information. Without asking the consultants, she discovers the purpose of the consultation through manipulating the rosaries. She provides details about the persons involved, their families, past history, the vicissitudes they have gone through, and the current illness or misfortune about which she is being consulted. All throughout the consultation period, the only type of question to the consultants, whom she does not regard, is to confirm or infirm the veracity of her discoveries (Lufuluabo, 1977).

Spiritualization through Ordination into Priesthood

Call to Priesthood: Under this title, we are speaking more specifically about individuals who have received a call to ascend into social statuses putting them in special relationship and contacts with the spirits and assuming functions whose performance make them entitled intermediaries between the living and the spirits. The qualifications generally include some moral character, some form of preparation or training, all culminating in some initiation ceremonies. Preparation may include a period of seclusion from regular living spaces, fasting, and taboo observances. It always includes abstention from sexual intercourse. Training may consist of intensive instructions and endurance-building physical performances. Initiation ceremonies implicitly or through formal ordination confer the power and authority to carry out religious services, handle sacred objects, and enter sacred spaces. From among the functions carried out by priests are: performing rites, making libation, offerings, and animal sacrifices. Ewe and Yorùbá priesthoods are known for being very much elaborate and socially effective. In addition to the above-mentioned functions, Yorùbá priests play active roles in king installations and chief making (Mbiti, 1970).

Yorùbá Priest: The Yorùbá have a complex system of priesthood. There exist several levels of priests, notably: the head of the compound, the head of the extended family, the leader of the ward, the chief, and the king. The compound is comprised of an elder, his wife or wives and children, his younger relatives, and absorbed foreigners. The extended family consists of a number of compounds whose heads are blood-related at some higher level and their respective established guests. The ward is a geographic community of non-related extended families. The chiefdom encompasses several contiguous wards. In turn, the kingdom is a collection of chiefdoms under the authority of the leader of a dominant chiefdom from among them. At the top of all Yorùbá kings stands the king of Ile Ifè, a kingdom believed to have been established by Odùdúwà, the legendary priest-king founding father of the Yorùbá people. The Yorùbá priesthood is believed to descend from Odùdúwà's priesthood. Each priest is associated with a cult to a particular divinity, called an *orìsà*. The *orìsàs* are spiritual creations of specialized appointed ministers in the government of Creator Olódùmarè on Earth. Sometimes there are more than one priest and more than a cult in a compound, notably when an incoming wife or a guest is already a practicing priest. Priesthood is acquired through heredity. Usually the most deserving oldest heir to the incumbent replaces him or her. There is no requirement for training for priesthood in Yorùbá religion. But the actual performance of priesthood functions presupposes some form of consecration which makes the candidate fit to perform sacred rituals. Through consecration, the devotee becomes an *Olóriyà*, one who possesses *orìsà* (divinity). This means that from now on there will be something of the divinity in him or her. The personality of the devotee will become impregnated with the personality of the spirit and manifest it. The priest's relation to the *orìsà* has a triangular dimension. The priest is the mediator between the human community and the sacred and holy world of the spirits. He or she has the double duty to offer up human's worship to the divinity or spirit and bless humans in the name of the said divinity or spirit (Idowu, 1994).

Dinka Priesthood: The Dinka of Sudan attribute the origin of their institution of priesthood to their legendary founding father Ayuel Longar. To help the Dinka people escape a devastating drought, Yuel Longar invited them to move with him to a land of rich fresh pastures. The elders refused. Yuel Longar departed alone. Unable to reverse the drastic situation, the Dinka decided to follow Longar. As they were trying to cross the last river, Longar pushed them back with his long fishing spear. One elder grabbed the spear, propelled himself out of the water to the shore; he struggled with Longar, gained control over the fishing spear, and helped others come out of the water. *Longar* distributed his fishing spears to the first men who came out of the water. The descendants of these men became the Dinka priesthood clans.

> "Longar gave the priests the power to invoke the spirits effectively and to perform animal sacrifices; he also gave them the power of his tongue to bless and of his spittle to curse. And he gave them a divinity named Flesh to inspire them and make their words true and effective" (Ray 2000, referencing Francis Deng 1980).

During sacrificial ceremonies, Dinka priests, empowered by *Divinity Flesh*, repeat words and gestures inherited from Longar while holding the spear over the head of the animal.

Journey to Consecration: The Luba culture values legitimate marriage and marriage stability, wealth achieved through personal hard work, and winning the race for the chieftaincy. In each case, if the ancestors are pleased with the accomplishments, they will call the achiever to seek spiritual anointing consecration from an authorized established achiever in the same domain. A successful marriage is one with a virtuous wife and abundant offspring. The delighted ancestors will request the dedication of the senior wife to the family guardian spirit *Nkambwa*. The achiever of wealth will be called to receive consecration from a qualified ordained achiever of wealth. The winner of the race for the chieftaincy will be authorized to receive investiture from a legitimate power-giver dignitary. The pursuit of each venue was a life project. The candidate began his achievement career as a young boy weaving mats and catching rodents from which he derived revenues allowing him to buy a baby chicken for raising. Faithful to the tradition, he would offer his first chicken to the ancestors through their representative living elder. It was expected that after receiving blessings from the elder in exchange for his tribute, the young man would raise chickens, ducks, and pigeons and eventually sell them to buy a goat for raising. The *Luba* are primarily agriculturalists. Before reaching this level of a livestock rearing, the young man was encouraged to begin tilling a field of his own separate from his father's. Quite often, it was thanks to revenues from farming that he was able to engage in more promising poultry raising. He was expected to offer the products from his field to his father who would offer them to the ancestor on his behalf. Just like with the first chicken, and the products from the field, the young man was expected to offer his first goat in tribute to the ancestors' representative among the living. Thanks to blessings received from compliance, he would prosper in rearing goats, sheep, and pigs to the point of assembling, through personal efforts, the necessary bridewealth for a wife. The ancestral law instructed him to offer the first wife acquired in this manner to the ancestors' representative. After receiving the wife in tribute, the elder would bless her and give her back to the donor. The latter would keep on working hard, this time with the help of two additional hands, his wife's. Together, they would labor in the fields while she would be rearing chickens in the house and he tending goats and sheep in the grass surrounding the homestead. Thanks to his strength and perseverance, he would marry more wives. Pleased with his accomplishments and the good character of his senior wife, the ancestors would call him to have the senior wife dedicated to the family's guardian spirit *Nkambwa*. Unselfish and mindful of the community, as he is expected to be, he would procure wives for his relatives as well. A community builder as a husband and father of many healthy children and a contributor to significant growth of the extended family, he would be called to be consecrated as an accomplished achiever of wealth, *Mukola*, a peer of past achievers, living and dead. Procuring many wives for self and relatives was the most praised accomplishment qualifying one to run for the chieftaincy. The race was a long and costly process. The candidate had to satisfy the incumbent chief's and power-giver dignitaries' immeasurable appetite for riches. Finally, victorious of this long and costly competition for the chiefdom throne, he was invested as Chief, *Mfumu*.

Dedication of the Luba Senior Wife: When the ancestors are pleased with a man's marriage, they invite him to have his senior wife dedicated to Ancestress *Nkambwa*, guardian spirit of the household. *Nkambwa is* the spirit of the husband's paternal grandmother. Through the dedication ceremony, the senior wife is ordained servant of the ancestress. The dedication ceremony, called *Kufikisha Mukaji ku Nkambwa*, takes place at the demand of the guardian spirit *Nkambwa* herself, usually after several years of marriage. Such a long period is needed for the candidate to give sufficient proof of being virtuous enough to serve the family guardian spirit with dignity. *Nkambwa* makes her request known by sending a dream in which the man sees a wandering woman carrying a water jug on her head and another jug in her left underarm. She may also send a sickness to the man or to one of his children that the diviner will interpret as an expression of *Nkambwa*'s request for the dedication to be carried out. If the diviner attributes the sickness to *Nkambwa*, the man will seek a confirmation by asking her to remove the sickness. If an improvement is observed in the condition of the sick person, everyone will be convinced that *Nkambwa* really requests the induction. In execution of the request, the husband will buy two live chickens. He will then invite over some inducted women from among the senior wives of his brothers and paternal cousins. The candidate for induction will welcome them with some money. She and her husband will confess themselves to their dignitary guests. Has he ever spoken against the induction? Has the wife ever sworn not to become the servant of the guardian spirit? In the affirmative, they will have to avow their faults and repair them by paying fines to the officiants. The officiants then will present the candidate to *Nkambwa* and ask the spirit to give them a sign of acceptance during the night.

The next day, in the morning or the afternoon, if *Nkambwa* has given favorable signs, the officiants will present the candidate to her again. To express her submission to the spirit, she will kneel down before the sacred tree and cover the inside of her arms and her neck with wet white clay. She will then buy all the privileges of being inducted by remitting some money to the guests of honor. Some of the privileges are: carrying the title of *Mukalenga Mwadi* (Senior Wife), being servant of the guardian spirit, and acquiring the authority to induct other senior wives. She will be asked to make vows of fidelity and submission to *Nkambwa*. When all that is done, one of the officiants, generally the senior wife of the eldest brother or cousin will kill the two chickens at the foot of the sacred tree. When the meal is cooked, the officiant who killed the chickens will once again implore *Nkambwa* to accept the servant that she has requested. Both she and the candidate for induction will crouch on a mat, facing the sacred tree. She will place the portions to be served the spirit on a *cikusukusu* leaf and put them in the hands of the candidate. Then, holding her two hands, she will present the food to the guardian spirit. The candidate will repeat after her each word of presentation. Together they will deposit the portions for *Nkambwa* at the foot of the tree. The participants will divide the meat among themselves. The officiant and the newly inducted senior wife will share the portions that were placed at the foot of the sacred tree for *Nkambwa*. It is believed that *Nkambwa* has mystically eaten by now. After the ceremonial meal, the man and the newly-inducted wife will be required to stay home and to behave themselves for the rest of the day. At night, they will perform the conjugal act to mark off the end of the taboo.

Consecration of the Achiever of Wealth: Consecration for achieving wealth through hard work is called *kutapisha mbuji wa bukola*. The *Luba* people believe that the achiever of wealth is obligated to pay tributes of the first fruits from his work and from his daughters' marriages in an expression of gratitude to the ancestors for his ability to work and to procreate. A corollary belief is that when the achiever has paid the first fruits from his labor and from his daughters' marriages to the ancestors' satisfaction, they will invite him to seek consecration as an accomplished achiever, whereby entering in fellowships with past achievers, living and dead. The ancestors communicate their will to the achiever in dream or by sending a misfortune to jeopardize his accomplishments, current and future. The misfortune may be sickness, sterility, loss of wealth, declining business, etc. In other cases, the achiever seeks consecration upon the advice of the elders. Whatever the case, the achiever consults the diviner on the matter before undertaking any action toward seeking consecration. Generally, the diviner confirms the suspicions of the achiever and his entourage that the ancestors really want the achiever to be consecrated. Once the decision is made, the achiever invites over a consecrated achiever, a *mukola*. The distinguishing mark of a *mukola* is the possession of the so-called *keela ka bukola*, achievement knife", which is used to slaughter sacrificial animals in consecration ceremonies. A person who possesses this knife has the authority to consecrate other achievers. Therefore, the culmination of the consecration ceremonies is the passing of the knife from the hands of the officiating *mukola* to those of the newly installed *mukola*. As with all major events, the ritual proper is preceded by some preliminaries on the eve of consecration. The candidate invites relatives, friends, and especially other achievers to his house. He welcomes each consecrated achiever with a present called *kupawula*, to clear the way. The achiever called to perform the consecration ceremony arrives that evening accompanied by a qualified peer of his choice. In a first move, he traces a circle on the ground at some point in front of the candidate's house with a piece of white kaolin held in his right hand. He orders the candidate to stand inside the circle. Then, he appeals to the candidate's ancestors, asking them to give a tangible sign that they really want their descendant to be consecrated *mukola*. He particularly requests the removal of the misfortune which prompted his invitation by the host. He promises to carry out the ancestors will as soon as the unfortunate condition has receded (Bamuinikile, 1975).

The candidate treats them to a chicken meal called *nzolo wa cibufuku*, night time chicken meal. That evening, women cook large quantities of food. In principle each crop grown in the area must be represented. A fireplace (*cyota*) is installed outdoors in the courtyard for people to sleep around. The officiant may choose to sleep at home if he lives nearby. But that night the officiant, the candidate, and the relatives must observe the taboo (*cijila*) of sexual intercourse. It is expected that at least one of the important participants will have a good dream that night. A good dream is anything that could be interpreted as a manifestation of joy, abundance, and success. In contrast, seeing a dead body, mourners, or fighters is considered a bad dream. In the latter case, the ceremony must be suspended and the diviner consulted so that the message contained in the dream may be known and appropriately addressed. If the night before consecration is blessed with a good dream, some improvement is observed in the deplored condition, everyone will see in it a positive response from the ancestors to the kaolin rite performed by the *mukola* on the eve, and the ceremonies will proceed. The officiant and his peers come from where they spent the night. The candidate for consecration welcomes them with presents. He is expected to be very generous on this day. His liberalities on the day of consecration are living proof of his qualification for the dignified title of *mukola*, an accomplished achiever. They are also an invitation to many more blessings of wealth to accrue to him (Bamuinikile, 1975).

Some of the guest achievers go into the wilderness to cut the tree that will be planted in commemoration of the candidate's elevation to the dignity of an accomplished achiever. They go and return in silence, carrying the ceremonial tree respectfully. The tree cannot touch the naked ground before it is planted. In the meantime, it is laid down on a mat specifically woven to this effect and appropriately spread at a selected site in the courtyard. While the tree lies on the mat, the candidate *mukola* has all his instruments of work—hoes, machetes, axes, spears, arrows, trading canes, etc.—gathered at a central place in the courtyard. Following this display, the officiant and the candidate proclaim all their accomplishments one by one. The officiant goes first. He briefly tells the attendance how he achieved his wealth. Following him, the candidate proclaims his accomplishments with the circumstances and manner in which he achieved each one of them. He must provide precise details about how he received the small initial capital that is at the origin of his wealth. This detail is important because only the fruits of his own work can enable him to qualify for consecration to the rank of *mukola* (Bamuinikile, 1975*)*.

After the proclamation of accomplishments, the candidate gives the officiant the animals to be sacrificed to the ancestors and to the spirits of past consecrated achievers. They may consist of one chicken and one goat. In most cases, however, there are more than one animal of each kind. The ideal number is three chickens and three goats. One of each kind is to be sacrificed in the name of the candidate's grandfather, one in the name of his father, and one in his own name. Glorifying one's ascendants before self is expected as a sign of filial piety. The Luba rationalize the expected subordination of children to their parents by figuratively saying: *Citunji kacitu cipita nshingu (*never will the shoulder grow taller than the neck), or blankly stating: *Mwana wa mumda katu upita nshandi* (a begotten child cannot outgrow his parents).

The sacrificial animals for the consecration ceremony are beheaded beginning with the chickens. The time of killing the chickens is a moment of great suspense. The beheaded chicken projects itself uncontrollably up and down until it dies. But it must die in a certain position for the consecration to be considered a success. At the time the chicken falls down to the ground for the last time to die, it must lie on one side (*mulaala kabavu*), or on the back (*mulaala cyadi muulu*: literally, laid chest up). A chicken that dies lying on the stomach with its face down is said to have experienced a bad death (*mufwa bibi*). A bad death signals some impropriety in the manner in which the candidate for consecration acquired his wealth. It may suggest that his accomplishments being celebrated on this day did not exclusively come from his own work. It may also mean that the taboo of sexual abstinence on the eve of the ceremony was violated, or that there is a pending case to be resolved first. To know for sure what the actual reason for the chicken's bad death is, a decision is made to consult a diviner, who will prescribe the appropriate course of action to be undertaken (Bamuinikile, 1975).

After the chickens' death, the officiant beheads the goat(s). All this time the tree of achievement is still lying on the mat and will stay there for a while longer. Following the beheading of the goat(s), the officiant puts the sacrificial knife head down in the hole dug to plant the tree. In this manner the heroic knife mystically participates in the erection of the monument to achievers that the tree is designed to be. When the meal is ready, the officiant serves the candidate first. This he does in a special manner as described hereafter. Holding the food in one hand and the candidate's principal instrument of labor (which created his wealth) in the other, the officiant runs in different paths around the homestead. As he proceeds, he calls the candidate by name and incites the latter to run after him. From time to time he stops to serve him some food on the head of the instrument. He does this with his arms crossed before him. The candidate must pick up the food with his teeth from the instrument. Each time the officiant calls the candidate by name, he adds the following exhortation:

> "Rise and run. The dawn is here. All your peers are up by now. It is time for you to go out to achieve wealth" (Bamuinikile, 1975).

The feeding rite ends in an atmosphere of generalized joy. The women present explode in joyful noises, singing and shaking bells. To the jubilant crowd the new *mukola* responds by throwing monies in all directions. Back to the center of the courtyard, the officiant serves some food to the family of the newly consecrated achiever. The guest achievers eat in a separate place. All those present, invited or not, are encouraged to partake in the feast. In the house of the *mukola*, everyone should feel at home, especially on this day. He enjoys seeing people happy about him. After the meal, the new *mukola* gives his peers presents, a signal that they may now leave if they so desire. To the officiant, now his ritual father (*tatwenda wa bukola*), he gives the required fees (*mabaka*) for his highly valued services. At this point, the officiant and the new *mukola* plant the tree of achievement together. At the request of the new *mukola*, his ritual father gives him the knife of achievement in exchange for a present in cash or in kind. The ritual formula for the passing of the achievement knife or any other authority symbol is:

> *Bute, bwate, bukaadi bweeba, kabucyena bwanyi:*
> Hold on to it, it is now yours, no longer mine (Bamuinikile, 1975).

Investiture into Chieftaincy: The investiture ceremonies include several acts of consecration elevating the incoming chief to a spiritual status. Below are the most important ones:

> The investiture proper is preceded by a period of trials during which the candidate to the throne, *Lwaba*, is subjected to fasting and sexual abstinence. He sleeps in an ad-hoc shelter or outdoors in places reputed to be haunted by spirits. During the entire period, he opens himself to inspiration, visions and empowerment by the ancestral spirits and the spirits of past chiefs and other prominent authority figures.
>
> To be acceptable in ancestral sight, the investiture rituals must be performed by *Notable Ntite*, or the equivalent. Only he holds the ancestral authority to confer the chiefly power to any candidate.
>
> On the inauguration day, the incoming chief is given a bath in water fetched from a river believed to be inhabited by the spirits of past chiefs and other prominent authority figures.
>
> Altogether, investiture rituals are believed to turn the incoming chief into the peer of the spirits of past leaders and them his partners in the governance of the chiefdom. Inauguration day's sacred meal of goats sacrificed to the spirits and served to the dignitaries and ordinary people is believed to be paralleled

by a mystical meal of human flesh in which the new chief, other mystical authorities of the chiefdom, the ancestors, and the spirits of past leaders participate. Individuals who die in the aftermath of the inauguration are the mystical sacrificial lambs of the inaugural day. Chiefdom's dignitaries and sub-chiefs execute dances in front of the new chief in an act of submission to his authority. Through them the supernatural powers they represent submit themselves to those of the new chief.

The inaugural procession includes a trip to the major market place of the chiefdom where a tree of power, *mulemba*, will be planted. Through the chief's visit and the planting of the *mulemba* tree, his ancestors and the spirits of past chiefs take possession of the market place, thus making it sacred. Fighting in the marketplace was prohibited. Individuals guilty of crimes against humanity, such as murders, were hanged in the market place.

In some *Luba* lineages, the inauguration procession includes a visit to the tomb of a past glorious chief. This was the case when Ngandu Mwana Kabamba became chief of *Beena Ngadajika* in 1974 (Mpyana, 1975).

Spiritualization through Death: The ultimate spiritual transformation occurs through death. In African thought, the deceased, liberated from the limitation of the physical body, becomes fully spirit and empowered, and journeys to the land of the ancestors in the underground word. Preparations are made to secure a good death and good reception of the departing among the ancestors. Among the Luba, preparations to this end are made through acts of confession (*ditonda*) and reconciliation (*kunwa cibalu*), and the farewell address to the dead (*kwela lusanzu*). When death approaches, the adults present, assembled around the departing, one by one in decreasing order of seniority, confess any acts of malice they might have committed and restate and recall any words of curse or bad wishes they might have uttered against the dying. The latter does likewise when his turn comes. They then, in symbol of cleansing of the hearts and reconciliation, chew white clay, spit it to the ground, and drink water from the same calabash ball. At internment, each adult, once again in his or her order of seniority, addresses the dead, sending greeting to the departed, declaring his or her innocence in the death, and challenging the deceased saying: "If I am responsible for your death, do not let one or two days pass without calling me to follow you there; but if you have brought death upon yourself by betraying a family member or by wronging somebody, you only have yourself to blame. And you will have to make your own case to the ancestors."

4. THE GIFTS OF IMMORTALITY AND REINCARNATION

Original Immortality and the Advent of Death

At creation, the human being was meant to live eternally. One would grow older and rejuvenate, be reinvigorated, and continue to grow in age. If one died accidentally, one would resurrect reinvigorated and go on living in permanent harmony and happiness. Heaven and Earth were joined at the time of creation. God and other heavenly spirits interacted regularly with humans and God's other earthly creatures. But for some reason this original harmony came to be disrupted. Different ethnic groups have their own notions of what happened and how it did. Some involve humans, others animals. In an Igbo story, the final actors are animals even though humans were involved at the start. The story relates that *Chukwu*, God, let humans and animals decide whether there should be death on Earth or not. All but a few, including *the crocodile,* said no. They sent the dog to deliver the no message to God. Unfortunately, *the dog* found some sweet bones along the road, spent his time eating them, and forgot about the mission. In the meantime, the crocodile took advantage of *the dog*'s irresponsibility and sent *the frog* with a message requesting that death should be allowed to exist on Earth. The Kono of Sierra Leone have a slightly-different story involving the dog as well. To honor a promise he had made to humans, the Creator sent the dog with a bundle of skins to deliver to them that they would wear as a protection against death. Imprudently *the dog* informed the other animals of the importance of the skins and his mission. Hearing that, *the snake* stole the skins and distributed them among members of his own kind. That is how it came to happen that mankind's death is definite whereas *snakes* die yearly but resurrect with a new skin and keep on living. In a Swazi creation story, the actors were animals also. *Mvelimqanti, The First to Appear* (God), *sent the chameleon* to humankind with a message of eternal life. Thereafter, He also sent *the lizard* with a message of death. The chameleon did not go straight to the target. Instead it stopped somewhere along the way to eat some berries, only to arrive after the lizard had already delivered the message of death (Ekechukwu, 1983; Jefferson and Skinner, 1991; Kuper, 1986).

In other stories, humans, rather than animals, were the actors. For instance, an Akan myth has it that Heaven above was as close to Earth below as a ceiling is to the house floor. So close was Heaven that one day a woman who was pounding some plantains to make the *fufu* meal hit Heaven with her pestle. God decided to move up higher to preclude future encroachments. Full of remorse, the woman had her children build a tower of mortars to reconnect Earth to Heaven. They fell short of one mortar. She advised them to remove the mortar at the bottom and place it at the top to close the gap. They did and everything collapsed. They perished in the process. And that is how death came to settle on Earth. In the above stories, the humans' actions that brought about death were accidental. In other stories, they were acts of disobedience instead. For instance, the BaManyanga, a subgroup of the Kongo, say that God made *Mahungu*, the first person on Earth, not only a very powerful human being, but another God-self. God entrusted to him the management of the whole creation and revealed to him secrets about His future plans. *Mahungu* became very pompous and lazy. Being very talkative, he divulged God's secrets to animals. In reprisal, God terminated His friendship with *Mahungu*, withdrew from the Earth, and stopped intervening in the affairs of the humans. But *Mahungu* became so helpless that God had pity for him and created death as a strategy for saving him and his descendants from endless helplessness (Bokie, 1993). The theme of arrogance is also found in the story of the Fang of Gabon. According to the Fang, *Nzame*, God, created the first man, *Fam*. He died as a punishment for becoming too arrogant and refusing to worship *Nzame*. Disobedience is also cited in a story of the Bambuti of Congo. The pregnant woman of the first man on Earth convinced her husband to give her for food fruits from the only tree in the forest the Creator had told them not to eat. He did it secretly at night. But the moon was watching and reported the violation to God. Angry, God sent them death in punishment (Abraham 1974, Gbotokuma, quoting "The Revolt against God", Mbiti, in Olupona 1991).

The Luba story has several versions of how death came into existence. In one version, Earth was initially connected to Heaven and located in *the Milky Way*. It came to pass that humans rebelled against the Creator. Generalized corruption settled in following the rebellion. Angry, *Maweja Nangila* expelled Earth and the humans from Heaven's proximity and destroyed the humans in punishment. However, by compassion and love for His creations, *Maweja Nangila* brought them back to life and redeemed the world from corruption by sacrificing his First-Born Son. In another version, *Maweja Nangila* placed the first couple in a land populated with palm trees and told them not to extract or drink wine from any palm tree, lest they die. They extracted and drank the wine anyway. When *Maweja Nangila* ordered man to bring him wine, it took him five days to respond. *Maweja Nangila* confronted him and punished by death all the creatures that had disobeyed him. All creatures became mortal as a consequence. In a slightly different version, *Maweja Nangila* created the sun, the moon, and man. *Maweja Nangila* brew beer, poured it in a jar, and warned them that whoever would drink it would die. During His absence, they drank the beer. Upon returning, *Maweja Nangila* found them crying. Their children had died. He confronted them: Did you drink my beer? The man said no; he was crying for nothing. *Maweja Nangila* punished man for his lie by making his children die for real. The sun and the moon told the truth: their children had died also. *Maweja Nangila* said they were only sleeping. To this day, the sun and the moon resurrect after each death; humans do not. According to still another version, God came with his people from East to settle them in a land filled with all sorts of plants they could eat from with the exception of fruits from the red tree. If they ate of the fruits of this particular tree they would die. When He came back, He found them eating fruits from the prohibited red tree. In his goodness, He still wanted to free them from the taboo. He told them to stay behind and to follow Him 60 days later. They stayed but never followed Him. Death and misfortunes stayed with them forever (Kalanda, 1992; Mudimbe, 1991; Mudimbe, 1991, quoting Fourche and Morlighem, and Theuws).

God's responses in the cases of human disobedience related above suggest that God's removal of original spiritual gifts—rejuvenation and immortality or resurrection—from humans is not seen as a rejection, abandonment or condemnation. The humans did not become evil in God's sight. Nor did they fall from God's grace. Instead, what occurred was simply a readjustment of the relationship between the two without a change to the being of the humans. Many groups, the Dinka for instance, believe that the Creator remains the parent of human beings. The change from immortality to death only applies to the body, not the spirit. Following death, the body perishes, but the spirit continues to live eternally. Now liberated from the limitations of the human body, the spirit of the departed enters in direct, unmediated, contacts with the Creator, divinities, and the ancestors. Their mutual spiritual interaction becomes more intense, whereby making the spirit of the recently deceased more powerful. Also, throughout life, humans are given opportunities to bring these spirits into their lives and be transformed into more spiritual beings with increased powers, through such mechanisms as trance, ordination to priesthood, or other forms of consecration (Carruthers in Beatty, 2001; Mbiti, 1970).

Reincarnation

Procreation as an Act of Reincarnation: The newborn baby is believed to be above all a returning spirit. The baby may or may not be of the same sex as the dead person in whose body the baby's spirit lived previously. For instance, the Illa people (Republic of Zambia) believe that the reincarnating spirit is sexless. It may seek manifestation in either the body of a man or a woman regardless of the individual's sex in a previous life. They say that, in common with the esoteric teachings of many other religious traditions, the incarnating spirit, the true self of each individual, provides the newly-born child with no memory of previous lives in the worlds of either spirit or matter. During life, the spirit animates the body but remains untainted by the vicissitudes of daily living (Rooke, 1980).

Reincarnation as Destiny-Making Renegotiation: The Igbo believe that at creation the individual receives his *chi*, soul/life force, from *Chukwu*, God, and along with it, his destiny across the various stages of the eternal cycle of time. The stages are life, death, and rebirth. At receiving the *chi,* the person makes a commitment to *Chukwu* about his destiny and course of time on Earth. Before entering the world, the person must cross a river where he or she is challenged by *Uhammiri*, goddess of water. The person must accept and defend his or her destiny from *Chukwu* or form a pact with *Uhammiri* for a new destiny and become a devotee of *Uhammiri.* If later in life the person wants to change the terms of agreement about his or her destiny unilaterally, ill fate will befall him or her in the form of illness, mental derangement, or continuous loss of children. At death, the person returns to *Chukwu*. Before reincarnating, *Chukwu* gives the person a new *chi,* which will be challenged again by goddess *Uhammiri* at the crossing of the river. Some of the after-birth rituals are devoted to determining who reincarnated in the newborn child. Improper identification may have fatal results for the person later in life (Jell-Bahlsen in Olupona, 2000).

Longing for Conception, an Invitation to Reincarnation: In Luba worldview, human life begins at conception. A complete human earthly life starts at birth. The Luba do acknowledge that the immediate cause of a conception is the encounter of a man's spermatozoid with a woman's egg during sexual intercourse. But they also believe in the existence of supernatural forces that can make such encounter possible or impossible. At the highest order of abstraction, such a force is said to be *diswa dya Nzambi*, God's will. Indeed, the Luba believe that all that exists, including human beings and their individual blessings, comes from God. However, the way they behave in many circumstances suggests that in their subconscious minds God has entrusted His many blessings to the ancestors and that it pertains to the latter to dispense them to their earthly descendents as they deem the latter deserving. For instance, a Luba man or woman living of tradition who wants a child, more often than not, will ask the ancestors rather than God. Also, when a child is born into a family, the parents will make sacrifices to ancestors in a spirit of gratitude rather than to God directly.

Other supernatural forces that can cause a particular conception to occur are the spirits of little children. The Luba believe that babies are re-incarnated spirits of bygone relatives, sometimes even those of non-related individuals. In their freshness and innocence, little children are more spiritual beings than they are physical ones. They still maintain camaraderie relationships with the pure spirits of their pre-birth world whence they came. A young woman who desires to become a mother is advised to be nice to little children so they may invite other spirits to be born to her. Sometimes, the supernatural force that brings a particular baby into a mother's womb is no other than that very child's spirit before conception. A mother may pray to her dead baby, imploring it to come back. The Luba bury their babies in the front porch or courtyard of the mother's house so the deceased baby may feel really wanted and eventually consent to come back. To invite the spirit of a deceased baby to be reborn through her, the mother would place a pot filled with white clay on the baby's tomb. Every evening, she would sit by the tomb with the palm of her left hand on the jaw in an attitude of sorrow, thinking about her baby, imploring the baby to return to her and praying God (*Mvidi Mukulu*) to send it back.

Determining the Baby's Spiritual Identity: Since children are returning spirits, Luba women are instructed to be very sensitive to the things occurring to their bodies or in their surroundings before and during pregnancy. Likewise, the midwife who assists with the delivery examines newborn babies carefully to detect the eventual marks of their spiritual statuses. Some babies do not have any special marks. Those who bear distinctive signs at conception or birth are called *baana ba bupangu*, special birth children. Distinctive signs are diverse (Katanga-Tshitenge, 1969):

> **Multiple births**: The most spectacular birth is that of twins, even more so triplets. The first of the twins is *Mbuyi*; the second *Nsanza* or *Nkanku*. The third of triplets is *Katuma*.
>
> **An event that occurred at the time of the child's conception**: the so called *Ntumba* baby falls into this category. This baby is born to a mother who has not menstruated between her first sexual contact with the baby's father and the baby's conception. It is believed that on the night a *Ntumba* child is conceived the parents will hear, during the sexual intercourse resulting in the conception, a big ceiling-shaking blow on the roof of the house. Hence this baby's full title: "*Ntumba wa Muulu*": *Ntumba* from the Sky.
>
> **The child's order of birth and relative sex** (the child's sex in relation to the sex and number of immediate older siblings). A child following three or four siblings of the opposite sex carries the birth title of *Ngalula*.
>
> **The position of the child's body or body parts during delivery**. For instance, a baby born lying on the stomach is titled *Cikudimena*, from verb *kukudimana*, to lie on one's stomach.
>
> **A distinctive physical mark on the baby's body**: *Kanjinga*. This baby comes to the world with the umbilical cord surrounding its body. *Kanjinga* means the one who is wrapped with a rope.

A Spiritual Being in a Physical Body

Physical Defect: The baby titled *Musangu* is a perfect example of a physical defect baby. Such a baby is born with a split lip, sometimes accompanied with crooked feet, a deformed spinal column, and partially grey hair.

Birth Rites for all Newborn Babies: Not all Luba babies are born with special birth marks. However, all are considered to be more spiritual and still emotionally attached to, and more participating in the life of whence they came than that of the world of humans they enter. They are very sensitive to the treatment that the parents give them. For these reasons, all newborn babies are welcomed with rites designed to make them feel wanted, grow normally in good health and become successful adults. Title babies have additional birth rites specific for their respective birth categories. Their welcoming rituals are discussed in Chapter 8. Traditionally in Luba society, a series of rituals were performed during the baby's first seven days of existence. To start with, when a child was born, the placenta and other amniotic substances covering the baby's body were secretly kept somewhere around the house. Until the umbilical cord was healed and detached, the child's feces were not disposed of. Instead they were preserved and kept inside the mother's house, in a corner under heating wood. Every morning, after sweeping the house, the mother would place part of the dirt, especially ashes, over the feces probably to dry them. The reason for keeping the child's feces so preciously during this time was perhaps the fact that they were considered more as wastes from intra-uterine nourishment received from the mother during conception than from earthly food consumed by the child after birth. In other words, they were part of the child rather than external to the child. Disposing them haphazardly could endanger the child's life. An evil hearted person disposing of supernatural powers could use them to kill the child or to spoil the child's future (Katanga-Tshitenge 1969:70-71, 125).

The next ritual within a baby's first seven days occurred at the time the stump of the umbilical cord detached. At this event, the father would provide the mother with a live chicken that she would present to the baby saying: *"Ki nzolu wa kukwakidila nenda eeu, wikala anu ne makanda*—This chicken is to welcome you, continue to grow in good health." When the chicken was killed and cut for cooking, the mother would bury the inedible parts such as the beak and the claws, along with the child's feces and the umbilical cord, at some spot behind her house. A banana tree was planted at the site. From this moment on, until the child became competent to go to the toilet alone, the baby's feces and the dirt from sweeping the house would be disposed at this burial place (*diyala*). When the chicken was cooked and the meal was ready, the mother would dip her finger into the chicken sauce and repeat the words of presentation made to the child earlier: *"Ki nzolu wa kukwakidila nenda eeu, wikala anu ne makanda."* "This is your welcoming chicken, grow in good health." She would then place the finger into the child's mouth to have the child suck the chicken sauce from it. She would also mash a tiny piece of the chicken liver with her fingers, wet it with the sauce and place it into the child's mouth. The mother and the older children would eat the rest of the chicken meal.

In some families, the umbilical cord was not buried at the time of its detachment from the child's body. Instead it was wrapped and the package was secretly kept somewhere in the roof of the mother's house. If the child had siblings, all the umbilical cords would be kept together. When facing imminent death, a mother who had not buried her children's umbilical cords, would entrust them to a close relative, sister or brother. Here again, the reason for burying the child's umbilical cord immediately, or for entrusting it only to a close relative in whom one has confidence, was the fear that, if left at the reach of everyone, a sorcerer might manipulate it to kill the child or to damage the child's ability to procreate (Katanga-Tshitenge, 1969:125).

A Luba mother would observe the post-partum sexual abstinence for about a year. During this time, she would wear a diaper of clothing material (*mukaya*) under her clothes to symbolize her state of abstinence. In general, she would also take less care of her own body in order to devote herself fully to the care of her child. She would neglect her physical cares also in order to make herself sexually unattractive to her husband. A woman in this state of abstinence and self-inflicted corporal neglect is called *muvyela*. When the time to resume sexual relations came, the husband would provide the *muvyela* with a chicken called *nzolu wa mukaya*, diaper chicken, which precisely was designed to symbolize the ending of the abstinence. Before killing the chicken, the mother would present it to the child saying: *ki nzolu wa kukujilula nenda eeu, wikala anu ne makanda*: "This chicken is to take you out of the taboo, be always in good health." When the meal was ready, she would reiterate this presentation before feeding the child with the chicken meat. It was believed that parents who resumed sexual relations without this ritual would expose their child to become mentally unstable and socially unsuccessful. To express this causality, the *Luba* speak of such parents as having damaged their child (*mbanyanga mwana*) (Katanga-Tshitenge, 1969:132).

Rites for Extraordinary Birth Babies: Welcoming rituals for all babies have been discussed in Chapter 1. Here we are concerned with extraordinary birth children only. Four types of birth are considered extraordinary: *Mapasa, Katuma, Ntumba*, and *Kabishi. Mapasa* are twins. *Katuma* is the third of the triplets. *Ntumba* is a child born to a mother who has not menstruated between the first sexual contact with her husband and the conception. *Kabishi* is a child born prematurely. These children are believed to be imbued with supernatural powers, with twins having the most extraordinary powers. Twins and other extraordinary birth babies are the objects of more complex birth rites. These children are generally sickly and difficult to keep alive. They are also said to cause numerous difficulties to their parents during pregnancy, including accidents, serious illnesses, and famine (Katanga-Tshitenge, 1969).

Two types of rituals, *nsasa* and *nsawu*, were common to these children. *Nsasa* was the name for a small shelter made of palm branches built by the front of the mother's house, generally in the veranda. During the first seven days of the child's (or children's in the case of twins or triplets) existence, both the mother and the baby would stay and sleep in this shelter. The purpose seems to have been to accustom the fragile child to the varying temperatures of day and night. The child's ability to survive these changes during the first week of existence gave hope for a longer survival. At the end of the seven-day trial period, the parents would call in the *mpamba* to introduce the child (or children) and the mother into the house. Like any other ritual in honor of children, this one would be accompanied with dances and chicken sacrifices, four in the case of twins, two for the others. From then on, the mother and the baby would sleep inside the house, sharing the mother's bed, as still is the case with all newborn children in

Luba villages. But the shelter would remain in place. Eight to twelve months later, the parents would once more bring the *mpamba* over. By this time, the baby was already crawling or walking. The *mpamba* would dismantle the shelter. The debris from the fallen shelter would be placed on *diyala*, the site behind the mother's house which served as the dumping ground for the baby's feces and the dirt from sweeping the house. Portions of the food, including some meat, would be placed on the debris to be buried with them. The shelter itself would be thrown away (Katanga-Tshitenge, 1969).

The last major rituals for a child of extraordinary birth took place when the child had started to walk. By that time, the parents were planning to cohabitate again. It was also the time for allowing the child to be taken to other houses in the village. Until that point, the child was confined to the parents' house and courtyard. Taking the child to other places would have exposed the child to the greed of sorcerers and the malevolence of evildoers, thus jeopardizing the child's health and life. To carry out the latter rituals, the parents would invite the *mpamba* and other women over. They would give her a goat and two chickens or two goats and four chickens, if they were parents of twins. The mother would dress in banana barks arranged in the form of a short skirt. She would have her body dotted with red clay kaolin and oil, and her hair braided and oiled. The husband would give her a chicken in order to allow her to throw away the calabash bowl in which the child's kaolin was kept. He would give her another chicken to allow her to throw away the diaper that she used to wear as a sign of sexual abstinence. After the ceremony, she would resume sexual relations with her husband. The husband would give her a third chicken to allow her to have her hair cut. If they were parents of twins, the number of chickens was doubled.

At this point, the one or two goats and the one or two chickens given to the *mpamba* would be killed. Then a house-to-house procession would be conducted throughout the village, during which the mother carried the head(s) of the goat(s) lifted up in her hand(s). Another woman would carry the child (two women in case of twins) being ritualized. At each house, the occupant would offer the child, or each child in case of twins, a present of cassava, corn, chicken, or money. After the procession, the chicken(s) killed previously and part of the goat or goats meat would be cooked for the mother, the officiating *mpamba*, and the other *mpamba*. Several other chickens would be killed and cooked separately for the non-*mpamba* mothers.

SUMMARY

The human being is an embodiment of divine properties. Every person possesses qualities of being that are similar to God's qualities, even though less perfect than God's. God is spirit. Through creation, God infused God's divine spiritual attributes into human, including the eternal presence of the spirit of God, the divine energy that permeates and animates the human body, holistic knowledge, including knowledge of things unseen in time and space; creative power, that is, the power to make things happen that were not there before; consciousness, imagination, wisdom soul and memory. In their conception of the build-up of the human self, ethnic groups across the continent of Africa, identify numerous metaphysical elements beyond the physical organs, the bone structure and the fleshy envelope. The invisible elements are manifestations or reflections of the inner divine spirit. The spiritual essence of the divine inner spirit and the cognate metaphysical forces remain inherent in severed organs as well as in extensions of the human body such as the footprint, the shadow and the reflection in water. They are susceptible to the strengthening or weakening powers of more powerful spiritual forces, such as the Creator, divinities, ancestors, nature spirits, witches, and sorcerers.

Even though humans lost their original supernatural powers when Heaven and God distanced themselves from Earth and humans, some individuals are still being born with spiritual powers above standard human powers. In most cases, such innate mystical powers are latent at birth and remain so until they are activated in adult age through mystical initiation. Fewer individuals acquire their superior mystical powers through initiation only. Some recipients of such powers, such as witches and haters, use them to harm the people they dislike for some reason. Others, notably diviners, medicine men and women, seers and healers, use theirs to do good, including counteracting the malevolent actions of the evildoers. The omnipresent threat of becoming a victim of the malevolent actions of the witches goes hand in hand with the prudence and wisdom to cover one-self with personal magical powers. Thanks to magical coverage, a hunted person could escape the enemy weapon, become opaque to its penetration, or simply completely disappear. One could also protect one's entire household and property. Additionally, magical powers could enable one to attract the marriageable women, the job, or the kinds of neighbors who would enhance one's chances of success in life.

Through creation, God endowed humans and the animal kingdom with the gift of immortality. People would grow older, rejuvenate, and keep on living. Immortality of the body ended when the original relationship of the inhabitants of the Earth with the Creator came to be altered in response to some inadvertent action by humans, animals, or both. The Creator also provides opportunities for individuals to be called to spiritual functions, which turn them into mediums of divinities communicating messages from the latter to the community of the living; and for spirits of the dead to reincarnate as humans through conception and rebirth. Many others are called to receive consecration and become the peers and fellows of powerful spirits and more capable of mystically protecting the households, the village community, or the nation. The ultimate call to spiritual transformation comes through death. The former human being becomes fully spiritual and enters an unmediated permanent contact with the Creator, the divinities, and the ancestors.

Chapter 2
A Moving Body Full of Vitality

1. Essential Existential Body Movements
2. Optimal Muscular Performance Aptitudes
3. Versatile Productive Hand Movements

An apt human body is a moving reality in its divine making and development processes, in its structural make-up, and in its functioning operations. It is capable of regularly engaging successfully in muscular performances requiring strength and endurance. It is also equipped with agile working hands capable of carrying out versatile productive activities.

1. EXISTENTIAL BODY MOVEMENTS

All that lives moves. Even the creation of the universe conveys ideas of movement. The making and unfolding of human life is portrayed in some African cosmologies as a series of cyclical movements patterned on the movements of the sun. The biological systems and vital organs which maintain life are animated by the constant circulation (movements) of the air, the blood, and the hormones. The human body is structured in such a way that several parts can be flexed at bone junctions making possible the movement of the trunk, the limbs, and the extremities. In addition, one can add the rhythmic body movements and melodic inflections of the voice which epitomize dancing and singing, respectively.

Creation Movements

The creation of the universe involves movements. For instance, in the cosmology of the *Dogon* people of Mali, all that exists is involved in two fundamental motions: the perpetual helical movement which is the principle of conservation of matter, and the zigzag movement which represents the perpetual alternation of opposites and reflects the principle of *twinness*. These primordial movements progressively took the form of an egg, the egg of the world (*aduno tal*). Life began when, *digitaria exilis*, a very small pair of male and female germs, animated by vibrations, busted the sheath envelop of the egg of the world and, moving in the form of a spiral, expanded to the outmost dimensions of the universe. *Digitaria* formed at the core of the egg of the world along with seven longitudinal internal segments of the egg of the word prefiguring the seven fundamental seeds of cultivation. *Digitaria* and the seven seeds are to be found in the organization and functioning of all domains of life: cosmos, human being, and society. For their part, the *Kôngo* of Congo DRC teach their children that Earth came into existence when the original eternal fire fusion mass, *Kalûnga*, cooled down and exploded into large fragments, including Earth, Sun, Moon, and countless stars. In the process of cooling, the fire fusion mass produced infinite water mass within the cosmic space. Earth floats on the *Kalûnga* water mass. Being a fragment of *Kalûnga* and in constant contact with the infinite *Kalûnga* water mass, Earth shares *Kalûnga's* life in its completeness and passes it over to all that comes in touch with Earth. *Kalûnga* is a force in motion. Consequently, Earth and everything in it is in perpetual motion.

Life Cycle Movements

Kôngo cosmology also portrays human existence as a change process patterned on the movement of the sun and having similar demarcation points: conception as midnight, birth as sunrise; maturity as mid-day strong sun, and death as sunset. At midnight, the sun begins the journey of the day but it is covered in the darkness of the universe. Likewise, following conception, the human being begins the life journey in the darkness of the mother's womb. Therein, the human-being in formation develops the capacity to breathe. The breathing and the beating of the heart accelerate the being's inner development in order for it to enlarge and expand its original environment, the mother's womb. At sunrise, the sun emerges into the physical world. Throughout the morning hours, the sun builds up strength as it journeys toward midday. At birth, the human being becomes the community's rising Sun, with a voice to speak and be heard; as well as with the capacity to hear and discern voices from the community. Hearing and being heard are the processes through which orders are given and received. Speaking and hearing also have the power to heal or curse, revive or kill (the power of words). At midday, the sun becomes the strongest it can be. For humans, midday epitomizes maturity, leadership, creativity, mastery, and great deeds. All in life is weighed to the scale of expectations associated with this stage: words, deeds, thoughts, movements, projects, meals, relationships. Initiation of adolescents is designed to produce adults who are mature, accomplished doers, and pillars of the community. After midday, the sun gradually weakens as it descends toward sunset. In humans, this is the aging process. At sunset, the sun disappears from the human eye. But it continues to live in the invisible world until it reaches the stage of rebirth at midnight. It is the same with humans: the dead do not stop living. To the contrary, they "persist as spiritual beings beyond the wall waiting for their probable return to the community of the living" (Fukiau, 2001). The spirit of the deceased becomes a stunted ancestor or a spiritually deified ancestor, based on the person's accomplishments and merits in the midday maturity stage.

Ancient Egyptians had a similar conception of life cycles, which is most known in its application to the sun-god and king. It was a custom of Egyptian kings to periodically retreat to the mountain to unite with the gods. They later built the pyramids to this effect. Symptomatically, the first pyramids were built with ascending steps. The pyramids were used as burial places. Here, the king would be united with the sun-god in order to fully participate in the daily cycle of death and resurrection. It was expected that when the king's powers declined he would go, through death, to a location in the underworld, where his *ba*, soul, would reunite with the corpse and enable the king to continue living. Various goods—implements, personal adornments, and provisions of food, often representing gods, sacred signs, and parts of the human bodies—were placed in the tomb to invigorate and protect the spirit of the dead king throughout the passage from death to resurrection. Placed in the tombs, also, were texts expressing messages of spiritual strength to the king for him to reach the heavens and take his rightful place in immortality among the gods in the retinue of god-Re. The acts of journeying from death to resurrection and immortality were symbolized by way of travel organs such as wings, road marks such as steps and ramps, and movement action verbs such as to fly, to rush, to leap and to go up (David, ND).

Optimally Functioning Biological Systems and Life Organs

A body in full vitality is everyone's dream. It is a constant subject of prayers to ancestors, to the spirits of protective heroes, and to God. Likewise, life diminution is feared and attributed to an evil spell, or to severe punishment for violation of a neighbor's sacred rights or for causing a physical or spiritual injury to someone (Mulago in Olupona, 1991:123). Students of human anatomy and physiology tell us that the human body is made up of interconnected, multi-functional biological systems and vital organs whose normal operation is necessary for survival. The essential biological systems are: circular, digestive, endocrine, immune, respiratory, urinary, lymphatic, nervous, muscular, reproductive, skeletal, and integumentary (skin). There are five vital organs: the brain, the heart, the kidneys, the liver, and the lungs. Individuals whose biological systems and body organs are fully operational have the ability to perform physical tasks demanding strength, endurance, and resilience. Constant movements—(circulation) of the air, the blood, and the hormones within and between the cells, the biological systems and the vital organs—are essential to existence.

A Flexible Bone Structure

The human body is structured in such a way that several parts can be flexed at bone junctions. Lower limbs are flexible in the toes, the ankles, the knees, the hips, and the waist. Upper limbs, the arms, are equipped with flexible fingers, hands, wrists, and elbows. The neck can flex back and forth, side to side, and rotate clock wise and counter clockwise. Flexibility allows for motion to take place. The human body can fold, twist, and rotate over the head or a limb. It can lie down or stand up, jump up and down; move to the left and to the right, forward and backward. Human beings can walk and run on short or long distances.

Countless Ordinary Daily-Living Movements

To live is to move. Each of the most elementary life functions, such as waking up from sleep in the morning, using the restroom, taking a shower, changing clothes, preparing and eating breakfast, is a complex combination of natural movements without which there would not be life. Suppose one is sleeping, lying on the back. Waking up involves movements such as lifting up the trunk while resting on the elbows and the palms of the hands, moving to the edge of the bed and sitting with the legs downward, then standing on the two feet and walking away by advancing the legs forwardly one after the other. If the next function is using the restroom and the door is closed, one has to turn the knob, pull the door, cross to the other side, and close the door behind oneself.

Chapter 2

Once near the toilet bowl, one lifts the lid, position oneself appropriately to use the restroom while standing or seated; afterward flush by extending the arm and pushing the lever down with one's fingers; then close the toilet bowl and walk away. The next function is washing the hands. This involves turning on the faucet, putting some soap on the hands, rubbing the hands and the fingers against each other under the running water, turning the faucet off when finished, reach out to a towel and drying the hands by rubbing the towel over them. Usually, in the morning, hand washing is followed by mouth rinsing and tooth brushing. Here one turns to the mouth wash container first to bring it to the mouth, let some drops in, put the container back where it stays, and rinse the mouth and toss the container. Then one reaches out to the toothbrush and the toothpaste and puts some toothpaste on the toothbrush. One then brushes the teeth by rubbing the brush over and under the teeth. To conclude tooth care for the morning, one washes the toothbrush and puts it away. One then scoops some water with a glass or a hand, takes it to the mouth and rinses the mouth. Usually, one then leaves the bathroom after washing and drying the hands one more time. Taking a shower is a complex of operational movements as well. It consists of movements such as taking the clothes off, opening or sliding the shower door, closing it, releasing the shower hose, turning the water on and pulling the water all over the body, reaching out to the soap, rubbing it all over the body or soaking a washcloth in soapy water and rubbing the body with the wet soapy washcloth; then running water all over the body again this time to remove the soap. The next shower-taking phase consists of stepping outside the shower, reaching for the towel, drying the body, putting on some deodorant and cream or lotion, brushing the hair, and putting on some minimal clothing before leaving the bathroom. Dressing for the day is usually done in the bedroom. To dress, one picks the clothing material from wherever it is and puts it over the part of the body it belongs to with one's hands and fingers. If it belongs to the bottom, it generally requires the cooperation of the legs by folding or extending as needed. Breakfast preparation requires walking to the kitchen, opening the refrigerator or the freezer, pulling out whatever is needed from there and closing it, bringing the cooking pots and other implements from the drawers, and closing the drawers. Most African meals consist of stews cooked in water. This means one has to put some water in a pot, put in the main item to be cooked along with seasonings, activate the fire, boil to satisfaction, manipulating with a spatula as needed depending on the nature of the meal. Serving, eating, drinking, and washing hands and dishes, all require movements of the hands. God has made it possible for the human body to coordinate all its body parts to complete these many tiny but important steps necessary to go through life.

Rhythmic Body Movements and Melodic Inflections of the Voice

African people customarily engage in patterned, rhythmic movements of the body and melodic inflections of the voice conventionally known as dancing and singing, respectively. Sound emissions can be weak or strong. The strong ones are manifestations of vitality and vigor. This section highlights African dancing and singing activities as manifestations of life vitality. Africans dance and sing with rhythm in all life circumstances: work, life cycle events, praise to authority figures, and popular entertainments. As a custom, they dance in circular line repeating some conventional steps. At points, individuals step out the line into the circle to exhibit personal dancing creativities. To end his or her improvisation moment, the person inside the circle invites someone else to come in by dancing in front of him or her. Selected instances when African men and women execute dances and songs include: collective work, a king's or chief's court dances, and religious ritual dances.

Collective Work Dances and Songs: African men often sing while collectively involved in some cumbersome activity to alleviate the burden of the task. For example, when tilling the land collectively, Luba farmers, at some peak moments, synchronize the movements of the hoes to produce a common sound and then harmonize the sounds of the songs with the sound of the hoes, saying:

> "*Twayi cinamina. Wakubanduluka, twamudya cibawu*"
> (Let us stick to the task while bent to the ground.
> He who straightens up his body will pay us fines").

In Nigeria, farmers, blacksmiths and women potters sing while executing their respective tasks (Falola, 2001). During the regime of King Leopold II (1885-1908) and the ensuing Belgian colonization (1908-1960), the Congolese were subjected to forced labor, including collective *corvées*. They were often summoned to haul heavy trees or stones attached to a long chain or rope. In *Bandundu*, the haulers, equally distributed along the chain, would pull the load to the rhythm of their bodies synchronized with the sounds of a popular song called *lunkamba* (rope).

Court Music and Dances: Court music is played in honor of a king, a chief, or another important dignitary. The making of a new king, renewal of the kingship institution, and the funeral of a king are some of the special occasions where court music and dances are performed. At the investiture of a new chief, Luba dignitaries and sub-chiefs execute before him the *kutomboka* dance which signifies power takeover by the new chief and submission to him by the outgoing chief, all sub-chiefs, dignitaries, and ordinary citizens. Where there existed strong kingdoms or large chiefdoms, praise music for the king or the paramount chief were more complex and more elaborate. Such was the case among the Mangbetu people who live between the Uele and Bomokandi rivers in Upper Congo. Court music reflected the power and splendor of the King. King Mbunza, who reigned in the nineteenth century, was a great king. Musical instruments symbolizing his power and greatness, such as the iron double bell, large ivory horns and certain types of slit drums were found in the king's court only. Numerous imposing musical ensembles performed for the king. Some were famous musicians personally invited by the king to live at the court while making a living from tilling lands provided by the sovereign (Demolin, 1990). The Tutsi King, *Mwami*, was praised with elegant dance and song performances called *Intore*.

Ritual Music and Dances: Some ritual music serves to purify society from evildoings. For example, the *ekpri akata* musical ritual among the Ibibio of Nigeria and the *Oro* ritual among the Yoruba are performed with the intent to restore morality and societal values. The players move around at night warning thieves and witches in songs and musical instruments to mend their ways (Falola, 2001). Birth rite dances are found all over Africa. Babies are believed to be returning spirits. They react to their parents' actions more as spirits than humans. Consequently they are generally welcomed with special ceremonies designed to make them feel wanted, to strengthen them physically and to ensure their future success in adult life. To this end, mothers perform baby welcoming rituals accompanied with songs and dances. One such dance-song that Luba mothers execute goes as follows:

Nyunyi wa Nsambasamba /A Flying Bird without Specific Destination

Cikololo nyunyi wa nsambasamba,	*Cikololo*, a bird that flies from place to place,
Usambila wasabuka Lubilanji.	Once flew across the Lubilanji River.
Ndelela penyi,	(She cried): Where will I give birth to my child,
Ntambwa wa ba Nkashama?	Oh Lion, fellow of the Leopard?
Ndelela penyi,	Where will I give birth to my child,
beena bulaba babenga?	since the masters of the land won't allow me to? (Mukenge, 2002)

Deaths are other occasions for celebrative dances and songs. Among the Lugbara of Uganda, the most elaborate funeral dances and songs tell of the dead man's life and way of dying, of the failings of other lineages and airing of grievances and disposing of grievances. A combination of personified drums – child (small drum), wife (middle-sized drum) and grandmother (large drum) are played throughout the singing period. Men and women participate in the dance, with most men inside the arena and most women at the outskirt. Dancers may carry spear and arrows (men), wands (women) and quivers (senior women). Dancers' teams are formed by generation, not by lineage. The oldest generation of the most senior lineage enters the arena first. Members of the same generation dance side-by-side (Middleton, 1965).

2. OPTIMAL MUSCULAR PERFORMANCE APTITUDES

Many human activities require muscular strength. Below, three types of daily activities are succinctly presented to illustrate this fact. They are: farming, physical fight, and sexual intercourse. A fourth illustration is taken from African history, notably: stone monument constructions.

Farming

Agriculture is the primary source of livelihood in African societies. The low-yielding technology of the hoe, the machete, the ax and even the stick dominates everywhere. African farming therefore is heavily dependent on the physical force and manual abilities of the farmer. Three illustrations are presented hereafter, notably from Luba villages in the Congo, Igbo towns in Nigeria and the Gikuyu region in Kenya. All three practice agriculture as a means of subsistence and a source of revenues. All members of the family—men, women, and children—participate in it, often with ethnic variations based on gender and age. Farming relies on rainfalls. In Lubaland, the rainy season runs from late August to late December, and February to May. Until Congo's independence in 1960, the repertoire of seasonal crops grown in Luba villages included cotton, corn, cassava, beans, groundnuts, sweet potatoes, green vegetables, and pumpkins. Two crops, notably millet and sorghum, once grown in Lubaland, had almost vanished by then. Cotton, a colonial export crop imposition, was abandoned in the years following independence. The other crops are grown both for domestic consumption and for generating income. Corn and cassava are the ingredients in the staple meal, *nshima* or *bidya*. Cassava leaves are the most popular green vegetable consumed on a regular basis in Luba families. Beans, sweet potatoes, and groundnuts are important supplements to *nshima*. Green vegetables are designed to accompany the staple meal. Pumpkin is grown for its fruit, its leaves, and its seeds; all three of which are edible. Several kinds of fruit trees grow in Lubaland: banana, plantain, orange, mango, papaya, and pineapple.

The hoe *(lukasu)*, the number one and multipurpose instrument of production, is used to clear and till the land, to uproot the trees, to make mounds or longitudinal platforms to plant seeds on, and to weed. For crops such as cassava, sweet potatoes, peanuts and yams, the hoe is also used to harvest. The machete *(mwela)* is employed to clear river banks in conjunction with a long wooden hook *(lobo)*, which helps separate the lianas from the trees and shrubs. In the past, a strong man could maintain three fields concurrently: a garden around the houses, a field in the savannah away from the residences, and a river bank field. Very often, some households had a fourth field, a cassava field from the previous year, located in the savannah, since cassava lasts longer underground without spoiling. Most of the above-mentioned crops grow in the three sites mentioned. Cultivation around the houses and in the savannah is practiced during the two phases of the rainy season: September through December, and February through April. In the dry season, May through August, these locations become too dry to produce anything. Cultivation in river banks is more appropriate then. Of the three types, savannah fields are the most important.

In Igboland (Nigeria), the farming cycle begins in January and February with men clearing the land with machetes and laying the green leaves on the ground to dry and be burned later to produce ash fertilizer. During the same period, men collect the sticks for staking the yams. March and April are first rain and planting months. Men make cylindrical holes with long-handle hoes. Whereas, women and children scrape the top soil with small hoes into the holes around yam seedlings forming a small hill around each seedling. In northern Igboland, men rather than women and children, make big yam hills of top soil. Yam is the top crop. Following the planting of the yam, the field is distributed to women individually for them to plant corn, melon and okra on the slopes of yam hills, and pumpkins, beans, cassava, and cocoyams in the spaces between yam hills. Concomitantly, men devote their time to staking the growing yams. Weeding is assumed by women, but harvesting yams is a man's prerogative. It is, then, the job of women and children to wash them and carry them home. Yams are stored in yam houses at home. A few people have a second storehouse in the field. Before storing, yams are dried in the sun (Uchendu, 1965).

The Gikuyu are former hunters and gatherers who gradually moved into farming.

Chapter 2

Men cultivated cocoyams and bananas, women sweet potatoes and millet. Sugar-cane is another men's crop. Corn, a recent arrival (early 19th century), has become a major crop grown by Gikuyu women for food and by Gikuyu men for sale. Today, Gikuyu's economy is much more diversified. More recent additions include dwarf beans, cowpeas, pigeon peas, kidney beans, lentil and garden peas, cabbage, tomatoes, onions, carrots, and kale. Impressive also is the variety of fruit plants cultivated by the Gikuyu, notably: papayas, mangoes, passion fruits, pineapples, oranges, plums and more (*Kikuyu* - Economy, ND). Planting takes place during the long rainy season (March to July) or the short rainy season (October to January) depending on the crops. Some crops take more months after planting to mature, notably ten months for the arum and 18 months for the sugar-cane. Women's work includes preparing the ground with a long digging stick, planting, weeding, and harvesting. Women are assisted by men in carrying out heavy works, such as clearing fallow grounds, cutting trees, and tilling new fields; and by children in growing legumes and cereals. Four women's crops dominated the Gikuyu diet: corn, the lablab bean, the kidney bean and arum. Two of the major men's crops—tobacco and sugar cane—were luxuries. Women are also responsible for unceasing daily chores, such as fetching water, grinding grains, gathering firewood, cooking, washing and taking care of children. Carrying loads befalls them too. They carry the loads on their backs tied to the forehead with straps (Presley, 2018).

Physical Fight

Human beings fight for a variety of reasons in a mutual agreement sport or in aggression and self-defense situations. Effectiveness in all these forms of fighting is predicated as much on physical strength as it is on skills. The *cibula*, *mbata* and *bisusu* fights of the Luba will serve as particular illustrations of a widespread cultural practice. The Luba are not known for being fighters. They value peaceful living. However, everyone is expected to be able to defend himself against attackers. A man must also be able to defend and protect his family, his property, and his village. Wrestling (*cibula*) and fist-fighting (*mbata*) were the most common forms of fight in Luba villages. Wrestling is perhaps the only form that seems to have been practiced following some rules. The fighters stand straight facing each other. Then, they place their arms around each other's waist. The fight consists of squeezing the adversary against one's own body, make him lose balance, and throw him to the ground lying on his back with the hero on top of him. Trips were not permitted. Nor was the use of hands. Either of these would disqualify the user. The muscular power of one's arms alone counted. Fist fighting (*mbata*, or *mankomu*, or else *makofi*) does not seem to have been subjected to any particular rule, except perhaps that most of the time fists were directed to the head and face area in a calculated manner. Wrestling and fist-fighting are men's fights. Women's equivalent of fist-fighting is *bisusu*. The impact of the fist is on the back of the closed fingers. The *cisusu* (singular of *bisusu*) reaches the adversary with the front of the hand, that is, the side where the closed fingers touch the palm. Men usually use the weaker arm to protect the head and the stronger fisted hand to aggress. Women fight with both hands, hitting the adversary's face wherever the hand can land. Men also fight with clubs, javelins, or spears. Women resort to whatever stick is accessible as well as to the pestle (*mwinshi*).

Clubs, javelins and spears were mostly used in corporate fights between members of different villages, lineages or clans.

The *cibula*, the *mbata* and the *bisusu* are person-to-person fights. King Shaka's conquest wars for the building of the Zulu nation were fought between Shaka's soldiers and the adversary ethnic groups' soldiers. Soldiers in each camp threw spears on the other camp's soldiers while running forward toward the enemies. King *Shaka* trained his soldiers in endurance and resilience by making them run bare-footed every day and in combat. He equipped them with a new weapon of war, the *iklwa*, short-stabbing spear in replacement for the *assegai*, the long-throwing spear. He also taught them a new fighting strategy consisting of running away from the adversaries in the form of a buffalo's horns, with the center running backward and the wings advancing outwardly while the enemies are throwing their spears in different directions. The strategy was to encircle the enemies after they will have used up their throwing spears and finish them up one by one with the short-stabbing spear (Davis, 1981; Omer-Cooper in Collins, ed., 1994, July 1992).

Sexual Intercourse

Virility is a physical, physiological, and psychological power. It is a mark of vitality sought after for pleasure, marriage, and procreation. Sexuality in marriage is considered more laudable than free-for-all sexuality. However, although legitimate, sexuality in marriage is felt misguided if it excludes procreation. More often than not, marriage is sought primarily as the proper context for legitimate procreation. African men and women marry with the goal to beget many children and to provide them with an environment that maximizes their chance to grow and become successful adults and parents of legitimate children. The Luba people express the high value placed on procreation by saying: *kulela ki panu*: to live is above all to procreate. The desire for prolific reproduction is often invoked to justify polygamy. The importance attached to marriage, polygamy, and procreation explains the concern with what the Luba people call *bukola bwa baluma*, literally, the strength of manhood, that is, *virility*. Men consume certain herbs and foods known to enhance virility and seek treatment from reputable medicine practitioners to fight impotence. Women use herbal medicines to treat infertility and engage in body treatment practices known only to women to increase their sensuality (Mukenge, 1967).

Stone Monument Construction

Several ancient African civilizations have left behind impressive architectural stone monuments. *Egyptian pyramids*, *Aksum stelae*, *Ethiopian Coptic churches*, and the *Great Zimbabwe Enclosure* in the ancient land of Mwene Mutapa, are the most known cases. The stones for building the Egyptian pyramids came from quarries along the Nile River; some close by, others hundreds of miles away. Most were transported on barges. Still, there is no doubt about the muscular nature of the operations involved and the colossal amount of physical strength required to execute them: e.g., breaking huge stones, loading them on barges, unloading them, hauling them to the construction site, lining them up side by side and stacking them one on top of the other line-by-line all way up to completion of the architectural structure; and thereafter smoothing the surface. Aksum stelae were stone pillars with a rectangular cross section and a pyramidal top erected as funerary monuments in honor of deceased members of the nobility. They consisted of single blocks of stones carved from hard rocks similar to granite. After carving, the stone blocks had to be transported to the construction site, and then worked on manually to be turned into smoothly surfaced artistic obelisks. All these were hard work operations requiring a large supply of muscular strength and stamina. Reportedly, there exist today 200 monolithic churches in Ethiopia, dating back to the reign of King Gebre Mesqel Lalibela (1181-1221) of the Zagwe Dynasty. Five famous churches are located north of the Jordan River in Tigray. These are: *Biete Golgotha Mikael, Biete Mariam, Biete Denagel, Biete Maskal,* and *Biete Medhani Alem.* Six famous churches are to the south of the river, in Mount Abuna Yosef, in Lalibela. They include: *Biete Lehem, Biete Gabriel Rafael, Biete Abba Libanos, Biete Amanuel, Biete Qeddus Mercoreus,* and *Biete Ghiorgis.* Adjacent to the churches, in each group, are tombs, catacombs, and storerooms pertaining to the clergy and connected to the church and to one another through a system of pathways and tunnels, whereas a system of drainage trenches and canals was built to prevent flooding from underground river and water tables. The churches and the accompanying structural facilities and communication and drainage systems were sculpted out of the volcanic rock mountain. It is well understood that breaking, chiseling, and smoothing rocks are hard muscular activities. In addition, going to these Ethiopian Orthodox churches is a monumental physical task all of itself. The churches are located toward the top of the mountain. Worshipers who attend the daily morning service climb on a risky walkway chiseled on the flank of the mountain. The pilgrims who come annually from all over Ethiopia, walk barefooted, many for several days, if not weeks (Luna, 2014; Barnett, 2013).

Other Activities Requiring Muscular Strength and Stamina

To make a living, Africans regularly engage in multiple activities requiring physical strength and stamina. Carpentry is one. Felling trees with an ax and cutting and splitting the wood with a machete or, in a smaller number of instances, with a manual saw, and making chairs, stools, or benches. All of these are exhaustive muscular performance tasks which can be effectively executed only by a body full of strength and stamina. What is true for carpentry is also true for wooden statue sculpture and canoe making. The canoes must in addition be hauled to the river or the sea. From among other competences, a person in an apt body has the stamina and endurance to walk back and forth to the fields or to the water spring. He or she can go into the bush to collect fire wood or to the marketplace to sell farm produce or purchase trade items from the city. They can participate in multi-day long-distance trade traveling parties. All these operations involve carrying loads in urns, baskets, or bags. Most African villagers only have their own bodies for cargo. They carry loads on their heads, backs or shoulders. Only an apt body can live up to such burdensome tasks. There is also running. The ability to run is a natural endowment inherent in an apt living animal or human body. Africans walk and run barefooted. Shaka, King of the Zulu, trained his soldiers to run strategically away from the incoming combatant enemies, encircle them and, then, run fast toward them to finish them up one by one with a short spear after they had used up their throwing spears. Today, East Africans, Kenyans and Ethiopians, in particular, are hailed for possessing the strength and stamina and mastering the speed for winning medals in international running competitions.

3. VERSATILE PRODUCTIVE HAND MOVEMENTS

Human hands and fingers are flexible and foldable. The ability to open and close the hand allows one to handle tools and operate on other objects; including making tools and practicing varied manual skills. This section examines African traditions in tool making, house building, weaving, and pottery. Emphasis here is on manual tasks. The artistic creativity dimension, where there is one, is discussed in Chapter 5 along with other manifestations of human mental power.

Tool Making

Tool making in Africa is traceable to divine creation. Creation was an act of empowerment, a divine project for human enablement. God made the first human creations with the potential for particular professional skills and endowed them with the ability to bring their potential to fruition. For instance, in the Bambara and Fulani creation story, *Maa Ngala*, the Creator, through speech and the blowing of a spark from His mouth, transferred to the first human being part of His own name, *Maa*, and something of himself consisting of the mind and of *Kuma*, the divine word that enabled *Maa* to activate his great potential. God equipped humans with instruments of labor. In the story of the Fon of Benin, for instance, the Creator *Nana Bukulu* had two twins: *Mawu* (Moon) and *Lisa* (Sun). *Mawu* had the attributes of a female; *Lisa* had those of a male. From their union a son, *Gu*, was born. He had the form of a tool that his parents used to shape the human form. After establishing humans on earth, *Gu's* parents - *Mawu and Lisa* - changed his shape to that of a metal blade embedded in a rock. They then sent him to earth to teach human beings how to make and use tools, thus enabling them to grow food and to build shelters. *Gu* is the patron god of the blacksmiths and metal workers (Carruthers, 1995).

That divine creation was an act of enablement is also portrayed in the story of the Luba of Congo and more extensively in that of the Dogon of Mali. In the Luba story, *Maweja Nangila*, Creator, equipped *Ngoi*, the first Luba man on earth, with an arrow for him to hunt animals for meat. He also sent him a wife, *Pamba*, to whom He (*Maweja Nangila*) gave flour, peanuts, beans and corn for food (Mudimbe, 1991). Flour, peanuts, and corn prefigure farming. In the *Dogon* story, not only did *Amma*'s creative word bring the human species into being, it also made them skilled in particular occupations. Among the created occupations were the weaver, the blacksmith, the tanner, and the speech master. The speech master assumed the function of teacher. Additionally, Creator *Amma*, made the fully developed speech and ordered the emerging of cloth weaving technology and instructions for crafting clothes. By this act, the Creator equipped the seven professionals with the ability to communicate meanings, to understand the laws of nature, and to enhance life through the application of technology. By enabling humans to bring to fruition the potential which exists in the power of technology, the Creator made them participants in the work of creation (Carruthers, 1995: 70-71). As a direct product of divine creation, the traditional African human was, and to some extent still is, occupationally polyvalent, versatile. He grew his own food, built his own shelter, and wove his own baskets, sleeping mats and fishing nets. He hunted, fished and gathered wild fruits, herbs and insects. Hunting, fishing and gathering could be individual or collective. Some occupations became specialized early. The blacksmith, the cloth maker, and the medicine man are among the most known.

Technology making in Africa goes back to Hominid evolution in East Africa, beginning with chipped pebbles by *Homo Habilis* in Oldowan Gorge, Tanzania, through the hand ax, scrapers, and use of fire by *Homo Erectus;* tools of bone and more refined stone knives, scrapers and spearheads by *Homo Sapiens*; and finally, the *microlith* (tiny stone) pointers, blades, awls, needles, and fish-hooks by *Homo Sapiens Sapiens* (Shillington, 1989: 6-9). Metal working was the next early technological development in Africa. Africa is the birth place of iron smelting. The trade of blacksmith was found all across Africa (Jackson, 1990: 60, 61, 63). Thanks to metal, early societies were able to make tools and weapons. Copper was the first metal mined as ore and smelted through heating. Saba, in what is today southern Arabia was economically and culturally integrated with Axum, today's Ethiopia. In Saba, copper was smelted together with tin. In the 10th century B.C. Saba was known as a major producer of gold. By the 6th and 5th centuries BCE, Saba craftsmen were manufacturing iron spearheads and axes, brass and copper products that they exchanged for ivory, tortoise shells and rhinoceros' horns from Aksum, Somalia, Kenya, and Tanzania. Gold was also in *Nubia*. Gold from *Nubia* was used in Egypt to make burial goods for the pharaohs' tombs and jewelry for the nobility (Shillington, 1989).

In West Africa, copper was extracted at Akjoujt, Mauritania, between 1000 and 500 BCE, as well as *at* Azelik and Agades in *Niger* (Shillington, 1989). Iron was smelted in trenches dug below the ground or in circular constructions elevated above the ground. Iron was an important trade item between Egypt and the rest of Africa. In Kush, iron ore production increased after the Assyrian invasion of Egypt (670 BCE) to strengthen the development of Meroe and to improve weapons of defense and spears and arrows for hunting (Shillington, 1989: 39-40). Evidence of iron ore smelting in Nigeria, Niger and Mali by 500 and 400 BCE are overwhelming along with terracotta figurines of the *Nok culture*. Evidence from Tanzania, Rwanda and Burundi are even older, dating back to the 7th century BCE. There are indications that the techniques used were invented locally without any foreign influence (Shillington, 1989: 53). Early Africans considered iron smelting technology as a divine gift. Iron ore "identification, extraction, crushing, smelting and forging" operations were always accompanied with "mystical rites and beliefs linking iron production to an immanent spiritual Power"(Davidson, 1969:33-34). Later working of other metals—copper, gold, and tin—was also practiced in an atmosphere of religious reverence. Production was equated with human reproduction:

> "…production was conceived as the fertilization of matter by energy, the blast furnace of ant-hill earth being the womb with the shaft of the bellows, which

were often paired as testicles, as the organ of transmission..." (Davidson, 1969:34).

The movement of peoples and nations impacted the dissemination of early technological practices. During the first millennium BCE, some of the *Bantu*-speaking groups from the Benue region in eastern Nigeria and western Cameroon, who had crossed the Equatorial Rainforest, settled in the Congo Basin south of the equator during the second millennium BCE. Some moved further south along the Congo River down to Angola and Namibia. Others, during the latter part of the first millennium BCE and the early part of the first millennium AD, headed northeastward to the *Great Lakes* region. From there, some later moved southward all way to South Africa. The Karanga, who built the Great Zimbabwe, are believed to have been part of this group (Spear 1994, July 1992). In the Congo Basin, the immigrants gave birth, near Lake Kisale, in what is today Katanga Province, in Congo DRC, to some of the early and most advanced copper mining and smelting states of their kind. Lake Kisale's flourishing fishing and mining industries, and dynamic states in fertile and well-watered grassland, allowed for population growth that created the need for a larger and more centralized state. Kongolo provided for this need with the founding of the Luba Empire near Lake Boa about 1400 AD. By its state formation strategies, conception of the kingship, and governing principles, the Luba Empire later influenced the creation and running of many similar states in southern Congo, Uganda, Rwanda, Burundi, Malawi, Zambia, Zimbabwe and the Congo-Angola area. Along with political influences, the immigrants spread copper and iron ore industries from the Lake Kisale region to their new host societies (Davidson, 1991).

House Building

Housing in Somalia: Every African country has a diverse population. This diversity in Africa is reflected in the variety of housing styles. Several housing traditions, materials and styles coexist in Somalia. Pastoralist nomads in Somalia's countryside live in portable homes, one per family. The construction procedures consist of assembling lightweight wood from the branches and roots of certain trees into a semicircular frame supported by a pillar. The frame is then covered with mats. The last phase is draping a tarpaulin on the top to prevent rain penetration. In Somalia's northern mountainous region, the stone dominates in home and storied building construction, whereas, in both old coastal towns and modern coastal cities, stone and adobe brick houses coexist side by side. Houses rebuilt on the rubble of old houses are a permanent characteristic of old coastal towns, whereas concrete roofs and pillars in storied buildings and colonnades and embellishments inherited from Italian colonization of *Somalia* abound in modern coastal cities and the capital *Mogadishu*. On the other hand, wattle and daub homes (made with thatched poles interwoven with reeds) dominate in the countryside just as round houses prevail in riverine areas (Abdullahi, 2001).

Housing in Nigeria: House construction in Nigeria is affected by income, climate and available building materials. For instance, in northern urban centers, even though using the same materials, the houses of the wealthy differ from those of the poor. The houses of the wealthy are large and made of thick walls and flat roofs of timber plastered with mud. Those of the poor are small, with conical thatched roofs and circular mud walls. There exist regional variances in dominant construction materials used:

South: Mats and straws from raffia palm leaves: Most available materials.

Yorubaland: Mud walls, grass or raffia leaves for the roof: Cultural preferences.

North: Flat mud roof on a square box-like structure; Insulation from intense heat, palliative for missing moisturizing trees.

Middle Country: Wood more used than mud; Less-intense heat environment.

Igboland: Lateritic soil, thatched roofs of raffia palm leaves supported by wooden poles: Lateritic soil is cohesive and requires minimal foundation (Adapted from Falola, 2001).

Architecture and House Design in Mangbetu Tradition, Congo DRC: The Mangbetu live in the Eastern Province of the Congo DRC. Mangbetu architectural technology has evolved over time. The most standard traditional houses of ordinary people were simple. The houses built in the grassland were different from those in the forest. *Grassland houses* were round and had thatched roofs. The walls were covered with mud, bark, or woven mats. *Forest houses* were made with wooden frames stitched together and covered from top to bottom with a layer of palm leaves inside and a layer of plantain leaves outside. This was supplemented by straw, grass, or many layers of leaves, which sealed the structure to keep water out. Usually, forest houses were smaller and less resistant than those in the grasslands. Houses in both settings had a pitched roof. They also had a spacious door, but no windows. It is reported that the structure was very strong and astonishingly resistant to the fury elements (Schildkrout and Keim, 1990).

This house building tradition changed gradually. By the 19th century, leaf walls had given way to walls of poles rammed with mud. House doors had changed also. Doors of handmade boards or old shields had come to prominence. Shield doors were covered with artistic designs similar to those previously found on the bark cloth. Thatched roofs offer the advantages of remaining dry and providing easy maintenance. Construction was time consuming and made in multiple steps, including cutting poles and digging holes in the hard ground, lashing horizontal bamboos or vines inside and outside the poles; building a framework of poles for the roof; adding a grid of smaller sticks to the framework; covering the roof with grass or leaves; leaving space between the roof and the wall free of horizontal sticks and grass or leaves to allow light and ventilation; stripping the vertical poles that are visible in the free space of the bark to spot termite tunnels and remove them before they destroy the poles. The above operations were carried out by the owner assisted by other men. Next, the women bring in water and mix it with earth for covering the walls. The plastering of the walls with mud is done by both men and women. When construction is completed, the owner offers a feast in honor of the participants (Schildkrout and Keim, 1990).

Weaving

Weaving Household Implements: Weaving was a vital productive industry in Ancient Egypt. Daily life implements—such as baskets, mats, ropes, tables, chairs, and mattresses—were made of woven papyrus reeds. Paper and clothes were made out of papyrus. Even fishing and commercial boats were first made of tightly woven papyrus reeds, and then of wood. The Luba of the Congo weave a variety of baskets:

1. Tubondo (singular: *kabondo*): small, tall round baskets used as containers and measurement instruments for such items as unshelled beans or peanuts, or else corn grains for milling.

2. Bibata (singular: *cibata*): large, round, short baskets, generally used to keep shelled beans or grains that still need sorting out. It is in *bibata* also that women sift corn flour and cassava flour from pounding or grinding.

3. Bisaka (singular: *cisaka*): elongated baskets with a hard edge and a hard bottom, the latter is always attached to a flat board designed to strengthen it. The major function of a *cisaka* is for women to carry loads on their heads.

4. Mitenga (singular: *mutenga*): large, round and tall baskets with holes all around which was mostly used to carry and store cotton wax.

The above items are made by men, but used by women. Men also weave fishing traps for women (*masungu*) and for men (*bisonso* or *bisakala*). They weave fishing nets (*makonda*, singular: *bukonda*), and hunting traps (*nkinda*, singular: *lukinda*), which by definition are for men's use. They also weave the mats (*byata*) that both men and women put in their beds to sleep on.

Weaving Fishing Nets: Fishermen in the Niger Delta make (1) surrounding nets, which are set into the water vertically to surround a whole school of pelagic fish, (2) throw or cast nets—circular nets which are thrown into the water and hauled back with the caught fish, (3) hand nets designed to scoop fish near the surface, and (4) dip nets, hand nets with a long handle used to scoop fish or crabs (Dyenye and Olopade, 2017). Fishermen in other parts of the Niger Delta use some more complex fishing systems including stakes erected in fences, enclosures of woven mats constructed in heart form, raffia screens, and traps with sliding gates and a trigger with a bundle of grasses attached, designed to keep the gate open (Abowel and Hart, 2008).

Pottery

Pottery making in Africa is traceable to 7000 BCE. African pottery has been primarily utilitarian, fulfilling such functions as carrying water, storing food and milk, cooking food, and serving and drinking water or other beverages. Since the invention of tools, hand-shaped forms and tool-carved designs have become almost inseparable in some artistic traditions. Spiritual designs are widespread and their symbolic messages are sometimes very complex. Ceremonial pots were generally housed in ad-hoc sacred spaces. Pot making is a long process, which includes mining and preparing the clay, mixing the clay with water, kneading ground sand, chopping dried grass and dung or other matter to the clay to decrease the shrinking that results from drying and firing. The final operations include coiling the pot around the base, and molding and smoothing the shape. Firing can be done in open air or in pits. When the pot is completely dried, decorations are made by adding shapes of human or animal figures or geometric or abstract forms; or by incising motifs with a sharp blade or comb (Contemporary African Art, ND).

Reportedly, Ghana has several long traditions of pottery making going back to 4000-3000 BCE. Pottery vessels were used to keep gold bracelets, necklaces and rings. These vessels were used for domestic purposes, notably fetching and storing water and performing religious rituals. The process of pottery production involves many manual operations: e.g., unearthing the dirt, mixing dirt with water, kneading to remove the water evenly, wedging the clay to remove the air, molding the clay, forming the clay into objects, drying, and finally firing. Sometimes parts of the vessel are formed separately and then joined afterwards with a wet slip of the clay body. The freshly made pot is dried in the sun, sometimes under hot ashes for a sturdier product (Adjei, 2013). The Luba practice clay pottery making. This is exclusively the activity of women. Luba women make cooking pots (*ngesu*, singular: *lwesu*). They make broad-mouthed water jars, (*nyingu* or *mabungu*), as well as bottle-neck jars called *nzaba* or *milondo*. *Nyingu* and *nzaba* are invariable; the singular forms for *mabungu* and *milondo* are *dibungu* and *mulondo*, respectively. Finally, Luba women make pots for babies and ceremonial-baths (*bizaba*, singular: *cizaba*). Both in Luba and in Ghanian societies, pottery is the specialty of women.

SUMMARY

African creation stories teach us that God created the universe and all that is in it as moving realities. Human existence is made through processes of growth and transformation at conception, birth, maturity, death, and in between. In the aftermath of divine creation, God's powers in terrestrial species were still in their fullness. Diseases and death did not exist. All living species—humans, animals and plants—were full of vitality. Heaven and Earth were located in one another's proximity. Humans and animals used to move around between earth and heaven and hold unity meetings to discuss matters of common interest. Physiologically, human life is maintained by constant flows of air, blood, and hormones within and between the major biological systems and the vital organs. The human body is flexible at many junctions allowing for body movements in all directions. They can move at will back and forth, up and down, and from side to side. They walk and run. They can spin on one leg and perform elegant choreographies and rhythmic dances and songs. Fully vital individuals have the ability to perform physical tasks demanding strength, endurance, and resilience. Farming, Africa's number one subsistence activity, uses a variety of tools. The productivity of such technology depends, to a large degree, on the physical strength, endurance, and resilience of the farmer. Fighting also, with or without weapons, requires strength, endurance and resilience. Virility and performance during sexual intercourse is a physical act of strength and a mark of vitality in the man's body. Humans, in full physical strength, are endowed with strong hands and can perform various manual tasks. They make varied tools out of stones, metal, ivory, and wood; they build houses out of a range of natural materials. They weave a variety of household implements and fishing and hunting traps and nets. They make vessels of clay or metal used to store jewelry, medicinal ingredients, food or drinks, to cook food and brew and store beer, or to perform religious rituals.

Chapter 3
An Inspired Speech Master

1. Sharpening Speech Articulation Skills
2. Identifying and Qualifying Subjects and Quantities
3. Inducing Behavior and Attitude Modification in Subjects
4. Expressing Feeling in Melodic in Songs

Articulate language is an essential element of human self which emanated from divine creation. Creation by the word was one of the methods employed by God in creating humans. Creation (or 'thingification') by the word of God means emergence, by the transcendental power of God's word, of a being or a thing with unique identity, form and properties. This mode, found in the creation story of the Dogon of Mali, for instance, is also known as creation by divine speech or creation by naming, or summoning. In some cases summoning was accompanied with gesture. In the Luba story, *Maweja Nangila* created animals by pointing his index finger forward and saying; "Let such animal species be." And the animal species emerged. To create human, *Maweja Nangila* combined His divine breath of life and the power of His word. He filled His lungs with his breath and forcefully exhaled on the Earth saying, "Let there be *Gentleman*" (*Mukalenga Muluma*), and the *Gentleman* appeared. *Maweja Nangila* filled His lungs with His breath again and forcefully exhaled on man, saying: "Let there be *Gentle Lady*" (*Mukalenga Mukaji*). And the *Gentle Lady* appeared (Kalanda, 1992). Not only did God create by the power of His divine word, He also equipped the human being with a vivid intellect capable of conceptualizing ideas, understanding meanings and expressing them in articulate spoken language. For instance, in the story of the Dogon of Mali, not only did *Amma*'s creative word bring the legendary ancestors of the human species into being, it also made them skilled professionals by the same token. From among the professionals, the speech master was created, who also assumed the function of teacher (Carruthers 1995). This chapter seeks to substantiate the characterization of the human being as a divinely inspired articulator of the spoken word. The Webster's Ninth New Collegiate Dictionary (pg. 626) provides three definitions of inspiration that are applicable to this chapter. These are: "a divine influence or action on a person believed to qualify him to receive and communicate revelation", (2) "the action or power of moving the intellect or emotions", and (3) "the act of influencing or suggesting opinions." The above modes of creation exemplify inspiration as a divine influence. The chapter's focus is on the power of the human intellect to conceptualize and express ideas in meaningful, clear, and effective forms of spoken speech. More specifically, the chapter consists of a survey of typical forms of speech articulation, or articulates, found across Africa. The following articulates are included in the discussion: meaningful words, names, numbers, counting rhymes, riddles and enigmas, proverbs, narratives/stories, repartees between rivals, call and response dialogue, and melodic songs. For the sake of presentation, the discussion is divided into four functional, non-mutually exclusive categories. The four functions are: (1) sharpening speech articulation skills, (2) identifying and qualifying subjects and quantities, (3) inducing behavior and attitude modification in subjects, and (4) expressing feelings in melodic songs.

1. SHARPENING SPEECH ARTICULATION SKILLS

For the sake of illustration, two types of articulate speech are examined in this category: (1) children's speech articulation games and (2) repartees between rival characters.

Children's Speech Articulation Games

Meaningful Words: Humans are endowed with a vivid intellect capable of conceptualizing ideas, understanding meanings, and expressing them in articulate speech. Meaningful words are the smallest units of articulate speech. In *Ciluba*, or *Tshiluba*, the language of the Luba people of Congo DRC, the words *muntu*, *mutu*, and *muntuntu* respectively, mean human being, head, and cricket. The word *udi* means "you are" whereas *tudi* signifies "we are." In Lingala, another language spoken in the Congo, *telema* means "stop, don't move." *Yaka* is the word for the imperative "come." In Kikongo, still another Congolese language, *bêtu* is "us"; *bênu*, "you" (plural). Grammatically, words assume different functions, such as nouns, pronouns, adjectives, verbs, or adverbs. Examples (in Ciluba or Tshiluba):

Nouns:	*mutu* (head)	*ciibi* or *tshiibi* (door)	*kabwa* (dog)
Pronouns:	*meema* (me)	*wewa* (you singular)	*yeya* (him/he/she)
Adjectives:	*mutu* **munena** (big head)	*ciibi* **citooka** (white door)	
Verbs:	*kudya* (to eat)	*kunwa* (to drink)	*kufwa* (to die)
Adverbs:	*leelu* (today)	*bulelela* (truly)	*penyi*? (where?)

African children customarily develop their knowledge and use of words by challenging each other in competitive games involving inversion of word syllables, counting rhymes, riddles and enigmas. Syllable inversions and counting rhymes stress spontaneity, speed, and verbal articulation. Riddles and enigmas require deeper thinking and understanding.

Inversion of Word Syllables: To foster the learning of words, African children, mostly boys, challenge each another verbally by playing inversion of word syllables. The game is intended to help one develop vivid audition, rapid processing and immediate comprehension, and readiness and suppleness of the tongue. The game is played in pairs anywhere since it does not require any particular setting. It usually starts with one player unexpectedly addressing the other in inverted form expecting for the latter to respond immediately in the right order of syllables. If two Congolese kids were fluent in both Ciluba and English, the first one would say, for instance:

Ciluba	English
Shampe kukoo yimâ.	*Vegi me meso terwa.*

The adversary should be able to enunciate the words immediately in the correct order of syllables:

Mpesha kooku mâyi.   Give me some water.

In turn, the latter player would challenge the former with words in right order of syllables for the adversary to invert them. He or she would say, for example:

Endela yeba.   Leave me alone.

-expecting for the other person to respond immediately without hesitation:

Ladene baye.   *Veli me neloa.*

The first challenger may charge again:

Langitamu pikwe?   *Rewhe rea you inghead?*

The expected immediate response is:

Mutangla kwepi?   Where are you heading?

In Turn, B might say:

Ku lusaci.   To the ketmar.

A would respond without hesitating:

Ku cisalu.   To the market.

Counting Rhymes: Counting rhymes are used to teach children important features of the living environment. In Luba villages, learning sessions were held in the evening around the fire in the courtyard of an elder. Children were asked one after another to count rhythmically, without hesitation or repeat, such things as ten names of animals, ten names of surrounding clans, ten names of rivers, ten names of important marketplaces, from among others.

Children's Counting Games' Rules: African children often challenge one another in syllable inversion, rhyme counting, and riddle and enigma games. All games require conformity to strict rules of competition. Failure is sanctioned with elimination. In syllable inversion and counting rhymes, the response must be immediate and correct, allowing no time for hesitation. Participation is sought as an opportunity for one to practice suppleness of the tongue, correct pronunciation, perception and discernment of sounds, and melody and rhythm. Riddles and enigmas require deeper thinking and discovery of meaning. The response demands longer time. The long-term educational goal of these children's intellectual games is to help young people master the spoken word, an important skill in judiciary art and reporting. Being value-laden cultural devices, these exercises and others are intended to inculcate social values deemed indispensable for cultural continuity (Mufuta 1974).

Counting wild animals: Rhymes are used in the teaching-learning of animals' names. Below, ten animals are presented in Ciluba alphabetical order: (1) *csumpa ntambwa:* panther, (2) *kabela:* wild cat, (3) *mbowa:* buffalo, (4) *mubwabwa:* jackal, (5) *nguluba:* hog, (6) *ngulungu:* antelope, (7) *nkashama:* leopard, (8) *ntole:* deer, (9) *ntambwa:* lion, and (10) *nzevu:* elephant. The left column, entitled "*Ku Nyama Ku Nyama eee*", means animal by animal and lists the animals by name. The phrase *Ntekumanga nte,* repeated in the right column, has no intrinsic meaning. Its sole function is to rhyme. The process goes like this:

Ku nyama ku nyama eee	*Ntekumanga nte*
1. Cisumpa ntambwa	Ntekumanga nte
2. Kabela	Ntekumanga nte
3. Mbowa	Ntekumanga nte
4. Mubwabwa	Ntekumanga nte
5. Nguluba	Ntekumanga nte
6. Ngulungu	Ntekumanga nte
7. Nkashama	Ntekumanga nte
8. Ntole	Ntekumanga nte
9. Ntambwa	Ntekumanga nte
10. Nzevu	Ntekumanga nte

The game is strictly regulated. If, for example, after citing *kabela* (wild cat) in number 2, a player cited it again in number 9, that player would be eliminated. The rule is that you cannot cite the same animal twice in the same round. A player would be eliminated also had he or she hesitated too long (long enough to break the rhythm) before finding an acceptable name.

Counting Clans: If children who live in the Mpoyi clan (*cisamba*, plural: *bisamba*) wanted to count the names of other clans in the *Ngandajika* Territory, they would go like this (For the sake of presentation, the clans below are grouped by geographic proximity):

Ku Bisamba ku Bisambeee	*Ntekumanga nte*
01. Kwa Manda	Ntekumanga nte
02. Ku Kaseki	Ntekmanga nte
03. Musakaci	Ntekumanga nte
04. Kwa Mulamba	Ntekumanga nte
05. Kwa Mpata	Ntekumanga nte
08. Ngandajika	Ntekumanga nte
09. Kwa Mpyana	Ntekumanga nte
10. Kwa Nsona	Ntekumanga nte

A player who would mention *Mpoyi* would be eliminated because the rule is that the clan in which you live cannot be considered. It is supposed to be known.

Counting Grasshoppers*:* Grasshoppers are delicious accompaniments to the *nshema* staple meal of the Luba people. A song named "*Ku Tupasu Ku Tupasu,*" literally "Grasshoppers One by One," attracts the attention of the listeners to varieties of grasshoppers living in the immediate environment, many of which are edible, as well as to a fundamental fact of life, namely, the fact that each variety is composed of a female element and a male element. The following version of grasshopper counting-song is derived from a tape published by the *Sangalayi* Group, a cultural organization of people from Kasai, Congo, living in Belgium. But the presentation is in alphabetical order of grasshopper variety names rather than the order in the *Sangalayi*'s song. Where a variety is known under two different names and both are mentioned in the song, only one appears in our nomenclature. *Mbevu*, a synonym for *dilaala (number 10)*, has been left out for this reason. Also, each announcement begins with "*Ku Tupasu ku Tupasu*" and ends with the repeated slogan "Ntolakanyii Ntolakanyi." "*Ku Tupasu ku Tupasu*" means Grasshoppers One-by-One." In real life *ntolakanyi* is the tiny flea found throughout Africa that, when it penetrates under human or animal skin, becomes a blood-sucking larva called *kabwasa* (plural *tubwasa*) in Ciluba, elsewhere known under several names, including chigger, chigoe, chigoer, and jigger chigoe . However, in the song, *Ntolakanyi Ntolakanyi* has no intrinsic meaning. Its unique function is rhyming. In singing, *Ntolakanyi, Ntolakanyi,* is the response by the audience. *Ku Tupasu ku Tupasu* and the stance thereafter by the leader constitute the call. The song goes as follows:

Ku tupasu ku tupasu: Grasshoppers One by One:
Cibutu mwana muluma A Male *Cibutu*
Mukwabo mwana mukaji And a Female *Cibutu*

Ntolakanyi Ntolakanyi Ntolakanyi Ntolakanyi

Ku Tupasu ku Tupasu: Grasshoppers One by One:
Citela mwana muluma A Male *Citela*
Mukwabo mwana mukaji And a Female *Citela*
Ntolakanyi Ntolakanyi Ntolakanyi Ntolakanyi

The remaining eight grasshoppers presented in the same manner are:

| *Cituma* | *Dilaala* | *Diyeya* | *Kamanyi* | *Mukumbi* |
| *Nkesa* | *Nkola* | *Ntondolo* | | |

Songs are natural channels used throughout Africa to convey call-and-response messages. The illustrations below include a narrative, repartees between rivals, epic songs, commemorative songs, and social critic songs.

Chapter 3
Riddles and Enigmas

Riddles and enigmas involve more meaningful thinking than simple counting and rhyming. Some ethnic groups designate riddles and enigmas by the same term. Others distinguish one from the other by name. The Yaka of the Congo, for instance, use the term *bitsimbwa* or *bitangi* (what is enunciated to be completed) for riddles and *biswekama* (what is hidden) for enigmas. In Ciluba, the terms *nkinda* (traps) and *nshinga* (questions) are used interchangeably. Riddles are stated in question-response form, for instance:

Question:	**Response:**
1. *Kwata aaku?*	*Mbakwaci.*
Hold!	I hold.
Mukalenga kayi udi ne dîsu dimwa? Kashingi	
What Lord has one eye?	Needle.
2. *Kwata aaku?*	*Mbakwaci.*
Hold!	I hold.
Mukalenga kayi udi mwambula kudi bantu basatu?	*Lwesu*
What Lord is carried by three porters?	Cooking pot
(The cooking pot sits on three stones)	
3. *Kwata aaku?*	*Mbakwaci*
Hold!	I hold
Mukalenga kayi udi ne mukolo umwa?	*Bowa.*
What Lord has one leg	mushroom

The objects of the above inquiries and responses have significance in everyday life. The needle used to remove chigoes from the feet or to stitch or repair clothes has one eye. Boiling is the most common cooking style in Luba families. The cooking pot sits on three stones. Mushrooms are somewhat a special kind of vegetables. The Luba people do not grow them. They pick them up from the wildness. Sometimes children are told mushrooms are some kind of meat since meat is scarce in the Luba country.

Other riddles imply more abstract thinking behind the obvious. Such is the case when two kids walk one behind the other: the one behind with its eyes closed is faced against the back of the one in front, and its hands on the latter's shoulders.

The One Behind:	***The One in Front:***
Twafiki anyi? To.	Have we arrived? No.
Mu njila mudi cinyi?	*Mudi cyula ne musodya.*
What is on the road?	A toad and a lizard.

This play is a lesson in information on safety. The presence of the toad and the lizard on the road means there are no snakes around. Snakes would have swallowed them up.

Repartees between Rival Characters

The most classic entertainment song and rhythm among Luba peoples who live in the former two Kasai provinces of Congo DRC is called *Kamulangu*. Just as in other African dancing songs, dancers in *Kamulangu* move rhythmically in a circle counter-clockwise. At moments, a dancer would move into the circle to express his or her creativity through improvised steps, body movements and gestures of his or her choice before inviting someone else to move into the center by dancing in front of him or her. The song tells of exchanges of insults between pairs of non-human rival characters, animals for most part, denigrating each other by pointing to each other's physical or behavioral abnormalities. It also shares deeper meanings which are explained further down. The version used here is a combination of what I know from my youth and older life among the Luba, and an adaptation from Professor Ngandu wa Kalonji (2002), whose own version is an adaptation from *Sangalayi,* a Luba literary choral group based in Brussels, Belgium, enriched with his own knowledge and innovations. Six pairs of characters are portrayed in Professor Ngandu's version: 1. Plantain versus Snake, 2. Pig versus Goat, 3. Duck versus Rat, 4. Cockroach versus Chicken, 5. Parrot versus Dog, and 6. Cat versus Turkey. The verses are rich in verbal repartee and demonstrate the wit of the Luba people.

Chapter 3

Table 2a: Repartees between Non-human Characters about their Imperfections

1. Dikonda Upenda Nyoka: Nyoka, udiswa kuyi mwakana; weewa wenda kuyi mikolo, ubanda kuulu kuyi maboko. Nyoka kupuwa e kwamba Bishi? Dikonda, umpenda kuyi mwakana; weewa wimita, ulela baana milongo kuyi muluma	**1. Plantain Insulting Snake:** Snake, you are arrogant, yet you are not normal; you walk without legs, and climb up trees without arms. Snake paused and said: Plantain, you dare insult me without being normal yourself; you conceive without husband and give birth to countless children.
2. Nguluba Upenda Mbuji: Mbuji, wadi mashinda uukutu, ukadi mulaala cyangadingadi. *Mbuji kupuwa e kwamba bishi?* Nguluba, umpenda kuyi mwakana, weewa mbidi manyanu, diulu divunga bu nkata.	**2. Pig Insulting Goat:** Goat, you ate too much grass and now you are lying down (on your back) with your belly up. **Goat paused and said what?** Pig, you insult me! Look at you: you have a dirty body and a nose that looks like a wreath rolled inside-out.
3. Mpatu Useka Mpuku: Mpuku, udya matala kuyi matuku, byakudya umina kuyi dintumbwa, difu diula kuyi mwimita; buloba bukoosha bipita cyaminu. *Mpuku kupuwa e kwamba bishi?* Mpatu, unseka kuyi mishiku, wewa musombela anu dikala nseka, mwinu mulepa kuyi mabola.	**3. Duck Laughing at Rat:** Rat, you eat corn grain all days of your life, with no gizzard to help you swallow; you have a big belly without being pregnant; always rubbing against the ground and getting overheated. *Rat paused and said what?* Duck, you are laughing at me but you have no lips; you are always scratching the soil looking for thrown-away grain parcels; you are mounted with a long beak without having missing teeth to hide.

Table 2b: Repartees between Non-human Characters about their Imperfections (Continued)

4. Kusangana Mpenzu Ubedya Nzolu: Nzolu, udila kuyi mukila; usenya nsonso kuyi ditaku; usaka baana kuyi cidika.	**4. Cockroach Facing Chicken with a Condescending Look:** Chicken, you cackle, but you have no tail; you wear pleated wraps but you have no buttocks; you push your babies forward but you lack audible motions.
Nzolu Kupuwa e Kwela Nyashi: Mpenzu, umbedya kuyi mifuba, mweba mwisu mukwata lubuwa, useka bantu kuyi kabewu.	**Chicken Paused, and Sneezed, and Said:** Cockroach, your condescension toward me is ridiculous; you have no bones; your face is caved-in like a pit; you mock people but you have no chest, no skin, and no pubis.
5. Nkusu Upenda Mbwa: Mbwa, umina kuyi mupodi; Usenya mbondya kuyi mukaba; Wewa mboyi wa kayi cikasu.	**5. Parrot Insulting Dog:** Dog, you swallow without blinking; you wear a pleated cloth on your hind without a belt. You do domestic dirt-cleaning tasks without a shovel.
Mbwa kwimana cya manga-manga: Nkusu, umpenda kuyi mwakana, musomba upela kuyi maboko; nsala muvwala kuyi mubaka.	**Dog Stood up valiantly and said:** Parrot, you insult me without being normal yourself, you sit down grinding food without having any arms; you wear a royal crown without being married.

Table 2c: Repartees between Non-human Characters about their Imperfections (Continued 2)

6. Mpusu Upenya Ndendu: Ndendu, unyema cya bukebuke Nzubu ulaala kayi mushiku Dyamba umina kuyi ludimi.	**6. Cat Pejoratively Grimacing at Turkey:** Turkey, you run leaning side-to-side without balance; you live in a closed-in house with no door; you swallow hard stuff without having a tongue.
Ndendu Kushala Ukenya Nak Mpusu, umpenya kuyi mwakana, mvita ufuna kuyi bulobu; mudimu usala kauyi mubota.	**Turkey, Silenced, with an Open Mouth:** Cat: You denigrate me but you are not whole; your martial arts demonstrations are valueless; you have no fighting might at all; your performances lack coordination.

Chapter 3

Possible Hidden Motives Inherent in the above Repartees

Several lessons can be drawn from these competitive insults. In the first place, they are exhibits of, and magnificent lessons in, astute observations of distinctive physical and behavioral characteristics of species that share humans' living spaces. On the moral plan, they are also invitations towards humility for those who only see other people's imperfections while closing eyes on their own. From an opposite standpoint, they are also invitations to never give in to character assassinations because those who demonize your shortfalls have their weak sides as well. Perhaps you can disarm your detractors by reminding them that you are aware of their own imperfections. Remember the Luba proverb:

> *Mulengela kabulal kalema, udi ne kenda kamulamata.*
> No good person is blameless; everyone has an indelible stain of some sort.

There are some other intellectually stimulating reflections one can make about the possible motive behind the opposition between the members of each pair of characters. Take the plantain and the snake. Both have an elongated form even though the snake is much longer. Neither have limbs; but the snake can move up and down along the tree, what the plantain cannot do. Maybe a snake climbing up a plantain tree while being pursued may cause the tree to be cut down and the fruits harvested unexpectedly. The plantain might not like that. Similarly, a harvested plantain is welcomed in the house whereas in no circumstance can a snake be allowed in. In the darkness of the night, a plantain on the floor can be easily mistaken for a snake, what probably the plantain would not like either. Such a mistake could expose the plantain to being eaten earlier than it would have otherwise survived.

The pig and the goat are livestock animals. The Luba prefer the goat to the pig. The goat is used in sealing marriage alliances, in sacrifices to the ancestral spirits, and in entertaining guests of honor. Both animals compete with humans to eat cassava roots and other food stuffs, and with each other for scraps that humans want to throw away. So, there is enough room for possible rivalry between the two. Likewise, as relates to the house rat and the duck: Rats are not liked; ducks are. A duck entering the house is sent back outside without cruelty, whereas a rat seen inside the house is pursued to be killed by throwing at it whatever object might be handy or by setting traps in the house corners. The cockroach and the chicken like to live in the house. The chicken is welcomed. The cockroach is not. Besides, the chicken pecks and swallows cockroaches. As to the parrot and the dog, both are loved pets. Each is endowed with some natural elegance to be proud of and be considered first. The dog has nice hind pelage and tail; the parrot has a nice royal crown. But each one has something important missing in order to be really first. A really beautiful African lady has the elegant pleats of her wrap spread along a belt tied around her waist. This the dog does not have. Likewise, a real African crowned-king cannot be single. He always has a first lady, which is not the case with the parrot. In spite of its natural shortfalls, the dog shares the master's food and is often praised for its accomplishments, which fact may explain parrot's denigrating altercation.

2. IDENTIFYING AND QUALIFYING SUBJECTS AND QUANTITIES

Identification is the process of designating subjects or quantities by names. The naming of quantities is called numbering. Naming includes identity, meaning, and significance of the subject or quantity. This section examines two types of speech articulates: personal names and numbers.

Personal Names

Some words or groups of works express personal names. Names are words or groups of words that identify persons, animals, or things. *Kwame Nkrumah* (Ghana), *Mudibo Keita* (Mali), *Séku Touré* (Guinea), *Patrice Lumumba* (Congo Kinshasa), *Jomo Kenyatta* (Kenya), *Julius Nyerere (Tanzania)*, and *Kenneth Kaunda* (Zambia) are personal names of African leaders who fought for the liberation of their countries and achieved political independence in the late 1950s and the 1960s.

Birth Names: Birth names -- *meena a ku cilelelu*, or *meena a munda* (names from the womb) -- are names parents give their children at birth. African names are relational in that they generally reflect the relationship of the carrier with significant others in the family or the clan. For instance, traditionally the Luba people did not have the custom of a father naming all his children after himself. Instead the children were named after different significant others from the extended family. The Luba being patrilineal, most children bore the names of the father's relatives. In general, the first son would carry the name of the father's grandfather, the second the name of the father's father, and the third the father's name. Sometimes the third son, but certainly the fourth, would be given the name of his mother's father. The first and second daughters are named after the father's grandmother and mother, respectively. The third daughter is generally given the name of her mother's mother. Children are identified and differentiated one from another by their birth names followed by the name of either parent preceded by a particle signifying "child of". Examples: *Mbuyi wa Masengu* (mother) or *Mbuyi wa Binunu* (father), *Ngoyi wa Bwakateta* (father) or *Ngoyi wa Muadi* (mother). Personal names in Bantu languages belong to different classes. In Ciluba, the language of the Luba people, all names of human beings belong to the same class. That is why particle *wa* is used in all cases indicating a relationship of belonging in which a single human being is the subject. The particle for plural human subjects is *ba*. Examples: *baana ba Mukenge* (Mukenge's children), *baledi ba Kalaala* (Kalaala's parents), *babeedi ba malaria* (malaria patients). In Kikongo, the language of the Kongo people, names of human beings belong to different classes and agree with different particles. Examples: Fu-Kiau **kia** Bunseki, Wamba **dia** Wamba, Munzele **wa** Maloko. Fu-Kiau, Wamba and Munzele are birth names (*nkûmbu yambutukila or nkûmbu yangudi*, in Kikongo). *Kia Bunseki, dia Wamba*, and wa *Makolo indicate* a relationship of belonging to their respective parents (Fu-kiau, 1991).

Birth Titles: Babies are incarnated spirits. They are given birth titles, that is, names that express the kinds of spirits they are and the circumstances, the condition, or the position in which they are born. For instance, the titles for twins (*ijeji* in Yorùbá, *mapasa* in Ciluba) reflect their order of birth. Among the Yorùbá, the first of the twins is named *Taiwo*; the second *Kehinde*. Their equivalents among the Luba are *Mbuyi* and *Nsanza* (also *Kabanga*, or *Nkanku*) respectively. Another Yorùbá birth name with an equivalent among the Luba is *AJayi*. An *Ajayi* baby is born with his or her face down. The *Luba* equivalent is *Cikudimena*: one born lying on his or her stomach. Twenty-seven (27) categories of title babies have been identified in the *Luba* nomenclature (Katanga-Tshitenge, 1969). The list of Yorùbá names reflecting circumstances or parents' wishes at birth is much longer. Here are just a few examples:

Abimbola	*Abiodun*	*Bankole*
Born into riches	Born on festival day	Build an abode for me
Babatunji	*Durojaiye*	
Our father has returned.	The one who awaits life's joys and blessings	
Ekundayo	*Erioluwa*	
My sorrows have turned into joy	Testimony of God's goodness	

(Ikande, Mary. ND.).[1]

Maturity Names and Initiation Names: In the *Luba* tradition, when a son becomes of age, he selects for himself a name to be added to the given birth name. Such names are referred to as *mêna bulungu* (singular: *dîna dya bulungu*). In the Congolese identification system, the latter name is called postname. In the examples above from the Luba, *Ngoyi wa Muadi* named himself *Kabwina*. From then on he was called Ngoyi Kabwina. Kabwina is his maturity name. *Ngoyi* is a man. Men become adults at adolescence. *Mbuyi* is a woman. A woman acquires maturity through birth giving. When *Mbuyi* got married and gave birth to a child called *Kalenga*, she became *Mbuyi mwa-Kalenga*, which means Mbuyi mother of Kalenga. Mwa-Kalenga is her motherhood name. The *Kongo* and many other African ethnic groups hold formal initiation ceremonies for adolescent children. The candidates undergo several weeks or months of training, often in isolated locations away from the village, and are given initiation names upon successful completion of the training program. *Fu-Kiau kia Bunseki* became *Fu-Kiau Kimbwandènde*. His full name came to be stated as *Fu-Kiau Kimbwandènde kia Bunseki*.

Clan and Totemic Names: In many African societies, members carry clan names as part of self-identification names. Some clan names are names of certain animal or plant species. These are totemic names. Totemic names express kinship relationships between the human community and the animal or vegetal species in question. Both often trace common descent from some legendary source. The members of each party are expected to protect those of the other. Killing each other or harming each other in any other manner is prohibited. Humans are not allowed to eat their totemic animal or plant or to hurt them in any fashion. For example, the Gikuyu are very protective of the sycamore tree which is identified with the spirit of their legendary founding father and protects them spiritually. Gikuyu neighbors, the Kalenjin, are relatives and allies of the leopard and the lion. These are their totemic animals. It is morally prohibited for a

Kalenjin person to kill either animal. Intermarriage is prohibited between carriers of the same totemic name, even if they are biologically distant (Kenyatta University, ND.).

Praise Names: The standard name for God in Ciluba is *Mvidi Mukulu*, which means the Eldest, Senior-Most High Spirit. But when praised for being the Omnipotent Creator, God is addressed as:

> *Mvidi Mukulu, Maweja Nangila, Dîba Katangila cishiki, Wakutangila Dyamwosha nsesa.* Most Loving God, You the Sun no one can dare look watching straight into it without having his eyes burnt by Your Rays.

Praise names for humans are extensions of birth names. Praise names stand for and accompany words of exhortation and encouragement. They are used to incite children to do great things or to congratulate them for their accomplishments. Praise names are evoked in lamentation cries at a person's death. For this reason they are called *meena a mu cibobo*, lamentation cries' names. The cries may be vocal or instrumental. Instruments such as the flute and the tom-tom are often used to send messages of cries. Actually, a praise name is an extended real name. For example, the praise name of a certain *Kazadi* is *Kazadi Lumembu lwa Butongo wa Ndaya*. Very often the praise name is the adulthood or motherhood name of the person one is named for. This person can be a living elder. A girl called *Kabedi*, who is named after an aunt whose motherhood name is *Kabedi ma Mulomba*, will be praised as *Kabedi ma Mulomba*. The person one is named after can be a historical hero: e.g., one of the lineage founders. For instance, the praise name for a person named *TsHemanga* is *TsHemanga Lwasa Mbuta*. The historical *TsHemanga Lwasa Mbuta* was one of the founders of the *Bakwa-Kalonji* chiefdom. If a person's name evokes that of an animal, his praise name will recall the character of that animal. For example, the name Mukenge evokes a kind of civet cat that captures chickens in millet gardens around the houses. To reach its target, the animal *mukenge* walks unnoticeably with its head down. Thus the praise name for a person named *Mukenge* is *Mukenge wa cyenda kabandubandu*, *Mukenge wa cyenda mu mponda*: Mukenge who walks with his head bent down, Mukenge who walks in millet fields. Praise names are not limited to humans. For example: the name for sweet potato in Ciluba is *cilunga*. To praise the sweet potato for being a life-saving crop in time of food scarcity, it is called "*Cilunga Panda Malaba*" – Potato the Earth-Breaker (often, during the dry season, the earth covering the sweet potato cracks). The *Ciluba* translation for leopard is *nkashama*.

The descriptive praise name is:

> *Nkashama wa bitole, bitole ku bilamba ne ku mutu.*
> Leopard the dotted one who carries dots all over the robe and the head.

Social Rank Titles: Titles are distinctive appellations associated with particular social ranks. Title holders expect to be and are called by their titles in front of their names. Titles are articulate messages of the social importance of the holders. Priests, notables, chiefs, and kings are addressed and referred to by their titles as marks of profound respect. The Yorùbá *Oba*, the *Kabaka* of Baganda, the *Mwami* of the Tutsi or the Bashi,

Chapter 3

the *Asantahene* of the Ashanti, the *Balopwe* of the Ancient Luba Empire, the *Mwant Yav* of the Lunda, and the *Mani Kongo* of the Kongo are most known historic titles of majesty. Muslim leaders who have made the historic pilgrimage to Mecca find great honor in being addressed as *Alhaji* (for men) and *Alhaja* (for women) (Falola, 2001).

Numbers

Yorùbá and Luba Numbering Systems: Numbers are names of quantities. Numbering is naming quantities. Some numbering systems are more complex than others. For instance, the number system of the Yorùbá of Nigeria is more complex than that of the Luba of Congo DRC. Single digits are alike in the two systems. Major differences are manifest in base numbers and the ten plus Number. Illustrations are found in Tables 2a, 2b, and 2c, respectively.

Table 3a: Single Digits in the Yorùbá and the Luba Number Systems

	Yorùbá		Luba	
Number	**Reading**	**Meaning**	**Reading**	**Meaning**
0	?	?	*cijengu*	zero
1	*ikan*	1*	*umwa*	1
2	*meji*	2	*yibidi*	2
3	*meta*	3	*yisatu*	3
4	*merin*	4	*yinayi*	4
5	*marun*	5	*yitaanu*	5
6	*mefa*	6	*yisambombo*	6
7	*meje*	7	*mwanda muteketa*	(junior quantity) 7
8	*mejo*	8	*mwanda mukulu*	(senior quantity) 8
9	*mesan*	9	*citeema*	nine

As can be seen in Table 3a, single digit numerals are simple denotations both in the Yorùbá number system and in the Luba number system; the names of numbers are distinct terminologies, which only express what the numbers are without implying any mathematical operations.

Table 3b: Base Numbers in the Yorùbá and the Luba Number Systems

Numbers	**Yorùbá**		**Luba**	
10	*mewa*	10	*Dikumi*	ten
20	*ogun*	20	*makumi abidi*	2 tens
30	*ogbon*	30	*makumi asatu*	3 tens
40	*ogoji*	20* × 2*	*makumi anayi*	4 tens
50	*adota*	50	*makumi ataanu*	5 tens
60	*ogota*	20* × 3*	*makumi asambombo*	6 tens

An Inspired Speech Master

70	adorin	70	makumi mwanda muteketa	7 tens
80	ogorin	20* × 4*	makumi mwanda mukulu	8 tens
90	adorun	90	makumi citeema	9 tens
100	ogorun	20 x 5	Lukama	hundred

In the Luba system, all the numbers are distinct denotations involving no mathematical operations. In contrast, in the Yorùbá system, the multiples of 20—*ogoji* (40), *ogota* (60), *ogorin* (80), and *ogorun* (100)—are expressed as multiplications, whereas the other numbers are distinct denotations. Also, it is said that intermediate numbers between multiples of 20, with the exception of 30, which is a distinct number, are reckoned as subtractions from the next multiple of 20. Thus 50 is enunciated as 10 from 60, 70 as 10 from 80, and 90 as 10 from 100. Likewise, 110, 130, 150, 170, and 190, are, respectively 10 from 120, 10 from 140, 10 from 160, 10 from 180, and 10 from 200.

Table 3c: Ten Plus in the Yorùbá and the Luba Number Systems

Numbers	Yorùbá		Luba	
	Reading	**Meaning**	*Reading*	**Meaning**
10	*mewa*	10	*Dikumi*	10
11	*mokanla*	1 + 10†	*dikumi ne umwa*	10 + 1
12	*mejila*	2 + 10†	*dikumi ne yibidi*	10 + 2
13	*metala*	3 + 10†	*dikumi ne yisatu*	10 + 3
14	*merinla*	4 + 10†	*dikumi ne yinayi*	10 + 4
15	*medogun*	-5† + 20	*dikumi ne yitaanu*	10 + 5
16	*merindilogun*	4 from 20	*dikumi ne yisambombo*	10 + 6
17	*metadilogun*	3 from 20	*dikumi ne mwanda muteketa*	10 + 7
18	*mejidilogun*	2 from 20	*dikumi ne mwanda mukulu*	10 + 8
19	*mokandilogun*	1 from 20	*dikumi ne citeema*	10 + 9

In the Luba system, all the numbers from 11 to 19 read 10 and 1, 10 and 2, 10 and 3, and so on. All are additions. In the Yorùbá number system, *mokanla* (11), *mejila* (12), *metala* (13), and *merinla* (14), respectively read: one above 10 or 10+1, two above 10 or 10+2, three above 10 or 10+3, and four above 10 or 10+4. These are additions. However, *medogun* (15) reads minus five plus twenty (-5† + 20), that is a combination of subtraction and addition. On the other hand, *merindilogun* (16), *metadilogun* (17), *mejidilogun* (18), and *mokandilogun* (19), respectively, mean four from twenty, three from twenty, two from twenty, and one from twenty. All these are subtractions (Zaslavsky 2017, AIRNET ND, Mathematicians of the African Diaspora ND).[2]

3. INDUCING BEHAVIOR AND ATTITUDE MODIFICATION

Some types of speech seek to induce behavior and attitude modification in the subjects. Such is the case with cradle songs, animal stories, proverbs, and the call and response dialogue.

Cradle Songs

Cradle songs—*lullabies*—are performed by the mother or the babysitter to get the baby stop crying and fall asleep. Below, an example from the *Kongo* and another from the *Luba:*

Kongo

Wa, wa, wa	*Quiet, quiet, quiet*
Mwâna wanlôngo e	*Oh! Sacred child*
Sangamani e	*Look at her/him*
Buta katominanga	*To be a happy mother*
Kala na ndezi âku e	*Should not one have a babysitter*
Sangamani e	*Look at her/him*
Wa, wa, wa	*Quiet, quiet, quiet*
Mwâna wanlôngo e	*Oh! sacred child*
Sangamani e	*Look at her/him*

(Fu-Kiau and Lukondo-Wamba, 1988)

Luba

Katende e Ncyo ncyo ncyo	*O! Katende, sing, sing, sing,*
Katende wa ba Kalanja	*Katende the fellow of the Kalanja*
Wa ba Kalanja	*The fellow of the Kalanja*
Ukaadi wenda nkayenda e	*Today walking alone*
Kayi bakwende	*Without his fellowshellows*

Katende (or *Katenda*) and *Kalanja* are birds. *Ncyo ncyo ncyo* is an onomatopoeia imitating Katende's sound.

Animal Stories

Animal stories are moralizing messages. The story of Chameleon and Leopard below comes from *Frobenius* (1983) who attributes it to the *Beena Kalambayi* (a Luba clan) of the Congo DRC. It draws attention to the importance of reading the signs and trusting one's first instinct. By the same token it warns one against the high price of credulity and inconsistency. Ultimately it says: "Trusting in the friendly words of a person who has threatened your life is stupidity."

> Leopard had befriended Chameleon by sealing a friendship pact and throwing a banquet in his honor. However, Chameleon was skeptical of Leopard's good intent. When Leopard visited Chameleon in return, instead of welcoming him, Chameleon climbed into a tree. When Leopard yelled at him to go down and greet his trustworthy friend, Chameleon threw down a stick, saying: "Here I am." Leopard jumped over the stick, caught it with his teeth, and broke it into pieces. Realizing that Chameleon had not really come down, Leopard asked him to do so in honor of their mutual pact. Chameleon told Leopard he was

afraid Leopard would do to him what he had just done to the stick. Leopard went back home. Chameleon paid Leopard a second visit, Leopard slaughtered a big goat and they feasted together. When Leopard visited for a second time also, Chameleon climbed into a tree again. Once again, when Leopard asked him to come down, he threw down a stick, which Leopard immediately broke into pieces with his teeth. Chameleon saysto say: "You see, what tells me you will not do to me what you did to the stick right now?" Leopard retorts: "Did we not seal our friendship over a meal?" On that note, Chameleon descends from the tree, whereupon Leopard jumps over him and breaks him into pieces. Chameleons have stopped jumping down from the trees ever since.

Proverbs

In Africa, life truths inherited from the ancestors are often expressed through proverbs. These are messages of wisdom expressed in condensed sentences. Proverbs are explained more extensively in the next section in regard to their functionality, that is, their implied expected behavioral adjustments. In the present section, proverbs are simply touched upon as a form of articulate speech. The few illustrations hereafter convey messages of unity.

Bravery, Being on One's Guard, Consistency in Dealing with Enemies, Real or Potential

1. *Bavwavwa abo, mbeena mulongo neba; wakutwa difuma, wamutuuta kabonga (kabwenge).*
2. Those assailers who are coming are your peers; if one pierces you with a spear, at least hit him with a club.

If you, your family, or your community is attacked, you should be able to defend yourself even with a meaningless object imaginable. Let them not damage you and go their way free of any harm.

3. *Kajiji munyoka, kapayi mputa, batuuta kajiji.*
   A hated fly gets swatted even where there is no wound.

Explanation: People who hate you will seek to destroy you even if you have done no wrong. Beware.

4. *Badinga kwela, wadinga kwepela.*
   If someone pretends throwing a stone at you, you better pretend to avoid that stone.

Meaning: Take seriously any threat to your life even if it seems like it is just a joke. Otherwise, the day the menace is real, the stone will hit you.

5. *Bulunda ne Ndunga munena, baana ba Ndunga utapa!*
   You claim being a good friend of the big Ndunga tree, yet you systematically chop down the baby *Ndunga* trees in your way!

The *ndunga* tree is tall, elegant and is liked for its large shade. Claiming love for the big tree while destroying the younger trees in your way to the shade is hypocrisy.

Message: *Be skeptical toward individuals who claim they love you for your goodness to them, yet cannot stand for the well-being of your children.*

Call and Response Dialogue

A well-known form of articulate speech common to African societies and cultures across the continent is call and response in public speaking, in singing, and even in enunciating phrases and proverbs. Call and responses are two-part statements: the speaker enunciates the first half, while the audience completes the statement with the second half. The call and response form of speech is intended to induce participation, energize the audience, and foster persuasion. The public speaker generally begins with a request of attention. Even this is rendered in two parts. A Lingala public figure, for instance, would go like this:

Speaker	Audience
Nye! Nyee!	*Nye.*
Quiet! Quiet!	Quiet.
Nye nyee!	*Nye.*
Quiet! Quiet!	Quiet.
Naloba?	*Loba.*
May I speak?	Speak.
Naloba?	*Loba.*
May I speak?	Speak.
Nabimisa?	*Bimisa.*
May I bring it into the open?	Bring it.
Nabimisa?	*Bimisa.*
May I bring it into the open?	Bring it.
Ya solo?	*Solo.*
True?	True.
Ya solo?	*Solo.*
True?	True.

Then, often after laughter by everyone, the speaker would proceed with the address. Often, in the course of the speech, he or she would seek and receive the approval of the audience with what he she is saying. A Ciluba speaker and the audience would say:

Speaker:	Audience:
Bataatu ne bamaamu, ki mmomu anyi ?	*Mmomu.*
Fathers and Mothers (Gentlemen and Ladies), isn't it so?	It is so.

They would end the address by saying:

Speaker:	Audience:
Twasangan kwamba anyi!	*Twamba.*
Thus, have we spoken!	Thus, have we.

A chief or a high-ranking religious leader would generally dismiss the audience with the latter's participation in the following terms:

Speaker:	Audience:
Wa mukishi kalaala!	*Wa muntu kalaala.*
As the departed sleep in peace!	So will the living sleep in peace.

Phrases and proverbs are enunciated in complete statements in general speech, but broken into two parts in teaching-learning gatherings or discussions of matter of community interest.

Examples:

1. In General Speech:
   Baya waya, washala washadilamu.
   Move with the movers, otherwise you stay behind forever.

In a Teaching-Learning Gathering

Speaker:	Audience:
Baya waya!	*Washala washadilamu.*
Move with the movers!	Otherwise you stay behind forever.

2. General Speech:
   Kwapwa kwa mudimi, kwashala kwa mudimina.
   Where the duty of the field tender ends, there begins the duty of the field owner
   (compensating the laborer).

In a Public Gathering:

Speaker:	Audience :
Kwapwa kwa kwa mudimi!	*Kwashala kwa mudimina.*
Where the duty of the field tender ends!	There begins the duty of the field owner.

3. General Speech:
   Mukulu kutumba, mmulela wa mwabi.
   For the oldest child to become famous, he must be a lucky one from birth.

In a Gathering Context:

Speaker:	Audience
Mukulu kutumba!	*Mmulela wa mwabi.*
For a firstborn child to become famous!	He must be a lucky one from birth.

4. General Speech:
   Kudya lukasa, nkupya mukana.
   Eating precipitously will burn your mouth.

In a Teaching-learning Gathering
Speaker:	Audience:
Kudya lukasa!	*Nkupya mukana.*
Eating precipitously!	Will burn your mouth.

4. EXPRESSING FEELINGS IN MELODIC SONGS

Three types of speech articulations can be identified as expressions of feeling in songs. These are: epic and lamentation songs, commemoratives, and social critics.

Epic and Lamentation Songs

The history of ethnic groups is often told in epic songs centered on heroic founding fathers who have become legendary figures.

The Keita Epic Song of the Mandinka is an example. The Mandinka people of Mali and similar peoples in West Africa have a historical epic song called *Keita* telling the legendary story of Sundiata Keita, leader of the small Kingdom of Kangaba, a Malinke subgroup, who became the founder of the great Mali Empire; and ruled from 1235to 1260 AD. The legend has it that the king of Kangaba, Sundiata's father, was told by an oracle that he would marry a very ugly woman after his beautiful wife. She would give birth to a crippled son who would rule over a large and powerful kingdom. As a crippled child, Sundiata was the object of mockery and beating by other children in the village. Both he and his mother suffered all kinds of humiliations by his father's beautiful senior wife. Sundiata came to adulthood at the time when the Ghana Kingdom had disintegrated and the provinces were fighting each other for new sovereignty. Sumanguru, leader of one of the fighting provinces, sacked Sundiata's village and killed all his 11 brothers. Only Sundiata's life was spared because of his infirmity. Over time, Sundiata's twisted legs grew stronger. He became a successful hunter, engaged in the war between the provinces and defeated all other contenders (Davidson 1991, July 1992, Shillington 1993).

The **Kasala Epic Songs of the Luba** is another example. The Luba society is divided into chiefdoms, large and small. Epic songs are executed at various occasions such as nostalgic events where they are sung as lamentations to praise the deceased person by invoking his or her ancestors' greatness; or at entertainment events to make people feel good about their ancestors' accomplishments and exhort them to strive for greatness as well. The purpose is not much to outdo others, but to let them know that "we too have a glorious past of which we are proud and that deserves to be proclaimed loudly." *Kasala* is the generic name for epic songs of Luba peoples living in the two Kasai provinces of Congo: Eastern Kasai and Western Kasai. Professors Mufuta Kabemba (Patrice, 1969) and Nzuji Madiya (Clémentine, 1967) have written classical works on the *Kasala*.

Ethnic Pride and Appeal to Unity: The Luba Kasala epic song just introduced praises heroes from particular chiefdoms, each one having its own kasala, praising its own ancestors. *Kasai wa Balengela* hereafter embraces all Kasai ethnic groups, most of whom are non-Luba and exhorts them all to work together as a family. Thus, says the chorus:

> 1. *Kasai wa Balengela, tudi beena muntu.*
> *Ooo, yaayee, tudi beena muntu.*
> Kasai Land of the Beautiful, we are family.
> That is right, big sister, we are Family.
>
> **2.** *Kasai se nditunga dya kwendela ntunku.*
> *Ooo, yaayee, tudi beena muntu.*
> Kasai is the land where we can walk shoulders up with pride.
> That is right, big sister, we are family.
>
> 3. *Kasai se nditunga dya kwenda mazengu.*
> *Ooo, yaayee, tudi beena muntu.*
> Kasai is the land where we can walk cool.
> That is right, big sister, we are family.
>
> 4. *Kasai se nditunga dya kwendela bwenyi.*
> *Ooo, yaayee, tudi beena muntu.*
> Kasai is that country foreigner's thirst to visit.
> That is right, big sister, we are family.
>
> 5. *Kasai se ncisamba cya kushinta dimiinu*
> *Ooo, yaayee, tudi beena muntu.*
> Kasai is that people whose seed others want to trade
> That is right, big sister, we are family.

The *Kasai wa Balengela* song is much longer than this. It includes a litany of various lineages, clans and chiefdoms who share the Kasai geographic space. Over the appeal to unity, the song exhorts and challenges the members to build their Kasai homeland and improve the lot of their people.

Commemoratives

The popular *Kamulangu* song of the Luba relates events and heroic figures from contemporary history of the Luba Lubilanji of Eastern Kasai, Congo DRC. The song is executed in call and response form. The repartees between rival characters presented previously are enunciated by the leader. Each is followed by a chorus sung by the participants. The chorus invites people to come and see how some authority figure is distributing medals. At many points in time, the *Bakwanga* locality has seen its status elevated to an important diamond mining center; a territorial administrative headquarters (1950); the major welcoming center for the 1959-1961 internally-displaced Luba people from Western Kasai and Katanga; a state capital during the South Kasai-secession period (1960-1963); and, since then, a provincial capital. The location is situated in the land of the *Bakwanga* lineage and borrows its name from the latter. The appellation Bakwanga is collective. An individual lineage member is a *mukwanga*. Mukwanga is one of the medal distributing-authority figures invoked in the *Kamulangu* song chorus:

> *Wa ba Mutambayi, vwakunwayi, nuvwa kumona mudi Mukwanga wabanya mpeta.* Brothers and sisters of Mutambayi come and see for yourselves how Bakwanga is distributing medals.

Mutambayi is a proper name among the Bakwanga people. The one evoked in the song is not specified. During the *South Kasai Secession* period (1960-1963), the Bakwanga locality became a major welcoming center for the internally-displaced Luba people from *Western Kasai* (1959-1961) and *Katanga Province* (1961-1962). From among the internally-displaced returnees to Lubaland, Albert Kalonji emerged as the number one leader of the Luba assembled from various regions of the Congo. Sometimes, Kalonji, rather than Mukwanga, is evoked in the song.

> People of all nations, come and see how Kalonji is distributing medals.
> *(Bakwa matunga, vwakunwayi nuvwa kumona mudi Kalonji wabanya mpeta.*

Long before the emerging of both Bakwanga and Kalonji, an important event had transformed life in the Luba region: the *Irebu-Kamina-Lubumbashi* railroad. Many Luba people migrated to Katanga mining centers in search for jobs and better life. Kamina was the first major stopover train station after leaving Lubaland. The railroad came to be referred to in the area as the *Kamina Railroad*. Instead of a medal-distributing authority figure, the classical chorus in the *Kamulangu* song invites people to come and participate in showing the personified *Kamina Railroad*.

> Come and let us show him the Kamina railroad.
> *(Vwakunwayi tumuleeja njila wa njanja ne wa Kamina).*

Sometimes, rather than inviting people to show the way, the chorus invites them instead to travel along with the personified *Kamulangu* by train on the Kamina railroad.

> Come and let us travel along with him by train on the *Kamina Railroad.*
> *Vwakunwayi tuya nenda njila wa njanja ne wa Kamina)*

Social Critics

Some songs express criticisms against certain sections of society, such as morally corrupt businessmen, oppressive colonial imperialists, power abusers, and possessive husbands, as illustrated below, respectively.

An Inspired Speech Master
Repulsive Corrupt Businessmen

A criticism song for disliked Nigerian businessmen goes as follows:

> "False man, Oh terrible man!
> The villain who looks like a beast:
> Massive chin, convex back.
> Insolent man, man of excess:
> His head is like that of an elephant,
> His cheeks are rotund" (Falola, 2001: 163).

In Lower Congo, the Kongo people invented a satiric song called *salanga*, (later corrupted as *salongo*), a protest song against exploitative treatments inflicted upon the Congolese people during the Leopoldian regime (1885-1908) and Belgian colonization (1908-1960). It was sung rhythmically synchronized with the movements of the body to relieve the pain and the anger. Each critique statement was preceded by a chorus saying: "Salongo, ee, alinga mosala"; which means: "Forced collective chores, yes, he (the black man) likes them." Here are some of the stanzas:

Salongo, ee, alinga mosala.
Forced Chores, yes yes, he likes them.

> *1. Biso tokoma baumba na bino, kotekisa biso na saki ya mungwa, lokola mosolo.*
> We have become your slaves, you traffic us for a sack of salt, as our selling price.

> *2. Biso tokoma banyama na bino, kokengela bino na porte ya ndako, lokola bapaya.*
> We have become your work animals, taking care of you, relegated to the house gate, like aliens.

> *3. Biso tokoma bangamba na bino, komemaka bino na mapeka na biso, lokola bampunda.*
> We have become your flunkeys, carrying you on our shoulders, like horses.

> *4. Mondele mobamaka biso, lokala banyama zamba. Likolo, mabele, bakoko batikala biso.*
> The white man kills us like beasts of the bush. This sky and this land, our ancestors have bequeathed them to us (Adapted from Fu-Kiau 2001).

Before meetings designed to discuss important social, political, and economic issues in the community, the Kongo people would execute a song designed to discourage dishonest enrichment and improper acquisition of property or exercise of power. It goes as follows:

Mu Kânda ka Mukadi
Within the Community There is No ...

> *1. Mu kânda ka mukadi mputu:*
> Within the community there is no room for poverty.

2. Mu kânda ka mukadi mvwâma:
Within the community there is no room for ill-acquired wealth.
3. Mu kâanda ka mukadi mpofo.
Within the community there is no room for blindness.
4. Mu kâanda kamukadi mfumu:
Within the community there is no room for order-givers
5. Mu kâanda ka mukadi n'nânga.
Within the community there is no room for slaves.
6. Babo mfumu na mfumu
All are masters, and only masters.
7. Babo ngânga na ngânga.
All are specialists, and only specialists.
(Fu-Kiau, 2001)

Women in Luba villages where I grew up had a song in which they expressed dislike for possessive husbands:

Taatu Kasomboyi wanyi/Dear Mister Kasomboyi

Uvwa kandelela anyi'ee	Were you born just for me,
Taatu Kasomboyi wanyi?	Dear Mister Kasomboyi?
Uvwa kandamika anyi ee,	Did you think you were glued to me,
Taatu Kasomboyi wanyi?	Dear Mister Kasomboyi?
Ukavu wa kashidianyi'ee,	Who told you I would be yours forever,
Taatu Kasomboyi wanyi?	Dear Mister Kasomboyi?

SUMMARY

The human mind is endowed with creative capacities such as vivid intellect, discernment and insights, and creative imagination. The human intellect can conceptualize ideas, understand meanings and express them in articulate language. This chapter demonstrated how the teaching of words allows the teaching of culture and social norms. African children enhance their wording skills by challenging each other in syllable inversion competitive games. Wording is a very important identification tool, and identifies persons, spirits, animals, plants, or inanimate objects. Names of praise are often multiple-unit compounds made of a basic concept and many attached attributes. Similarly, some numbering systems are more complex than others, as was illustrated by the complexity of the Yorùbá system over the Luba system. Luba children practice counting by rhyming ten-by-ten names of animals, names of clans, or of grasshoppers. Africans communicate through many other forms of articulate speech, such as riddles and enigmas, animal stories, proverbs, and call and response dialogues. To facilitate learning and retention and promote solidarity, Africans also articulate verbal messages in songs. Narratives, repartees between rivals, epic songs, commemoratives, and social critics are such often sung forms of articulate verbal speech discussed in this chapter.

(Endnotes)

1   Ikande, Mary. ND. "Yoruba names for twins boy and girl". *Legit.* https://www.legit.ng/1117190-yoruba-names-twins-boy-girl.html. Retrieved 6-8-2020.

2   Zaslavsky, Claudia. 2017. "Mathematics of the Yoruba People and of their Neighbors in Southern Nigeria." https://www.jstor.org/stable/3027363. Retrieved 4- 23-2020.

AIRNET. ND. "Number System of the Yoruba." *Number Systems of the World.* http://www.sf.airnet.ne.jp/ts/language/number/yoruba.html. Retrieved 4-23-2020.

Mathematicians of the African Diaspora. ND. "Yoruba Numerals" 17th to 19th century Nigeria. *Nigeria Mathematics Today*. http://www.math.buffalo.edu/mad/Ancient-Africa/mad_nigeria_pre-. Retrieved 4- 16-2020.

Chapter 4
A Creative Mind

1. Insights, Discernment, Judgment, and Behavioral Adjustments
2. Creative Imagination and Symbolic Representations

Articulate language is a particular manifestation of human mental creativity from divine creation. At Creation, God also equipped the human mind with built-in faculties of (1) insights, discernment and judgment, together allowing for mental penetration of intricate situations and perception of nuances, and inspiring personal behavioral adjustments to meet optimum community standards; and (2) creative imagination, that is, the ability to generate ideas and turn them into symbolic representations in the form of concrete actions or physical objects. This chapter explores these sets of attributes of the human mind through proverbs; animal stories and legends, cultural practices, royal customs, religious rituals, and artistic productions from across the African continent.

1. INSIGHTS, DISCERNMENT, JUDGMENT, AND BEHAVIORAL ADJUSTMENTS

Insights are illuminating ideas about an intricate situation. Discernment is the ability to grasp and comprehend such a situation in its totality and internal nuances. Judgment is the thought process that leads to a decision. Together these faculties invite for personal behavioral adjustments to some optimum community standard. The habit of regularly putting these mental powers into practice in the best collectively desired way is called *wisdom*. Parents sensitize their children to the complexity of human life on Earth, pointing to a whole range of situations where wisdom must prevail. In Africa, life truths embodying wisdom inherited from the ancestors are often expressed through proverbs and animal stories and legends. The illustrations discussed below are taken from Luba thought. Below, sample proverbs are grouped by the desired types of wisdom they promote.

Courage, Bravery, and Preparedness in Dealing with Life Hardship

Hardship, be it exhausting work, mystical assaults by witches, or demands by protector spirits, is inevitable as long as one lives on this planet. One better be prepared to face it victoriously. Courage, bravery and preparedness are necessary equipment.

1. ***Panu mpasangana pakola, masela ne bilunda mbisangana bimena.*** Hardship on Earth preceded man. The tall grass and the short grass in the fields preceded the farmer.

    The tall grass is wet and covers the farmer with water while walking to the fields and at work trying to unearth it. The short grass has a large base, is deeply rooted and hard to unearth.

2. ***Kudya wa Mbuyi, Kudima wa Ndaya, Kudya kulengela, Kudima kubi.***
   Eating and farming food are inseparable cousins born of two sisters—Mbuyi and Ndaya. However, eating is pleasant and invigorating whereas farming is unpleasing and exhausting.

   Message: If there is no struggle there cannot be victory.

3. ***Kadima Minu ne Kadima Ntonku***
   One farms with finger gestures while the other scratches the soil with a hoe.

   ***Explanation:** Kadima Minu and Kadima Ntonku are two characters. Kadima, of kudima "cultivate," means the "one who cultivates." Minu means "fingers." Kadima Minu is a character who spends his time pointing with his fingers how far his field will go. Ntonku comes from kutonkona "to scratch, to hoe." Every day, Kadima Ntonku clears some land with his little hoe, whereas Kadima Minu continues to point to the big trees to which he will extend his field. Not before long the first rains of the season will come; Kadima Ntonku will be able to plant some corn whereas Kadima Minu will still be describing with his hands how big his field will be.*

   This is the story of the talker versus the doer. If you keep postponing tasks you will accomplish nothing in life. Rather do something every day no matter how small.

4. ***Mutwenzenzabu, baloji batwasa nzadi, bakishi ku bulaba batulomba nshima.***
   This is how supernatural forces treat us: Agents of evil pinch us all the time, whereas the ancestral spirits always ask us for food.

   Life is a constant battle. To live in peace, you will have to learn how to fight evil powers while complying with the demands of the protective spirits.

Carefulness, Skillfulness, Caution and Diplomacy in Marriage

An important area of life requiring lots of wisdom daily is marriage. Married men are exhorted to exercise extreme carefulness and skillfulness to be able to preserve their marriages.

5. ***Dibaka ncisaka cyambula mwena meeji, cyambwila kahumba, ciicikila mu mâyi.*** Marriage is like a basket on the head of a wise person crossing a river (on a bar). If carried by the unwise one, it will spill into the water.

   Explanation: Unless one is extremely wise, one cannot be successful in marriage. Sometimes it takes a little misstep for a marriage to be irreparably broken.

6. **Mbanza ya mpangu yidi ne bilumbu.**
   Polygamous compounds are nurseries of disputes.
   Africans practice polygamy. Disputes, open or latent, between the husband and each wife and among the wives with one another are everyday realities in polygamous compounds. This proverb sensitizes polygamous men to the risks that are inherent in multiple marriages.

7. *Sela basatu, nanku ufwa lukasa.*
   Marry three wives, and die early.

Life itself is a struggle. Marriage brings in more struggles. Multiple marriages aggravate them all. The polygamous man may become victim of conflicts between his wives under the weight of compounded pressures or by taking side with the one who is guilty in the eyes of the ancestors. He must exercise extreme caution and diplomacy.

8. *Wasela muteketa, kulekedi mukulu; mukulu nukadi nenda lungenyi bula bumwa.*
   If you marry a younger woman, do not overlook your older wife; the older wife and you have reached the same wavelength.

   There is no guarantee that you and the younger wife will get along for very long. It would be very unwise to neglect the older wife with whom you have learned to adapt to each other's thoughts and behaviors over the years.

9. *Mudya nenda ki mmufwisha, wamubenga ne moyo waya.*
   A woman you have shared life with is not to be led into death, rather let her go away alive instead.

   The ideal is for any marriage, monogamous or polygamous, to be stable. But when the situation becomes untenable, do not cause your wife to die; send her away alive.

Awareness of One's Insecurity While Away from Home

10. *Kwa benda nkulu kwa muci.*
    Living in a foreign land is like being perched way up in a tall tree.
    Meaning: Your possibilities for actions beneficial to you are limited.

11. *Mvula uleejile Kaluma kwabo.*
    Severe rains once showed Kaluma the way back home.
    Meaning: Threats to life in a foreign land will make you value your own homeland more and want to return to it for more security.

12. ***Wamwangala kutuulu njilu, wadya kupingana mweba mu nkolu.***
    When you move away to live, do not unearth the eggplants (a rescue vegetable) from your current garden, you might come back to your roots in a time of food scarcity.

    Explanation: When you move out of the community or upwardly in social hierarchy, do not sever your current good relationships. Who knows? You might fall back and need their support.

Measure, Moderation, Patience, Balance

13. ***Kabwa ka lubilu kashila nyama panshi.*** The fast running dog will pass by the game without seeing it.

    Meaning: Do not act precipitously. Take time to examine the situation first. Otherwise you will miss the essential.

14. ***Kudya lukasa nkupya mukana.*** He who precipitously eats hot food will burn his mouth.

    Meaning: Instinctive, unchecked actions will hurt you. Take time to think so you can behave responsibly.

15. ***Wadya cyakanangana ne muminu.*** Only eat the portion that can pass through your throat.

    Meaning: Do not assume too many responsibilities, whatsoever pleasing they may be. Too many unfulfilled responsibilities will choke you just as too much food in your throat will do.

16. ***Bakwana kudya musabu, ukaadi wenda ne muni mukonya.***
    Even if you are admired for being a great porridge lover, do not go around with your finger scooped.

    Explanation: The Luba people eat porridge with their fingers, an curved mango leaf, or a spoon. They generally scoop out the very last quantity at the bottom of the bowl with the index finger curved.

    Message: Do not let the love of something become an obsession, an addiction. Temperance is in order.

Justice, Equity, Fairness

17. ***Tuyaya kwa ba mwanda, katwena tuya kwa ba wetu.*** (In the court of law) we

are guided by the nature of the case, not by our kinship relationships (with the litigants).

Message: Objectivity and impartiality must prevail in all legal cases.

18. ***Biyaya mu lwabanyinu, kabyena biya mu bakaji bungi.*** The rule of equitable distribution for collective work does not count the number of wives.

    Explanation: Hunters have conventional rules for distributing game from collective hunt. The person whose weapon reached the animal first, the first assessor, and the person who finished up the animal are entitled to specific parts of the game. The rest is distributed equally among the other participants. It would be unfair to privilege a member of the team who has more mouths to feed, such as multiple wives, at the expense of a more deserving contributor who only has one wife or none.

19. ***Wateeka cyanza pa keeba, pa kabenda wakeba diyoyo.*** Only put your hand on what is yours, otherwise you get yourself in trouble.

    Respect of private property is expected of all. Violations are punishable. Restitution is often required and fines imposed.

20. ***Muntu wa cilema tumubelela pa bantu.*** Counsel the ill-behaved person in public.

    Message: Offenses against the community must be rebuked, sanctioned and repaired publically. Private counseling is cover-up.

Alertness

21. ***Babela mwan' a muntu, mwan'a mufu wateelela.*** When the son of the living is being advised, you, son of the dead, listen carefully.

    Explanation: Orphans have no excuse for lacking in their community's social and moral education. They should listen to, and take advantage of advices that living parents give their children.

22. ***Badimusha kasha, bukwa nyama bwonso bwadimukilapu.*** A warning to the animal *kasha* is a warning to all animals.

    Explanation: Kasha, a kind of deer known for being the fastest running animal, is being admonished that its speed may be insufficient to escape the danger if it does not begin early and runs faster than usual. If that is true for the fastest runner, a greater sense of urgency should be expected of all others.

23. ***Mudimuka umvwila hampenga, mupota anu wa mutuuta mu cyadi.*** The

attentive person hears distant echcoes, the inattentive one only hears knocks on his chest.

Meaning: Stay on alert so you can act proactively, lest you be surprised and find yourself with no time to do anything.

Open Mindedness, Realism, Good Sense

24. ***Diudyadya cyula ki ndiudi umena mpusu.*** The day you eat the toad is not the day pimples grow over your body.

    Explanation: Luba parents tell their children that the reason humans do not eat the toad is that eating the toad would cause pimple irruptions all over their bodies. At the same time they warn the skeptical child from trying because even if the effects are not immediate it does not mean they will never occur.

25. ***Futa mabanza ushala kumuna.*** Pay off your debts, and then launch your livestock-raising business.

    Explanation: If you really want to prosper in your business, free yourself from indebtedness first. Otherwise debts will hamper your progress.

26. ***Kabwa wa nsenu, bavwa kumpala bakaadi panyima.*** Slippery stone, those who were ahead are now behind.

    Explanation: Human life is haunted by innumerable uncertainties. Success in one day may turn into failure in the next. Do not look down on those of a lower socio-economic status than yours. Tomorrow they may be ahead of you.

27. ***Kubenga milaala nkumona ya mudilu pa kapya.*** Turning down leftovers only makes sense when fresh food is cooking on the stove.

    Explanation: Milaala and *ya mudilu* in this proverb stand for *nshima*, the Luba staple food. Leftover *nshima* is hard and disliked for this reason. Generally, it is eaten by children in the morning hours while the parents are away taking care of household chores, sometimes by women in the fields before returning home. It makes no sense turning down an opportunity if a better one is not certain.

28. ***Kajadikila beena bilowa, bya mwenda bishaala bisendama.*** She straightens up other people's calabashes, while her own remain leaning.

    Explanation: Luba women brew a beer called *cibuku*. They sell it in calabashes (*bilowa, bibungu*) or in urns (*nzaba, milondu*) at their home. They also sell it in the marketplace, along an alley specially reserved for beer sellers. The calabashes, or urns, are seated on crowns *(nkata)* made of rags. Sellers who sit together usually take care of one another's business, including telling those whose calabashes seem to be losing balance to straighten them up. This proverb is addressed to individuals who are busy telling other folks how to carry out their business, while their own continue to be in shambles.

29. ***Kajiji ka bundu bakajikila ne citalu.*** A shy fly ended up being buried with the corpse.

    Explanation: A fly was afraid of becoming the object of mockery by other flies who eat flesh meat from game, if it was to be seen flying away from a human corpse. So it hid in the sleeve of the dead man's shirt and was buried with him. The lesson is: Do not be so ashamed of an embarrassing situation that you necessarily put your life at risk.

30. ***Bidi mwetu tenta, anu keeba peeba.*** Saying "there is plenty in my village" does you no good, unless some of it belongs to you personally.

    Explanation: It is right to be proud of the successes of your community. But know that other people's prosperity will not elevate you. Only your own accomplishments will make you somebody.

31. ***Waya ku Bakuba kwanji kuteya, wamona Bakuba muteyateyabo.*** If you move to Kubaland, set no traps until you observe how the Kuba people set theirs.

    Explanation: Locals are the primary experts in patterns of interaction in their environment. You, outsider, consult with them first. It will spare you unnecessary trials and errors.

2. CREATIVE IMAGINATION AND SYMBOLIC REPRESENTATIONS

Creative imagination is the ability to conceive ideas and to turn them into meaningful concrete actions and or physical objects. Presented below for illustrations are: selected cases of ideas embodied in actions and objects, figurative monuments, architectural monuments, and aesthetic decorations.

Symbolic Actions

In "La dance de la fôret", writer *Wole Soyinka* talks about a multi-ethnic rally to be held at the occasion of a country's independence. The villagers decide to erect a big totem and ask a well-known sculptor, *Demoke*, to make one, while praying to the gods to only send to the rally the noblest and most prestigious ancestors to represent the past. Instead, the gods sent an old soldier in rags and a "nobody" pregnant woman. Disappointed, the villagers reject the latter. In this fictive story, sculpting operations by *Demoke* and prayers by the villagers are actions. The totemic sculpture, the soldier in raggedy clothes and the pregnant woman are physical embodiments. All three are materializations of ideas conceived by the villagers (Soyinka 1971, quoted in Yoka 1990).

The Luba Kunwa Cibalu: An adult Luba man who has had an argument with a close relative, such as a brother, in the courtyard of the latter, and has left the brother's courtyard while still angry at him, will come back to the brother's house before the day is over, ask for a drink of water, and take it on the spot. The argument, the anger and his departure in anger have broken the good relationships that are expected to reign among family members. His return to, and drinking of the water from the brother's house clean his heart, wash away the anger, and remove the barrier that had started settling between the brother and him, thereby restoring the normal brotherly relationships between them. Traditionally, the Luba serve drinking water in a vessel called *cibalu* made out of a pumpkin calabash. The drinking of the heart-cleansing and reconciliation water is called *kunwa cibalu*. The *kunwa cibalu* for a more severe violation, such as a physical fight with one's senior, or one that has settled in for some time, includes chicken sacrifice or, depending on the gravity of the case, chicken and goat sacrifice to the ancestor; a recall by both parties of all words of malice or hatred uttered in the argument; and the drinking of the cleansing water by both parties from the same *cibalu*.

Symbolic Objects

Egyptian Pharaohs' White and Red Crown, Statues and Engraved Images: The rulers of ancient Egypt introduced several symbolic representations of pivotal ideas. King *Menes* or *Narmer*, Dynasty I, the conqueror who unified Upper Egypt and Lower Egypt, symbolized the unification by combining on his own crown the white crown from Upper Egypt's kings and the red color of Lower Egypt's kings. The kings left behind statues and engraved images to memorialize themselves. The statue of King *Khufu* found in the Great Pyramid is an example. The *Sphinx*, a monument in the form of man-lion, was built near Memphis in honor of King *Khafre*, *Khufu*'s son, believed to embody *Re*, the highest of the sun-god trinity and Horus, the god of kingship. The pharaohs received their authority to rule from the *Sphinx* (Gore 1991, Lehner 1991). *Ramses the Great*, *Ramses II*, Dynasty XIX, had his name engraved on a pillar and in many other places on the building of the Temple at *Abydos* that he completed in honor of his father, King *Seti* (Gore 1991).

Aksum Royal Inscriptions and the Ghanaian Royal Stool: *Aksum* was ancient Africa's next largest civilization second to Egypt. Upon conversion to Christianity, King *Ezna* (320-350) had his inscriptions of thanksgiving to God for his victories engraved in public monuments in several languages: e.g., *Ge'ez* (the mother language of the Ethiopian *Amharic*), South Arabian and Greek. He issued golden coins inscribed in crosses. He is believed to have brought to *Aksum*, precursor of present day Ethiopia, *the Ark of Covenant* on which God gave the Ten Commandments to Moses (Millard 2001). When in the 17th century A.D, the three *Akan* states – *Bono*, *Akwamu*, and *Asante* – decided to unite into a more powerful confederacy, Leader *Osei Tutu*, under the tutelage of his mentor *Okomfo,* magician and priest, instituted the golden stool as the symbol of unity of the *Ashanti* nation. The stool represented the spiritual and political powers of the Ashanti people. All of the *Ashanti* owed loyalty to the stool and the *Asantehene,* King (Collins 1997, Davidson 1997, Osae et al, 1973).

The Lukasa Memory Board of the Luba: During the Luba Empire (15th-19th centuries), the Luba people who lived in what is now North Katanga Province of the Democratic Republic of the Congo, developed a wooden device called *lukasa.* The *lukasa* is curved and has the shape of a woman, with its interior resembling a woman's torso. It was used as a storage of significant king-related events in the history of the kingship; hence its nickname as memory board. The storage contained objects such as beads, shells, and bits of metal attached to the board as well as designs of human heads carved into the wood. Some marks look scattered pell-mell. Others, particularly the heads, were arranged in round, linear, or other configurations. Some configurations could be identified as forming paths leading to some historical locales where some significant event in the history of the kingship once took place, uniting the king with his people. Both the torso-like interior of the *lukasa* and the back were embellished with scarifications, just as *Luba* women were. The back resembles a tortoise shell. The tortoise represents, for the king, longevity, patience and a source of power. The woman's body is also portrayed on royal tools, covered with scarifications as well. The woman, seated or standing, carries the body of the king. Some of the ideas embodied in the *lukasa* relate to the conception of the world, respect for social hierarchies and protocols, the origins of the kingship and greatness of particular kings. By their colors, shapes and distribution over the woman's body, the scarifications, the incised designs and the shells, express beauty, grace, elegance, spirituality and sacredness. They symbolize prudence and good counseling for the king. The knowledge stored in the *lukasa* is only directly accessible to historian specialists and members of the Mbudie Secret Association who recount the marks by touching and feeling, and interpret them to the public. The events they commemorate are also enacted through dancing and singing rituals (Roberts 2011, Tissières 1998, Moss. ND).[1]

Symbolic Representations of Relationships between Humans and Spirits

The Cult of Ancestors among the Dogon of Mali: *Dogon* practitioners of ancestral veneration symbolize communication between the living and the dead by small wooden objects in Y form with notches all along one side representing steps. The ladder-like objects are placed near the ancestral altar along with other cult objects such as cooking pots to enable the soul of the dead being honored to ascend into heaven first and then come back to consume the food prepared for them. The Y-form represents the pubis and reproductive power. Sometimes the Y-form ladder is placed on a tomb to allow the spirit of the dead to climb back up to the surface in the land of the living and reincarnate in the body of a future descendant (Zahan, in Olupona 2000).

Deity Osun and Goddess Uhammiri/Ogbuide: *Osun,* god of medicine and herbs in Yorùbá religion, is the patron of medical professionals. The followers of *Osun* who are priests and traditional medical practitioners at the same time combine in them the spiritual power of the priesthood and the natural power of medicinal plants. On the other hand, the *Oba,* King, is the embodiment of spiritual powers protective of his people. On occasion, priests/medicinal health specialists who are the *Oba*'s medical providers make complex variable arrangements of iron staffs, including "flames, birds, chameleons, and snakes" for him to carry and be empowered to fight witches and evil forces, thereby protecting and securing the well-being of his people and the nation (Kaplan, 2000). In Igbo cosmology, the human being is a perpetual traveler passing through several critical stages, notably: transition into childhood through birth and naming, transition into adulthood through initiation at puberty, initiation in old age into titles and priesthood, and transition into the afterlife through death and funeral. Through death and funeral, the departing is born into the afterlife and keeps on traveling passing through similar transitions until rebirth. All the transitions are marked by special ceremonies involving the water goddess *Uhammiri/Ogbuide* who is the goddess of the crossroads, and displaying her color, white, more specifically white limestone. It symbolizes the washing away of the person's old identity and instauration of a new one, otherwise marked by name change. The invocations of the goddess, the displaying of her color, and the ceremonial performances are intended to strengthen the person and enable him or her to pursue their travel successfully (Jell-Bahlsen, 2000).

Shrines as Channels of Communication between the living and the departed are omnipresent throughout the continent. There exist natural shrines such as forest groves, particular trees, and rocks. The great majority of shrines are man-made and are found everywhere. The shrines stand for crossroads between the ancestors and their descendants; as well as instruments of unification among the living, as groups of adepts assembled at the altar make offerings to, and execute rituals in honor of the spirits to restore broken relations and or secure blessings for the participants and their progeny. Sometimes, ritual dances and songs may lead the priests and people to go into trance and embody the venerated spirit. The spirit communicates his or her will in a coded language that only the priest can decode and interpret to the lay persons (Ray, 2000).

Masks are another physical form through which the ancestral spirits can be involved in the actions of their living descendants. Mudiji Malamba Gilombe has studied the masks among the *Phende* of Congo DRC used in initiation rituals (*mukanda*) marking the transition from youth to adulthood. According to him, the *Mukanda* initiation is practiced not only by the *Phende* of the Congo and Zambia, but also by several other ethnic groups. The mythical origin story of the *mukanda* is that a young man (*Malenga*) dressed in *G-string*, dared traveling to the river in the forest in group of his mother, his sisters and other women. He got wounded by a sharp reed to the prepuce in their presence and to their view. In panic, the women cried out to men, who came running. The most intrepid one from among them cut off the prepuce with a sharp razor. The men built a shelter camp in the forest and stayed there until *Malenga*'s wound healed. At that point, they invented formidable masks named *minganji* to watch over the camp. They invented a different category of masks which they named *mbuya* by summoning the face, nose, eyes, and the rest of the body to come out of the trunk of a tree. Upon reentering the village, the women asked them what they had done in the forest; they showed them the *mbuya* masks in response. At that occasion the ancestors decreed that every male person should be circumcised in the *mukanda* initiation rite (Mudiji, 1989).

Initiation begins with separation of the candidates from the world of women by placing them in shelters under construction, where they are served a farewell meal along with a sacrificial meal of fresh chickens provided by the candidate's father and maternal uncle. Each father gives his son advice and instructions of good conduct and commits him to God's will. Ancestral spirits are served their share of the sacrificial meal to secure their protection. The maternal uncle rubs the candidate's body with the kaolin of blessing while uttering words which means "Happiness! Let your eyes see clearly and your legs move swiftly." The next stage in separation consists of special dances in a rally camp built in the savannah away from the village, prohibited to lay people. Had-hock planted palm trees, a periodically resounding bell and a buffalo *mbuya* mask guard the access to the camp. In the camp, the candidates are initiated to major men's skills: hunting, fishing, extracting palm wine, martial arts, and a special task designed by the initiators. They also receive theoretical information about the history of the *mukanda* initiation and the knowledge of the environment in an esoteric language. After two months or more the camp moves into the forest for circumcision in a special shelter built for the circumstance. The candidates who have seen the sex of a woman or an adult man are asked to avow and are given a purifying concoction to drink. There is a circumciser per village painted in white and red kaolin spots all over his body and wearing red feathers of a particular bird on his head. One by one the candidates are presented to him by their fathers and godfathers. The circumcision is done with a sharp razor. The event is announced in songs and rhythmically ringing bells. The operation ends with all the newly circumcised prostrated before the circumciser camouflaged in a leopard mask (Mudiji, 1989).

Symbolic Representations of Relationships among Humans, between the Living and the Dead, and the Living and the Ecology

A *Luba* man's compound is a complex of symbolic representations of ideas about relationships among humans, between the living and the dead, and between humans and the ecology. The dominant idea is the protection of the homestead as a whole, including the people and movable and immovable property. Ancestral protection over the homestead includes protection against natural calamities. It is often symbolically reflected in the position of the shrines and actively solicited through gatherings around the shrines for offerings, supplications or trance dances. Ancestral protection over the homestead is primarily symbolized through the positioning and orientation of the houses and the shrines in a polygamous compound. The following ideas are explained below: preeminence of the senior wife among her co-wives, spiritual fortification of the senior wife's house, strategic positioning of the senior wife's house, and the senior wife's house as the center of the universe.

Preeminence of the Senior Wife among Co-Spouses. Usually, the senior wife enjoys a higher social status than her co-wives. She is often the first one to have married the common husband. For this reason she is generally the oldest as well. By respect for her seniority as co-wife and for her age, the other wives of the common husband call her *Yaaya* (Big Sister), or *Maamu* (Mother). The ancestral tradition requires that the common husband spend more days with her than with each of the other wives in his her sleeping rounds with them. She is generally the one who is dedicated to the ancestress *Nkambwa* and keeps the protective taboos for the entire household. Perhaps for this reason the husband is expected to spend the last night before going on trip and the first night upon returning from trip in her house. The senior wife's higher social status in relation to her co-wives is transferable to her children. Her children are the ritual seniors of their half-siblings regardless of their chronological age. They are entitled to replace the father in receiving the tributes of the first fruits that his children owe him for their ability to work and to sire and raise marriageable daughters. The oldest child by the senior wife replaces the father by primogenitor right. Generally, when he dieshis siblings replace him in decreasing order of age. If there are no survivals among siblings, then his children by the senior wife replace him in their chronological age.

Fortification of the Senior Wife's House. The ancestral spirits are the major family guardians. This role is most symbolically expressed in the strategic location and orientation of the shrines for male ancestors (*Bakishi*) and the sacred tree representing the female family guardian spirit (*Nkambwa*). Both abodes are located by the house of the senior wife, making it a veritable spiritual fortress. If the man had some fetishes, they were generally located in or by this house as well. Hidden meanings are to be found in the position and orientation of the shrines in relation to the sacred tree, and in the location of both the shrines and the sacred tree in respect to the house. The sacred tree, abode of the ancestress *Nkambwa,* is planted west of the senior wife's house, near or at a distance. The shrines for male ancestors, consisting of one or two small huts, are situated to the east, toward the front, facing both the house and the sacred tree. The location and orientation of the shrines and the tree symbolize conjugal responsibilities between male ancestral spirits identified with the Luba husband and the female spirit *Nkambwa*, identified with the senior wife. The location of male ancestors' shrines to the east of the senior wife's house and their westward orientation toward the house and the sacred tree, suggest their mystical identification with the powers of the ascending sun. As a result of this empowerment, the male ancestral spirits stand in a position of strength and keep a watchful eye on the female spirit, as a husband watches over his wife. On the other hand, the location of the sacred tree to the west of the house identifies the abode of the ancestress *Nkambwa* with a restful home to which a tired husband returns when the journey is over. Thus, when the sun moves toward sunset, the Luba say: *"dyatangidi kwa Muadi"* (King Sun is moving toward the Senior Wife's House) or *Dyayi kubwela kwa Muadi* (He is about to enter the Senior Wife's House). The Luba generally make sacrifices to the ancestral spirits during the mid-morning hours. The westward orientation of the shrines means that, when addressing the ancestral spirits, the worshiper would be facing the sun. The practice of carrying out ancestral rituals in mid-morning hours and the westward orientation of the shrines are reminiscent of a now defunct worship to God symbolized by the sun. Luba tradition tells that the Luba once venerated God the Creator directly. As a rule, the ritual was carried out during mid-morning hours when the sun had become strong (*diiba dya nkankala*). To perform this ritual, the officiant, a man, would first open a pathway in the wildness near the house. Next, he would stand in the pathway facing the sun while holding a white rooster in his hands. Then, he would raise the rooster to the sun and address the Creator *Maweja Nangila* as:

A Creative Mind

"Diiba Katangila Cishiki Wakutangila dyamwasa Nsensa (The Sun that No One Can Dare Look in The Eye without Being Dazzled by His Rays).

Strategic Positioning of the Senior Wife's House: A Luba man can marry as many women as he can afford. But a compound of four wives is considered a complete one. By ancestral rule, each wife must have her own house, located in a particular corner of the compound commensurate with her seniority in relation to her co-wives. When tradition was still respected in the Luba country, the house of the senior wife was always located in the northwestern corner of the compound facing south. The house of the second wife stood diagonally to the right, facing north. The house of the third wife occupied the southwestern corner, in front of the senior wife's house, looking north. The house of the fourth wife was situated to the right of the senior wife's house, in front of the second wife's, and oriented to the south. Thus there were two houses to the north facing south (senior wife's and fourth wife's), and two houses to the south looking north (second wife's and third wife's houses respectively). In some compounds, a guesthouse (*beesa*, or *ndaku*), generally bigger than the other houses, occupied the middle of the rectangular courtyard separating the four houses. Each co-wife bears a title designating both her rank in the compound hierarchy and the position of her house in the compound layout. The title or rank of the first wife is *Mukalenga Mwadi* or *Mwadi Mukulu* (Senior Wife). The second wife's title is *Cikala Mwadi* (Deputy Senior Lady). The third wife is titled *Ntomena* or *Citumbatumba* (literally, Functionless Corner*)*. Finally, the fourth wife is *Kalami ka Mukalenga Mwadi* (Senior Lady's Bodyguard).The orientation of the houses, more specifically the senior wife's house, was a fieldwork puzzle for me. Why does the house of the senior wife always face north? This question remained unanswered for long time during my fieldwork. I still have a fresh memory of asking several informants the question and not obtaining any response. They were young and old. They simply did not know. I interviewed some individually, others in groups. Still, no one seemed to know. It was almost miraculously that one day a certain *Barthelemy Kalala,* a man in his thirties, a native of *Beena Manda*, living in *Beena Mpoyi,* my village of origin, gave me the answer. He answered my question rhetorically: "*Misulu eeyi mmitangila kwepi*?" (Can't you tell in what direction the rivers run?) What was a mystery to me seemed so obvious to him. *Kalala*'s response opened my eyes to connections between the ecology of the compound and the physical geography of *Lubaland* through the double mediation of Luba linguistics and belief system. Gradually, piece by piece, once hidden meanings began to unravel. His exclamatory question: "Can't you tell by the direction of the rivers" made me realize that the four major rivers that cross the *Luba* country run south to north in the area. From east to west these rivers are*: Sankuru, Kalelu, Mbujimayi* and *Lubi*. This discovery enabled me to understand the terminology used to designate the position of the senior wife's house. Her house is called "downstream the compound" (*kwinshi kwa lubanza*). Indeed, in respect to the direction of the four rivers in the area, her house is located downstream, in opposition to the houses of the second and the third wives, which are located upstream. The location of the fourth wife's house alongside the senior wife's house is an ecological anomaly. The anomaly is legitimated by assigning her the symbolic role of being the Senior Wife's Body Guard, as expressed in her title:

Kalami ka Mukalenga Muadi.
Sociologically, the senior wife alone is identified as being downstream (*kwinshi kwa lubanza*). The second, third and fourth wives are collectively termed upstream the compound (*ku mutu kwa lubanza*). The opposition downstream-upstream has many implications. Upstream wives are juniors. The downstream wife is their senior as her title of Senior Lady so rightfully proclaims it. Co-wives' statuses in relation to one another are extended to their respective children. The senior wife's children are ritually seniors to their half-siblings regardless of their chronological age. For instance, after the common father passes away, the children of the senior wife replace him in receiving the presents of first fruits that their half-brothers owe the father. The moving of the tributes from the children of other wives to the children of the senior wife is equated with the running of spring water from upstream to downstream. Their respective children are likewise characterized as downstream children and upstream children, respectively. There is a supernatural dimension to the downstream location and upstream orientation of the senior wife's house. Her house is located downstream facing upstream because of the spiritual powers it embodies and the protective role it is called to play for the family community. In Luba mentality, rivers are carriers of scourges. On the other hand, the house of the senior wife, as we already know, was the headquarters of the family's protective forces. The shrines for male ancestral spirits and the sacred tree, abode of the ancestress *Nkambwa*, stood by this house. If the husband had some fetishes, they resided in the senior wife's house as well. Being thus empowered, the house of the senior wife faced upstream the rivers so it could perceive from distance the various calamities that are carried down by the waters and ward them off the family community before they got near.

The Senior Wife's House, Center of the Universe. Together, the location of the senior wife's house downstream the compound and its upstream orientation, the location of male ancestral spirits' shrines to the east of the house and their westward orientation, along with the location of the sacred tree, abode of the female spirit *Nkambwa*, to the west of the house, instruct us of Luba notions of the cardinal directions:

Ku Mutu kwa Ditunga (Upstream the Country), South
Kwinshi kwa Ditunga (Downstream the Country), North
Kudi Diiba Dibanda (Toward the Ascending Sun), East
Kudi Diiba Dipweka (Toward the Descending Sun), West

Resoundingly, not only do the above observations underscore the preeminence of the *Mukalenga Mwadi* (Senior Wife) among her co-wives and the centrality of her house in the geopolitics of the compound, they also portray this house as the site where North and South, and East and West meet. In other words, her house is the center of the universe.

Figurative Monuments

Figurative monuments are artistic productions in human figures. Human statues and faces dominate in African art. Pharaohs' statues fall in this category. Deities occupy a preponderant place among figurative productions by African artists. In the Yorùbá *Ifa* religion and its Brazilian offspring, *Candomblé*, Creator *Olódùmarè*, has entrusted the government of the Earth to a core of ministerial spirits, the *Orixás* (in Portuguese) or *Orìṣàs* (in Yorùbá), each assuming one or more ministerial functions, such as fertility and procreation (Deity *Oxala, Oṣala),* metals and metal workers *(Ogum)*; land, agriculture, and property (*Omulu* or *Obaluaye*); medicinal plants and herbs (*Ossayn*); justice and lawyers (*Xango, Ṣango*); wild animals, hunters and forests (*Oxossi, Osossi*); the sea and sea travelers (*Yemanja*); and more (Idowu, 1994). These deities and others are represented in human forms in masks and or statues and venerated by their adepts in songs and dances and are offered special foods and sacrifices. The sacrifices to the *Orìṣàs*, called *ebọ*, are designed to restore broken relations or secure protection or other favors. Their nature and quantity depends on the problem at hand and the deity involved. They may involve such items as money, fruit, drink, kola nuts, and more. They necessarily include animal blood in life–and–death situations, in initiation ceremonies and other important matters. For example, one may sacrifice sheep and pigeons for long life; rooster, male goat, or ram to overcome enemies; or ducks, roosters, hens, and female goat for the blessing of many children and grandchildren (Neimark, 1993).

Some of the best known artistic traditions in the Congo DRC are *Kongo, Kuba, Luba* of *Katanga, Hemba, Yaka* and *Mangbetu*. Human motifs prevailed in all these traditions. They include ancestor figures, divination, initiation and healing spirits, human faces, and others. The summary below is taken from Mukenge's *Culture and Customs of the Congo* (2002). Statues occupy a preponderant place among ancestor representations. Kongo funerary monuments are among the well-known ancestor representations. Funerary monuments portray different characters. One, a thoughtful-looking man, sits with his left hand supporting his cheek and the right hand holding the hip. Another, a symbol of maternity, represents a seated mother holding her baby in her lap. Kongo funerary monuments were made in stone. Elsewhere statues featuring ancestor figures were made in wood instead. The Hemba people, a branch of the Luba of Katanga, produced some of the most beautiful ancestor figures; so did the Suku of Bandundu. Suku artistic productions include an ancestor figure with a special hairdress dominated by a crest and the line of the stomach dominated by the navel. The Yaka, an ethnic group living in Bandundu had wooden ancestor figures among their artistic productions. They were adorned with beads and cowries. Under the influence of Christianity, Kongo artists of the past have left behind in the *Mbanza Ngungu* area metal crucifixes dating from the seventeenth century. Some statues with human figures were inhabited by sprits other than ancestors. These spirits were invoked for protection or divination. Among the Yaka of Bandundu, Congo DRC divination statues were covered with a bag except for the head and the feet. The Holo people, who live in Bandundu at the border of Angola, had a statue representing a spirit called *Nzambi*, to whom they addressed their prayers. Rather than whole bodies, some arts portray human faces only. Human faces are found on a variety of artistic productions, including stone bracelets, trumpets, fly whisks, knife handles and combs. The upper end of a Yaka slit drum used in divination and healing ceremonies consisted of a woman's head wearing earrings and necklaces. The Luba of Katanga had a rectangular wooden divination instrument with a human head. During divination, the instrument was seated on the ground or on a stool while both the diviner and the client held it. The oracle (revealed knowledge) was delivered when the instrument began to shake.

Architectural Monuments

Egyptian Pyramids and Temples: The kings of ancient Egypt, the pharaohs, believed they were gods and will live eternally. The transformation into gods would take place in the mountain during an encounter with deities from the sky. The pharaoh, being the strongest ruler on Earth, identified with the sky's strongest god, the sun. Rather than going to the natural mountain, the pharaohs decided to create their own mountains, the pyramids, on locations of their choice. The ideas of the king being deified during encounters with sky gods on the mountain, and eternal life after death, were put into action through the processes of mummification and pyramid construction. The Kings' mummified dead bodies were meant to live eternally. Indeed, to the present day, many mummies have, as they are still being found intact in the tomb through archeological excavations. King Djoser, Dynasty III, built the oldest stone building, the Step Pyramid at *Saqqara,* designed by Architect *Imhotep.* The steps were the ladders for the deified king (pharaoh) to climb after death in journey toward the sky to be unified and live forever with departed deified kings (Roberts, 1995). Other pharaohs built more pyramids and temples to their glory. The Great Pyramid, completed around 2550 B.C.E., in honor of King *Khufu,* Dynasty IV, is the greatest architectural accomplishment in ancient history. The Great Pyramid is located on the Giza Plateau, along with two smaller pyramids: the Pyramid of *the Queens* and the Pyramid of *Khafre, Khufu's* son. Each pyramid was accompanied by a temple constructed near the Nile River and a mortuary temple at the base of the pyramid. From the Nile River, funerary boats, one carrying the mummified body of the king, would be carried to the mortuary temple, where the body would be entombed for eternity (Gore, 1991). The ideas of the king's deification and eternal life were thus put into action through the following processes: pyramid, temple, and boat building, mummification, solemn procession and entombment. Whereas, eternal life was embodied in the mummies and the pyramids. Other Egyptian temples were built in locations other than Giza. Ramses II, *The Great,* was considered a god and a descendent of the man-lion *Sphinx.* In the very year of his enthronement (1279 B.C.E.), he had the base of the *Sphinx* reinforced with freshly cut stones. He also completed the construction of the unfinished temple to *Osiris,* begun by his father, *Seti,* in the sacred city of Abydos, in northern Egypt. Thereafter, he built a temple to himself at Abydos, a large city called *Pi-Ramses* (House of *Ramses*) in the Nile Delta, and the temple of *Abu Simbel*, in Nubia, carved into the hillside and four huge statues of himself carved into the rock (Gore, 1991).

Aksum Stela Towers: Remarkable architectural development took place in the ancient Kingdom *of Aksum,* precursor of present-day Ethiopia. Rich Aksumites built palaces, temples and impressive tombs. The kings built tall stone tower monuments called *stelae,* in the form of *obelisks*. An obelisk is an upright, 4-sided monolithic pillar gradually diminishing in size as it rises up above the ground. It generally terminates in point. The stelae were built on the ground lying horizontally and erected after construction. They are believed to have served as markers for underground burial chambers. The Aksumites built stelae in the hundreds. A few still stand in the city of Aksum. The King Ezna's Stela, named after King Ezna, 4th century A.D., is suspected to have been the last built of all. The most massive stela tower and also the world largest single-stone obelisk, now fallen, looked like a 13-story building and was 100 feet tall and weighing 500 tons. Some impressive obelisk towers still survive in the City of Aksum, Ethiopia, including the one named Obelisk of Aksum, weighing 160 tons and ending in a semi-circular top, once enclosed by metal frames (Millard 2001, Shillington 1993); **(Khair ND. UNESCO. ND.).**[2]

Mali Adobe Mosques: Some major developments took place in the 13th and 14th centuries' West Africa. Mali became a glorious empire and largest political formation following the fall of the ancient Kingdom of Ghana. Included in the empire to the east, were *Timbuktu* and *Gao*. The empire reached high levels of prosperity. Mali's rulers and their great empire became known and respected everywhere. They converted to Islam and made the compulsory pilgrimage to Mecca, but they did not force their people into Islam. The *Koran* grew in importance and served as a constitution. Law, order, and safety reigned throughout the empire. Islam increased literacy and the availability of schools for the study of the *Koran* and *Sharia* (Islamic Law). *Niani*, Mali Empire's capital (after 1300) and Timbuktu (after 1400) became major learning centers. Niani and Jenne had many mosques with priests and professors teaching in them. Foreign scholars also lived and taught in Jenne (Davidson, 1997). Upon returning from *Mecca*, Mansa Kankan Musa, the most famous emperor of Mali, brought scholars from Egypt to Timbuktu. As-Sahely, who designed mosques in Timbuktu and Gao and built a palace for the emperor, was among them. Other North African and Egyptian scholars came on their own to visit or practice in Mali. Timbuktu became a major university, with a curriculum spreading from theology and the Koran, to law and administration, history and geography, and a whole range of science and humanities disciplines. The courses were dispensed in different locations throughout the city, but administrated from three departments—*Sankore, Jingaray Ber* and *Sidi Yahya*—each housed in a different mosque. But the University of Timbuktu is most known as the University of *Sankore*. The three mosques, other mosques in the city of Timbuktu and elsewhere in Mali, and even ordinary houses are built in adobe bricks. Adobe bricks are made of sun-dried clay or other sun-dried earth, mixed with materials from tree trunks, straws and others. In Timbuktu, one also finds adobe mausoleums, that is, large buildings with places for entombment above ground. In short, Timbuktu architectural landscape was, and still is, one of adobe houses of all shapes, sizes, and heights. From among them were prestigious Islamic houses of worship and scholarly training centers, mosques. The University of Timbuktu, the famous University of Sankore, was housed in three adobe Mosques: *Sankore, Jingaray Ber* and *Sidi Yahya*. (Khair, ND.).[3]

The Great Zimbabwe: The present country of Zimbabwe derives its name from a historic state and historical buildings that once existed on the Mashonaland plateau and adjacent lowlands, between the Zambazi and the Limpopo rivers. Both the state and the buildings were founded by the Karanga, a branch of the Shona people, the largest ethnic group in Zimbabwe. Farming and especially cattle raising were the major economic activities in the region, but Zimbabwe kings derived their wealth primarily from controlling gold trade with the Indian Ocean. There were no goldfields in the

Zimbabwe state proper, but trade routes passed through its territory and its rulers had great power and influence in the region which they used to impose taxes on the traders. The Karanga built over 250 stone buildings between Zambezi and Limpopo, going all way to the Indian Ocean. Building in stones began around 1100 A.D. The *Acropolis,* in the valley, goes back to this period. The zenith was reached with the construction of the *Great Zimbabwe* somewhere between 1300 and 1500 A.D. The last constructions, such as the elliptical enclosure, the adjacent embankment and a conical tower below the *Acropolis,* came into existence in the 18th century. *Great Zimbabwe* consists of three areas of stone constructions: (1) the *Hill Ruin*, situated on a rocky hill, built around 1250 A.D. with cylindrical towers and carved monoliths on its sides and surrounding high walls, once stood on a cave believed to have been a sacred residence for the king and his family; (2) the *Great Enclosure*, also called the *Elliptical Building*, is the largest and most complex enclosure; it consists of a series of enclosure walls made of stone blocks of granite laid horizontally and carved to fit accurately without cement; it had the form of cattle kraals and encircled the community of the ruling class in a series of curving ellipses. (3) The *Valley Ruins*, a cluster of structures in enclosures, are likely to have been used for commercial exchange and long-distance trade. The *Great Zimbabwe* may have served as defensive fortifications to protect the community within it. The inside was divided into passageways and rooms. The ruling class directed the affairs of the state from the Zimbabwe sites. Ordinary people lived in mud dwellings outside the enclosures (Beach, 1994); (Demerdash, ND.).[4]

Aesthetic Creations

It is human nature to value and appreciate beauty. The human mind is endowed with the power to create beauty. Many individuals in many cultures have achieved higher levels of sophistication in creating meaningful pieces of beauty. The examples below highlight beauty in the form of wall engravings, body decorations, beautiful hand-made implements, colorful jewelry, and house paintings.

Decorative Scenes Carved in the Walls of Pharaohs' Tombs: In Ancient Egypt, decorative scenes were found carved into the walls of Pharaohs' tombs in Giza pyramids showing workers hauling large granite blocks to build the pyramids, members of the elite at banquets being served by ordinary people, and musicians playing flutes, harps, and bone clappers with beautiful young people dancing. In addition to being excellent works of art in of themselves, Egyptian boats were decorated with beautiful scenes, such as Egyptian nobility hunting birds and hippopotami found in abundance in pharaohs' tombs at Thebes in Upper Egypt (Miller, 1988). Images of these very boats were used as decorations on other objects: e.g., a vase found in King Khufu's tomb. In South Africa, in the defunct city and state of Mapungubwe, members of the royalty have been found buried upright, in a sitting position, wearing gold and copper ornaments and glass beads (Roberts 1995, El-Baz 1988). (*Kingdoms of Southern Africa*: Mampungubwe, ND).[5]

Somali Aesthetic Hand-made Implements: The Somalis are praised for their extraordinary aesthetic art skills. Their hand-made implements, be they caved combs, wooden milk vessels, woven mats, worked leather, gold ornaments, nomadic portable homes, or building walls carry impressive marks of embellishments consisting of lines and geometric patterns. Somali women are skilled beauty makers using ordinary materials. They combine fiber filaments, strings, and colored thread in the weaving of the *kabad*, a rug with plush fibers on one side and a smooth upper surface. The *kabad* is multifunctional, as it is used as an inner wall mat in the making of the portable home (*aqal*) as a seating mat, and a protective cover for the back of the pack camel. Women in pastoral areas weave mats using bamboo, grass, and colored ribbons from worn-out clothes. The mats are used as the exterior cover of the portable house. Somali women also once wove beautiful hand bags out of acacia fibers. Somali textiles manufactured in Mogadishu were renowned in the Mediterranean and Indian Ocean rim countries before the 19th century's introduction of cheap American cotton cloth (*maraykaani*) (Abdullahi 2001).

Body Decorations. Examples from contemporary Africa abound. We have already discussed the *lukasa* of the Luba of Katanga, in Congo DRC, with its elegant woman's torso form, scarifications, and varied decorative objects. Scarifications and these other aesthetic objects were and still are worn by Luba women. The Surma people of southern Ethiopia cover the entire body with fine artistic clay and water paintings designed to frighten the adversary in ritual battle simulations. Images found on rocks in Chad portray tall women with their bodies covered with elaborate engraving patterns. The Mangbetu of Ituri, Congo DRC, and their Azande neighbors were prolific producers of decorative arts. Both groups produced many items with human faces or complete human figures with artificially elongated heads, symbols of beauty in their culture. For their part, the Tuareg women of the Air Mountains, in Niger, accentuate their natural beauty by adding make-up made of powdered stone on their faces to the traditional indigo hue on their heads. In Yorùbá religion, *Orìṣà Eṣu* is known for his/her love for brightly colored clothes. Sometimes, female *Eṣu* is portrayed ornamented with a hairdo made of medicine bottles. During festivals, Yorùbá kings and chiefs dress in their majestic garments decorated with royal regalia, such as a red cross and a white sword. A priest's adornments during rituals may include a white cloth, a shirt covered with cowry shells, and a wrapper with coral beads, shells, and brass charms attached. Altars are richly decorated with figures representing deities and many other designs (Neimark, 1993). In Nigeria, modern aesthetic artists, building on ethnic traditions, have produced decorative carved panels, cement relief screens, metal relief, and portraits commissioned by church, government and individual patrons of the arts. They have produced decorative chairs, recliners, church pews, and more. Nomadic Fulani women of West and Central Africa travel wearing gold and silver earrings, rings, bracelets, and necklaces. They also wear beautiful glass and amber beads in their hair. (Coulson 1999, Schildkout and Keim 1990, Webster 1999, Falola 2001); (*Africa Facts*: "Fulani Earrings." ND).[6]

Colorful Hand-made Jewelry by Maasai Women of Kenya and Tanzania and Ndebele and Zulu Women of South Africa: Maasai women design bead jewelry, making pendants, bracelets and necklaces as a woman's daily duty. Traditionally they used natural materials such as bone, clay, wood, copper and brass. Since the 19th century, with the coming of the Europeans, glass has become increasingly dominant. By their colors and structure, Maasai beaded necklaces are social indicators of age, social status, marital status, and one's children's gender.

Chapter 4
Maasai Woman's Status, Jewelry, and Occasion

Unmarried Girl: Large flat beaded disk around the neck while dancing.

Woman on Wedding Day: Very elaborate and heavy beaded necklace hanging down to the knees.

Married Woman: Long necklace with blue beads indicative of her married status. (Adapted from *Africa Facts*. ND. "Maasai Bead Jewelry")[7]

The colors of the jewels are chosen for their symbolic meanings in reference to cattle, the highest economic prestige and spiritual value in Maasai society and culture.

Black: Symbolizes the people, their struggles to protect people land and cows.
Blue: Represents Energy from the sky that provides the rain, source of water or cattle.
Green: Stands for the land that provides food for the cattle.
Orange and Yellow: These are colors of the cow skin on the guest bed.
Red: Means bravery, strength, unity; it is the color of the blood of the cow slaughtered when the community assembles.
White: Evokes purity, color of the milk from the cow, the purest animal on Earth.

(Adapted from *Discovered*. ND. "The Story Behind the Maasai Beaded Jewelry")[8]

Traditional Ndebele women's adornments were symbols of their changing social status: from little girl to marriageable young woman after initiation, or newlywed before having a house of her own, to established wife in a home provided by the husband, to a mature married woman, to mother of a son who has reached manhood through initiation.

Ndebele Woman's Changing Social Status and Corresponding Bead Jewelry

Little girl:
beaded aprons or beaded wraparound skirts.

Marriageable girl after initiation or newlywed before having her own house:
hoops of twisted grasses covered in beads around her neck, legs and arms.

Established wife in her own home built by the husband:
a blanket over her shoulders; copper and brass rings around the arms, the legs and neck provided by the husband, symbolizing her bond and faithfulness to him; and more elaborate dresses.

Mother whose son has reached manhood through initiation:
highest status in society marked by her wearing long beaded strips.

Every married woman:
simple beaded headband, a knitted cap, or an elaborate beaded headdress in respect for her husband. (Adapted from Vuk'uzenzele, 2007).[9]

Ndebele men wore ornaments also, but to a much lesser extent than women. The principal one, given to the man by his father at initiation as a symbol of manhood, consisted of a breast-plate made of an animal skin, decorated with beads around the top, worn hanging from the neck. The others included animal skin bands worn around the head and the ankles and an animal skin around the shoulders to keep warm (Vuk'uzenzele, 2007).

Zulu women's hand-made bead jewelry is beautiful. The shape and the colors of the beads are used as communication devices between the sexes. All jewelry beads are triangular, but the positions of the triangles within a particular beadwork convey different messages. A beaded work with downward triangles worn by a woman means "I am single." Whereas upward triangles signify "I am single" for a man. The beads are of variable colors: black, blue, green, pink, red, white, or yellow. Each color has a positive message but may have opposite meanings in certain contexts.

Zulu Bead Jewelry Colors with their Positive and Negative Meanings

Color	Positive Message	Negative Meaning
Black	marriage	death, despair, sorrow
Blue	faithfulness	hostility, ill feelings
Green	contentment	illness
Pink	firm promise	poverty
Red	strong emotion	anger, impatience
White	love	no negative meaning
Yellow	wealth	badness.

(Adapted from *Africa Facts*. "Zulu Bead Jewelry")[10]

Ndzundza Ndebele House Painting: The Ndebele people of South Africa are famous not only for their multicolored, message-carrying beadworks, but also for their house painting tradition going back to the 18th century. Mud-walled houses became the standard during that century. The Ndebele began wall painting after losing the war against the Boers, Dutch-origin Whites, who took control over South Africa and submitted the Ndebele to harsh treatments for having opposed them most furiously. The paintings on these house exteriors were used to express grief and communicate messages of cultural resistance among the African people in the area. Wall painting, like bead weaving, was done by women and passed down from mother to daughter, generation after generation. A well-painted house spoke to the character of the female head of the household as a good wife and a good mother. The houses were painted on the front and side walls. Similar patterns were replicated on the gates. The original patterns consisted of finger-painted natural brown and black pigments on top of a limestone whitewash and dominated by a V-shape and a triangle on a large shape of color. It came to be replaced with patterns of brushes of bundled twigs with feathers. Geometric patterns and shapes are laid out grouped together, filled in with colors, and then repeated throughout the design. The significance of the painting is in the intensity of the color. Most used colors include blue, green, red, yellow (or gold), and pink to a lesser extent. The emphasized symbols may stand for marriage, the homeowner's status or power, prayer offering, or a protest (JC Roman, 2015).[11]

The Tiebele Tiny Village in Burkina Faso: Tiebele, a tiny circular village in the southwest region of Burkina Faso, West Africa, is known for windowless, all painted, very beautiful houses called *sukhala*. The inhabitants, the Kassena people, in Burkina Faso since the 15th century, are the oldest ethnic group in the nation. They regularly, from a long tradition, decorate their homes and mausoleums for the dead with intricate painting designs made of colored mud and chalk. The ornaments consist of varied geometrical drawings, works of women using local black, white and red clay, kaolin and coal. The external designs serve to protect the walls; whereas, the entire configuration, with thick walls, small doors and lacking windows, is designed to protect the village against bad climate and human enemies (Goran, 2016).[12]

SUMMARY

In addition to the intellect that conceptualizes ideas and expresses them in articulate language, the human mind is endowed with insights and the faculties of discernment and judgment conducive to behavioral adjustments and balanced life. The encompassing concept for such mental capacities is wisdom, that is, the ability to mentally confront conflicting or confusing situations, discern differences, similarities and nuances, and make appropriate behavioral adjustments. African wisdom is often expressed in proverbs. Some of the situations addressed in proverbs of wisdom are: life hardships, marriage, insecurity of being away from home, and dealing with enemies. Some wisdom proverbs simply promote socially accepted virtues, such as the spirit of unity, moderation and balance, justice and equity, alertness, and open mindedness, realism and good sense. Another important human mental power is creative imagination, that is, the ability to conceive ideas and to turn them into meaningful concrete actions and objects. Rituals surrounding the contracting of loyalty oaths, baby welcoming rituals, royal rituals, and funeral rituals are some of the common symbolic actions. Royal regalia, memory boards, shrines, and masks are widespread symbolic objects. This study has highlighted figurative monuments, architectural monuments, painted rocks, and painted houses, among widespread symbolic representations of major historical significance. Body decorations also occupy a major place in African cultures across the continent.

(Endnotes)

1	Moss, Juliet. ND. "Lukasa (memory board) (Luba peoples)." https://www.khanacademy.org/humanities/ap-art-history/africa-ap/a/lukasa-memory-board-luba-peoples. Retrieved 3-12-2020.

2	Khair, Zulkifli. ND. "Obelisk of Axum." https://search.yahoo.com/yhs/search?hspart=sz&hsimp=yhs-001&type=type7036981-sv7-. Retrieved April 3, 2019.
UNESCO. ND. "Aksum." UNESCO World Heritage. https://whc.unesco.org/en/list/15/. Retrieved 3-12-2020.

3   Khair, Zulkifli. ND. "The university of Sankore, Timbuktu." http://muslimheritage.com/article/university-sankore-timbuktu. Retrieved 5-6-2019.

4   Demerdash, Dr. Nancy. ND. "Great Zimbabwe." GoogleClassroomfacebookTwiter. https://www.khanacademy.org/humanities/art-africa/southern-africa/zimbabwe/a/great-zimbabwe. Retrieved 5-7-2019.

5   Kingdoms of Southern Africa: Mapungubwe. https://www.sahistory.org.za/article/kingdoms-southern-africa-mapungubwe. Retrieved 3-12-2020.

6   Africa Facts. ND. "Fulani Earrings." https://interesting-africa-facts.com/African-Jewelry/Fulani-Earrings.shtml.

7   Africa Facts. ND."Maasai Bead Jewelry." https://interesting-africa-facts.com/African-Jewelry/*Maasa*i-Bead-Jewelry.shtml. Retrieved 5-15-2019.

8   Discovered. ND. "The Story Behind The Maasai Beaded Jewelry." https://blog.discovered.us/maasai-beaded-jewelry-explained/. Retrieved 5-14-2019.

9   Vuk'uzenzele. 2007. "Ndebele Traditional Dress." Capetown, South Africa: Government Communications. https://www.vukuzenzele.gov.za/ndebele-traditional-dress. Retrieved 5-14-2019.
10   Adapted from Africa Facts. "Zulu Bead Jewelry". https://interesting-africa-facts.com/African-Jewelry/Zulu-Bead-Jewelry.shtml. Retrieved 5-14-2019.

11   Roman, JC. 2015. "Ndebele House Painting - South Africa." In *Community Culture Visual Arts* / 1. April 5, 2015. http://myartistslist.com/ndebele-house-painting-south-africa/. Retrieved 5-17-2019.

12   Goran, David. 2016. "Tiebele, Burkina Faso – The African one-of-a kind village with unique and stunning painted houses." August 8, 2016. https://www.thevintagenews.com/2016/08/08/karni-mata-temple-rats-temple-india-crawling-thousands-holy-rats-protected-worshipped/. Retrieved 5-16-2019.

PART TWO

HUMAN SELF IN INTERACTION WITH THE SPIRITS

Chapter 5. A Firm Believer in God
Chapter 6. A Fervent Devotee of the Spirits

Chapter 5
A Firm Believer in God

1. Belief in the Eternal and Omnipotent God
2. Belief in Divine Creation
3. Belief in Divine Providence

1. BELIEF IN THE ETERNAL AND OMNIPOTENT GOD

A fundamental belief common to African societies is that there exists a unique God, Creator of the universe and all that exists in it, visible and invisible, who is eternal, omniscient, omnipresent and omnipotent. To an authentic African, non-obliterated by some foreign influences, challenging this truth is blasphemy. Africans confess God the Creator as unique in God's category. For one thing, Humans cannot really understand who God is. They represent God with physical approximations that their limited minds can understand. They express God's uniqueness through God's names formed by resorting to physical personifications. God is unique also in that God's powers are self-emanated, unlimited, and sovereign; whereas the powers of other forces emanate from God's, are limited, and are subordinate to God's powers. This chapter shares manifestations of these beliefs from ethnic groups across Africa.

Essential Aspects of Being Unique to God

Eternal: God alone is eternal. God has no beginning and has no end. God has always been and will always be. Three additional major attributes of being distinguish God from all other beings. God alone is omniscient, omnipresent, and omnipotent. African peoples express God's uniqueness in respect to these capacities in various ways. The following sample is taken from Mbiti's classic *African Religions and Philosophy* (1970: 39-41).

Omniscient: God knows everything. Nothing can escape God's vision, hearing, or knowledge.

Peoples	God's Attributes as the Omniscient One
Akan:	He who sees all.
Yorùbá:	He sees both the inside and the outside of man.
Barundi:	The Watcher of everything.
Ila:	God's ears are long.
Baganda:	The Great Eye, the Sun which beams its light everywhere.

Omnipresent: God is everywhere. No one can hide from God.

Peoples	God's Attributes as the Omnipresent One
Ila:	There is nowhere and no when God comes to an end.
Barundi and *Kono*:	God is met everywhere.
Shilluk and *Langi*:	God is like wind and air.
Yorùbá and *Kono*:	Wrongdoers cannot escape the judgment of God. No hiding place is unreachable to God.

Omnipotent: God's power is above all powers.

Peoples	God's Attributes as the Omnipotent One
Zulu:	He who bends down even the majesties.
Ngombe:	He who clears the forest without difficulty.
Banyarwanda:	The plant protected by God is never hurt by the wind.
Kiga:	God, the One who makes the sun set.
Gikuyu:	The one who makes mountains quake and rivers overflow.

Names Expressing the Creator's Uniqueness

The names of God in many African societies express God's uniqueness and superiority. Some of the anthropomorphic attributes expressing the uniqueness of *Olódùmarè*, the God of the Yorùbá of Nigeria are: Creator of all; the Owner of days and nights; the King whose works are mighty, done to perfection; Alone perfect in wisdom; Judge over all; the Mighty, Immovable Rock that never dies; and Invisible King. *Deng*, the God of the Dinka of Sudan, is universal, parent of Humanity, educator and sovereign. He is really and absolutely the truth. His name conveys the notions of uprightness, righteousness and justice. He listens to the word of divinely inspired leaders, the Masters of the Fishing Spears. The Zulu of South Africa call God *uZivelele*, "He who is of Himself, the Self-existent One." *Engai,* the name of God among the Maasai of Kenya and Tanzania, means the Unseen one, the Unknown One. The Unknown One is also the meaning of *Hounounga*, the name of God among the Tenda of Guinea. One of God's names among the Igbo of Nigeria is *Ama-Ama-Amasi-Amasi*, "He Who is known but never fully known". The most common name of God among the Akan of Ghana, *Nyame*, means "The Alone Great God". *Otumfuo*, among the Asante of Ghana, means the Mightiest and Most Powerful by Right and Fact. *Maa Ngala*, God among the *Bambara/Fulani* of West Africa, is "uncreated-infinite" and "unknowable". Likewise, *Kalûnga*, God's Name among the *BaKongo* of Congo, means immensity that no one can measure and the source and origin of life; divine principle of change and force that continually generates. For the Bagbamba of northern Ghana, "Nothing can be compared to God". God is Chief of Chiefs and has the "capacity and choice to make and destroy, to uplift and bring down, to provide and withdraw, to make rich and make poor. For the Boro of Burkina Faso, God, *Wuro*, is veiled. No one is an immediate witness of Him. He is only known through mediators, Human or spiritual. Once His name has been evoked, God withdraws from the affairs of the World. He becomes aware and let things pursue their course (Idowu 1994, Abraham 1962, Mbiti 2007, Fu-Kiau, 2001, Carruthers 1995, Chernoff, in Olupona 2000, Sanon 1990).

Table 4: *A Sample of God's Names and Exclusive Attributes*

Ethnic Group	God's name	God's Attributes
Akan	*Onyame*	The alone Great God is invisible but is present everywhere. Is directly accessible. He is eternally creating.
Bakongo	*Kalûnga*	Is immensity that no one can measure and the source and origin of life; divine principle of change and force that continually generates.
Bambara/Fulani	*Maa Ngala*	Is uncreated, infinite, and unknowable, is self-named and sovereign (What *Maa Ngala* says is).
Bobo	*Wuro*	Is veiled. No one is an immediate witness of Him. He is only known through mediators, Human and spiritual. Once His name has been evoked, God withdraws from the affairs of the World. He becomes aware and let things pursue their course.
Dinka	*Deng*	Is universal, parent of humanity, educator and sovereign. Is the truth, really and absolutely so. His name conveys the notions of uprightness, righteousness and justice. He listens to the word of divinely inspired leaders, the Masters of the Fishing Spears
Gikuyu	*Ngai*	Has no father, mother, no companion of any kind; works in solitude; and is in constant communication with nature.
Igbo	*Chukwu*	Is *Ama-Ama-Amasi-Amasi*: the one who is known but not really known.
Yorùbá	*Olódùmarè*	One who is supreme, superlatively great, incomparable and unsurpassable in majesty, and excellent in attributes"
Zulu	*Unkulunkulu*	The Oldest Deity (Mbiti 2007, 3 of 12).

Physical Personifications of God

The human mind cannot really understand who God is. To compensate for their limitations, humans often resort to personifications of God in forms of powerful earthly natural phenomena such as thunder and earthquakes, or physical configurations like mountains and waterfalls; or else heavenly objects such as the sun, the moon, and the stars. Thus, among the *Bobo* of Burkina Faso, the word *Wuro*, God, connotes multiple celestial phenomena situated in the heights such as thunder, flash of lightning, and lightning. The Kongo story summarized in the section below consists of a series of personifications of the powers of *Kalûnga*, God, through natural phenomena corresponding to the different phases of the creation process (Sano 1990, Fu-Kiau 2001).

> Physical formations are vehicles through which the Creator communicates with Humans. The Gikuyu of Kenya, for instance, believe that Ngai, God, communicates with the inhabitants of the earth through such manifestations of his powers as the sun, the moon, the stars and rain. To the Igbo, Sun and Moon are God's traveling messengers who bring to him knowledge of what is going on across the universe. Stars and other bright heavenly bodies play a similar role in the Luba interpretation of God's omniscience: They are eyes that surround the Creator's entire body and enable Him to see everything everywhere (Carruthers, 1995, quoting Jomo Kenyatta; Ekechukwu, 1983, Kalanda 1992).

In Ancient Egypt, the sun and the Earth, the sky and the air, and water were believed to be part of God's being and were recognized as sources of life. At Memphis, Ptah (i.e., the Earth) personified God's creative power. At Heliopolis and Hermopolis, *Re* (i.e., the *Sun*) was the personified God's creative power. In other places, the Creator was identified as *Khnum*, (i.e., the *Ram*). Also, a particular God's name could be praised for different powers or superior attributes. For instance, Sun was praised as the Creator when his life-giving powers were being stressed, whereas the morning's rising sun indicated victory of light over darkness and victory of life over death. It symbolized God as a resurrected son. For its part, the sun's unchanging course through the sky was a symbol of justice. These identifications were not mutually exclusive. At times, *Khnum* and *Re* were joined to represent the Creator as God *Khnum-Re*. Likewise, God *Amon, Amun* (i.e., *Air*) was imminent, hidden, in nature and manifested his divine power in wind and breath. He was later identified as *Amon-Re* when he rose to the status of supreme God. These gods and others were sometimes represented in human or animal forms to stress their various attributes. Thus, for instance, as a power in nature, goddess *Heqt* appeared as the moon, whereas as one who assisted women in childbirth, she was represented by the toad. Likewise, depending on the body or element of whose God's powers were identified with, God was called *Ptah (Earth), or Re (Sun), or Heqt (Moon)*, or else *Amon (Air)* (Frankfort, 2000).

Who God is to the Luba

God's Names: The Luba of Kasai call God *Mvidi Mukulu,* a name that stresses both God's spiritual nature and God's anteriority to all deities. *Mvidi* or *Mvidye* means "Spirit, Deity." *Mukulu* means the "Oldest of all." In other words, *Mvidi Mukulu* is the Most High who has existed before any other spirit. *Mvidi Mukulu* has other names that stress God's other attributes. As the Creator, He alone is called *Maweja Nangila*. Maweja may be an evolution from *Mwena Meeji (also Mwedi wa Meeji)*, the Owner of thinking, the Thinking One, the Intelligent One. *Nangila* evokes verb *kunanga*, to love; or *kunangila* or *kunangidila*: to love ceaselessly, to keep on enjoying doing something. Thus, *Maweja Nangila* would signify the Thinking and Eternally-Loving One. His other names stress His other attributes, such as the Omnipotent and Omniscient One.

A Firm Believer in God

Luba ancestors used to express their subordination to the Creator by recognizing Him as the most potent being that has ever existed, while offering Him rooster sacrifices during the mid-morning hours as they faced the ascending sun. They would present the sacrifice to Him with words of praise such as:

Luba Personifications of God's Greatness

> *Diiba Katangila Cishiki, Wakutangila Dyamwasa Nsensa*
> The Bright Sun Whose Rays Blind Anyone Who Dares Watching Him Straight (onwards).
>
> *Ngabu Wancimuna Bilobo.*
> The Impenetrable Shield Against Which Even the Weapons of the Most Indomitable Warrior Fail.
>
> *Ciibi Wammona Lubidi, Umona Mpala, Umona Nyima.*
> The Omniscient Door Who Sees from the Front and from the Back.
>
> *Nzevu Kendela mu Nshinda, Anu Badi mu Nshinda Banyema.*
> Elephant Who Cannot Stop in the Middle of the Road without Causing all Travelers to Run Away.
>
> *Nkashama wa Dyenda Dîtu, Cyenda Nkaya, Mwena Buloba.*
> Leopard Who Lives in the Forest of His Own, Lone Walker, Master of the Land. (Van Caeneghem 1956, quoted in Mulago 1973)

God's Superiority to All Created Powers

God's powers supersede all other powers. The powers of divinities, ancestors and witches are derived from and subordinate to God's power.

Divinities: In African traditional religion, created spirits are more intensely involved in people's daily lives than the Creator. Divinities are among such created forces. However, the fact that the created spirits' presence in Human lives is more pervasive than God's does not belie the fact that the Creator is regarded not only as higher than divinities, but also as one who is alone in His category. Divinities have a beginning whereas the Creator has always existed. Divinities are products of God's making whereas God is self-existent. Never will a product equal its maker. In addition, divinities are often seen not as acting independently, but rather as particular manifestations of the Creator's powers. For instance, the *Orishas* in the Yorùbá religion are ministers of the Creator *Olódùmarè* who has vested them with specific functions. For example, *Olódùmarè* entrusted to Arch-Divinity *Orìshà-nlà* the mission to complete the creation of the earth. The Fon, the Ewe, and the Igbo, just as the Yorùbá, venerate divinities to which the Creator has assigned particular responsibilities toward Humans. The Fon and the Ewe acknowledge a divinity named *Sakpata* whose role is to protect people from smallpox. The Igbo venerate *Anyanwu*, a sun-divinity who makes crops and trees grow, and *Ala*, an earth goddess who is the spirit of fertility and guardian of morality. In the latter capacity, goddess Ala mystically sanctions abominations such as incest, adultery of a woman, and eating and killing 'totem' animals. For the Akan of Ghana, minor divinities are avenues to God's magnificence and bountiful protection, lieutenants of the Supreme Being and almost the expression of his omnipotence (Uchendu 1966, Ekechukwu, 1983, Abraham 1962).

Ancestors: Of all spiritual forces, the ancestors are the most intensely involved in individuals' daily lives. Ancestors are sprits of past relatives. Through death a person's life principle separates from the physical body and becomes a ghost. It is believed that the ghost of a person who has lived and died with dignity joins the spirits of deceased forebearers to become an ancestor like them. Mystically, ancestors continue to share life with their earthly descendants as elders. They also become mediators between the descendants and the Creator, taking their petitions to him and bringing His blessings back to them. Ancestors are present and honored in all African religious traditions. But their powers are delegated by God.

Witches: A belief shared by Black Africans across the continent is that some individuals possess supernatural powers derived from divine creation. Existing in a potential state at birth in most cases, such powers generally become active later in the holder's life after he or she has undergone some sort of mystical initiation. Some holders of such supernatural powers, witches in particular, use them destructively to cause misfortunes, including sickness and death, to individuals they dislike. But it is also held as an absolute truth throughout the African continent that God is so powerful that no mystical power can resist Him. A Luba proverb stresses this truth by stating that the witch can neutralize the killing power of the poison, but he cannot escape God's sword:

> *Mwena mupongo wakafu mulungu, anu mwela wa Muweja ki udi umutwila*
> (Van Caeneghem 1956).

The Omnipotent God is also the good shepherd who extends his divine protection to all those who belong to Him, protecting them against their enemies. When an agent of evil surprises God's protégées and identifies them as such, he leaves them alone unharmed:

> *Mwena mupongo wavu, ukenketa baluma, ukekenta bakaji, ukupa mutu, wamba ne: "Aaba mbantu ba benda ba Mvidi Mukulu."*

> The witch came over; he examined men and women, then shook his head and backed off, saying: "These are God's people" (Van Caeneghem 1956).

2. BELIEF IN DIVINE CREATION

Modes of Creation

African societies have various versions of how the Supreme Being's work of creation unfolded. But all conclude with the creation of the human being. Dominique Zahan reports four modes of creation derived from stories collected across Sub-Saharan

Africa:

1. The exteriorization of signs and thoughts actually conceived within the divinity
2. The "thingification" of the Word of God
3. The manual act, and
4. Creation through vomiting by the Supreme Divinity (Zahan, 2000)

Mode 1, "exteriorization of signs and thoughts actually conceived within the divinity", means emergence of a being that has never existed before and that is brought into existence by the mere fact of God conceiving the existence of that being. Elsewhere, this mode of creation is called metamorphosis, or self-emanation. Thingification of God's Word, Zahan's Mode 2, means emergence, by the transcendental power of God's Word, of a being or a thing with unique identity, form and properties. This mode, found in the creation story of the Dogon of Mali, for instance, is also known as creation by divine speech or creation by naming or summoning. In some cases, summoning was accompanied with gesture. Creation by a manual act, identified in Zahan's Mode 3, involves manipulation of some already existing, God-created matter. *Olódùmarè*, God, among the Yorùbá, created Earth by sending Arch-Divinity *Orìshà-nlá* with a bucket of dry soil and the pigeon and the hen to help him spread the soil over a marshy land. As to Zahan's Mode 4, creation by vomiting, the author insists that it is rare and is found only among the Bakuba of the Congo. As told later in this chapter, creation in Kongo cosmology illustrates creation by metamorphosis whereas the Luba case presents a combination of metamorphosis, summoning and gesture (Mudimbe 1991, Fourche and Moringhen1973, Kalanda 1992, Carruthers 1995, in Beatty 2001; Idowu 1994).

The Creation Process in Ancient Egyptian Myths

A version of Ancient Egyptian creation myths relates that in the beginning there was an uncreated, infinite, unorganized matter. It contained the essences of the body of the future beings, notably, sky, stars, earth air, fire, animals, plants, and Human. The primordial infinite matter was identified as divinity *Nun*. It contained *Khepera*, who is both a divinity and the law of transformation. Acting on matter through time, *Khepera* enabled the beings that until then had only existed in essence to become realities. In a later time, *Nun* came to identify Himself as God, *Ra*, whose methods of creation include the word and simple vision, the representation of the future beings in the divine conscience of *Ra*. The latter method means Ra created beings by the mere fact of conceiving them. Through this method, *Nun* transformed Himself into three beings: *Nun*, *Shu*, and *Tefnut*. In turn, *Shu* and *Tefnut* gave birth to Geb and *Nut*. Geb and *Nut* begot *Osiris, Seth, Isis,* and *Nephthys*. Thus, *Nun*'s primordial creations included:

Shu (Air) and *Tefnut* (Water)
Geb (Earth) and *Nut* (Heaven)
Osiris (Man) and *Isis* (Woman): the fertile Human couple that will beget Humanity
Seth (Man) and *Nephthys* (Woman): the sterile Human couple that will introduce evil into Human history.

These and Nun's other creations first existed in potentiality as three principles before the formation of the world: the being, intelligible essences; the place, space, and generation, and the act by which *Ra* engenders the first beings *Shu* and *Tefnut*. Over time, potentiality evolved into actuality (Diop, 1991). Another version of the Egyptian story holds that Atum (Khepera) Chepri created Shu and Tefnet by spitting (Parsons, ND.). [1]

The Creation Process in the Luba Story

Belief in Divine Creation is the cornerstone of Luba religion. Existence in heaven, on Earth and elsewhere in the universe began with divine creation. *Mvidi Mukulu*, Supreme Being, is the Creator of the universe and all that exists in it: tangible and intangible, material and spiritual. Men and women raised in Luba tradition share this fundamental belief. For the Luba and, for that matter, Africans in general, not believing in divine creation is blasphemy. Nonetheless, ordinary Luba people do not know how the work of creation unfolded. The Belgian colonial government and Christian missionaries in the Congo discredited traditional education and fought against African religious practices as paganism. The elders who knew about traditions gradually took them to their graves. The few initiates who survived longer kept them in secrecy by fear of persecution. Some used them as means of social control. However, Luba men and women know the Creator by many names through proverbs and maxims of praise, as demonstrated in the preceding section (Kalanda 1992, Lufuluabo 1961).

Creation in Four: The Luba Creation story exhibits aspects of metamorphosis (Mode 1) and naming (mode 2), and adds Creation by the gesture and Creation by exhaling the breath of life. The Creation story is part of revealed knowledge retained by a minority of initiated members of particular mystical societies. Kalanda (1992) and, before him, Fourche et Morlinghem (1973), interviewed some of these members as part of their research. According to them, *Maweja Nangila* created the world in stages.

Four Lord Spirits: Four is a complete number. Through the process of metamorphosis, God first created two hermaphrodite spirits who share his divinity to the highest level. He placed the one who appeared first to his right to assist him in the capacity of First-Born Son and the second to his left to assume the position of Senior Lady. Thereafter, God created another lord spirit in the capacity of Emissary. The four Lord Spirits share the title of Maweja: (1) *Maweja Nangila*, The Creator, (2) *Maweja wa Cyama*, the Firstborn Son, (3) *Maweja Cyama*, the First Lady, and (4) *Mulopo Maweja*, the Emissary Spirit. The Son Lord Spirit's name *Maweja wa Cyama* means *Maweja* son of *Cyama* (the First Lady Spirit), even though there never existed a biological tie between the two of them and in spite of the fact that The Firstborn-Son appeared first in the order of creation. Sometimes, the Son is called *Kapinga wa Cyama* (Kalanda 1992).

Four Lord Spirits
Maweja Nangila: Creator
Maweja wa Cyama: Firstborn Son
Maweja Cyama: First Lady

Mulopo Maweja: Emissary Spirit

Four Senior Spirits and Four Junior Spirits: *Maweja Nangila* next created other spirits. First from among them were a set of four Senior Spirits and a set of four Junior Spirits:

Four Senior Spirits	**Four Junior Spirits**
Nkimba	*Lumanya*
Mule Mwedi	*Mwadyamvita*
Mushikuluje	*Cyela-Mpungi*
Muntu-Lufu	*Kadya-Bilumbu*

(Mudimbe 1991, Kalanda 1992).

Other Creations in Four: *Maweja Nangila* also created countless minor spirits, all in series of four, and is still creating more until today. God even made non-spiritual creations in series of four. For instance:

Four Types of Wind	**Four Types of Earth**	
The breath of life	Red clay	
The breath of death	Rock	
The wind that brings in the rain	White clay	
The wind that brings in dry cold	Black soil	

Four Types of Water	**Four Types of Color**	
Magical waters of certain lakes	*Difiika*	Black
Salted waters of ocean waves	*Dikunza*	Red
Warm spring waters	*Ditooka*	White
Fresh river waters	*Lubidibidi*	uncertain color

(Kalanda 1992, Fourche et Morlighem 1973)

Lubidibidi, the uncertain color, designates many colors for which the *Luba* people do not have specific names, such as grey, purple, and mauve. However, three of its variances are identifiable by names: *difiikuluka*: blackish; *dikunzubila*, reddish, and *ditookoloka*, whitish (Fourche et Morlighem 1973).

Creation in Pairs of Seniors and Juniors: *Maweja Nangila* made many of His creations in pairs, each composed of a senior element and a junior element. The senior element represents strength, the junior element weakness. For instance, fire and water belong to the same pair. Water is senior and stronger. Fire is junior and weaker. Water extinguishes fire. The Sun and the Moon form a pair, of which the Sun is the stronger element, the Moon the weaker element. Good spirits are senior; bad spirits are junior. Darkness is senior, light is junior. The rainy season is senior. Occult (revealed) science is stronger than lay science (using human senses).

Chapter 5
Sample Pairs of Senior and Junior Creations

Senior	Junior	Senior	Junior
Fire	Water	Sun	Moon
Good Spirits	Bad Spirits	Darkness	Light
Rainy season	Dry Season	Occult science	Lay science

Each of the three basic colors for which the *Luba* have specific names, has a senior tonality and a junior tonality. The *Luba* term for color is *diikala*. The terms *difiika* (black), *dikunza* (red) and *ditooka* (white) respectively stand *for diikala difiika, diikala dikunza*, and *diikala ditooka*. In addition to being the generics of the colors they represent, the terms *dikunza, ditooka* and *difiika* designate the junior, weaker, tonality. Their respective senior tonalities are *teeteete* or *cididii* for *dikunza, zeezeeze* for *ditooka* (Fourche et Morlighem, 1973) and *fitutuu* for *difiika*.

Senior and Junior Colors

Senior	Junior
Fitutuu (very black)	*Difiika* (Black)
Teeteete or *Cididii* (Very Red)	*Dikunza* (Red)
Zeezeeze (Very White)	*Ditooka* (White)

Creative Powers: *Maweja Nangila* created the Lord Spirits who share His divine power to the highest degree through the process of direct emanation, *dyalu*. Through this process, the Creator mystically derived the other sprits from Himself without any external action, but by ejecting them out of Himself by the power of his will while remaining the same and losing none of His initial properties. He brought forth other creations by resorting to three specific powers inherent in Him: the word, the gesture, and the breath of life. *Maweja Nangila* created things that do not blink, such as the rain, stones, grass, and trees by the power of His word alone. For example, He created rain simply by saying: "Let there be rain," and rain appeared; "Let there be trees," and trees appeared; "Let there be grass," and grass appeared. As to creatures, other than Humans, that have eyes and can see. *Maweja Nangila* created them by way of making a gesture followed by the naming word. Thus, He created insects by slowly moving and extending His lips forward while holding his breath, and finally saying: "Let such insect species appear." And the insect species instantly appeared. He created animals by pointing his index finger forward and saying, "Let such animal species be." And the animal species appeared. By his breath and the power of His word, *Maweja Nangila* created the Human being. He filled His lungs with his breath and forcefully exhaled on the earth saying: "Let there be Gentleman" (*Mukalenga Muluma*), and Gentleman appeared. *Maweja Nangila* filled His lungs with His breath again and forcefully exhaled on man, saying: "Let there be Gentle Lady" (*Mukalenga Mukaji*), and Gentle Lady appeared (Kalanda, 1992).

3. BELIEF IN DIVINE PROVIDENCE

In most African creation stories, the making of the human being occurs at the very end of the process, suggesting that God wanted to make the human being the finishing touch and primary beneficiary of the fruits of divine creation. "It is as if God exists for the sake of man." The Batammaliba people of Togo and Benin say that *Kuiye*, God, created humans because He felt Himself lonely and incomplete, like a tree without branches. It seems that to accommodate His special branches, the Creator Tree made sure that the world would be a suitable dwelling place for humans to live in and bloom in harmony with other species and with easy access to plentiful life amenities (Mbiti 1970, Ray 1999).

A Planet Where Organic Life Would Be Possible

Kalûnga: Before creating Humans, God made sure there will be a suitable world for Humans to live in comfortably. The creation process in the cosmology of the Bakongo of Congo/DRC, exemplifies God's special attention to the well-being of humans in the making of the terrestrial world. *Kalûnga*, God, first existed as Divine Fire-Force. Creation consisted in Divine Creative Fire-Force gradually self-scaling down through a series of personifications of His powers, all the way down to the state of reduced fire intensity where life on Earth, including human life, became possible (Fu-Kiau 2001).

The Physical World's Creation Processes as Manifestations of *Kalûnga's* Powers

Eight stages can be identified in the process of the creation of the physical world. Each stage represents particular manifestations of Kalunga's powers.

> ***Stage One: Emptiness***: In the beginning there was emptiness *(mbûngi)*, not without life, but filled with active invisible forces and waves.
>
> ***Stage Two: Fire Force***: *Kalûnga* emerged from within the infinite emptiness as a fire-force complete by itself and the source of life on what was to become Earth.
>
> ***Stage Three: Projectiles***: *Kalûnga* fired up. His heated huge mass of projectiles dominated the emptiness, thereby becoming a symbol of force, a process and principle of change.
>
> ***Stage Four* (a): *Sun, Moon and Stars***: The fire force blew up. Some particles remained hanging in the upper space and became Sun, Moon and Stars.
>
> **Stage Four (b): Fusion**: By the same token, the explosion produced a huge mass of fusion *(luku)*.
>
> ***Stage Five: Mountains/Waters***: While cooling, the mass of fusion produced

mountains and the water that gave birth to rivers.

Stage Six: Solidified Mass/Earth: By cooling, the mass in fusion became a solidified mass (*kînda*), forming Planet Earth.

Stage Seven: The Physical World: With the solidification of *luku* and the resulting formation of earth, the world became a physical reality (*nza*).

Stage Eight: Endless Water: At the end of the above processes and as a result thereof, *Kalûnga*'s powers manifested themselves in the form of endless water within the cosmic space. On this endless water floats *nza*, the physical reality.

Terrestrial Life and Submarine Life: Half of the physical world expands above the water to sustain terrestrial life: plants, animals, rocks and humans. The other half lies at the bottom-end of the water and nurtures submarine life. The spiritual world lives in the submerging half as well.

Ocean: As a manifestation of *Kalûnga*'s powers, Ocean serves as a door and a wall between the terrestrial world and the spiritual world. (Adapted from Fu-Kiau 2001).

An Environment Where Humans Would Grow and Prosper

According to the Yorùbá creation story, the planet Earth we live on was preceded by a wet marshy waste. Before creating Human-beings, *Olódùmarè*, God, sent Arch-Divinity, *Orishà-nlà* with a leaf packet of dry soil along with a hen and a pigeon as work tools. As the divinity threw the soil on the marshy ground, the two birds spread it all around them until the entire marshy waste was covered. Upon receiving a positive task-completion report from *Orishà-nlà*, *Olódùmarè* sent chameleon to inspect *Orishà-nlà's* production and submit an independent assessment report. The inspector first reported that the covered land was vast enough but needed to dry some more. After a while, *Olódùmarè* sent chameleon back to Earth for a second inspection. This time, chameleon was satisfied with the Earth's state of dryness and capability to support life. Pleased, *Olódùmarè* sent *Orishà-nlà* back, this time in company of Counselor Divinity *Òrunmìlà*, along with a palm tree to provide drink (wine), oil (seeds), and food (kernels) and other trees valued for their sap (drink). He created lagoons for humans to farm fish in. *Olódùmarè* sent back also the hen and the pigeon, this time with the mission to multiply and serve as continuous sources of meat for humans. It was only when all had been done to His satisfaction that *Olódùmarè* sent Divinity *Orèlúéré* at the head of a delegation of heavenly hosts who became first humans on earth. In the *Abaluyia* belief system, "God created man so the sun would have someone for whom to shine" (Idowu 1994, Mbiti 1970).

A Land Where Spiritual, Human, Animal, and Vegetal Species Would Coexist and Support One Another

The Yorùbá creation story has shown us how God had divinities collaborate with the hen, the pigeon and the chameleon in the creation of Earth. All throughout Africa, human creation is almost always announced in association with that of animals and plants, as having occurred at the same time as, prior to, or, in most cases, after the latter. Whatever the case, creation stories suggest that in the post-creation era, humans, animals and plants lived together in conviviality and harmony, sharing life concerns and collaborating in search of solutions to situations of common interest. At the time, Heaven, abode of God and spirits, and Earth, land of the humankind, fauna and flora, existed in close proximity of each other. Mutual visits and other forms of communication exchanges between the two worlds were frequent. For instance, the Dinka of Sudan say that in primordial times, the inhabitants of Earth used to climb up to Heaven, home of the Creator *Nhialic*, suspended to a rope. Particular animal species are credited with having played life-and-death messenger roles between Earth and heaven. For instance, many groups relate that the lizard was the messenger the Creator sent from Heaven to Earth to announce the advent of death. Prior to the lizard, God had sent the chameleon with the message of immortality, but the chameleon got distracted somewhere along the way only to arrive to his destination after the message of death had been delivered. The Igbo story relates that *Chukwu*, God, left it to humans and terrestrial animals to decide about the existence or nonexistence of death. All but a few, including the crocodile, said no to death. They sent the dog to deliver the no message to God. Unfortunately, the dog found some sweet bones along the road, spent his time eating them, and forgot about the mission. In the meantime, the crocodile took advantage of the dog's irresponsibility and sent the frog with a message requesting that death should be allowed to exist on earth (Ray 1999, Mbiti 1970, Ekechukwu 1983).

Cooperation and mutual support between human and other species appear to have been meant to persist beyond the primordial times. Animal and plant totems are a good example of this dynamic. Animal species are believed to have played community-building and protective roles as totems among members of particular clans. The ancestors of such clans are believed to have established brotherhood, blood relations with particular animals engaging not only them, but their descendants as well. The members of the clan and their totemic animal are morally committed to protecting each other from any harm. They must repudiate all acts of aggression toward each other. Clan members cannot kill or eat their totem (Magesa, 1997). For example, a study of eight Akan clans lists a different totemic animal for each clan with its valued qualities. Alphabetically these are:

Totemic Animal	**Quality**
bat	bravery and diplomacy
buffalo	uprightness
crow	purity of heart and eloquence
dog	humility and friendliness
hawk	confidence and patience

leopard	bravery
parrot	eloquence and frankness
vulture	intelligence and stamina (Lumor, 2009)

The *Gikuyu* of *Kenya* provide a good example of human-plant mutual support from Creation. After creation, *Ngai,* God, took the founding ancestor of the *Gikuyu* to the top of *Mount Kiri*, later called *Mount Kenya* during British colonization. From there, *Ngai* showed him a vast plain beneath and around the mountain populated with a wealth of beautiful plants and animals, which *Ngai* bestowed to him and his descendants. *Ngai,* then, directed this first man to a grove of fig trees in a nearby location to the south of the mountain. Here lived a huge fig tree called *Mukuyu* (Sycamore Tree). The founding father took for his own name, *Gikuyu*, a derivative of *Mukuyu*, which means Tree of Origin. His descendants inherited his name as *Gikuyu* people. Near the *Mukuyu* fig-tree, grew another large fig-tree species, *Mugumo*. By the fig-tree grove, Gikuyu found a woman named *Mumbi*. *Gikuyu* and *Mumbi* became husband and wife and established their first homestead nearby. Ngai instructed them to pray any time they needed facing *Mount Kiri Nyaga* (*Mount Kenya*), or pray and make a sacrifice of goat to *Ngai* under the *Mukuyu* fig-tree or the *Mugumo* fig-tree. *Ngai* and *Mumbi* begot 10 daughters. To find husbands for his older nine daughters, *Gikuyu* consulted with Ngai, who instructed him to make a sacrifice of a spotless ram under the *Mugumo* fig-tree, and have each daughter cut a straight rod of her height from a *Mukuyu* fig tree. Next morning, young men, with the respective height of each daughter, came and took them into marriage. Ever since, *Mukuyu* and *Mugomo* fig-trees have been *Gikuyu* men and women's sacred sacrificial trees. During religious sacrifices to *Ngai* under the *Mukuyu* fig-tree, dancers paint their bodies with white ashes from *Mukuyu* tree branches (Mukuyu, 2008).

A Land Endowed with Abundant Natural Diversity

Fauna and Flora. In the belief systems of Bantu peoples—animals, plants and minerals, by God's will—only exist for the purpose of augmenting the vital force of humans. Material possessions are seen as provisions from God (Mbiti, 1970: 76). Testimonies of God's blessings to African societies from Creation abound. As pointed out in the previous section, in the *Gikuyu* story, *Ngai*, God, took the *Gikuyu*'s ancestor to the top of Mount Kenya and from there He showed him the country's bounty that was going to be his and his descendants' as a gift from Him, the Most High. The country had abundant varieties of plants, animals, rivers, plains, and meandering hills. All in it was beautiful and splendid. In the last stage of preparing Earth for human life, *Olódùmarè, God* of the Yorùbá people, sent His right-hand Arch-Divinity *Orishà-nlà* in company of the Counselor Divinity *Òrunmìlà*, along with the hen and the pigeon whose mission was to multiply and serve as continuous sources of meat for humans. He also gave them the palm tree to be planted for the purpose of providing humans with wine for drink, oil for cooking and kernels for food (Jefferson and Skinner 1990, Idowu 1994).

Africa is the epitome of plentiful, diverse natural resources to sustain and enhance human life: the animal kingdom, plants, and aquatic species. This bounty speaks to the favor God has placed on man and the land that will sustain him. Even the semi-desert country of *Niger* is home to 136 mammal species and over 500 species of birds, of which over 450 live in the National Park (500,000 acres). Niger reportedly has over 2100 plant species, of which 210 have nutritional value, including the *baobab, kapok, bastard mahogany, shea tree, prickly grass,* and *acacia tree*.[2] Some of the animal species found in Niger are rare for the country's dominant climate, for example:

African bush elephant	stripped hyena,	Northwest African
cheetah	waterbuck	African Leopard
West African lion	antelope	common warthog
scimitar oryx	hippopotami	

Some other rare species found in the Niger River are:

horned vipers	lizards	pythons	manatee
Nigerian giraffe	dama	gazelle.	

In Africa, the highest levels of biodiversity and species unique to the area are found in the Congo Basin; the coastal mangrove, the Albertine Rift highlands, and the eastern lowland forests of the Democratic Republic of the Congo.[3] The Congo Basin is home to 600 tree species and 10,000 animal species. Of the 10,000 animal species, 3,000 are found in the Congo only. Also unique to the Congo are 1,000 bird species, 400 species of mammals, over 210 species of reptiles, more than 900 species of butterflies. The most known mammals from the Congo Tropical Rainforest are:

monkeys and apes	gorillas	chimpanzees,	bonobos
okapis waterbucks	buffalos	elephants	wild pigs
pigmy hippopotami			

Many other animal species live in the Congo's savannah forest and grassland:

leopards	lions	hyenas	deer	antelopes	zebras.

The Tropical Rainforest occupies almost the entire northern half of the Congo. Countless vegetation species—roots, mushrooms, all kinds of leafy vegetables—grow naturally everywhere in this immense region. The forest houses a myriad of medicinal plants. Various palm trees, including the palm oil tree, the Raphia tree and the Copal tree, live here. Wood for making furniture and for construction is omnipresent in all kinds, shapes, and sizes.

Trees of Life: In the Yorùbá creation story, God provided humans with the palm oil tree to grow for food (kernels), wine (sap), and oil. Africa's most common palm species is *Guineensis*. Native to West and Southwest Africa, from Angola to the Gambia, this palm tree species provides multiple amenities and uses. The many uses of the palm oil tree in Luba villages, where the present author grew up, are a case in point:

Chapter 5
Uses of the Palm Tree in Luba Culture (in alphabetical order):

Table 5: *Palm Tree Uses In Luba Society*

Part	Product	Function
Branch (*cikoolo*, plural: *bikoolo*)	Poles (*mikoolo*)	Used in building house roofs
Branch with palms at the upper end	Long broom (*cikombo*)	Used by men to sweep the courtyard between the houses in a compound
Branch slats (*mbaala*)	Bird cages (singular: *musasa*, plural: *misasa*)	To keep or carry chickens, ducks or pigeons
	Maracas (*masaka*, singular: *disaka*)	Musical instrument used in child welcoming and other rituals
	Hard, strait mat (*lusaala*)	Laid on the bed between the slats and the upper, soft/folding sleeping mat
Flower (*miselekete*)	Concoction (*mufita*)	Substance made of dried palm flower burned into ashes, then moistened with water and mixed with salt. Is used to treat the eruptions of the throat and the mouth.
Heart of the palm (*bula*)	Vegetable	Eaten in time of hardship
Kernels (*misa*)	Cream (*mushinda*)	Pimple treatment
Larvae (*mposa*)	Delicacy (*mposa*)	When eaten fried
Nut skin (*ngaji*)	Oil (*mafuta*)	Traditionally the only kind of oil known in the land of Luba Kasai people.
	Soap (*nsabanga*)	Good for treating pimples, but not very much appreciated because it melts easily and tears clothes. Hence its symptomatic pejorative name: nsabanga wa cibombo: melting soap.
Palm (*dilala*, plural: *malala*)	Makeshift bags (*mikundululu*, singular: *mukundululu*)	Used to carry fresh meat, gathering products, or small game
Sap	Wine (*maluvu*)	Used for human consumption, and for sealing marriage alliances and in religious rituals among the Kanyok.
Stalks (*tupungu*)	Sifters (*tusengulu*, singular: *kasengulu*)	Used for cassava and corn flour or as strainers for indigenous beer (*cibuku*) made out of palm stalks (*tupungu*)
	Toothpicks (*tupungu*)	Practically the only type in the past

| Thorns (*meeba*) | Pins | Can be used as pins to remove jiggers (*tubwasa*) from the feet. |

Other Important Trees of Life: The palm oil tree is a rainy-wet-climate plant. Southern Africa's Kalahari Desert and the Sahel-Sahara region in West Africa above the Equator receive little rains annually. By divine providence, the Creator has endowed these areas with drought-resistant plants like *the African Peyote Cactus* that grows in the Sahara Desert and the *Umbrella Thorn Acacia* found in Southern African and the Sahel. Kalahari Desert's *Camel Thorn Tree, Shepherd's Tree, Tsmamma* (Kalahari Water Mellon), and *Ghaap, Hoodia Cactus* are Africa's other trees of life from divine creation.[4]

The *Baobab* Tree is the most acclaimed tree of life found across Sub-Saharan Africa Africa. The *baobab* measures up to 60 feet in girth: 75 feet in height, and in thousands of years—2,000 to 3,000—in longevity. Legends from various African areas where the tree grows provide an explanation of the tree's upside-down look. The *baobab* became too arrogant and disrespectful of other trees, denigrating them as midgets. The latter complained to the Creator, who, to teach the *baobab* a lesson in humility, uprooted the original tree and replanted it upside down. Indeed, the *Baobab* is called the upside-down tree because of its root-like, dry-out-looking leafless branches. Nowadays, there exist eight species of baobab in the world. Six species are native to Madagascar.

Adansonia Grandidieri,   *Adansonia Madagascarensis,*
Adansonia Periieri,   *Adansonia Rubrostipa,*
Adansonia Suarezensis,   *and Adansonia Za*

There are countless ways that the *Baobab* can meet human needs. A few examples should suffice to make the point.[5]

Baobab Uses:

The whole tree is the sacred home of founding fathers' spirits; gathering space to debate community issues; a protective watchtower to scout threats from the surrounding area.

The stem is thick and can hold water for long periods of time.

The wood can be used for lumber.

Bark fibers are used to make fishnets, ropes, cloth, baskets, strings for musical instruments, mats, and hats.

The leaves are edible and reputed to be rich in Vitamin C.

The fruit is eaten as fruit or porridge, or else pressed into drink. The pulp is a rich concentration of nutrients, including minerals and vitamin c. It can be dried and turned into a highly nutritious powder or used as soap.

Chapter 5

The sprouts are a famine vegetable.

The *baobab* is also praised for the medicinal value of its various parts, notably: the bark for malaria, the fruit for dysentery, fever, diarrhea; the leaves for treating diarrhea, fever, the kidneys, bladder, blood cleansing, asthma; the pulp for coughing; the seeds for dysentery, fever, diarrhea; and the roots for malaria and cleansing sores.

Minerals: As further example of God's generosity to the African continent, practically every African country hosts several important minerals. Below are selected examples[6]:

Table 6: *Sample Minerals per African Country*

Angola:	Oil	diamonds	manganese	gold	uranium	wofram
Chad:	sodium carbonate	gold	wolframite	bauxite	uranium	silver, alluvial diamonds
Cote D'Ivoire:	gold	oil	copper			
Ethiopia:	gold	emerald	tantalum	nubium-columbium		
Ghana:	gold	bauxite	diamond	manganese		
Guinea:	bauxite	iron ore	uranium	diamonds	gold	
Nigeria:	oil	gold	bitumen	lead	zinc	
Rwanda:	gold	tantalum	tin	gold	tungsten	
Sierra Leone:	diamond	bauxite	gold	iron		
South Africa:	diamond	gold	chrome	manganese		
Zimbabwe:	gold	silver	chrome	nickel		

The Democratic Republic of the Congo, DRC, is known for being a mineral wonder given its immense reserves. The gamut of its most known mineral resources includes the following[7]:

beryl	bauxite	cadmium	cassiterite
charcoal	cobalt	coltan	copper
diamond	germanium	gold	iron
ore	malachite	manganese	petroleum
platina	rheunium	tin	uranium
zinc	walframite		

River Fisheries: God has endowed Africa with numerous rivers and prolific natural habitats of all kinds of fish, mammals (hippopotami), amphibians (turtles), birds, reptiles, and insects.[8] The *Congo Basin Complex* in Central Africa, the *Limpopo Complex* and the *Orange Complex* in Southern Africa and the *Niger Complex* in West Africa are populated by countless numbers of these species and their breeds. Reportedly, the *Congo River Basin,* that is, the *Congo River* is home to over 1200 fish species and 400 mammal species. The elephant fish family dominates. Some of the other important fish families represented are the lungfish, the killfish, the cichlid fish, the bichirs, the characins, the upside-down catfish, and the minnow/carps. In West Africa, the Niger River and the Senegal River are home to varieties of fish that are important not only for human nutrition but also for the nutrition of the ecosystems in which they live, from among them: the African butter fish, the *barbus baudoni,* the featherfin squaker, and the electric catfish. In Southern Africa, the rivers of the Limpopo Basin are filled with several varieties of catfish, perch, elephant fish, trout, and more. For its part, the Orange River is home to various fish species, including minnows, yellow fish, mudfish, catfish, tilapia, eel, philander, anguila, and others.

Lake Fisheries: There are lakes with impressive fisheries all over Africa.[9] Lake Tanganyika, the world's longest, is bordered by the Congo DRC, Burundi, Zambia and Tanzania. It is a major fishery and exporter of fresh fish to East African countries. It harbors special kinds of cichlid fish, sardine, and catfish. *Uganda*'s lakes—*Victoria, Albert, Kyoga, Edward*, and *George*—are major fish reserves and suppliers, with Lake Victoria being the largest supplier both for domestic and external markets. Lake Edward belongs to the Congo and Uganda. Its important harvest consists of tilapia, catfish and lungfish. Lake Albert, also shared by the Congo and Uganda, hosts a great variety of fish, mostly consumed locally.

Marine Fisheries. Many African countries have an oceanic coast and active marine fisheries.[10] South Africa is located at the meeting point of the Atlantic Ocean, to the west, and the Indian Ocean, to the east. Together the two coasts host over 10,000 species of marine plants and animals recorded. The country's coastline is over 3000 km long with major fisheries on each side. Commercially exploited varieties of marine life from the Atlantic coast include hake, anchovy, sardine, horse mackerel, tuna, rock lobster and others; and squid and linefish, from the Indian Ocean side. Tanzania's 850 km-long stretch of coastal marine fishery contains over 500 fish species, including, from among others, emperors, snappers, groupers and goatfish. Reportedly, Namibia's marine fishing grounds are among the most productive in the world. The most productive zone—Exclusive Economic Zone—contains 20 different species, including pilchard, anchovy, mackerel, monkfish and lobster, from among others. Hake, another important species, is marketed in European Union and to other international markets.

SUMMARY

As can be derived from the creation stories, belief systems, and life practices, the African man or woman is a profound believer in God's existence, eternity, omnipresence, omniscience and omnipotence. God is, God was and God will always be. God has no beginning and has no end. God is everywhere and sees and identifies everything by name, visible or invisible, known or unknown to humans. God's powers are above any creature's powers. God's powers supersede the powers of divinities, ancestors, and witches; as well as those of the natural forces of the universe and most powerful animals of the land or of the sea. God created the universe and all that exists in it, material or immaterial, visible or invisible, known or unknown to humans. God alone created the spirits and celestial bodies—sun, moon and stars—by the power of God's will. God created Earth and the terrestrial world through various methods, including: creation by the power of God's thought, God's word, and God's gesture. In some cases, God created through some appointed mediator spirit empowered by God to this effect. Unique to the creation of Human, God infused himself into human by exhaling the divine breath of life into Human directly or through a conduit such as the vapor through the combined mouth of the *Nummos* twins in the *Bambara* story. The God of the African Human is a generous provider who ensured that Earth would be habitable, and endowed with waters, plants and animals for Human's comfortable living and prosperity. Africa, destined to become a land of abundant living, is blessed with trees of life even in the Sahara and Kalahari deserts, with numerous animal species living in the continent's forests and savannah lands and unimaginable numbers of water-life species in the rivers, lakes and coastal waters. These are all manifestations of God's generosity.

(Endnotes)

1   Parsons, Marie. ND."Creation". In: *Egypt: Egyptian Creation, A Feature Tour Egypt Story. From Religion in Ancient Egypt ed. By Byron E Shafer.* http://www.touregypt.net/featurestories/creation.htm. Retrieved 11-29-2020.

2   Wikipedia. ND. "Wildlife of Niger." https://en.wikipedia.org/wiki/Wildlife of Niger. Retrieved 7-9-2019.

3   Wildlife of the Congo. ND. https://wwf.panda.org/knowledge_hub/where_we_work/congo_basin_forests/the_area/wildlife/. Retrieved 7-11-2019.

4   Hoyt, Richard. 2017. "What Plants Grow in the Kalahari Desert?" September 21, 2017. http://www.gardenguides.com/95331-plants-grow-kalahari-desert.html. Retrieved 2-23-2020.

5   Sevier, El. 2015. "*Adansonia digitata* L. (baobab): a review of traditional information and taxonomic description." *Asian Pacific Journal of Tropical Biomedicine.* Volume. 5. Issue 1.January 2015. Pages 79-84. https://www.sciencedirect.com/science/article/pii/S222116911530174X. Retrieved 3-1-2020.

6   "For country-by- country location of mineral resources in Africa." See, from among others: Mining Africa. ND. "Natural Resources of Africa." https://www.miningafrica.net/natural-resources-in-africa. Retrieved 3-4-2020.

Mining Africa. ND. "Mining Countries of Africa". https://www.miningafrica.net/mining-countries-africa/. Retrieved 3-4-2020.

For an extensive historical description and geographic locations of Congo's immense mineral resources, see:

Euromin. ND. "The Minerals of the Democratic Republic of the Congo: The History of the Congolese mineralogy, Exhibitions of Congolese minerals in Belgium, Minerals described for the first time in the Congo." http://euromin.w3sites.net/Nouveau_site/gisements/congo/GISCONe.htm. Retrieved 3-4-2020.

7   The following are some sources on river fisheries in African countries:

Harrison, Ian J, Randall Brummet, and Melanie L. J. Stiassny 2016. "The Congo River Basin Abstract." *From the Wetland Book*. Pp. 1-18. Posted 1 August 2016. https://link.springer.com/referenceworkentry/10.1007%2F978-94-007-6173-5_92-1.

Sawe, Benjamin Elisha. 2017. "Native Fish Species of Mali." *World Atlas*. April 25, 2017. worldatlas.com/articles/the-native-fish-species-of-mali.html.

Limpopo River Awareness Kit. ND. "Fish Species of the Limpopo." www.limpopo.riverawarenesskit.org/LIMPOPORAK.COM/EN/RIVER/ECOLOGY_AND_BIO DIVERSITY/AQUATIC_ECOLOGY/LIFE_IN_AQUATIC. Retrieved 6-15-2019.

Ecology and Biodiversity. ND. "Fish Species of the Orange Senqu River." http://www.orangesenqurak.com/river/ecology+biodiversity/aquatic+ecology/liae/classification+of+organisms/Fish+Species+of+the+Orange+Senqu+River.aspx?print=1. Retrieved 7-13- 2019.

8   On lake fisheries in Africa, see: Wikipedia. ND. "Lake Tanganyika." https://en.wikipedia.org/wiki/Lake_Tanganyika. Retrieved 3-3-2020.

Wikipedia. ND. "Fishing in Uganda." https://en.wikipedia.org/wiki/Fishing_in_Uganda. Retrieved 3-3-2020.

Wikipedia. ND "Fishing in Chad." https://en.wikipedia.org/wiki/Fishing_in_Chad. Retrieved 3-3-2020.

9   The information on marine fisheries in Africa is taken from the sources listed below:
South Africa Government www. gov.za. ND. "Fisheries." https://www.gov.za/about-sa/fisheries. Retrieved 7-10-2019.

Jiddawi, Narriman Saley and Marcus C. Ohman. 2002. "Marine Fisheries in Tanzania." Abstract. *Ambio: A Journal of the Human Environment*. 31(7-8)::518-527. December 2002.

FAO. 2007. "The Republic of Namibia». FAO Fishery Country Profile." http://www.fao.org/fi/oldsite/FCP/en/NAM/profile.htm.

FAO 2004. "FAO Fishery Country Profile – The Republic of Angola." http://omap.africanmarineatlas.org/BIOSPHERE/data/fishes/fisheries/CountryCatches/Fishery%20Country%20Profiles/FAO%20Fishery%20Country%20Profile%20-%20Angola.htm.

Diallo, A. 2000. "Status of Fish Stock in Senegal." In: Abban, E.K. et al (Eds). *Biodiversity and sustainable use of fish in the coastal zone*. Dakar: Centre de Recherches Oceanologiques de Dakar-Thiaroye. pp 38-40.

Chapter 6
A Fervent Devotee of the Spirits

   1. Divinities and their Mediating Roles
   2. Ancestors as God's Mediators and Family Elders
   3. Devotion to Protector Spirits

God's provisions for the well-being of humans on Earth include care by God's mediator spirits, namely divinities, ancestors, and nature spirits. Divinities are God's highest-ranking spiritual creations. Ancestors are spirits of family members who have passed away. Nature spirits are earthly spirits that, unlike ancestors, have not lived in human form. In addition to describing these mediators and their protective roles among the humans, this chapter discusses the acts of devotion that African peoples across the continent exhibit toward God and these mediator spirits.

1. DIVINITIES AND THEIR MEDIATING ROLES

Before any other beings, God created Lord spirits, also known as divinities, whom He invested with high powers second only to His own. God appointed a select few divinities to assist Him in the completion of the work of creation. Some from these appointees are said to have become incarnated as humans. To other divinities the Creator assigned specific functions as God's ministers watching over the humans in particular areas of need. Some divinities entrusted with such missions are actually deified spirits of famous human beings who died heroically. This section provides illustrations of these four categories of divinities: God's assistants in creation, God's ministers in charge of particular functions among the humans, incarnate spirits, and deified spirits (human heroes).

Assistants to the Creator in the Creation Process

In African traditions delegation of power is highly valued. Despotic power is resented. To achieve effectiveness in governance, a good king or chief delegates responsibilities to most deserving dignitaries. In many creation stories, God created some divinities and made them partners in carrying out the creation process. The *Nummo Twins* in the creation story of the Dogon of Mali are an example. One can also cite Arch-Divinity *Orìsà-nlá* and Divinity *Orunmìlà* in the Yorùbá story, and *Maweja wa Cyama and Maweja Cyama* in the case of the Luba.

  The Nummo Twins: For the Dogon of Mali, *Amma*, God, first created the *Nummo Twins*, male and female, united by the mouth. Then, step by step, *Amma* ordered the rest of creations to come out through the *Nummo Twins'* combined mouth. In the first place, the twins released vapor. This made the existence of nature possible. The original vapor was the anticipation of the wind, the language by which nature communicates. At a higher level, *Amma* summoned the appearance of the human creative speech that brought into existence technical skills, the ability to use them, and practitioners such as the weaver, the blacksmith and the tanner. At the highest level, *Amma* ordered the appearance of articulate and meaningful human speech, which is the most advanced form of communication. It enabled humans to fully understand laws of nature, enhance technology, and contribute to the development of the human community (Caruthers, 1995).

Arch-Divinity *Òrìṣà-nlá*: In the case of the Yorùbá of Nigeria, God's number one partner in the work of creation was *Arch-Divinity Òrìṣà-nlá*. *Olódùmarè*, the Creator, charged *Òrìṣà-nlá*, a product of His creation, to fill a preexisting wet marsh with dry soil to transform it into Earth. Along with him, the Creator sent the hen and the pigeon to help him spread the soil. *Olódùmarè* also gave *Òrìṣà-nlá* palm trees to plant in anticipation of humans' need for oil, wine, and food for subsistence. *Olódùmarè* later charged *Òrìṣà-nlá* to build the physical structure of the human body that *Olódùmarè* himself animated by breathing into it (Idowu, 1994).

Orunmìlà, another Yorùbá divinity, is the Deputy Minister in charge of matters pertaining to omniscience and wisdom. He was with *Olódùmarè* at the beginning of creation; he knows all about the work of creation, and was charged by *Olódùmarè* to serve as Counselor to *Òrìṣà-nlá* (Idowu, 1994).

***Maweja wa Cyama* and *Maweja Cyama*:** The creation story of the Luba relates that *Maweja Nangila* created Lord Spirits, celestial animals, celestial bodies—the sun, the moon, and the stars—and basic celestial elements—such as air and thunder—all by Himself. But He created life on Earth, including humans, with the assistance of *Maweja wa Cyama*, Firstborn Son, and *Maweja Cyama*, First Lady, the two highest most Lord Spirits, products of His creation. Each time *Maweja Nangila* brought a particular type of creatures into being, *Maweja wa Cyama* organized them the way the first born son organizes the goods of his father, and *Maweja Cyama* made them grow as the senior wife takes care of her husband's property (Mudimbe, 1991). In other words, the Creator represents the *Action-Generating Principle*, the Son is the *Supreme Action Principle*, and the Senior Lady Spirit is the *Nurturing, Conservation, and Growth Principle*. To the role of these three one must add that of *Mulopo Maweja*, the Emissary Spirit, who represents the *Contradiction and Change Principle* (Kalanda, 1992).

God's Ministers in the Governance of Life on Earth

***The Òrìṣàs*:** Some divinities are assigned by the Creator to particular functions among humans. The *Òrìṣàs*, in the Yorùbá religion, are believed to be ministers of *Olódùmarè*, the Creator, whom He has vested with particular functions. There exists a considerable number of *Òrìṣàs*. The three below are some of the most important ones (Idowu, 1994).

***Èṣú*:** This character is the special-relation officer between Heaven and Earth and the inspector general who reports regularly to *Olódùmarè* on the deeds of divinities and humans. A versatile character, *Èṣú* also has the mission of trying humans' sincerity and putting their religion to the test, checking and making reports on the correctness of worship, in general, and sacrifices, in particular. *Èṣú* is the right hand of *Orunmìlà*, the

High Counselor to *Arch-Divinity Orìṣà-nlá*. Always present where *Orunmìlà* is, *Èṣú* is also the one who brings about calamities to punish those who disobey *Orunmìlà*.

Ògún: Divinity *Ògún* is very important in the lives of the Yorùbá as the controller of all iron and steel. He was a hunter even before the firm land was formed. He used to descend on the spider's thread to hunt on the primeval marshy waste that *Orìṣà-nlá* later solidified into Earth. *Ògún* was the only one with the implements needed to cut the forest and is the one who goes first to prepare the road to others.

Olókun: The creation of Earth in the Yorùbá story included two bodies of water respectively known as the Lagoon and the Sea. They are located in *Ile-Ifẹ̀*, the creation city and cradle of the humankind in Yorùbá worldview. The two are the original sources from which come all the waters of the Earth. *Olókun*, one of Creator *Olódùmarè*'s ministers, is the goddess of the sea.

Anyanwu, Ala, and Amadioha: The *Igbo* also venerate many divinities. One, *Anyanwu*, a sun-god, makes crops and trees grow. Another, *Ala*, an Earth goddess, is the spirit of fertility and guardian of morality (Uchendu, 1965: 96). In the latter capacity, goddess *Ala* mystically sanctions abominations such as incest, adultery of a woman, and eating and killing 'totem' animals. A third divinity, *Amadioha*, god of thunder and lightning, personifies "the wrath of God". He carries out punishments against wrongdoers, such as witches and sorcerers (Ekechukwu, 1983).

Ay-Situ: Pregnant women in Pre-Islamic Somalia used to hold fertility rites and make offerings to *Ay-Situ* (*Mother Situ*), the equivalent of goddess *Isis* (3s.t) in ancient Sudan and Egypt, for the purpose of easing delivery. This practice has been incorporated into Islam. Now, fertility offerings are being made to *Fatima*, the daughter of Prophet Muhammad (Abdullahi, 2001).

Incarnate Deities

The Pharaoh: Some divinities are known to have existed in physical bodies. In ancient Egypt, gods were believed to incarnate in natural objects, animals and humans. God *Horus* was incarnated in the sun and in the pharaoh. Consequently, the king was man, God, and sun at the same time. *Horus* was a major divinity in Egyptian religion. An outgoing king passed the title of god *Horus* to his successor (Frankford, 2000). Thus, through coronation, each incoming pharaoh acquired the divinity's powers, and name of *Horus* as well as special powers from the insignia he received. Through the process of coronation, the king became a divine ruler. As a result, a king's actions would become divine and reflecting the will of the gods. Horus would be speaking and acting through the king. The king would also become a spiritual mediator between the gods and the people. Some versions present *Horus* as the son who ascended to the throne of his father *Osiris*. In other versions, *Horus* is god *Atum* metamorphosed into a son. In both versions Horus is identified as sun-god and coronation is equated with creation. Through creation god *Atum* metamorphosed himself into Re, Sun, with all his divine powers, by the same token establishing himself as the supreme ruler. By this act *Atum* became the father of Re. The pharaoh, being identified with Re, became son of *Atum* (Frankford 2000; David, 2002: 78). In managing the affairs of the state that affected people's lives, the king was subject to *Ma'at*, the principle of balance personified as goddess of justice and order (David, 2002).

Kabale, Benda and Mikombo wa Kalewu: In Luba creation myths, there are also cases of Lord Spirits incarnated in human forms. *Kabale*, *Benda*, and *Mikombo wa Kalewu* (*Kalowa*) are such incarnations. All three are said to have derived from and equal to *Maweja Nangila*, the Creator. References to *Kabale* present him as God or God's Son, or else, *Kabale wa Tshilele*, meaning *Kabale* Son of *Tshilele*, a woman who survived persecution after persecution and all kinds of life challenges. Kept under special divine protection, she escaped numerous traps designed to kill her. *Benda* is presented as God, as well as the spirit, voice and counselor of Creator *Maweja Nangila*. *Mikombo wa Kalewu* means *Mikombo* Son of *Kalewu*, a woman. *Mikombo* is claimed to have begotten himself in Kalewu's womb, hence his full name: *Mikombo wa Kalewu Nkayende Mudifuka* (*Mikombo* the Self-Created Son of *Kalewu*) (Mudimbe 1991, quoting Van Caenegem 1956). Today, in Kasai, *Mikombo* is only known through a popular epic song telling the allegoric story of how humans hated him, mounting plot after plot to kill him, but each time *Mikombo* escaped death at the last minute thanks to the assistance of some uniquely talented and skilled animal member of his inner-circle of followers. Finally, *Mikombo* ascended into heaven triumphantly assisted by the entire animal kingdom.

Deified Spirits of Past Heroes

Odùdúwà: Deified spirits of past heroes are another category of divinities found in some African religious traditions. A certain oral tradition of the Yorùbá tells that *Odùdúwà*, who is one of the major divinities today, was once a powerful immigrant who founded a particular branch of the Yorùbá people. As a man of strong repute and a very capable leader who lived *in Ile Ifè*, he had great influence not only on the city but also on a large part of the hinterland. Surrounded by powerful warriors, he united several peoples who came to be known as Yorùbá. Today, he is acknowledged as the founding father of the Yorùbá people. The various Yorùbá clans are believed to have been founded by his descendants. After his death he came to be honored both as an ancestor and as a divinity (Idowu, 1994).

Balubaale: The *Balubaale* in the religion of *Baganda* were believed to be the spirits of persons with exceptional attributes on Earth who became glorified in death. They are identified with particular functions among humans. In this respect, they are comparable to the *Òrìṣàs*, God *Olódùmarè*'s ministers in the Yorùbá pantheon. The *Balubaale* were the highest-ranking spiritual creations of *Katonda*, God. *Katonda* was believed to live among the *Balubaale* and behaving just as one of them. Each had a specific function, as indicated in the sample below (Musoke, 2018)[1]:

Sample *Balubaale* and their Functions

Katonda	*Kiwanuka*	*Kawumpuli*
God of the sky	God of lightning	God of plague

A Fervent Devotee of the Spirits

Ndaula	***Musisi***	***Musoke***
God of small pox	God of earthquakes	God of the rainbow

Kitaka
God of Earth

Ṣàngó: This and the next deified human being are examples of famous individuals who died of a humiliating death. The example comes from the Yorùbá once more. The next is from the Bashi of eastern *Congo* and related ethnic groups in *Rwanda, Burundi*, and Tanzania. *Ṣàngó* is today revered as the manifestation of the "Wrath" of *Olódùmarè*. He is distinct from those who have been divinities from creation. They are of the heavens. He was all terrestrial. He once existed on Earth as a strong man, a powerful hunter and versed in magic. He became king of *Oyo*. He gained the infamous reputation of being cruel and passionate for carnage. His subjects resented him very much. Once challenged by his courtiers to a point of no escape, he committed suicide by hanging. In revenge and to save his face, his followers consulted a powerful medicine man who attracted lightning and calamities to the area. They changed the suicide story to one of live ascension to heaven. The intensified occurrences of lightning and calamities befalling the kingdom were his acts of vengeance against his slanderers who had spread the suicide story. *Ṣàngó* came to be venerated as the one god who controls thunders and lightning (Idowu, 1994).

Lyangombe: The story of *Lyangombe* in Bashi religion is similar to the above story of *Ṣàngó* in the Yorùbá religion. The Bashi of Congo and related peoples in other countries of the Great Lakes of East Africa—*Uganda, Burundi, Rwanda* and *Tanzania*—have a cult to a great spirit called *Lyangombe*. This hero was a great magician living in Rwanda, consulted by monarchs from the region. He succeeded his father at the head of a religious sect called *man-duwa*. He died in a hunting party, killed by an antelope after having had a dispute with *King Ruganzu Ndori* (RuganzuII) of *Rwanda*. It was a shame for a hero warrior of his caliber to be killed by an antelope. His followers promoted a different story: they claimed he was killed by a buffalo and that his followers and hunting partners committed mass suicide in a spirit of loyalty to him. A severe epidemic befell Rwanda during the reign of *King Mutara I*, son of Ruganzu II. It was the revenge of the sacred death of *Lyngombe* and his fellow heroes. The king ordered the initiation of the entire Rwanda to the cult to cool down the anger of the formidable spirits. The cult became a national religion. *Lyangombe* gave birth also to a secret society, *kubandwa*, to which adolescent males are initiated periodically (Mulago, 1973).

2. ANCESTORS AS GOD'S MEDIATORS AND FAMILY ELDERS

Two beliefs underlie veneration of the dead: survival of the individual after death and the interchange of relations between the living and the dead (Mulago, in Olupona 1991: 120-121). In general, ancestors are relatives who have passed away and are credited for having died of a good death. By becoming pure spirits through death, ancestors move closer to God whereby increasing in spiritual powers. As family members, ancestors continue to live among the living as family elders using their increased divine powers to bless their descendents for good behaviors and chastise them for wrongdoings.

Two Fundamental Beliefs about Ancestral Veneration

From creation, the human being is spirit and body. At death, the body perishes whereas the spirit continues to live indefinitely. In the minds of African people, the spirits of the dead do not abandon their earthly family. Instead, they mystically continue to share in their lives as invisible members of the extended family or the clan, and are ostensibly venerated with invocations, rituals, offerings and animal sacrifices on all occasoions of significance: birth, initiation, marriage, investiture, and death (Mbiti, 2007). The ancestors are principles of life of bygone relatives. Having been liberated from the limitations of the human body through death, ancestors increase their supernatural powers, which they use to guide, help, and protect the living; thereby increasing descendants' life forces. Both the *mangara* principle (spiritual force)—resulting from the union of the ancestor's spirit with the person's physical body at conception—and *buzimu* (physical strength, propriety of the living) areis shared by the dead and the living (Atal 1997, Gyekye, in Mario Beatty 2001; Kalu, in Olupona 2000, Jahn 1961).

Also, as pure spirits and elders, the ancestors occupy a higher social rank in the spiritual realm and, therefore, are closer to God than their earthly descendants. By becoming pure spirits through death and closer to the Creator, they even increase in knowledge and power to exercise such an influence. They become the natural mediators between their descendants and God, taking their petitions to Him and bringing His blessings back to them. In other words, the ancestors' relationship with God is transacted into a deputizing role. For instance, the Dinka traditional society is governed by a council of elders, *the Masters of the Fishing Spears*. In the Dinka belief system, *Longar*, the ancestor of *the Masters of the Fishing Spears*, is the one who sets up the behaviors for attaining the good life. Likewise, among the Sotho and Tswana of southern Africa, the founding fathers of the clans are the intermediaries between *Molimo*, God, and their descendants (Tempels 1965, Kalu, in Olupona 2000, Carruthers 1995, Beatty 2001).

Who Becomes an Ancestor?

Some societies differentiate between the spirits of the dead who become revered ancestors and those who do not based on their respective social statuses and moral achievements or lack thereof. The Akan of Ghana make a distinction between deserving deceased who become ancestors and undeserving ones who are deprived of this honor. The spiritual part of the human being that may eventually become an ancestor is called *mogya* before death and *saman* after death. The Akan identify three categories of *saman*:

1. **Samanpa**: Good Ghost, ghost of a person whose death is followed by good events or cessation of bad ones.

2. **Saman Tween-Tween**: Bad Ghost, ghost of a person whose death was followed by bad events befalling the family or the community.

3. ***Tofo:*** *Ghost of a person who died violently* (Abraham, 1974).

Only *samanpa* ghosts could become venerated ancestors and sources of blessings for their descendents. *Saman Tween-Tween* ghosts were not accepted into the land of good ghosts. They stayed on Earth in temporary or permanent punishment, hanging around dark corners and haunting the living. *Tofo* ghosts did not live with the good ones either. Instead, they walked around with their faces painted with white clay and boldly aggressing people (Abraham, 1974).

Among the BaKongo of Congo, just as among the Akan, not all ghosts of deceased family members qualify to be honored as ancestors. The Kongo recognize three categories of spirits of the dead—*bakulu, matebo,* and *bankita*—and one category of nature spirits: *bisimbi*. Together the four categories are sometimes referred to as spirits of the land.

> ***Bakulu:*** These are the spirits of individuals who have lived nobly on Earth and now live in the ancestral village underneath the Earth near the forest or rivers, organized in clan communities similar to earthly villages.
>
> ***Matebo:*** Are called *Matebo,* the spirits of relatives who lived undeserving lives and sorcerers who have harmed people with their supernatural powers. They live by springs and frighten people.
>
> ***Bankita:*** These are the spirits of individuals who died tragically. They live with the founding fathers of the clan who died in conquest wars.
>
> ***Bisimbi:*** This name is given to water spirits. They live by creeks, springs, and ponds. They crouch underneath stones and roots and make individuals who step on them sick (Van Wing 1959, quoted in Mulago 1973).

The *Shona* of Zimbabwe distinguish between several categories of intermediate spirits between Creator *Mbari*, or *Musika vanhu*, and the humans, notably *mhondoro, vadzimu, shave, ngozi,* and *muroyi,* as explained hereafter:

Mhondoro: These are the spirits of the founding fathers of the clan. They oversee the clan community and its land as a whole. One of their major gifts to the clan is rain. When starting a new village in a different location within the ancestral lands, family heads ask for *mhondoro*'s intersession to higher spirits, for protection and abundant crops. At the time of succession, they consult *mhondoro* to give them a good chief. Traditionally, a particular day of the week, *chisi*, determined by the phase of the moon, was set aside to abstain from working in the fields.

Vadzimu: The *vadzimu* are the spirits of closer family protector ancestors. They protect the household and the homestead from harm, sickness, and witches. Often, prayers to the *vazimu* are not directly addressed to God, even though admitting that ultimately whatever they are asking for will come from God. The *vadzimu*, along with the *mhondoro*, are called upon to redress infractions against family moral values, such as incest, adultery, and molestation of a minor girl.

Shave: These are the spirits of talented foreigners, *matebele*, or *senna*, who died in *Mashonaland* longtime ago and were interned without proper burial. Such spirits were condemned to wander until they could find hosts through spiritual possession, to whom they revealed themselves and who accepted their talents. Acceptance was expressed through prayers, ritual ceremonies, and wearing special garments. Compliant professional hosts, such as hunters and healers, become endowed with the spirit, the spirit's talents, and efficiency in the exercise of their profession.

Ngozi: These are the avenging spirits of deceased persons who were wronged while on Earth, neglected, or murdered. In revenge, the *ngozi* afflict entire families with sudden death or untreatable illnesses.

Muroyi: Evil spirit of an evil person who lived and passed away long time ago and is passed from parent to offspring generation after generation (Gefland, Arntsen).[2]

Nganga: The *nganga* is possessed by a special spirit of healing and of divining and is said to have originated from a person with these gifts many generations ago when the clan was founded. The original person whose spirit now possesses a *nganga* knew how to treat disease and to discern its spiritual cause. This special *nganga* spirit remains in the family and when a *nganga* dies his healing spirit selects one of his children who, in his turn, becomes a *nganga*. This spirit is a good one and can contact the ancestral spirits of any family and thereby discover what has annoyed them and what is necessary to make amends.

Have All Ancestors Lived Morally Exemplary Lives while on Earth?

The view that the term "ancestors" is reserved for those forebearers who lived morally exemplary lives has been challenged by some scholars of African religion. Kwame Gyeke rightfully argues, for instance, that there are among people to whom we refer as our ancestors, chiefs who are known to have been corrupt and tyrannical rulers who led morally unworthy lives. *Ṣàngó*, a major divinity in Yorùbá religion, is perhaps the best example in this respect. *Ṣàngó* was a strong man and a powerful magician and hunter. He became king of *Oyo* and was resented by his subjects because of his cruelty and passion for carnage. But he died shamefully. To avoid capture by his challengers, he committed suicide by hanging. Unhappy with this degrading kind of death, his followers sought revenge by consulting a powerful medicine-man who attracted lightening and calamities to the area. Also, to save his face, they changed the suicide story to one of live ascension to heaven. Furthermore, they convinced the population that the intensified occurrences of lightening and calamities befalling the kingdom were his acts of vengeance against his slanderers who had spread the suicide story. *Ṣàngó* came to be venerated as the one god who controls thunders and lightening. He is also considered as a manifestation of the "Wrath" of *Olódùmarè*, the Creator (Gyekye, in Beatty 2001, Idowu 1994).

Like elsewhere in Africa, the ancestral spirits (*Bakishi*) in Luba society continue to share earthly life with their descendants. They acquire greater supernatural powers through death by passing from the human state to a purely spiritual state. They use these powers to protect and bless their descendants in many ways: giving them the capacity to work, to procreate, and to achieve many other forms of success. In return for these blessings, the descendants bear the obligation to share food, shelter, and other enjoyments with their benefactors. To the believer, ancestral obligations are not optional. Violations may attract misfortunes on the perpetrator, his progeny, or his possessions. This belief in ancestral intervention in human lives is the foundation upon which Luba ancestral veneration is built. The Luba tradition, however, is silent on the issue of whether or not all spirits of the dead should be honored as ancestors. However, the burial of two categories of individuals was handled in a way that prevented their reincarnation into the family. Traditionally, the Luba buried adult men in the courtyard of their compounds and adult women behind their houses. They buried children in the verandah of their mother's house to make them feel still loved and to motivate them to be reborn to the same mother. Mechanisms explicitly designed to encourage the spirits of deceased adults to reincarnate did not exist, even though it was and still is believed they do. However, the burial of individuals who died of certain diseases excluded them from the community. Such was the case with people who died of belly swelling or leprosy. These two categories of deceased were laid on top of a mound in the wilderness, away from the village, and left there to rot, thus preventing their reincarnation (Mukenge, 1967).

3. DEVOTION TO PROTECTOR SPIRITS

Prayer to God

Relationship of Dependence: Communications with the Supreme Being are established through representations and various verbal expressions, such as invocation prayers, proverbs, and sayings. The relationship of the Supreme Being to humans implies dependence, notably, relation of Creator to creature, Father to child, Protector to protégé. For instance, God's names among some Congolese ethnic groups begin with the morphemic prefix *sha, shya or sa*, which means father. Among many others, the Luba and the *Songye,* for instance, God's names express God's spiritual nature, invisibility and transcendence. Often, communications with God begin by invoking God's titles of glory, such as:

- ***Lulemà***: The Powerful one who causes the mountains to tremble (*Vira of Congo DRC*)
- ***Olódùmarè***: Supreme, Superlatively Great (Yorùbá),
- ***Deng***: Parent of humanity, educator and sovereign (Dinka of Sudan).
- **uZivelele** "He who is of Himself, the Self-existent One" (Zulu of South Africa)

- ***Engai***: The Unseen one, the Unknown One (Masaai *of Kenya* and Tanzania).
- ***Ama-Ama-Amasi-Amasi***, "He Who is known but never fully known" (Igbo *of* Nigeria).
- ***Nyame***: "The Alone Great God" (Akan of Ghana)
- ***Otumfuo***: The Mightiest and Most Powerful by Right and Fact (Asante of Ghana)
- ***Kalûnga***: Immensity that no one can measure and the source and origin of life (Kôngo of Congo DRC)
- ***Mvelimqanti***: The First to Appear (Swazi of Swaziland)

Drawing from Ancestors' Experiences: Prayers do not spring out in a vacuum. Instead, they are nurtured by life experiences and spiritual responses of the ancestors and of the family or personal experiences. Prayer reactivates these experiences (Gravrand, 1990).

Circumstances Prompting Community Prayers to the Supreme Being: Prayers to the Supreme Being are held in circumstances affecting the entire community. Several Congolese ethnic groups have been found to address collective prayers to the Supreme Being:

- In times of abundant harvest to express gratitude and joy
- In times of drought to ask for rain
- Before an undertaking with potential danger or uncertain ending, such as a hunting party, to ask for protection and luck
- In times of epidemic or collective calamity, to ward it off the community
- When faced with sickness and infertility. (Mufuta, 1990)

Similarly, speaking of the Sérèer of Senegal, H. Gravrand reports that prayers and other spiritual protections are often the first reflexes:

- In times of sickness or death, or else following dreams,
- In preparation for marriage, in matters relating to fecundity, birth, or growth of children
  In work, school, or sport competitions,
- In political races or upon assuming power or entering the government. (Gravrand, 1990)

Reportedly, among the Dagbamba of Northern Ghana, at every important event, the drummers start the history of the drum by beating a number of proverbs praising God, affirming God's omnipotence, omnipresence, and omniscience. The refrain is always: "Truly, it is the Chief of chiefs" (Chernoff, 2000).

Appropriate Time, Location and Personnel for Prayer to the Supreme Being: In general, anyone in need may address a personal prayer to God any time, but only group leaders holding ancestral powers may speak on behalf of the entire community. For the Pelende of Congo, the head of the household, the elder member of the group, or the clan elder assumes this function. Generally, prayers to the Supreme Being by the community are ceremonial and held in particular locations and times by a designated person in a particular social position. Examples:

- In the forest, under a sacred tree, or on a rock (*Bemba*)
- In a cave located near a cataract, during 7 days, generally at night (*Binja*)
- In the evening, at the foot of a sacred tree, planted inside a fence, behind the king's house (*Chokwe*)
- Around a tree in the center of the village (*Lunda*)
- At the crossroad or under a palm tree called divinity tree, early morning (*Kete*)
- Around a tree in the forest or in the bush in the evening (*Songye*)
- On the edge of the forest, on a river bank, or in the abode of the chief or an elder, at dawn (*Soo*). (Mufuta, 1990).

Examples of Prayers to the Supreme Being

The Pelende of the Congo:
Oh, God, You created us, you begot us,
when a misfortune befalls us,
when a problem hits us, we turn to you for help.
If happiness comes our way, our thanksgivings will go to you.
Today, we are confronted with a misfortune,
Help us, your children;
Take this calamity away from us (Mufuta, 1990).

The Luba of Katanga, Congo:
If it is by the will of God, that will happen,
I have not eaten (killed by witchcraft) anyone.
If I have, let The Supreme Being punish me (Mufuta, 1990).

The Bemba of Congo:
God Creator of all things,
Have compassion for us,
as you did for the wasp
when you spared it from breaking into two pieces (Mufuta, 1990)

The Igbo of Nigeria:
Prayer to *Chukwu*, the most important God:

"God eat *cola*
God of the universe eat *cola*,
Sun, and King of the sky eat cola
Earth deity greeting!
Sky deity greeting!
Eat *cola*

First, second, ancestors
Up to last three generations
Greet grandfathers
Eat *cola*..." (Uzukwu, 1990)

Devotion to Great Spirits

The spirits are God's highest-ranking creations. God created the spirits in hierarchies of seniors and juniors, major and minors. God called some spirits to assist in the work of creation, others to become God's mediators to the humans on Earth. Some spirits took the human form during their God's assignment to Earth. On the other hand, some humans died heroically and were deified after death. This section examines the attitudes and actions of the humans toward the great spirits, also called divinities (Kalu 2000, Mudimbe 1991, Idowu 1994, Kalanda 1992).

Uhammiri/Ogbuide Water Goddess of the Igbo: The Igbo live off farming, fishing and trading. Local sources of livelihood include crops such as yam, cassava, plantains, rice, beans, vegetables, and palm oil; and meat from fish, goats, sheep, and poultry. *Uru* towns are interconnected by a network of waters including the Ogbuide Lake and the Niger River and its tributaries. Non-standard seasonal variations of water levels and their unpredictable influence on productive activities create an atmosphere of livelihood uncertainty. Flood unpredictability and life uncertainty foster people's dependence on *Uhammiri/Ogbuide Water Goddess* and on other water deities for favors. Priests and priestesses seek to obtain such favors for the community by maintaining shrines and paying homage and making offerings to the spirits in a timely manner. Traditionally, the Igbo people measure the time in multiples of four. They have a four-day week: *Nkwo, Eke, Orie,* and *Afor*. Life is regulated by a four-day market cycle. Each day is a market day in a member town of the network. Seven cycles of any market day make 28 days, that is, a lunar month. Each market day is dedicated to a particular deity that is honored on that particular day (Jell-Bahlsen, in Olupona 2000).

The Great Spirit Mindiss of the Sérèer of Senegal's Sine Valley: Myths are a major reservoir of a people's ancestral experiences drawn from various sources and transmitted through oral tradition in forms of narratives or fables. As an example, *Mindiss*, founding father of the Fatik population over a thousand years ago, is one such myth among the Sérèer of Senegal's Sine Valley. *Mindiss* disappeared in the river leaving his sandals on the bank of the river but his footprints on the river itself. He couldn't be found anywhere in the river but showed up in the form of seacow. A cult and prayer site built on the river bank then has existed as such to the present. In the XIVth Century, a new city ruling family took charge of the shrine. In the XVth Century, a renowned spiritual leader, Khodar Ndiaye, saw *Mindiss* in a dream and convinced the new king, Wassila Faye, to build a second shrine to *Mindiss*. But Ndiaye did not assume the priesthood of the new shrine, *Mindiss* having turned violent toward him. A brother of the king became *Mindiss's* priest instead. Since then, *Mindiss* became the object of two cults: one by the former people and leaders, the other by the new class of leaders. On the *Mindiss* day, multitudes come in hundreds and pray to end their pain, to obtain assistance or to meet various needs. The prayers are addressed to the Supreme

Being who has power over the strong waves that drove *Mindiss* away, and addressed to the waves for occasioning *Mindiss*'s transformation from great human leader to God's mediator spirit, and also to *Mindiss* as a heroic divinity vested with great powers and a spiritual mediator of the Supreme Being in relations with humans (Gravrand, 1990).

The Cult to Great Spirit Lyangombe: The Bashi of Eastern Congo and the Banyarwanda of Rwanda practice a cult to a great spirit called *Lyangombe* for various purposes, including the following (Mulago, 1973):

1. To obey a divine order by the Great Spirit when the latter deems it opportune to make the request
2. To obtain healing from a sickness cast by cult followers or by spirits in concert with them
3. To prevent a sickness that diviners have declared imminent or predicted will hit the ground in some time to come.
4. To secure protection over resources of the land: harvest and cattle
5. To secure mutual understanding with neighbors, triumph over the enemy, or protection against witches
6. To fulfill a promise made by ancestors, but which they failed to carry out while on Earth
7. To enjoy the public recognition given to *Lyangombe* initiates
8. To preserve a family tradition thereby pleasing and appeasing ancestors

Devotion to Ancestral Spirits

Ancestorship and Eldership: Igor Kopytoff has pointed out that African people's practice of honoring the ancestors has been erroneously called ancestral worship. The Gikuyu are very clear on this issue, he argues. The words "prayer" and "worship"—*gothaithaiya, goikia-mokoigoro*—are never used in dealing with the ancestors' spirits. These words are reserved for solemn rituals and sacrifices directed to the power of the unseen and are not applicable to animal sacrifices made to the ancestors. These are rather "tributes symbolizing the gifts which the departed elders would have received had they been alive, and which the living elders now receive." Rather than worship, Igor Kopytoff (2008) proposes that the service in honor of the ancestors be called *eldership* instead. His argument is that ancestors are intimately involved with the welfare of their kin-group structurally through elders who are their representatives among the living and whose authority is related to their close link to the ancestors. Living elders are mediators between the ancestors and the kin-group. The statuses of ancestors and living elders are so close that the Suku simply apply to the former (ancestors: ascendants, forebears) the regular term for the latter (elders), *bambuta:*

> "The *Suku* have no term that can be translated as 'ancestor'. These dead members of the lineage are referred to as *bambuta*. Literally, *bambuta* means the 'big ones', the 'old ones', those who have attained maturity, those older than oneself; collectively, the term refers to the ruling elders of a lineage" (Kopytoff, 2008).

Community of the Living and the Dead: The behavior of ancestors in their capacity as elders reflects not their individual personalities but the particular structural positions they occupy in the kin-group hierarchy. In virtue of the functional role the ancestors retain among the living, African kin-groups are generally portrayed on the religious plan as communities of both the living and the dead in which the ancestors occupy the position of authority and exercise their increased supernatural power derived from their closer proximity to the Creator:

> "In all ceremonies of any significance, on the occasions of birth, marriage, death, funeral, or investiture, it is the ancestors who preside and their will yields only to that of the Creator" (Mulago, in Olupona 1991).

For instance, among the Suku, at the coming-out ceremonies for infants and at marriages, the dead members of the lineage are informed of the event; pleas are made for their approval and their efforts in ensuring the success of the newborn or of the marriage and the children that will be born to it. Before the large communal hunts of the dry season, the dead members are asked to extend good luck to the enterprise. They are told that the people are hungry for meat, they are reprimanded for not granting enough meat, and they are shamed that their own people should be eating less well than other lineages. To rephrase Victor C. Uchendu, speaking of the Igbo, the ancestors are the invisible father-figures whose countervailing powers the living appeal to against the powers of malignant and non-ancestral spirits. In reverence for the ancestors' role of invisible father figures, Suku living elders always refer publicly to dead members of the lineage on all ceremonial occasions involving the lineage as a unity (Kopytoff 2008, Uchendu 1965).

Communication with the Ancestors: Elders assume ancestors' physical place in ceremonies. The specific individuals who assume this function, the locations where and the manner in which they conduct rituals to the ancestors vary from one group to another.

The Suku: Among the Suku, this role belongs to the lineage head and the older men. The Suku do not have a permanent place or arrangement set aside for honoring the ancestors. To address the ancestors, the lineage head and the qualified elders gather at the grave of the most recently dead older man they remember or at a pathway crossing (Kopytoff 2008). The communication with the ancestors takes the form of a conversational monologue. The elder says, for example:

> 'You, [such and such], your junior is ill. We do not know why, we do not know who is responsible. If it is you, if you are angry, we ask for forgiveness. If we have done wrong, pardon us. Do not let him die. Other lineages are prospering and our people are dying. Why are you doing this? Why do you not look after us properly." (Kopytoff, 2008)

A Fervent Devotee of the Spirits

The Binja used to address the following prayer to ancestral spirits:

> "You all who have preceded us, look over here on Earth where we still are. You know well how we live. Don't let us continue to live like this. Where will we go? God of the universe, who gives grace even to things, we your children on Earth are suffering. Help us to solve these problems." (Mufuta, 1973)

The Kôngo: In the conception of the Kôngo of Congo, at death, the person's spirit moves to *ku masa*, a location by the water where life is eternal. *Ku masa*, departed elders and noble members of the clan who have lived exemplary lives on Earth, become *bakulu*, ancestors. They now live a peaceful and happy life in the ancestral village, underneath the Earth near forests and rivers. Here, life is organized on a model similar to human villages, with men and women, chiefs and subjects, all fulfilling the same functions as they did on Earth. The ancestral spirits are very active in the lives of their terrestrial descendants. Each Kôngo clan had a day of the week designated as a holiday. On that day, the priest of the ancestors would bring a small calabash filled with palm wine into the ancestors' house. He would plunge some leaves from a certain tree into the calabash and sprinkle the wine on the ancestors' basket. Then, he would kneel down, pour some wine on the ground, pick up some wet soil and rub his chest three times. Before vacating the house, he would greet the ancestors three times by clapping his hands. The ancestors are the providers of everything, including success in reproduction, farming, business and hunting (Fu-Kiau, 2001).

Four-legged animals are ancestors' property. The hunter who has killed such an animal must show respect for, and gratitude toward the ancestors by honoring all hunting traditions concerning that particular animal species. The chief selected the day for such hunts and the day and time for supplication prayers in the ancestral cemetery before the hunt. Hunters would bring their dogs and guns to the cemetery, the chief would pour palm wine on each tomb and, with all the hunters on their needs behind him, he would address the ancestors as fathers, mothers and elders, inviting them to drink the wine and imploring them to bless their descendants with fecundity and success in the enterprise of the day by making the game available to the hunters and reachable by their weapons. Everyone would greet the ancestors with a triple hand clap and then leave for the hunt (Van Wing 1959, in Mulago 1973).

The Luba do not have a specific permanent physical location separate from the village, venerated as the ancestors' residential community. Also, they are more individualistic in their approach to the ancestors. Each adult male head of the household who practices ancestral veneration honors his immediate ancestors in his own compound, particularly the spirits of his paternal grandfather, his paternal grandmother and his father. In the ritual, each honoree is identified by his or her family status and personal name, however, not in isolation, rather as a member of a community of peers. For instance, the officiant addresses supplications or offerings to *Grandfather Ngoyi* and all grandfathers; to *Father Kazadi* and all fathers; or else to *Grandmother Ngomba* and all grandmothers (Mukenge, 1967).

The Igbo: Important ancestors are sometimes assigned attributes similar to God's. Igbo priests, at the occasion of masquerade, address the ancestors as omniscient and powerful protectors before placing specific petitions. Kalu (2000) provides the following two prayers to make the point:

> "Please, we solicit for your protection. As you have returned, our lives are in your custody. Never will you accept any evil to befall us. You are the great kings of the great town. You are aware of all that happened in the past, in the present and the ones that will happen in future."

> "*Odo*, you are welcome. Protect us. Give us good life. Give us long life. Give us prosperity…"

Offerings and Sacrifices to the Ancestors: Devotion to ancestral spirits includes offerings and sacrifices. The inventory of Igbo people's offerings to *Ancestor Odo* includes: "tender palm fronds, eagle feathers, kola nuts, palm wine, richly cooked food, goats, cocks, rams, cows, and articles of clothing…" Among the Luba, the regular service to ancestral spirits consists of sacrifices of chickens at minor occasions such as moving into a new compound, the birth of a child, or to honor a specific request of a chicken sacrifice by the honored ancestor. At major occasions, such as lineage-unity celebration or reparations for a physical fight with an elder, a goat was sacrificed instead. In rituals to male ancestors, only the father and the grandfather are identified by name. However, these spirits are not venerated in isolation. Instead they are always addressed as members and representatives of the grand family of deceased relatives. In sacrifices, the invocation to the spirit of the father is immediately extended to all departed fathers. Likewise, a call to the grandfather is immediately extended to all grandfathers. Not only are the ancestors honored as a community, but also the descendents of the same father or paternal grandfather form a community of venerators. They share the same beliefs, religious practices and divinities; they partake of the same sacrificial meals (Kalu 2000, Mukenge 1967).

Ancestor Shrines: Shrines assume the functions of symbolic crossroads between the world of the living and the world of the dead and instruments of social unification as altars. Shrines can be small. Among the Nuer and Dinka of Sudan, the shrine consists of a forked tree branch stuck into the ground with the limbs upwards. The offerings include bracelets, horns, corn, and animal skins hung to the sacred tree branch. The tree-branch altar is reminiscent of the Tree of Creation to which offerings are still being made. Among the Ndembu of Zambia, the shrine for initiation into a cult called *Chihamba* consists of:

> "a bundle of medicinal twigs set into the ground; a clay pot containing tree bark and medicinal leaves, water and beer; a large section of a cassava root near the pot; and seeds of beans and corn planted around this assemblage (Ray 2000).

The Luba of Kasai have small shrines as well. The term *Bakishi* (the ancestral spirits as objects of veneration) shares the same singular form (*mukishi*) with *mikishi* (ghosts, spirits in general). Additionally, *Bakishi* is mostly understood in the sense of male ancestral spirits, again as the objects of veneration. In the latter sense, *Bakishi* does not include the spirit of the paternal grandmother in its semantics. When thus distinguished from the male spirits, the spirit of the grandmother is called *Nkambwa*. The plural of *nkambwa*, *bankambwa*, however, designates the ancestors in general. Thus, as objects of veneration by their descendents, the spirits of male ancestors (*Bakishi*) and the spirit of the paternal grandmother (*Nkambwa*) are differentiated both from the spirits in general (*mikishi*) and the ancestors in general (*bankambwa*). Lastly, the term *bakishi* applies also to the shrines for sacrificing to male ancestral spirits. Likewise, *nkambwa* is also the name for the sacred tree that houses the spirit *Nkambwa*. To distinguish these spirits (*Bakishi*) and (*Nkambwa*) from their respective abodes (*bakishi* and *nkambwa*), we have chosen to spell the former with capital initial letters, and to write the latter totally in low cases (Mukenge, 1967).

There exist large shrines as well. The Igbo of Nigeria build a house-like large shrine called *mbari*. From the front of *mbari*, a doorway leads to a central inner room. The doorway is generally closed. As a custom, a large picture of the divinity sits in the front of the doorway. The central inner room is surrounded by a wide porch populated with painted sculptures of men, women, deities, and animals. Ganda royal shrines are another example of large shrines. The kings of the Baganda people, in Uganda, have left behind large shrine buildings, once designed to house the spirits of the royal ancestors. The buildings are conical-shaped, two-story high, identical to the palace of the living king. The rear section of the building, called *forest*, is reserved to the spirits. It is sacred and inaccessible to the public for this reason (Ray, 2000).

Nature Spirits and their Involvement in Human Lives

Nature spirits have never existed in human form. They were created as spirits and continue to live as spirits. Their primary role among some African ethnic groups is carrying to God messages and offerings from the humans. Sometimes they substitute for God either because God is inaccessible or in the name of the economy principle, which limits direct access to God to exceptional circumstances. Water divinities and spirits are very popular in Africa. They can be welcomed as beneficent providers of water, healing herbs, creative inspiration, children, women's beauty, success in business, and wealth. They can also cause misfortunes, such as drowning, infertility, or madness (Mulago 1973, Wicker 2000).

***Mongo Bilima*:** The veneration of nature spirits was quite widespread among the Mongo people who live in the Equator Province, in Congo, DRC. Mongo nature spirits, called *bilima*, were believed to live sometimes in village communities as husbands, wives, and children. The most generous *bilima* favored human beings with abundant progeny; they were addressed as grandmothers. It is a quite widespread African custom for a person who is a source of generosity to be affectionately referred to as mother even if that person is a male. Grandmothers here is used in the sense of those who have provided for their offspring unceasingly and for a long time (Hulstaert 1961, in Mulago 1973).

Nature spirits resided in mysterious locations, such as whirlpools, springs or steep slopes. They exercised supernatural powers to the benefits of humans, such as helping them to discover thieves, take revenge on an enemy or achieve success in hunting and fishing. The greatest gifts expected from these spirits were fertility and progeny. In general terms, their role was to intercede before God for the humans and obtain for them success in their undertakings and all kinds of blessings. By their social position, some individuals could establish alliances with particular spirits, to whom they would regularly make presents of food. Sometimes, an individual would give food to a spirit just for survival. Such a gift was different from offerings of food (not sacrifices) made at the home of the spirit for the specific purpose of obtaining blessings for the children (Hulstaert 1961, in Mulago 1973, Vansina 1965).

Examples of Prayers to Nature Spirits: The Kuba of Congo, DRC, used to sing a prayer to a great spirit identified as *Ncyedy*:

> "*Praise Ncyedy.* Yes, praise, *praise Ncyedy* the Great Spirit. Great Spirit, you are the one we have followed. Yes, it is you that we all have followed" (Mufuta, 1990).

The Luba of Katanga also used to identify nature spirits by name. For example:

> "You, our shepherd and protector, open your home to us. Ô! *Kalombo*, our guide, we are in your domain. Answer our supplications" (Mufuta, 1990).

Not all water spirits are nature spirits. Some are spirits of victims of water disappearance deified after death. Sea fishermen, among the Sérèer of Senegal, before embarking, pray to request the protection of *Maady* and *Peel Ndiaye*, two famous fishermen who died during a marine fishing expedition. Remember the story of the *Great Spirit Mindiss*, from the Sérèer people also (Gravrand, 1990). Chokwe hunters recite the following prayer to ancestors before setting off:

> "To you our ancestors, you who reigned without flaw, you who begot us, you who brought us here to Earth, we are asking you to give us games. When we will be hunting, please remove all ferocious animals away from our path" (Mufuta, 1990).

SUMMARY

God created the great spirits and minor spirits, and heavenly bodies and elements, all by the power of God's will, that is, just by thinking about doing it and it was done. In the creation of Earth and its inhabitants, however, God appointed some lord spirits to carry out specific tasks. The assigned task could be filling in a primordial marsh with soil to create the hard land that became Planet Earth. It could be to serve as a conduit through which God's creative power was channeled. Assigned tasks could also be ordering God's fresh creations and nurturing them to full maturity. Assisting God in the creation process seems to have been reserved for selected few great spirits. Most divinities entrusted with specific assignments were appointed to serve humans in particular areas of need. Some of such God's spiritual ministerial envoys became incarnate. Others have existed or continue to exist as spirits. Other than divinities, God entrusted custody of humans to ancestors, spirits of relatives who have passed away. African ancestors are not gone. Instead they continue to be active in the community of the living. By becoming pure spirits through death, they have incorporated more divine powers. In their double capacity of God's ambassadors and family elders, ancestors regulate their descendants behaviors, carry their petitions to God and bring God's blessings to them. They reward the descendants with blessings for good deeds and sanction their wrongdoings with misfortunes.

(Endnotes)

1	Musoke, David. 2018. "Uganda: The Ganda Tradition." *Southworld Culture,* February 2018. https://www.southworld.net/uganda-the-ganda-tradition/. Retrieved 3-5-2020.

2	Gelfand, M. ND. "The Shona Religion." *Michigan State e-Library.* http://digital.lib.msu.edu/projects/africanj. Retrieved 3-7-2020.

Arntsen, Hilde. ND. "Shona and Ndebele Religions." http://www.postcolonialweb.org/zimbabwe/religion/arntsen1.html Retrieved 3-7-2020. At writing, Hilde Arntsen was Lecturer in the Department of Medias and Communication, at the University of Oslo.

PART THREE

HUMAN SELF IN INTERACTION WITH FELLOW HUMANS

Chapter 7. An Ethic-bound Community Member
Chapter 8. A Family-Kinship Builder
Chapter 9. A Compassionate Caretaker of Fellow Humans
Chapter 10. A Freedoom Seeker and Nation Builder

Chapter 7
An Ethic-bound Community Member

1. Endowed with Sacred Natural Rights
2. Subject to Moral Restraints
3. Accountable for Moral Transgressions
4. Addressing Moral Violations: Illustrations

Joseph Mbiti, the renowned scholar of African religions, identifies five categories of behaviors that constitute the body of African religious ethics:

(1) the ethical order given to humans by God through creation which consists of laws, rules, customs, traditions and taboos for people to live by in their relations within the family, in the community, toward the surrounding world and toward the departed;

(2) moral offenses which include disrespect toward the elders, murder, stealing, robbery, telling lies, causing bodily or property harm, use of sorcery or witchcraft, and sexual immoralities such as incest, rape, adultery and sexual intercourse with children or a person of the same sex;

(3) punishment by the community in the form of shame, fines, banning from the community, beating or death; by the ancestral spirits by causing sickness or failure in undertakings; and by God bringing epidemics, famine or drought upon the entire community for collective moral offenses or offenses committed by the leaders;

(4) channels for instilling moral values: initiation ceremonies, stories, proverbs, taboos, and others; and

(5) restoring a morally broken community through drumming, singing, dancing and eating (Mbiti, ND. "General Manifestations of African Religiosity").[1]

This chapter focuses on (1) *the ethical order given to humans by God through creation*, and (2) *moral offenses that call for sanctions*. In general, social values and moral principles in African traditional contexts place communality above individuality. Human identity is inconceivable outside of the family, the community, and the union of the living and the dead. Joseph Mbiti's slogan: "We are, therefore I am" has greatly contributed to popularizing this view. However, it is important to stress the fact that, as a product of divine creation, every human being possesses qualities of being that are similar to God's qualities, with the difference that God's qualities are more perfected and constitute the ideal that African believers strive for in their religious endeavors. Qualitative similarities with the Creator make the human being a special creation. The human being, no matter how low his or her social status may be, is endowed with inalienable sacred natural rights that everyone else, in or outside the community, is morally bound to respect. In other words, by virtue of a person's human nature, that person's inalienable sacred natural rights put moral restraints on the community's or any individual's behaviors toward him or her. Laurenti Magesa discusses the following aspects of African morality from among others: taboos, incest, wrongdoings, affliction, punishment, redress, and shame. We have ordered them to fit the Luba nomenclature, notably: the human being as endowed with sacred natural rights, subject to moral restraints, and accountable for moral transgressions (Oosthuizen1991, in Olupona 2000, Zahan, in Olupona 2000, Kalanda 1992, Magesa 1997). This chapter includes principles, traditional stories, songs, and prayers which relate norms about morality and integrity.

1. ENDOWED WITH SACRED NATURAL RIGHTS

Moral Confrontation
(***Lusanzu,*** *pronounced: Loo-sah-nzoo*)

It is a common practice in Luba culture to confront an individual who is experiencing some misfortune with his own conscience. A sick person whose condition has taken turn for the worse is often asked to tell whether he has wronged anybody. Each adult relative present is publicly confronted with his own conscience as well. Has he kept bad feelings toward the sick person for some wrongdoing the latter might have committed? If death occurs, the person will be morally confronted again at internment. In the eulogy, it will be repeated to him that if the cause of his death is a punishment for some wrongdoing on his part, he only has self to blame and will have to make his own case to the ancestors. A dying female is morally confronted likewise. Also, each adult present at the internment must call death upon himself if he has in some way betrayed the departing person. Refusing to do this is admission of guilt. Why would an innocent person resist testifying to his or her innocence while afflicted by such a terrible tragedy as the loss of a relative? Here both the individual and the community are confronted with their potential shortcomings vis-à-vis the values and norms of behavior anchored in society's basic moral traditions defining what is and what is not acceptable (Magesa, 1997).

Self- Examination / Declaration of Innocence
(***Kudyela Lusanzu,*** pronounced: *kood-ye-lah loo sah-nzoo*):

Kudyela lusanzu is moral confrontation of self, thus self-examination, which often takes the form of a declaration of innocence. The occasion is often some threat to life. Life threatening sickness or any other serious misfortune is often used as a wake-up call to moral self-examination. For instance, in Luba villages, a man who has lived up to the moral standards of the Luba society, but who finds himself facing a life-threatening misfortune for which he has no explanation, would examine his behaviors in reference to internalized moral principles of the Luba society. If complete, his declaration of innocence would include the following elements:

1 - *Cyena mushipa muntu.*	-I have not killed anyone.
2 - *Cyena mubunda muntu.*	-I have not assaulted anyone.
3 - *Cyena mupala muntu byakudya.*	-I have not denied food to anyone.
4 - *Cyena munyanga luumu lwa muntu.*	-I have not slandered anyone.
5 - *Cyena mupepeja bakulu.*	-I have not humiliated my elders.
6 - *Cyena mubenga bwa kufuta milambu.*	-I have not refused to pay the first fruits.
7 - *Cyena mushipa bibindi.*	-I have not committed incest or indecent acts in the family
8 - *Cyena mwangata mukaj'a benda.*	-I have not taken another man's wife.
9 - *Cyena munyanga mwana wa muntu.*	-I have not molested anyone's child.
10 - *Cyena mwiba cintu cya muntu.*	-I have not stolen anyone's property.
11 - *Cyena muteka mikalu mu njila.*	-I have not erected barriers on public roads.

(Adapted and expanded from Kalanda 1992)

Sacred Natural Rights
(***Bumpyanyi bwa kwa Maweja***; pronounced: *Boo-mpyah-nyee bwah kwah Mah-'wə-jah)*

The above self-examiner declares his innocence relative to the required respect for other people's natural rights derived from divine creation. The Luba term used here to express natural rights is *bumpyanyi*, more specifically *bumpyanyi bwa kwa Maweja*. *Bumpyanyi* means inheritance. *Bumpyanyi bwa kwa Maweja* means inheritance from Maweja (God). An inheritance is an entitlement. It confers one right, claim, and prerogative over that which is inherited. Legitimacy of claim over an entitlement is called *bukenji*. One could speak of *bukenji bwa kwa Maweja* referring to such man's rights from creation. To each statement of innocence above there is a corresponding natural right one can claim:

Chapter 7

Table 7: *Statements of Innocence and Corresponding Natural Rights*

Statements of Innocence	Corresponding Natural Rights
1—I have not killed anyone.	1—The right to life.
2—I have not assaulted anyone.	2—The right to physical integrity
3—I have not denied food to anyone.	3—The right to food
4—I have not slandered anyone.	4—The right to human dignity
5—I have not humiliated my elders.	5--The right to one's juniors' respect
6—I have not refused to pay the first fruits	6—Elders' right to their juniors' tributes of first fruits
7—I have not committed incest or any indecent act toward a family member	7—The right to relatives' respect for one's sanctity
8—I have not taken another man's wife.	8—The exclusive right to intimacy with one's spouse
9—I have not molested anyone's child.	9—The right to preserve one' virginity until marriage
10—I have not stolen anyone's property.	10—Sovereignty right over one's property
11—I have not erected barriers on public roads.	11—The right to freedom of movement in public places

Sacred Natural Rights Explained

1&2. Rights to Life and to Physical Integrity: Human life is the most sacred value on Earth. Every human being has the right to full life, to physical integrity, and to human dignity. Respect for an individual's physical integrity is perhaps the topmost moral principle. Noone has the right to take away or undermine someone's life, not even one's own. Killing, beating, torture and even suicide are violations.

3. Right to Food: Food is essential to life and physical integrity. Food deprivation imposes suffering on the body and diminishes life. Instead, sharing food is expected of all. Men in Luba villages eat from common bowls, sitting on chairs or stools, or squatting, in a location where passersby can see them and eventually join the circle. To encourage them to do so, someone from among the partakers would yell in their direction saying:

Maja a kabuta, mwanyisha wavwa kuja.

This statement means: "Eating is like a nightjar dance, he who wishes is welcome to join the circle any time." In Luba mentality, there is no meal too small to be shared with at least one relative. That sharing food is expected from everyone is expressed in the saying:

Byadima umwa, Byadya bangi.
Literally: "Cultivated by one, but consumed by many."

The obligation to share food binds the invitee as well. Turning down an invitation to eat while the food is being served in one's presence is asocial. It amounts to telling the person who is offering the food: "When you come to my place, do not eat even if you are invited to." Even more damaging, it is equivalent to wishing *cishoto* to the person offering the food. *Cishoto* is the curse of failure in food production activities such as hunting, fishing, trap setting or commercial transactions.

The obligation to share food extends to ancestral spirits. In Luba tradition, ancestral veneration consists in most time of sacrifices of chickens or goats made to ancestors at special family occasions for the purpose of sharing the enjoyments associated with said occasions with departed relatives. Each Luba man is obligated to share the joys of family blessings such as the birth of a child, a daughter's marriage, or the release of a brother from prison with the spirits of his paternal grandfather, his father, and his paternal grandmother. The specific ancestor to whom a particular sacrifice is made is supposed to share it with his or her peers. For example, in presenting sacrifices to the spirit of the father, the invitation to accept the sacrifice and pour out the expected blessings is addressed to the father and all fathers. Likewise, in sacrifices to the spirit of the grandfather, the latter and all other grandfathers are invited to respond favorably.

4&5. Right to Human Dignity and Respect by One's Juniors. Every human being deserves to be treated with dignity. Humiliation, calumny, slander, and vilification are infringements on the human value in the individual. Such acts must be avoided. Violations will sooner or later bring some misfortune upon the offender, his family or his undertakings. Close to the right to human dignity is the right to respect by one's juniors. A person's senior status and the respect it commands are innate prerogatives. Violations offend not only the individual who endures them, but also the Creator who instituted eldership, and the ancestors whom that senior represents among the living.

6. The Right to One's Juniors' Tributes of the First Fruits: A man's power to work and accomplishments therefrom are gifts from God made possible by ancestors' intercession on his behalf. He owes to these spiritual benefactors, through the family elder who represents them among the living, the first fruits from his labor. The Luba live off agriculture. It is expected that with revenues from farming one would raise goats and that over time farming and goat raising would enable him to unite sufficient income for bridewealth. The family law requires that he pay tributes of first fruits with the first crops, first goat and first wife acquired through his labor. At each stage the receiving elder would ritually appropriate the gifts, present them and offer sacrifices of roosters to ancestors. The ability to procreate is another gift from divine creation received through ancestral mediation of which accomplishments are subject to the rule of first fruits. Each Luba man owes his ancestors through their living representative elder the bridewealth from his first daughter's marriage (tribute to the grandfather) and his second daughter's marriage (tribute to the father). The tributes received by the elder on behalf of ancestors are not necessarily his to use as he sees fit. He returns the junior's bride received in tribute to him and uses the bridewealth from his juniors' daughters' marriages to procure wives from male family members in their order of seniority.

7&8&9. Right to the Integrity of One's Sexual Sacredness: A woman's body is sacred. Her intimate life is strictly sacred. Access is reserved to the authorized individual in appropriate time and circumstances according to accepted community moral standards (Mbiti, 1970). Intimacy with a married woman is an exclusive prerogative of the legitimate husband. All other men must abstain. A minor's entire body is sacred. Her virginity is even more so. It must be kept intact and respected until marriage. Sexual intercourse with a virgin minor before marriage is malicious, ignominious, and condemned as child rapechild molestation (*kunyanga mwana*). One's relatives' sexual life is a sacred *taboo*. Incestuous relations are condemned. Among the Luba, multiple circles of kinship identify large ranges of relatives among whom sexual relations are considered incestuous. The Luba are patrilineal. For a particular individual the smallest circle of close relatives is the patrilineal extended family, that is, all the descendants of Ego's grandfather all the way down to the generation of Ego's great grandchildren. Members of this circle are identifiable by specific kinship terms denoting generation distances among them in relation to Ego. This same prohibition of sexual relations among members applies to the extended family from the mother's side. Ego's sexual relations with a member of either of these two descent groups is prohibited as incestuous. The Ciluba word for incestuous relations is *bibindi*. However, this concept encompasses more than actual sexual relations or lustful desires, looks, or touching. It includes engaging in sexual acts, legitimate or illegitimate, in one's parents' home, even in their absence. Parents having sexual relations in their son's or daughter's home is even more abominable. Language or gestures alluding to sex, revealing or provocative dress in presence of parents are *bibindi*. They are even unimaginable *bibindi* if perpetrated by parents in their children's presence. An outer, larger circle of unmarriageable relatives encompasses a number of like extended families tracing descent from a common ancestor identified as the founder of the clan, *dîku*. Each person is biologically related to the father's *dîku* and to the mother's *dîku*. Sexual relations and marriage with a member of one's father's clan or one's mother's clan are prohibited (Mukenge, 1967).

10. Sovereignty Rights over One's Property: Material things can be possessed individually. A house belongs to the individual who built it, or for whom it was built, or else to whom it has been legitimately transferred. Products of a person's work belong to him or her. A person's possessions are other people's *bijila*, restraints. All other individuals must abstain from appropriating them unless authorized by the owner.

> *Wateeka cyanza pa keeba, pa kabenda wkeba diyoyo.*
> Only put your hand on what is yours, taking another person's property will put you in trouble.

Violations of property rights, such as stealing, robbery, and physical destruction are morally condemnable. They cause prejudice to the being of the owner by taking away something that contributes to his or her self. They are prohibited even among relatives.

> *Kantu kalengela kweba ku nzadi, kwambi ne kadi kwa mwanetu nkangata.*
> Only count on the property in your own hands, not on that in your brother's.

11. Right of Access to Public Places. Access to public places is everyone's inalienable natural right. The Luba society recognizes three kinds of collective property: the road, the market place, and ancestral lands. The road belongs to everyone. Market places belong to the chiefdom. They are open to everyone under the supervision of chief's appointed supervisors. Chiefdom's lands belong to its constitutive lineages. Lineage members have free access to lineage lands by birth right. Non-members must secure permission from authorized members. The road, marketplaces and ancestral lands, including forests and rivers, are inalienable. Traditionally, they could not be the object of a commercial transaction. Neither did they fit the notion of being vulnerable to theft (Kalanda, 1992). In brief, freedom of movement is a natural right. Luba morality prohibits denying someone access to public places.

2. SUBJECT TO MORAL RESTRAINTS

Moral Restraints
(Bijila: pronounced: Bee-jee-lah)

One's sacred natural rights are sacred moral restraints (*bijila*) for others. Africans across the continent believe in the existence of an ethical order given by God that regulates interpersonal relations in the family and the community and between the living and the dead. The ethical order is expressed through laws, rules, customs, traditions and taboos that identify and set boundaries between right and wrong. Moral values are instilled through initiation ceremonies, stories, proverbs, and wise sayings. Through teaching, monitoring and sanctioning moral principles, the individual is very much exposed to the community and anonymity is almost impossible. Moral restraint is thus prohibition of what African Religion expresses by the concept of "wrongdoing", "badness", or "destruction of life", to use Laurenti Magesa's terminology. A generic term for moral restraints is taboos. Taboos may relate to certain persons, things, acts, or situations (Mbiti, 1970; Magesa 1997, quoting Hutton Webster). Examples include:

Persons: **Mother-in-law:** The mother of the bride is a special-category parent to the groom. Physical proximity with one's mother whose violation would approximate incest is even exaggerated with the in-law. In Luba custom, the marriage alliance is concluded in the bride's family. It is then that the groom and the mother–in-law would meet face to face and look at each other. Thereafter they would avoid close proximity and looking at each other.

Chief or King: Due to his association with the spirits of past rulers through investiture ceremonies, the chief or king becomes a sacred, therefore, taboo person. Usually, ordinary people do not touch him. His food is cooked separately; his death handled differently and secretly by authorized dignitaries only.

Things: *Bakishi,* male ancestors' shrines; *cikusukusu*, the sacred tree that houses the female guardian spirit *Nkambwa;* and the horn or pot that contains healing medicine and into which the spirit of good health has been invited to dwell are sacred, therefore, taboo objects to everyone, except special individuals qualified and authorized to handle them. Sacred also are the chiefs' or kings' majestic stool or chair, and ornaments. Ordinary people do not touch them.

Acts: eating the meat of one's clan's totemic animal, committing rape or adultery, assaulting or killing someone are all prohibited and morally abhorred.

Situations: A chief's or king's death is a sacred situation. No hunting operations can be carried out on the kingdom's lands before the official burial and mourning period closure. The senior wife is entitled to handle sacred objects and cook sacred meals. Handling sacred objects or cooking sacred meal during her periods is a major taboo. Even a more stringent taboo is for any man to have a sexual intercourse with a menstruating woman.

3. ACCOUNTABLE FOR MORAL TRANSGRESSIONS

Moral Transgressions
(Bibawu: pronounced: Bee-bah-woo)

A moral transgression or moral offense is a behavior that breaches the boundaries between right and wrong as defined by one's society's moral code. Behaviors such as disrespect and rudeness towards elders, murder, stealing, robbery, telling lies, deliberately causing bodily or property harm are moral violations. Also, morally reproachable are sexual improprieties such as incest, rape, adultery, and intercourse with children or with a person of the same sex. Disrespect to persons of higher status is a moral transgression also (Mbiti, 1970). These violations are sanctioned as moral transgressions (*bibawu*). The corresponding transgressions to the above moral restraints are:

1—Attempting to take someone's life, with or without success
2—Assaulting someone
3—Denying someone food
4—Slander, denying an individual's right to human dignity
5—Humiliating an elder
6—Refusing to pay the tributes of the first fruits
7—Breaking the incest taboo
8—Taking someone else's wife
9—Molesting a child
10—Taking someone's property
11—Denying someone access to public places

Violations of life can be physical or mystical. A physical violation involves an actual contact, direct or mediated by an instrument, between the aggressor and the victim. Inflicting suffering on somebody through beatings or injuries is a physical violation of that person's being. Human blood channels the divine principle throughout the body, thus making it sacred. Consequently, blood effusion desecrates the divine in the victim and diminishes his or her vitality. Luba morality condemns such acts. Mystical violations are affected without any actual physical contact. They are the work of individuals who can control supernatural powers of some sort. These violations include not only physical harms such as murder and bodily harm, but also mystical harm by sorcery or witchcraft.

Sanctions, Punishment
(Dinyoka: pronounced: Dee-ño-ka)

The breaching of the ethical order calls for punishment, not only by the community of the living, but also by the ancestors and God. The community of the living punishes immoral acts by having the perpetrator or his family suffer shame or pay fines, by ostracism (banning from the community), or by beating. In the past the violator could even be stoned or burned to death depending on the gravity of the offense. Morality therefore, belongs to the public domain. It is normative that moral transgressions be treated in public. The Luba people say in this respect:

"*Muntu wa cilema tumubelela pa bantu*"
"Always counsel a wrongdoer publicly"

In situations of theft, stolen goods must be restituted. An unknown thief will be caught one day or will experience some misfortune sooner or later. In general, thefts were dealt with severely and swiftly. Adultery was once punished very severely. Violators were subjected to severe beatings. They could be beaten to death, especially when caught in the act. In other circumstances, the woman could have her life spared, and then she was repudiated. The man, if not killed, could be emasculated through a process called *kwela lusala*, which consisted of plunging a feather into the spermatic canal and straining out the sperm content and, with it, the ability to experience an erection. When not caught in action, he was tried in the chief's court and sentenced to pay *bibawu*, fines. If the husband repudiated the wife, the accomplice in adultery could be forced by her relatives to marry her. Nowadays, divorce is practically the only punishment for adultery still in effect (Kalanda, 1992).

Fines, Redress
(Bibawu: pronounced: Bee-bah-woo)

In *Ciluba,* Luba peoples' language, the term *bibawu* applies both to transgressions and to the fines to repair them. Redress is the correction or reparation of the wrongful act, such as restitution in case of theft or recalling disrespectful words and apologizing in case of disrespect toward an elder. Higher level violations, such as the theft of a goat or adultery require the intervention of public authorities such as the chief or the judge. Family violations generally involve the ancestral spirits both as members of the offended party and the redressers of the wrongful act. In such a case, fines include chicken or goat sacrifices depending on the magnitude of the violation.

Respect for seniority is a major norm. Luba parents teach their children to love one another. They tell the older ones to protect the younger ones and the latter to respect the former. They assign the children tasks whose execution requires knowledge and respect for age hierarchy. In Luba families, people eat the starch *nshima* and the accompanying vegetables from a common calabash bowl or wooden bowl, but they distribute the meat, a rare commodity in the Luba territory. The ethic that regulates eating habits requires that meat be consumed parsimoniously (*kulobelela*). The seniority principle requires that the portions served to elders be proportionately larger than those to their juniors, but that everyone be served equitably. At the time of meal, the parents may assign a child to distribute the meat. Gradually children learn to apply the expected rules of sharing with mastery.

As children grow in age, the parents make them understand that respect for the elders is demanded by the ancestors. Persons who humiliate their elders by insulting or beating them offend not only the humiliated elder and other living elders, but also the Creator who instituted the hierarchy between seniors and juniors and the ancestors who continue to live among the living as invisible family elders. They must repair their violations in words and in deeds. Among other things, they must acknowledge their wrongdoings in front of the ancestral shrines, reiterate and withdraw their words of violation, and offer reconciliation sacrifices to the ancestral spirits. Without reparation and reconciliation, some misfortune will befall the violators sooner or later that will be seen as the punishment for their failure to repair violations of the required respect for elders.

Supernatural Sanctions
(Bibawu bya ku Bakishi: pronounced: Bee-bah-woo byah koo Bah-kee-shee)

In the Bantu conception of human integrity, violations of a person's natural rights are major infringements on life. They constitute attacks on the life force, the victim's life-sustaining principle. Therefore, through violations and because of violations, life is diminished due to the fact that every physical or spiritual injury to the individual adversely impacts the life force, that is, the victim's being. Any injustice to God's supreme gift that the life force represents calls for reparation commensurate with its importance. In African religion, reparations for violations of human integrity are not limited to legal and other social sanctions. They involve supernatural sanctions (*bibawu bya ku Bakishi*) that sooner or later will be administered by the ancestral spirits on the perpetrator, his family, or his undertakings. The ancestral spirits send bad dreams as warnings or deterrents and punish the offenders by causing sickness and failure in undertakings. From time to time, God punishes the whole community for collective and severe moral offenses and offenses by the leaders by sending calamities such as epidemics, drought, war, and famine. Supernatural punishments, such as lightning, could be used against the criminal. Here, the chief of the perpetrator's lineage would give some white clay, *lupemba*, the Luba equivalent of a "green light", to *Notable Ntite*, highest authority in the chiefdom, second only to the chief. The *Ntite* controls lightning. In case of adultery, the *Ntite*, after receiving the *lupemba*, passes it over to the chief or the offended husband's village to obtain a green light. At the time of lightning, the man would have his sex cut off (Tempels, 1965, Mulago, 1991, Mbiti, 1970, Kalanda, 1992).

Moral Imprecations

Violations of a person's innate sacred rights desecrate the divine in that person, offend the Creator, call for ancestral sanctions, and confer to the victimized person the moral authority and power to utter words of imprecation capable of causing harm to the perpetrator, his property or even his progeny (Kalanda, 1992).

Mucipu (Moo 'chi-poo). A typical example of words that are imbued with supernatural powers is what the Luba call *mucipu*, a noun derived from verb *kucipa*, to curse. The *mucipu* is uttered by an individual who is besieged by the feeling of having been wronged in the exercise of some natural right socially acknowledged to him or her. Such feeling is so damaging that the person experiences *kanyinganyinga* (deep-seated, depressing anger), or *dijita* (an urge to take revenge by the most destructive means available). The violated natural right is the justification for the uttering of the *mucipu* and for the latter to produce the intended supernatural effect on the violator. The *mucipu* curse is stated in a conditional, if-then, form. For example, parents have authority over their children by divine and ancestral right. By this right, they have a claim over their children for respect and obedience. A father who has been gravely humiliated by a son may say: "So and So, you have humiliated me so badly. If, as your father, I deserve your respect, then, let misery fall upon you." On the other hand, parents have the obligation to love their children and care for them. A child who has been mistreated by the father or the mother may utter an imprecation that can have damaging effects on the mother or the father at whom the *mucipu* is targeted. The victimized child may say: "If, as your son or daughter I deserve the love that you have denied me, let you never love any living child of yours." An innocent person who has been victimized can speak likewise to the victimizer. He would say: "If I am guilty, let death strike me. But if I am innocent, let you die with your eyes wide open" (*meesu matonona*). Sometimes, a conditional *mucipu* is directed at self. A person who takes a public oath, would say, for instance, "Let death fall on me if I break this oath" (Kalanda, 1992).

Mulawu (Moolawoo). Whereas *mucipu* is enunciated in conditional form, *mulawu*, a close form of curse, is stated affirmatively at the presumed culprit. A *mulawu* target can redeem himself or herself by repairing the wrongdoing blamed on him or her. Reparation preempts the effect of the curse. This reparation-reconciliation always includes recognition of the wrongdoing and payment of some fines by the person seeking redemption. It also includes recall of the cursing words by their author and a sacrifice of chickens or goats to the ancestral spirits provided by both parties. The sacrifices are designed to undo on the supernatural plane the separation created between the two parties on the human plane. If the person who pronounced the curse dies before reconciliation takes place, a relative of the same kinship status will substitute for the dead person in quality of father, mother, or older sibling, according to the case, regardless of his or her sex. For example, a maternal uncle can stand in for the mother and a paternal aunt for the father (Kalanda, 1992).

Chapter 7
4. ADDRESSING MORAL VIOLATIONS: ILLUSTRATIONS

Sung Complaints or Condemnations

Taatu Wambilee. The one example hereafter is taken from the Kanyok of the Congo DRC. It tells of a slave entrusted with the orphaned son of his deceased master. On the way to taking the boy to a relative who was living in a distant village, as instructed by the master before his death, the slave decides to abandon him alone by the river stripped of his clothes, thumb piano, and walking cane. He proceeds to the village where he presents himself as the chief's son. He is welcomed with fanfare by the whole village. The abandoned son, since he had no clothes on, waited for the night to come before walking into the village. He does so while singing the song below, which I learned in my youth as part of the audience in gatherings around the evening camp fire. The song tells the story with detailed descriptions of the thumb piano and the walking cane. The young man arrives while the villagers were singing and dancing around a big fire in honor of the imposter. The story and the descriptions were so moving and so convincing that the villagers arrested the imposter, clothed the boy, and organized an even bigger feast in his honor. Here is the song:

Taatu wambil ee, Kabungam!.	*Dya lufu kunkwat ee, Kabungam.*
My father to say: O'Kabungam!	When I die, O' Kabungam!
Waya kw'Itond ee, Kabungam!	*Ki kudi mwanenu ee, Kabungam!*
Go to *Itond*, O Kabungam!	There lives your kinsman, O Kabungam!
Twabuk Yabuy ee, Kabungam!	*Kahik ne cibengu ee, Kabungam!*
At crossing the *Yabuy*, O'Kabungam!	The audacious servant, O' Kabungam!
Kamfula bivwalu ee, Kabungam!	*Cisanj'a matumb ee Kabungam*
To take away my clothes, O' Kabungam!	My loud-sounding thumb piano, O'Kabungam!
Ne dikombo dya mizel ee, Kabungam!	And my metal-decorated walking cane.

When this song is sung in a gathering, *Kabungam* is the response by the audience. The statement before *Kabungam* is the call by the leader. Note that the call ends with "ee", pronounced long "a" like in paste, made, or fame. Its role is simply to add melody to the call.

Ngabidiela and Zelemani, Noel and Wanga. Some songs accompanying young people's evening games convey moralizing messages. The Congolese writer Batukezanga Zamenga relates two stories from game songs of his youth which criticized community members who had secretly engaged in forbidden activities, thinking no one would know about it. One song talks about *Ngabidiela* and *Zelemani*, who had tested jackal meat in secret. This meat is forbidden, as the jackal is identified as wild dog. Their excuse was that the jackal is not really a dog, since the dog is domesticated while the jackal lives in the wilderness. The song reminded them that a dog is a dog whether it is domestic or wild. The other song denounced two boys, *Noel* and *Wanga,* who had stolen a big rooster and were caught busy cooking it in the forest. They pretended it was an eagle. The song confronted them with two undeniable facts: one, the feathers of the two birds are different; two, even if their bird were an eagle, the forest is not the place humans cook and eat their game meat. Humans cook and eat their food in the village, not in the wilderness (Batukezanga, 1999).

Mwa Cizenzenzebele. Luba youth sung a story of thievery involving a plucked bird with no tail. The perpetrator, *Cizenzebele*, had set traps in the wilderness to catch birds. One day, he had no luck at all. On the way back, he saw someone else's trap with an ostrich in captivity. He took the bird, plucked it, cut off the tail, and hid the feathers and the tail underneath some bush. Back at home, he told his mother, *Mwa-Cizenzebele,* which means *Mother of Cizemnzebele,* that he had purchased the bird just like that from the marketplace. The mother was skeptical; she did not cook the wonder bird right away. The trap that had captured the ostrich happened to have been set by a ghost. Shortly after, they heard a singing voice from nowhere saying:

Mwa Cizenzenzebele,	Mother of *Cizenzenzebele*
Mwa Cizenzenzebele,	Mother of *Cizenzenzebele*
Mwa-Cizenzenzebele	Oh! Mother of *Cizenzenzebele*
Ambilanu mmwaneba	Tell your son
atwalanu ntubanyi.	to return my ostrich.
Ntuba uvwa ne mulundu.	The ostrich had a tail and feathers

They went out, looked around, but saw no one. Once inside the house, they heard again:

Mwa Cizenzenzebele,	Mother of *Cizenzenzebele*
Mwa Cizenzenzebele,	Mother *of Cizenzenzebele*
Mwa-Cizenzenzebele	Oh! Mother of *Cizenzenzebele*
Ambilanu mmwaneba	Tell your son
atwalanu ntubanyi.	to return my ostrich.
Ntuba uvwa ne mulundu.	The ostrich had a tail and feathers.

The mother and the community confronted *Cizenzenzebele*. He finally told the truth after lying repeatedly. People accompanied him to the place where he had hidden the tail and the feathers. They took them to the trap, and deposited the bird, the tail, and the feathers into the trap. They went back home, performed expiation rituals and returned to normal life.

Chapter 7
In the Land of the Dead: A Legend to Discourage Theft

The Kalutshi and Kapongo Legend was told to the youth in Songye villages, in *Congo DRC*, to discourage laziness and thievery. It warned people of after-death torments awaiting perpetrators of social and moral offenses as explained in the title, "in the land of the dead." This is the story of an individual called *Kalutshi*, who had been stealing people's crops and other property. Each time he would escape earthly justice by practicing magic. Finally, he was expelled from the village after a boy testified that he had seen him stealing a chicken. He went into the forest. There, a voice called him, asking him to come closer. He did so, but all he saw was a big tree standing in the pathway. It had a large hole on the trunk near the base. The voice invited him into the hole, which proved to be the tunnel that led to the village of the dead. The village was vast. *Kalutshi* found all the people from the village who had died over the years, including his mother, father, and brother. All were very short. Their hair fell down to their shoulders. Their feet were reversed, that is, with the heels in the front and the toes in the back.

The mother served him beetles and warms, but he did not touch them. The mother told him: "That is what people eat over here." The mother told him she had to hide him since the people in the land of the dead did not like the living. At night, the mother hid *Kalutshi* in a pit, under a mat. Later, the father returned home. He was very small, his feet were reversed, and his hair was very long. The father sat on the mat, just on *Kalutshi*'s neck. *Kalutshi* thought he was going to die of discomfort, but the father did not get up. The mother murmured to *Kalutshi*, warning him that he would be killed if he cried. After a while, the father stepped out. The mother quickly put *Kalutshi* in a basket and hid him in the attic and again warned him against crying, saying that he would be finished if he did.

The father came back and lit the fire. The smoke drifted up into *Kalutshi*'s eyes. *Kalutshi* began groaning: "I cannot stand it anymore. I am dying, I really cannot stand it, I am dying." The father brought the neighbors over. They searched and found *Kalutshi* hiding in a basket in the attic. When *Kalutshi* came down, his father asked him: "Who hid you?" *Kalutshi* said: "My mother did." The father convened everybody in the village. The full number gathered. They were all very small, and they all wore long hair, falling down to the shoulders. All had feet with the toes in the back and the heels in the front. They grabbed *Kalutshi* and killed him. They told the mother to go way. For hiding someone who had committed crimes against the community, her place was no longer among them, so they expelled her.

The mother left, heading toward her former village among the living. However, everyone who saw her ran away, including her surviving son, *Kitenga*. People were scared by her appearance. She was very old and excessively short. She had long hair and her heel where her toes should be. They panicked, ran away, and deserted the village. To make things worse, a torrential rain began to fall. It took away everything: houses, banana trees, and fields. *Kalutshi*'s mother arrived at the site of the village, but it had disappeared completely. She became an errant spirit (Frobenius, 1983).

The Power of Imprecation

In 1998, a Luba man who lives in the United States sent some money to relatives in *Eastern Kasai, Congo-Kinshasa*. They were internally displaced and had been expelled from *Katanga Province* during the 1992-1993 ethnic cleansing of the *Kasaians*. The money was sent with specifications regarding the receivers and the amounts. In 1999, the sender received a letter informing him that the money had caused divisions within the family. His cousins were not speaking to his brother any more. Reportedly, the brother, who is the eldest living member of the extended family, ignored the instructions and used the money to buy himself a house and some goats to raise. Not surprisingly, the other would-be beneficiaries were infuriated. The one next in age to the person who had misappropriated the money uttered a *mucipu* at the culpable one saying: "If all the money invested in your house and goats was destined for your exclusive use, live in peace. But if any portion of it was meant to be mine and you have arbitrarily taken it away from me, let the house and the goats perish." At some point after the curse, according to the letter, the house crumbled and the goats died.

Violations of Seniority Rights

Beating and verbal abuse of one's senior are among the most commonly recognized forms of disrespect to be avoided. Below are two eye-witness stories to illustrate how such disrespect is dealt with when it occurs. *Mukenga Mudiabuloba* and his two younger brothers, *Ngoyi Tantamika* and *Kapiamba Binunu*, were very close. Whenever one moved to a distant place to stay, the other two would join him. But one night, when they were living in *Tshamba*, a village between *Luputa* and *Tielen St. Jacques Mission Station*, the two brothers had a fight. *Mukenga Mudiabuloba* intervened in favor of the older of the two, *Ngoyi Tantamika,* by throwing the younger brother, *Kapiamba Binunu*, to the ground. That was the end of the fight. Thus, by respect for him as an elder, the two brothers stopped fighting the moment he ordered them. Furthermore, the next morning, the younger of the belligerents paid a goat to the older one for hitting him. The goat was sacrificed to the ancestors to repair his violation on the spiritual level.

The other example shows how respect for older family members is extended to non-family older people. It involves a third grader, *Tshifwa Bubela*, his younger sister Kabedi, and a by-passer adult called *Mutombo*. One day, *Tshifwa Bubela* had a fight with the younger sister, *Kabedi*. He fled to the back of the house. *Kabedi* was recalcitrant. She kept following him to continue the fight. It was around noon. A certain adult man called *Mutombo*, who was living up the street, passed by on his way from work. He slapped *Tshifwa Bubela* to stop him from beating his sister. The boy seized him by his shirt, in protest. As *Mutombo* was trying to take the boy's hands off his body, *Tshoba*, the older sister with whom both *Kabedi* and *Tshifwa Bubela* were staying, heard the noise and came to separate them. The incident occurred in *Luputa*, a town along the Port-*Franqui-Katanga-Dilolo* railroad. It rained that night. Three young men from *Mwene-Ditu*, another town along the railroad, who were visiting a relative of theirs in *Tshifwa Bubela*'s neighborhood, got fatally struck by lightning. When the news spread out the next morning, *Tshifwa Bubela* went to see them. The popular explanation for their death was that they had beaten up an older man. *Tshifwa Bubela* got very scared. Around noontime, he went to wait along the street, behind the house, until *Mutombo* passed. *Tshifwa Bubela* greeted him nicely, and he responded with a smile. The boy was relieved. Thus, among the Luba, the respect that is expected of younger relatives for their elders is extended to all adults. Violations are believed to always mystically provoke some punishment sooner or later, unless immediately repaired and some form of reconciliation is achieved.

SUMMARY

The human being is an embodiment of divine properties. Every person possesses qualities of being that are similar to God's qualities even though less perfect than God's. By virtue of a person's human nature, that person is endowed with inalienable sacred natural rights which put moral restraints on the community's or any individual's behaviors toward him or her. Moral restraints are inscribed in one's conscience through conception in a latent state and reinforced in life through socialization mechanisms by the family and the community or loyalty pacts between friends, neighbors or political allies. On an individual basis, moral restraints are often reactivated through confrontation by a third party or self-examination in life-threatening situations. From the Luba moral code, we have identified eleven moral restraints, as well as the social sanctions for violating them. These can be material sanctions such as corporal punishment, imprisonment or fines. They can also be mystical like imprecations and witchcraft.

(Endnotes)
1   Mbiti, John. ND. "General Manifestations of African Religiosity." An Exploratory Paper at the meeting of the Standing Committee on The Contribution of Africa to the Religious Heritage of the World. http://www.afrikaworld.net/afrel/mbiti.htm. Retrieved 8/8/2007.

Chapter 8
A Family–Kinship Community Builder

1. The Individual and the Community
2. The Family Community
3. The Kinship Community

Community building is traceable to divine creation. Historically, Africans have built communities on the basis of marriage alliances, the kinship bond, collective sacred rituals, and nationalistic control policies. This chapter elaborates on community building as a natural phenomenon in African culture, specifically the family community and the kinship community.

1. THE INDIVIDUAL AND THE COMMUNITY

Divine Creation and the Making of the Human Community

The roots of the human community are embedded in the creation process. In many instances, God created communities rather than isolated individuals, as can be seen in the creation myths presented in this chapter, of the Mande of Mali, the Yorùbá of Nigeria, and the Luba of the Congo DRC.

The Creation Myth of the Mande: Take the case of the myth of the Mende of Mali who claim descent from King Sundiata Keita of the 13th century AD. According to the story, *Mangala*, God, began creation with a seed. God rejected it in favor of two new twin varieties of seeds, to which God subsequently added six more, bringing the number of seeds to eight. Each pair was comprised of a male seed and a female seed. *Mangala* then organized the eight seeds in the form of the cardinal directions reflecting the world formed of a pair of twin seeds of opposite sex in each corner. Afterwards, *Mangala* placed the whole configuration in a single seed, the egg of God or egg of the world, the conception womb of the world, containing two previous pairs of twin seeds, with a male seed and female seed in each. *Pemba*, one of the eight male seeds, broke off the egg prematurely and descended on a piece of the placenta, which became Planet Earth where it stopped. *Pemba* did not break off alone; he took along eight males seeds from the same placenta of the world. He planted them in the Earth (the fallen piece of the womb of the world in which he was conceived), thereby impregnating his own mother, an incestuous act. The Earth, the fields, and the harvest became impure. To purify the world, *Mangala,* God, sacrificed *Faro*, one of the two initial male seeds in the womb of the world, prior to the arrival of the eight, by cutting him into 60 pieces and scattering them all over the world. Later*, Mangala* resurrected *Faro* and sent him to Earth on top of an arc along with the eight female seeds that remained in the womb when *Pemba* stole the eight male partners, as well as the ancestors of the four pairs of twins from the cardinal points. The place where the arc landed came to be called *Mande*. While still in the sky, *Faro* had the form of twin fish called *mannogo,* which now pullulate in the

Niger River. Faro's descent to the Earth was followed by the creation of the rain, the construction of the first altar, the revelation of the word, and the planting of the eight female seeds from the egg of the world in a special field around the altar. *Faro* caused inundations to invade the fields where *Pemba*'s sister, *Mousso Koroni*, had planted the seeds. *Mannogo* fish swallowed the seeds and turned them over to the altar. The inundations caused by Faro became the *Niger River*, which represents Faro's body, with *Lake Lebo* as the head. Humans in the same *Mande-Dogon* story, were created as a community also. Humans were created by *Amma*, God, through the combined mouth of the *Nummo* twins, a male and a female. By the power of His speech, *Amma* created seven professionals with complementary skills and the ability to articulate language for the express purpose of enabling them to communicate meanings, another necessary ingredient in making the human community effective. From among the seven were the tanner, the weaver, the blacksmith, and the teacher and speech maker (Dieterlen 1957, 1955; Carruthers 1995).

The Yorùbá story: In the Yorùbá creation myth, even the very act of creation was a cooperative undertaking. The Creator, *Olódùmarè,* assigned Arch-Divinity *Òrìṣà-Nlá* the mission to complete the creation of Earth that *Olódùmarè* himself had started. *Òrìṣà-Nlá* would drop loose soil from a packet on a pre-created marshy wetland. Along with *Òrìṣà-Nlá* , the Creator sent the hen and the pigeon to assist *Òrìṣà-Nlá* by spreading the loose soil over the marshy land. Upon their return, *Olódùmarè* sent the chameleon to inspect the work. Chameleon's report was praiseworthy. *Olódùmarè*, then sent *Òrìṣà-Nlá* on a second Earth-creation mission. This time he would be carrying a palm tree for the humans to grow as a source of food, oil, wine, and clothing. *Olódùmarè* further instructed *Òrìṣà-Nlá* to carry along lagoons that would serve as permanent water reservoirs. *Òrìṣà-Nlá's* last assignment was to build the physical structure into which *Olódùmarè* himself would blow the divine breath of life to create the human being. All throughout the aforementioned creation processes, *Òrìṣà-Nlá* was receiving spiritual advice from Divinity *Òrunmìlà.* Finally, to people of the Earth, *Olódùmarè* dispatched *Orèlúéré*, another of his divinities, with a party of heavenly hosts who became the first human beings on Planet Earth. Creation stories also state that the Creator gave humans rules and instructions to live by as communities. Indeed, moral restraints and obligations considered as presents from God conspicuously converge toward strengthening life in community. Community building is thus for humans a life goal instituted by the Creator (Idowu 1994, Mbiti 1970).

The Idea of Community in the Luba Story: Creator *Maweja Nangila* first metamorphosed self into three Lord Spirits: *Maweja Nangila* (Self), *Maweja wa Cyama*, Firstborn Son, and *Maweja Cyama*, First Lady. Thereafter, *Maweja Nangila* created *Mulopo Maweja*, the Emissary Spirit. *Mulopo Maweja* rebelled against the Creator and was expelled from the Sky of the Summit, abode of the Creator and Lord Spirits, of which the sky that we see is only a reflection. *Maweja Nangila* then created superior spirits in groups of four, each time four seniors and four juniors. These spirits and the celestial bodies - Sun, Moon, stars - *Maweja Nangilla* created them and placed them where they are all by Self. As to other creations, *Maweja Nangila* created them with the collaboration of the Son and the First Lady. He made them in pairs of two, each one comprised of a senior element and a junior element. As *Maweja Nangila* created them, the Son ordered them, as a firstborn son is expected to put in order and organize his father's property; and the First Lady took them into care, nurturing them and multiplying them, as a first lady is supposed to care for the family property (Morlighem and Fourche 1973, Mudimbe 1991, Kalanda 1992).

The Individual and the Community in African Philosophy of Life

Joseph Mbiti qualifies the basic philosophy of life in Africa as one based on the principle "I am because we are." Because of this philosophy, the person is the center of existence, not as an individual, but as family, as community. There is a community dimension to practically everything people do in pursuit of individual destiny. In Kongo cosmology, at creation, the human-being emerged endowed with many potentials, including the potential to grow, develop, mature and achieve a great many things in multiple fields of life, including becoming a strong community pillar, well-willed and helpful community member, a community healer, leader, and agent of justice (Fu-Kiau, 2001).

Descent is the most pervasive community organizing principle. Chanoine Mulago expresses this reality in the following terms:

> The fact that we are born into a family, a clan, a tribe immerses us in a specific current of life, "incorporates" us and molds us to the fashion of that community; it modifies all our being "ontically" and orients us to living and behaving in the manner of that community (Mulago, in Olupona 1991).

This individual-community togetherness is symbolized by the circle in the houses, in dancing, in singing, and in having meals in circle. The African community is to be seen under two aspects: as a community of blood, a primordial element; as well as a community of property that concomitantly makes life possible. In the latter respect, community refers to communal ownership of ancestral lands which is common to African traditions across the continent.

2. THE FAMILY COMMUNITY

Marriage

A Divine Institution: In various African traditions, God instituted marriage by His very acts of creation. In some instances, He created a couple made of a male and a female. Such was the case for the Lugbara of Uganda and the Mende of Sierra Leone. Likewise, the Abaluyia of Uganda say that God created the husband first and then the wife so the man could have someone to talk to. In the case of the Ekoi of Nigeria, *Obassi Osaw*, God, made a man and a woman and placed them upon the Earth. In the story of the Fong of Gabon, God made man a participant in the creation of the woman. They say that *Nzame*, God, created the first man, *Fam*. He did not live long. He died in punishment for becoming too arrogant and refusing to worship *Nzame*. *Nzame* then created a second man, *Sekume,* whom he ordered to make himself a wife from a tree. *Sekume* made wife his *Mbongwe*. In still other stories, God sent an already created woman to an already existing man. According to the Wakaranga of Zimbabwe, for instance, the first man, *Moon*, became very unhappy from living alone. He wept and wept. In consolation, God sent him *Morningstar* to live with him for two years as his wife. At the conclusion of the two year period, God sent *Morningstar* to live in the sky. *Moon* wept and wept again. God gave him *Eveningstar* as his substitute wife to live with him for another two-year period, to the term of which he would die. For the *Bushmen* of Southern Africa, in the beginning, people and animals lived underneath the Earth with *Kaang, the Great Master and Lord of All Life.* Their life was one of happiness and harmony with *Kaang* and with one another. After furnishing the surface of the Earth with all that man would need, *Kaang* helped man climb up to the surface through a hole. Up there, man sat down on the edge of the hole. Then, the woman came to him through the hole as well (Roach, 2008). We are aware of two versions to the Luba story as relates to marriage. According to one version, *Maweja Nangila* created man by inflating his lungs with air and forcefully exhaling on the ground saying: "Let there be Gentleman." And Gentleman there was. Immediately, the Creator filled His lungs with air again and forcefully exhaled on the man saying; "Let there be Gentlewoman." And Gentlewoman there was. The second version states that *Maweja Nangila*, the Creator, sent *Ngoi*, the first man, to live by the river. Afterwards, He sent *Pamba,* the woman, to live with him there (Mbiti 1970, Roach 2008, Mudimbe 1991, Fourche et Morlighem 1973, Kalanda 1992); (Gbotokuma ND.)[1].

Marriage Preparations: Marriage was taken very seriously in traditional African societies. Marriage stability was a major concern. Marriage preparations could take very long to this end. *Igbo* marriage, for instance, was a multi-stage process beginning with the *"Asking the Girl's Consent"* phase. This task was carried out by the parents in arranged marriage of minors; or by friends and relatives in the so called *"Send Me a Wife"* program, for distant marriage candidates. In second place, middlemen were assigned to consult the diviner on whether the marriage would be auspicious and investigate the families on hereditary diseases and incidences of premature deaths and divorce. Then came "the exchange of presents" between the two families, of which the high point was the groom's family periodically bringing a pot of raffia or palm drink to the bride's family until the required amount of bridewealth was made available. During "the testing character" period, the girl was sent to live in the groom's parent's home. She was to be examined on her character and ability to carry out women's tasks. When satisfied with her, the groom's parents sent her back to her parents with rich presents. Following was the settlement of the bridewealth through a long debate and negotiations until an agreement was reached and a reasonable part of it paid (Uchendu, 1965).

Couple formation was a long process among pastoral *Somalis* as well. The lookout for a mate could be initiated by the girl or the boy. A young woman desirous to meet a would-be husband would lead a water-camel to the well, dressed in her nicest clothes. There, she would find a slew of young men anxious to converse with her and help her fill the water jars and load them on the camel. A young man on lookout mission for a bride, would dress well and go around visiting neighboring settlements accompanied by a trusted relative or friend. Together they would engage the targeted young woman in conversation showing the best in them: oratory skills and ability to solve enigmatic questions, for instance. Several day-long marriage dances were the greatest occasions for rural young men and women to meet, exhibit their poetry, music and oratory talents, and converse and attract mates. Watching the sheep near the settlement was another opportunity for a young woman to converse with a young man, although feared since disapproved by the parents and the community. Formal preparation began when the young man convinced his father or another responsible older relative to contact the parents of the desired bride and the contact visit was successful. For sake of the stability of their son's marriage, the parents of the groom were principally concerned about the reputation of the bride and her family, whereas the bride's family's preoccupations were the groom and his family's ability to provide for the daughter and the couple's future family. (Abdullahi, 2001).

The Bridewealth: African marriage is an alliance between two lineage communities. Bridewealth transfer from the groom's family to the bride's family is the bonding mechanism, the *sine qua none* condition of marriage existence and legitimacy, as well as the legitimacy of children to be born out of it. The bridewealth is also conceived as a mark of appreciation of the bride's parents for work well done in raising a woman who is going to be a valuable investment for the groom's lineage through her work and reproductive power. The nature, composition, and quantity of the bridewealth differs from ethnic group to ethnic group within the same country. For instance, in Nigeria, the bridewealth consisted of food items, such as yam, cattle, clothes, drinks, money, cola nuts, and holy books depending on the areas' traditions (Falola, 2001). Among the Yorùbá, in particular, it consisted of yams, *kola* nuts, logs of firewood, cowry shells, and currency paid in several predetermined stages. In the Congo, the bulk of the bridewealth was paid in goats among the Luba and in arrows, knives, and copper rings among the peoples of the Central Basin region. Whereas, the Bashi, the Nande and other pastoralist peoples of Eastern Congo paid their bridewealth in cattle. In most cases the bridewealth was essentially symbolic. Nowadays it has been commercialized and is principally paid in money and trade items (Bascom 1969, Mukenge 1967; Cuypers, in Vansina 1965, Vansina 1965).

The Kinship Bond between the Groom's Family and the Bride's Family: African marriage creates a kinship bond between the two allied families. The spouses and the relatives from both sides acquire new kinship statuses. Among the Luba, the relatives of one spouse are *baku* in relation to the other spouse's relatives. The parent, male or female, of one spouse becomes *civyela*, in relation to the parent, male or female, of the other spouse. Brothers and sisters of one spouse designate those of the other spouse as *babukonda* (singular: *bukonda*), brothers-in-law/sisters-in-law. In general, the husband addresses the wife's parents by the same terms she uses. Vice-versa, the wife addresses the husband's parents by the terms he uses. These are: *taatu* for the father and *maamu* for the mother. By respect, they sometimes do likewise for the big brother *tuutu,* and the big sister, *yaya.* The kinship bond between the two families lasts beyond the death of one of the spouses. Widow inheritance by which the brother of the deceased becomes his wife's new husband was largely practiced in Africa. So was the fact for a man to marry the sister of his deceased wife. Among the Luba, such a wife was called *mukaji wa mpinga,* replacement wife. A man who married his brother's widow was called *muluma* wa *mu bumpyanyi*, husband by inheritance. Widow inheritance and marrying a deceased wife's sister were most practiced when children were involved. It was meant to ensure that the children grow with two parents (Mukenge, 1967).

Gender Roles in Marriage: Economic Activities: Economic roles are played through carrying out activities of production, exchange, and consumption of goods and services. The most common unit of production is the individual family, that is, a man, his wife or wives, and their children. So is it in Igboland in the production of palm oil and palm kernels. Men climb the tree with a rope to gather the fruit, the children separate the nuts from the husk, and the women supervise the extraction of oil. The process includes the boiling of the nuts in water by women, the pounding of the nuts in a large mortar by men, and the separation of the nuts from the fibers by women and children. When the oil pressing is over, women take possession of the kernels. They crush the nuts between stones to pull out the kernels. In Kenya, since their conversion from hunter gatherers to farmers, Gikuyu men cultivated cocoyams and bananas; Gikuyu women grew sweet potatoes and millet. Corn, introduced in the 19th century, is cultivated by women for household consumption and by men for commercial exchange (Countries and their Economies Forum, ND).[2]

Gender Roles in Farming: Agriculture is the dominant economic activity in Lubaland. Luba men and women participate in all phases of production—clearing the land, tilling, weeding—with the exception of the harvesting of food crops, which is essentially a woman's activity. However, during Belgian colonization both men and women did the harvesting of cotton, a commercial crop imposed by the colonial power. Peanuts are another exception: men and women, adults and children, participate in their harvest. Perhaps, one reason for men's participation in harvesting peanuts is the latter's high risk of germinating and spoiling if they are not unEarthed quickly. The peanut's commercial value is a second possible reason. In fact, peanuts play a secondary role in Luba diet and are more often than not grown for supplementary income. In addition to cotton and peanuts, men and women share in the harvesting of bananas and plantains. Actually there is not any harvesting problem with these products. The Luba do not plant them systematically or in any large quantities. When a bunch of bananas or plantains has matured, a man or a woman may cut it off. This is not a difficult task at all. These fruits are harvested by felling the tree, an operation that can be executed very easily because the tree is soft.

Gender Roles in Marketing: In Nigeria, on market day, Igbo women bring palm kernels and their other farming produce and artwork products, such as clay pots. They bring men's products also, notably, hoes, wooden mortars, knives, and iron traps, from among others. In trading, women dominated in selling domestic products in local marketplaces, men alone practiced long-distance trade. Busting markets existed in all Yorùbá towns. Market women sold their husbands' farm products as well as their own. They also sold on behalf of other producers in capacity of commissioned agents. Some women entered in agreement with a palm wine tapper to sell wine on their behalf. If the wine had to be sold in three days to avoid spoilage, for example, the revenues of the first two days were for the owner; those of the third day went to the wine tapper. In Luba villages, men and women practice marketing somewhat differently. Women sell and buy most produce and freshly gathered products. Women sell indigenous beer and hard liquor, of which they are the only producers, whereas men are the major consumers. Men sell fresh cut meat. Both men and women sell dried fish and import products such as sardines. Both sexes sell the most commercialized type of caterpillars in the nation, *mansamba*. More women than men sell live chickens, but more men than women sell goats (Uchendu 1965, Bascom 1969, Mukenge 2002).

Gender Roles in Practicing Crafts. As previously discussed, Igbo women made clay pots, whereas Igbo men produced wooden mortars and metal implements such as hoes, iron traps and knives. In Luba villages, clay pottery is also a woman's craft. Luba women make cooking pots, water jars, and baby bathing pots. Only men practice weaving and metal working. Men weave a variety of baskets, fishing nets, sleeping mats, and carrying bags. Traditional metalworking has almost completely disappeared from Luba villages to the benefit of industrially produced imports from overseas or from other regions of the Congo. Hoes, machetes, spears, axes, and knives used by the Luba are no longer of their own making.

Gender Differences in Fishing: Men and women can be differentiated from each other by the way they fish. The only form of fishing that Luba women practice is the so-called *kutuwa* method. It involves the following:

1. damming a creek in order to contain the water upstream, then fencing spots of the reduced water downstream the dam;
2. hauling the remaining water out of the fenced spots with a utensil called *luupu*;
3. then finally capturing whatever fish are entrapped in the spots.

Men practice various types of fishing as well. They may angle, set traps, or use canoes and nets.

Gender Roles in House Building: The Mangbetu of the Congo built houses of poles rammed with mud. Men were responsible for – 1) cutting the poles, digging the holes, lashing horizontal bamboos or vines inside and outside the poles; 2) building a framework of poles for the roof, adding a grid of smaller sticks to the framework; 3) covering the roof with grass or leaves; 4) leaving space between the roof and the wall free of horizontal sticks and grass or leaves to allow light and ventilation; 5) stripping the vertical poles that are visible in the free space of the bark to spot termite tunnels; and 6) removing them before they destroy the poles. The women brought in water and mixed it with Earth for covering the walls. Both men and women did the plastering of the walls with mud. House building and farming were the first skills expected of a young man before he was authorized to marry. He had to demonstrate his ability to take care of himself as a proof that he will be able to provide for his wife and children. Luba houses are square or rectangular with a pointed roof. The walls are built of standing poles planted into the ground and tied to a beam at the top. The roof is made of poles descending from the top of the home—where they are tied to a pillar supporting the frame—and go down past the beam and are also tied to it. The poles for both the walls and the roof are surrounded at equal distances by horizontal reeds tied to them. The roof is covered with straws. The walls are plastered with wet mud. Among the Luba, house building is a man's job, with the exception of plastering the walls with wet mud, which is a woman's responsibility. Women also help carry the straw for the roof (Schildkrout and Keim 1990, Mukenge 2002).

Gender Roles Livestock Raising: Gender-based differences can be identified in livestock raising. In the Nigerian Nasarawa State, women dominate in raising poultry and goats, but are a small minority in cattle production. Their greatest participation is in feeding animals, cleaning of pens and cages, and provision of water. Among the Luba, women raise chickens and ducks, men tend goats and sheep. The Luba do not raise cattle. Pigs, when available, are fed by both men and women but they are considered a man's livestock. Building the stable or the manger and keeping the animals indoors are men's responsibilities (Ayaode et al., 2009).

Moral Foundations for Marriage Stability: Marriage is a morally regulated institution. Luba marriage, for instance, operates under the moral authority of the husband's ancestral spirits (The Luba are patrilineal—they trace descent through the fathers; as well as patrilocal—in general, the married couple lives among the relatives of the husband). The ancestors regulate both the behavior of the husband and the behavior of the wife.

Regulations of the Husband's Conduct: When a Luba young man reaches the age of maturity, he builds himself a house. Upon marriage he and his wife will live in this house that he has built by his own hands. However, the ancestral tradition prohibits housing a legitimate wife in a house that one has reviled with extra-marital affairs, or one in which he has lived with another legitimate wife. Luba tradition also finds it morally inappropriate for a husband to house two or more wives under the same roof. Therefore, whenever, on his own initiative or upon advisement by his relatives, or even by his senior wife, a Luba man living of tradition decides to take on an additional wife, he will build her a separate house. In marriage, Luba ancestors do not prohibit man's infidelity explicitly. However, they do not permit him to return to the house of a legitimate wife and sleep therein the same day he has been with another woman.

A Luba husband's behavior is regulated by two additional sets of norms. One applies to repudiation. In the eyes of the ancestors, verbal repudiation does not count. True repudiation occurs when a man throws his wife's cooking utensils, clothes and other personal belongings out of her house. The husband does not have to account to the ancestors for divorcing or repudiating her in this manner. But, once he has done this, he has disrupted the marriage bond and cannot bring the wife he has rejected so ostentatiously back in without primarily apologizing for his misconduct. Apologies to the wife or internal regrets do not count. He must express his apologies to the ancestors verbally in front of their shrines and pay fines (*kufuta bibawu*) by sacrificing a rooster to them. Also prohibited is the fact for a man to refuse the conjugal bed to his wife, for example, by making her sleep on the floor following a dispute. Doing this is equivalent to establishing a separation (*mukalu*) between the two of them. And this, Luba ancestors do not condone. When it happens, it must be repaired.

A final set of norms affecting a man's conjugal behavior has to do with his relationships with a wife who has violated an ancestral norm. No man is allowed to stand between the ancestors and such a wife, for example, by taking her defense. Worse, he would become an accomplice had he to treat a wife who is sick by ancestral punishment. For this reason, many traditional Luba men did not mourn their wives unless they were sure that her death was not a punishment from the ancestors.

Regulations of the Wife's Conduct: The principal ancestral norm binding a Luba man's wife is the prohibition of infidelity. The Luba value procreation more than anything else in the world. However, the prohibition of a married woman's infidelity applies even in the event of proved sterility of the husband. In no circumstance is it permissible for a married woman to have an intimate relationship with a man other than the legitimate husband. Whatever the motive may be, a wife's extramarital sexual relations remain a crime (*cibawu*). This prohibition stands even if the bridewealth has not been paid in full. A woman accused of adultery is generally the object of serious beatings by her husband and his relatives, both men and women. In the past, she could be beaten to death, especially when caught in action. Also, since infidelity of a married woman is prohibited not only by the living, but also by the ancestors, an adulterous wife who cooks the sacred meal without primarily avowing and expiating her crime exposes herself to death. Even if she obtains the clemency of her husband and his relatives, she must pay fines to the ancestral spirits to be reinstated as a spouse.

Just as it is against the ancestral law for a man to keep his wife from sleeping in the conjugal bed following an argument, by tradition it is not permissible for a woman to refuse to sleep in the conjugal bed in discontentment with her husband. Likewise, it is prohibited for a married woman to pack her utensils, clothes, and other belongings and walk away in protest against her husband. In case of an argument with her husband, the ancestral tradition allows for her to seek refuge with her or his relatives, but she could take along no more than the clothes that she had on at that time. Taking her other belongings along was a declaration of divorce. Such acts create a separation between husband and wife and call for reparations. A woman who is responsible for such a separation must pay fines to the ancestral spirits before returning to the conjugal bed in the former case, and before reintegrating her house in the latter.

There is another ancestral justification to the prohibition of a wife's walking away from the matrimonial home. The senior wife is the living representative of the family guardian spirit *Nkambwa*. Taking out her utensils and walking away is equated with throwing *Nkambwa* out of her home. This act must be repaired ritually by paying fines and imploring *Nkambwa* to come back into the house first.

Procreation

Africans, like other peoples, know that conception occurs during copulation when a spermatozoon from the male partner connects with an egg from the female partner. But they believe in the existence and power of other factors that can produce or qualitatively affect a particular conception and the child therefrom. Two of such intervening factors have been discussed in a previous chapter: procreation as a destiny-making moment in the Igbo conception, and procreation as an act of reincarnation of the spirits of the dead as believed by African peoples across the continent. This section highlights two aspects of human procreation: procreation as a mission from divine creation and procreation as a genetic package transfer.

Procreation as a Mission from Divine Creation: Not only did God create man and woman and unite them as husband and wife, He also enabled them to procreate. As parents, the first human beings on Earth sent their children away with the mission to procreate, multiply, and cover the surface of the Earth, thus prolonging the divine mission to procreate. The ability to procreate is a gift from divine creation. In many creation stories, the Creator made species that were hermaphrodites, that is, they had the potential to perform and reproduce as males or females. Such was the case with *Mahungu*, the original ancestor of the *BaManyanga*. He possessed both genders. In other stories, couples became parents after they had been together. Thus, in the Wakaranga story, after *Moon* (man) slept with *Evening-Star* (woman), the latter became pregnant and gave birth to animals, birds, and human sons and daughters. In the story of the Tetela of Congo, *Onya*, God, after giving life to the first two human beings on Earth, a blacksmith and his wife, by breathing into them, placed them in His compound where they lived in immense joy and gave birth to many children. Gikuyu, the legendary father of the Gikuyu people, was also predestined by the Creator to become the father of many. The Gikuyu say that, *Ngai*, God, after giving *Mount Kenya* and the beautiful country surrounding it to their founding father, promised him, pointing to the mountain, that out of the marvelous bowl on which he (*Gikuyu*) was standing, his sons and daughters would roam and multiply. The beauty and the fruits of the land around the mountains were blessings that *Gikuyu,* his offspring and their own descendents would enjoy wherever they would go. There are also cases in which the Creator delegated the power of fertility to some of his assistant deities. Earth goddess *Ala* assumed this function among the Igbo. In the Igbo patrilineal system, where group identity and access to ancestral lands are acquired through the fathers, *Ala* is responsible for man's fertility and land productivity. Being a merciful mother, *Ala* also intercedes for her children with other spirits. A version of the Luba story has it that the first man, *Ngoi*, and the first woman, *Pamba*, gave birth to two children male and female, two months after they had been together. Another two months later, they had a second set of twins, a male and a female also. They sent their children to live and procreate by other rivers (Bockie 1993, Anyang 1997, Jefferson and Skinner 1990. Uchendu 1965, Mudimbe 1991); (Gbotokuma ND).[3]

Procreation as Genetic Package Transfer: Fu-Kiau stresses the importance of the parents' genetic package, behaviors, and states of mind at conception and during gestation for their children's well-being. At conception and during gestation parents transfer to the fetus a complete genetic package, with all its strengths and all its weaknesses. The transferred genetic package includes all they have inherited from their own parents, grandparents, great-grandparents, and so on; and what the parents themselves have built up in their system through: (1) What they are taught, constructive or destructive; in the family, at school, or on the street; through the spoken word, reading, television, or movies. (2) What they eat, that is, anything they have introduced into their bodies through the mouth such as food, drink, tobacco, and drugs; through the skin like beauty products, or through the nostrils, like air, gas, and smoke. (3) What they see, which feeds their minds with pictures. These pictures will be perpetually reproduced throughout life, often unconsciously, particularly those of heroes. (4) What they believe in, that is the beliefs of the entities to which they belong, such as parents, groups, associations, institutions, and societies. These beliefs can make them strong or weak physically and spiritually (Fu-Kiau, 1991).

Socialization

Responsible procreation as a contributor to community building goes beyond bringing a child into the world. It by necessity includes transmission of foundational social values to younger generations through culturally sanctioned socialization processes. Five socializing agencies are outlined below: (1) familial forums for transmitting knowledge of circles of identity and resources of the environment, (2) memorials of cultural heroes to perpetuate ethnic pride, (3) initiation camps to teach foundational virtues essential for productive manhood or womanhood, and (4) sample proverbs fostering sociability.

Familial Forums for Transmitting the Knowledge of Circles of Identity and Resources of the Local Environment: In Luba villages, routine socialization sessions are held after the evening meal around the family fire in the courtyard of an elder. Children are asked to tell their names, their parents' names and their genealogies. They are taught the hierarchical circles of identity (patrilineal in the case of the Luba) to which they belong by birth from the largest to the smallest and proper terms of address and of reference for relatives from the father's side (patrilineal), the mother's side (matrilineal), and relatives by marriage (affinal relatives). They learn clan totems and taboos and about marriageable and non-marriageable co-descendents. The children learn about the life-sustaining resources of the surrounding environment: animals, plants and neighboring clans and ethnic groups. They learn the territorial entities in which they reside. Nowadays, these include the village, the territory, the district, the province and the country. In schools, they learn about the geographic location of their country: for example: the Congo is located in the center of Africa and that Africa stands in the center of other continents separated by many oceans.

Memorials of Cultural Heroes to Perpetuate Ethnic Pride: African ethnic groups have epic songs, songs of exhortation and ethnic pride celebrating the accomplishments of legendary cultural heroes. The *Mande* of Mali sing the *Sundjata Epic* to the glory of *Sundjata Keita,* a heroic man, a buffalo's prophesy made true, who conquered birth infirmity, family rejection, childhood bullying and community denigration to become the founder of the 13th Century historic great empire of Mali, after militarily subjugating one after another much larger kingdoms than his own. The Luba of Kasai have the *kasala* song which glorifies the founding fathers of their chiefdoms and the achievements of their other famous ascendants. Some ethnic groups organize pilgrimages to particular locations deemed sacred due to their identification with revered heroic ancestors. Yorùbá youth dream of a life-time pilgrimage *to Ile Ifè*, the birthplace of the Yorùbá nation, in anticipation of possibly having a personal encounter with the spirit of *Opa Oranyan*, the heroic son of *Odùdùwà,* the deified original king of the Yorùbá nation; if not *Opa Oranyan* himself, at least his staff and the statues of other heroic ancestors. In the remote town of Lalibela, Ethiopia, sits eleven rock-carved Christian churches belonging to the Ethiopian Orthodox Church, dating back to the fourth century AD. To date, these churches attract large crowds of pilgrim worshipers, including blind and disabled persons, from far and from near. The roads are hilly; many pilgrims walk bare-footed. The painstaking journey can take several days or weeks. Through it all, the faithful, full of excitement, joy, and hope, spend several days and nights on the church compound praying, reading religious texts, and attending daily worship services to receive spiritual blessings (Hilliard 1998, Faik-Nzuji 1967, Mufuta 1969, Idowu 1994);

(Barnet 2013).[4]

Initiation Camps to Teach Foundational Virtues Essential for Productive Manhood or Womanhood: At puberty, *Kongo* children are led into seclusion in the forest for ceremonies of initiation into manhood or womanhood. These ceremonies stress and dramatize, for life-long enforcement, secrets about the sacredness of manhood and womanhood and responsibilities to the community, notably: 1) the role of the individual as the core of the fundamental circle of identity, the family and the clan; 2) stewardship over natural resources: land, water and forest; and 3) leadership. Through initiation, the novices are introduced to the knowledge about the formation of the universe and planets, the developmental process of human life from conception, birth, maturity, and death; and the rise and fall of social systems. During the initiation period, young Gikuyu were taught significant values, meanings and responsibilities associated with adult life. The period culminated in circumcision of the candidates. Undergoing circumcision was a test of courage, a bravery building trial. Crying was not permitted, unless one wanted to remain a child all throughout life. Through initiation, the young men acquired the status of warriors, defenders and protectors of the community, its people, its lands, and its resources. As circumcised, they could marry and have children, fundamental rights that the uncircumcised could not achieve. Circumcision spared them the misfortune of fathering children who would be rejected as unfit by the community and believed rejected by God and the ancestors as well. Also, it was inconceivable for an uncircumcised person to be invested village or clan elder (Fu- Kiau,2001; Jens ND).[5]

Proverbs Fostering Sociability: Humans have natural penchant toward forming friendships and engaging in cooperative acts. Some African proverbs seek to reinforce this inclination in young people and discourage isolationist behavior and situations. Below are illustrations taken from Luba culture.

1. Mumu umwa kautu wangula nkusu.
Never will a single finger be able to pick up a louse.

Lesson: *There is not much you can accomplish working as a loner.*

2. Nkunda ya bangi yibobela ne mate.
With the cooperation of many, beans can get cooked with saliva.

Explanation: When many individuals take turns blowing on the fire, beans can get cooked even if out of exhaustion each participant's breath is filled with splashes of saliva.

Lesson: With the participation of many, no task is too hard to be accomplished.

3. Padi tutenda tutwilangana ke paditu tutendangana.
When *tutenda* birds gather, they sing songs of praise to one another.

Explanation: Gatherings with members of one's own kind are precious occasions for praising each other's accomplishments and instilling into one another feelings of greatness and commitment to the common good.

Lesson: Family reunions are better spent building each other up.

4. *Bakufinga bantu, kabakufingi nsona.*
You better be covered with people rather than with straws.

Explanation: You better be alive in company rather than dead and lonely in a straw-roofed tomb.

Lesson: Rejoice rather than complaining about having many people around you. Solitude belongs to the dead, not to the living.

5. *Luswa lumwa luboleshila nswa yonso.*
One spoiled flying (edible) ant can cause a basketful of ants to spoil.

Meaning: One individual's bad behavior can ruin the reputation of an entire community.

Legends Designed to Impart Self-Control: One of Frobenius's stories, which he attributes to *Beena Kalambayi*, talks about some plateau dweller folks who one day, while hunting in the wilderness, came across footsteps of some forest dwellers: i.e., spirits. Forest dwellers are masters of hunting game—wild animals that humans need for meat. Humans produce food crops but have to negotiate with the spirits of the land for successful hunting. Seeing forest dwellers' footsteps while hunting for game in the wilderness was unusual. The hunters began yelling asking if there were any forest dwellers around. As a matter of fact, an old forest dweller showed up. The hunters proposed to exchange with the old forest dweller their *nshima* staple food for his meat. The exchange was concluded and executed on the spot to the satisfaction of both parties. They returned to their respective living quarters and were welcomed by their kin with great jubilation involving eating, singing and dancing. The next day, older plateau dwellers sent some young people into the wilderness for another exchange of *nshima* for meat with forest dwellers. They instructed them to be polite and respectful. But the young people, after calling the forest dwellers a couple of times without immediate response, became impatient and rude, ridiculing them as uncivilized carnivores. Insulted, the forest dwellers turned down the trade offer and sent the young people back home with their *nshima* without meat. Disappointed of the young people's behavior, adult plateau dwellers went to the wilderness with apologies, but the forest dwellers did not change their mind. The damage was done. As a result, to date, game meat is scarce in Luba villages. The mishaps of one member can damage the reputation or jeopardize the future of a whole community. Disrespect and condescendence will never be grounds for building enduring relationships (Frobenius, 1983).

Some other Frobenius stories talk about individuals who were born and lived in poverty and were mocked or despised. Due to some mysterious intervention, their condition improved gradually: they acquired the instruments of labor they desired; were able to produce abundant crops and raise a large livestock of chickens, ducks, sheep and goats. They married several beautiful and faithful wives who lived in nice large houses. They became chiefs. Many people settled around their residences and became their subjects. Some of the people became sub-chiefs who bowed before the chief, offering them due tributes. In brief, the once marginally surviving individuals became famous chiefs. They organized popular celebrations in which sub-chiefs and subjects sang, drummed, and danced to the chief's honor. One of the conditions from the mysterious destiny maker who had brought them from poverty to fame was that when the subjects dance in honor of the chiefs, the latter should not join the dance; or if they danced, they should not dance with their full body as the subjects would do, but only with one side of the body, that is, not as well nor with the same freedoms of movements as the subjects would do. In each case, during celebrations, the dancers were marvelous, with participants full of excitement and acclamations. In each case, the chief could not contain himself. Ignoring reminders by the first lady of the prohibition by the mysterious destiny maker, he jumped into the circle and danced to the best he could, even attempting to outdo his subjects. Once the dance was over, the subjects, the sub-chiefs, and the chief's wives abandoned him. All his wealth vanished, and he became less than an ordinary man, an indigent (Frobenius, 1983).

One lesson that could be drawn from this summary is that often individuals who are catapulted into positions of honor and glory mishandle them. Above all, the stories are lessons in self-control, a quality highly required of individuals in a position of chief or king and of leaders in general. Leaders are expected to act by reason rather than by emotions and to control their impulsions particularly in public. It is not because a public event is exciting that one got to inject oneself into it. If this is true for anybody, it is even more so for a leader, particularly a sacred leader like an African chief or king. Another, lesson, also fundamental, relates to the pursuit of success: Build your success around the blessings you already have. Be content of the successes inherent in your status. Do not envy those of others. For a chief, organizing great celebrations in which his subjects and sub-chiefs sing and dance to his honor is a mark of success and greatness. Singing, drumming and dancing in chief's honor is for ordinary people an opportunity to achieve success and greatness. A chief who overlooks his own greatness to compete for that of his subjects debases himself beneath the subjects. He does not understand what chieftaincy's greatness and success really are. Lastly, the chief's behavior in the four stories violates a cardinal principle of governance in African political systems: the principle of division of labor and limitation of power. The chief must delegate responsibilities in particular sectors of life to his collaborators. In the Luba political system, for example, it is not expected for a chief to be a witness to a crime, an investigator or a prosecutor. A chief who has witnessed the commission of a crime will not mention it or issue an investigation. He will wait for his officer in charge of justice to bring up the case. Sometimes, when he is the only witness, he might describe the details surrounding the commission of the crime and pretend that the ancestors or the spirits of past chiefs showed them to him and thus induce the criminal into denouncing himself.

3. THE KINSHIP COMMUNITY

Biological Kinship

God, in creation stories, gave the first couples the mandate to procreate, multiply and live in harmony with one another. Biological kinship is African societies' basic organizational principle. Kinship groups are African societies' major building blocks, and their members' solidarity is a constant preoccupation and nurturing force. Some African societies trace descent through the fathers (patrilineal descent), others through the mothers (matrilineal descent), and still others through both lines (bilateral descent). In patrilineal societies, identity, group membership and inheritance rights are transmitted from father to children. In matrilineal societies, these attributes are passed to children through the mothers. In bilateral kinship, some rights are inherited through the mother, others through the father.

African descent-based communities may consist of bands, lineages, clans or chiefdoms. Bands are temporary communities of nuclear families. Bands were found among the Pygmies of the Congo, the Twa of Rwanda and the Bushmen of Southern Africa. Bands lacked permanent political leadership. They elected leaders by consensus for specific tasks, such as a hunting party. Bands societies subsisted on hunting and gathering. Lineages are sedentary groups of extended families of common ancestry. Members of a particular lineage lived in a village community on collectively owned lands bequeathed by the ancestors. They had free access to ancestral lands under the supervision of the elders. They owned the products of their labor, but the land continued to belong to the community as a whole. The lineage was headed by an elder assisted by a council of elders. In most cases, lineages are sub-groups of larger social entities, such as clans or chiefdoms. The Lele of Congo were organized in sovereign lineages. Clans are sedentary groups similar to lineages. Unlike lineages, clan unity was based on more factors than common descent. Clan members identified themselves with a particular animal, carried its name (totem), and abstained from eating it (taboo). Marriage was often prohibited among clan members. Some clans had branches with their own ancestral lands in distant locations, but still refrained from intermarriage. An elder and a council of elders supervised the affairs of the clan. In the foregoing types of societies, the lineage or the clan was the highest level of political affiliation. No common authority linked them together. In most *Bantu* societies, lineages and clans were incorporated into larger units, chiefdoms. In a chiefdom, a dominant clan exercised political control over the others. The Tsong and the Yansi of Congo are good examples of such chiefdoms. In some societies, the Luba of Kasai for example, selected clans rotated at the head of the chiefdom (Vansina 1966, Mukenge 1967).

Strengthening the Kinship Bond

Several practices serve to strengthen and perpetuate the kinship bond among relatives. One is the required respect for seniority at all levels: younger siblings for older siblings, children for parents, commoners for authority figures, the living for the departed, the ancestors and divinities for the Creator. Respect toward the carrier of a particular social status is extended to his or her peers in that status. For example, the respect owed one's mother is extended to other mothers of her generation. Sharing among relatives is another powerful community bonding practice operative in African societies. It takes various forms. Co-parenting is one. This is the practice whereby one raises younger siblings, cousins, nephews or nieces without filling any official adoption request and the services are free of charge. Sharing common clan names, totems and taboos or names of common ancestors is another unifying factor of descent-based groups. Participating in common ancestral ritual under the leadership of authorized elders is another pervasive form of sharing. For example, among the Luba, all male descendants of a common grandfather owe him through his living representative elder, the first fruits from their work and from their daughters' marriages in gratitude for their ability to work and to procreate. The receiving elder offers sacrifices of chickens and goat to the ancestral sprits and all participate in the ritual (Mukenge, 1967).

Use of Appropriate Kinship Terminology: Every African ethnic group has appropriate kinship terms for relatives. The Luba people identify seven generations of relatives by specific kinship terms: Ego, the speaking person, male or female, siblings, and first cousins are the middle generation, Generation Zero (0). There are three older generations: parents (+1), grandparents (+ 2), and great-grandparents (+ 3); and three younger generations: children (-1), grandchildren (-2), and great-grandchildren (-3).

Luba Kinship Generations
Generation + 3: *bakaaku wa bwikulu*   great-grandparents
Generation + 2: *bakaaku*   grandparents
Generation + 1: *baledi*   parents
Generation 0: *baana beetu*   siblings
Generation - 1: *baana*   children
Generation - 2: *bankana*   grandchildren
Generation - 3: *tunkanunwina*   great-grandchildren

Kinship Terms in Various Generations: Two principles dominate in the use of kinship terms: respect for seniority and extension of terms for close relatives to distant relatives of the same generation. You call your seniors or elders by terms stating their kinship status in relation to yours and expressing your respect for them. Your seniors are all those born in generations before yours and those born before you in your generation. Great grandfather and great-grandmother are *taatu wa bwikulu* and *maamu wa bwikulu*, respectively. Literally, *taatu wa bwikulu* or *maamu wa bwikulu* means father or mother by the relationship of grandparenthood. The term for grandparent is *kaaku*. There exists a joking and equality relationship between alternative generations, which fuses the two generations into one. Through this process, the grandchild becomes a fictive brother or sister of the grandfather or grandmother. Symptomatically they often address each other as *kaaku*.

A Family-Kinship Community Builder

Table 8a: *Appropriate Kinship Terminology by Generation*

Generation + 3: Great-Grandparents			
Terms of Reference: Singular & Plural		Terms of Address Singular & Plural	
taatu wa bwikulu great-grandfather *maamu wa bwikulu* great-grandmother	*baataatu wa bwikulu* great-grandfathers *baamaamu wa bwikulu* great-grandmothers	*taatu* father *maamu* mother	*baataatu* fathers *baamaamu* mothers
Generation + 2: Baakaaku /Grandparents			
kaaku muluma grandfather *kaaku mukaji* grandmother	*Baakaaku baluma* Grandfathers *bakaaku bakaji* grandmothers	*kaaku* grandfather *kaaku* grandmother	*Bakaaku* grandfathers *Bakaaku* grandmothers
Generation + 1: Baledi /Parents			
taatu or *taawu* father *maamu, maawu,* or *baaba* mother	*baataatu* or *baataawu* Fathers *baamaamu, baamaawu,* or *baabaaba* mothers	*taatu* or *tawu* father *maamu, mawu,* or *baaba* mother	*baataatu* or *baatawu* fathers *baamaamu, baamawu,* or *baabaaba* mothers

Table 8b: *Appropriate Kinship Terminology by Generation (Continued)*

Ego's Generation 0: Baana Beetu /Siblings			
Terms of Reference: Singular & Plural		Terms of Address: Singular & Plural	
tuutu kampanda big brother So & So *yaaya kampanda* big sister So & So	*baatuutu kampanda* big brothers So & So *baayaaya kampanda* big sisters So & So	*tuutu* big brother *yaaya* big sister	*baatuutu* big brothers *baayaaya* big sisters
mwakunyi wa baluma: younger brother *mwakunyi wa bakaji* younger sister	*baakunyi baa baluma:* younger brothers *baakunyi baa bakaji* younger sisters	*dîna dya muntu* personal name *dîna dya muntu* personal name	
Generation minus 1: Baana /Children			
Terms of Reference		Terms of Address	

mwananyi my child	baana banyi my children	personal names
mwanayi wa baluma my son	baana banyi baabaluma my sons	mêna personal names
mwanayi wa bakaji my daughter	baana banyi baabakaji my daughters	mêna personal names
Generation minus 2: Bankana /Grandchildren		
munkananyi my grandchild	bankana banyi my grandchildren	personal names (or *kaaku*)
Generation minus 3: Tunkanunwina /Great-Grandchild		
mwananyi wa bwikulu my great-grandchild	baana banyi baa bwikulu my great-grandchildren	personal names

Kinship Term Extension: Kinship terms applicable to a particular generation or particular statuses within a generation are extended to their peers. For example, Ego calls *kaaku*, grandparent, not only the grandfather or grandmother, paternal or maternal, but also their siblings and first cousins. Likewise *taatu*, father, applies to the biological father, his male siblings and first cousins, and other relatives of their generation. *Taatu mukaji*, paternal aunt, term of reference and address for the father's sister, is extended to his cousins. *Taatu mukaji* literally means female father. *Maamu*, mother, is used for the biological mother, her sisters, and her brothers' and cousins' wives. A step-mother, a father's brother's or father's cousin's wife is called *maamu,* mother, also. The Luba term for child is *mwana*. Ego refers to each one of his or her children as *mwananyi*, my child. This term is also applicable to the children of Ego's siblings or cousins. By respect, juniors among siblings and cousins call their seniors of the same *generation tuutu (big brother) or yaaya* (big sister*)*.

Other Categories of Specific Kinship Terminology: The Luba people are patrilineal. They trace descent through the fathers. The terminology described above applies to male *Ego* and his agnatic relatives, meaning relatives from the father's side. There exists a distinct terminology for uterine relatives—mother's relatives—and another for affinal relatives, that is, relatives by marriage. The three categories of kinship terminology overlap to a large extent. Mother's sisters are *baamaamu* (singular *maamu*), that is, mothers. Her brothers are *bamanseba* (singular *manseba*). *Manseba* means male mother. Ego's mother's father and mother are *baakaaku*, just as his father's parents are. The generic term for the in-laws is *baku*. The collective term for the wife's siblings and cousins is *baabukonda* (singular *bukonda*). *Bukonda* is both a reference and an address term and applies both to her brothers and to her sisters. As a term of address, *bukonda* is reciprocal: the husband addresses his brother in-law or sister in-law as *bukonda*;

each one addresses him as *bukonda* also. The wife's mother is referred to as *mamwenu*, but addressed as *maamu*, or *mawu*, or else *baaba*, mother. The wife's grandparents, *baakaaku*, are *baakaaku* to the husband also.

Mbôngi: Kinship-Based Community Politics

Mbôngi, in Kikongo, the language of the Bakongo people who live in the *Lower-Congo Province*, DRC, designates a community house in which members meet periodically to discuss matters of common interest and take decisions, generally by consensus, which affect the well-being and destiny of all community members. Issues such as land security, social conflicts, marriage, initiation, property, livestock, leadership, public conduct, health, sickness, medicine, death and practically all others are debated in *Mbôngi* for the common good. *Mbôngi* is training center for *Mbôngi*'s own leadership and assistants (*Bambuta, bakuluntu*) as well as the youth whose participation is required to this effect. Through the universality of the topics addressed, popular participation, and intensive discussions, *Mbôngi* operates as a powerful community unifying force. The spirit of unity that *Mbôngi* promotes and *Mbôngi*'s unifying power and attributes are expressed through special names of significance and multiple proverbs. Depending on the proverbs, *Mbôngi* means many things expressed by different names: call to collective problem-solving action (*boko*), house verandah or mother-bird's wing that covers and protects (*yemba*), or the gathering place of community members and storage and transfer center of accumulated experiences (*lusanga*), or else life-sustaining breath (*kioto*) (Fu-Kiau, 1985).

Scheduling Mbôngi Events: *Mbôngi's* community-building role is also apparent in the scheduling *(landu)* of events of importance to the community and its members for discussion. A special appointee called *Na Makolo* marks the dates commonly agreed upon by tying knots on a rope representing the number of days or weeks before the event. The knot rope of agreements is called *Mabika*. Every day or every week, depending on the agreement, *Na Makolo* unties a knot from *Mabika*. The *Mabika* for initiation was among the most important ones. Programs for various initiation sites were carefully recorded. Contracts with other *Mbôngis* or communities were marked by special knots. Sometimes cuts were made on a piece of wood instead of knots on a rope. The *Na Makolo* was expected to know the meaning and history behind every knot on the rope or cut on the wood. All important knotty ropes or cut-bearing pieces of wood were turned over to the *Ne Masamuna*, the community griot, that is, oral historian. They could also be deposited in the "*Nzo-Bakulu*", the house of ancestors. The coming of scheduled events was announced with fanfare by the *Ne Mabika* and celebrated in large crowds of young and adult members of the concerned constituencies (Fu-Kiau, 1985).

Mbôngi Leadership: *Mbôngi* leadership is comprised of many other specialists than the *Na Makolo*, the event scheduler. First from among them is the *Mfumu Mbôngi*, Chief of *Mbôngi*, that is, *Mbôngi*'s CEO. He must be a stable individual in the local system, not a temporary resident or an outsider professional. In his absence, the *Lândi kia Mfumu-Mbôngi*, Deputy Chief of *Mbôngi*, replaces him. *Mbôngi*'s basic constitutive units are extended families. *Mfumu-dikânda*, elder of the extended family, is their chief of delegation in the *Mbôngi*. He is the entitled spokesperson for his lineage both to the *Mbôngi* council of the living and to the invisible council of the *Bakulu*, ancestors, who are the fully accomplished elders. He is responsible to both councils for the compliance of his household (extended family). In this double capacity, the *Mfumu-dikânda* is the harmonizer and peace maker who helps keep the relationships between the three communities—the lineage, *Mbôngi,* and the ancestors—in balance. As a participant in the spiritual world of the ancestors, *Mfumu-dikânda* has the power to see and counteract the secret harmful actions of the witches. *Nzônzi*: a wise, respected skilled debater and negotiator, versed in language nuances and expressions; expert in truth finding techniques. He may be from outside the community, therefore must be knowledgeable in legal systems and practices of the region and in information gathering. He is the speaker of the *Mbôngi* and the community. It is his duty to explain the law and the policies to the community. *N'Swami:* security personnel, operate clandestinely. They spy and collect information about the *Mbôngi,* its constitution, and individual behaviors within the *Mbôngi* and in the community. They serve as counselors to the leaders and to the community. They operate in various specific capacities. The *N'kengi* focuses more on individual behaviors while the *N'suni* investigates the persons suspected of causing disorder in the community. The *N'langi* concentrates on the boundaries of the community's land and the activities conducted on the land, the forests and the waters; and community's inalienable real estate of which the palm tree, other special vegetations, and the animals are constitutive elements. Finally, the *N'neki* collects secret information from outside the *Mbôngi* and the community (Fu-Kiau, 1985).

Kinship-Based Collective Sacred Rituals

The Ancestors and the Living: In African worldview, the ancestral spirits continue to share Earthly life with their descendents. Freed from the limitations of the human body through death, the spirit of the deceased moves closer to God and thereby appropriates more divine power. It joins the spirits of bygone relatives and becomes an ancestor among them. Ancestors use these powers to protect and bless their descendents in many ways: giving them the capacity to work, to procreate, and to achieve many other forms of success. There exists a fundamental belief among the Luba*,* and for that matter among other Africans, according to which all the blessings a person can enjoy on Earth—life, strengths and talents, progeny and wealth, power and fame—ultimately come from the Creator. Traditionally, however, people who were desirous of these gifts and blessings would, in most cases, address their petitions to ancestors rather than to God. The underlying belief, conscious or subconscious, is that God has delegated the handling of these matters to ancestors and does not have to intervene personally in each case. In return for the blessings so received, the living bear the obligation to share food, shelter, and other enjoyments with their immediate mediators and benefactors, the ancestors. To the believer, this ancestral obligation is not optional. Violations may attract misfortunes on the perpetrator, his progeny, his possessions, or his undertakings. The belief in ancestral intervention in human lives is the foundation upon which ancestral veneration is built (Mukenge, 1967).

Kinship-Based Rituals: All throughout Africa spiritual rituals were performed to ancestral spirits, to divinities, and to God the Creator to promote the well-being of the community beyond the nuclear family. Ancestors are venerated deceased relatives who are believed to continue to share life with their Earthly descendants. Most often rituals are performed by the elder of the extended family on behalf of the entire lineage or clan. Violation of the ancestral code of conduct stains the whole clan. To restore the relationship with the world of the spirits, the violator must recognize his wrong-doing in a public confession in presence of the clan chief and other members. Among the BaManyanga of the Congo, such a ceremony is held in the ancestors' burial place. The whole village and other clan members living nearby are expected to attend. The entitled elder will offer sacrifices of goat and wine to ancestors seeking mercy and forgiveness for the entire community. This is an example of the "redress" or "repair" function of African religious rituals. The elders also intervene as intercessors of ancestral blessings for the entire community (Bokie 1993; Magesa 1997, quoting Aylward Shorter).

The Woyo people who live on the Atlantic shores of Congo-Kinshasa and the Enclave of Cabinda engage in a series of rituals designed to bring them happiness and success in farming and fishing. Their perception and formulation of the material needs of the group are structured by their conception of the sacred. Their vision of well-being, happiness, and man's relation to land, the major means of production, is conditioned by these factors as well. Woyo people are agriculturalists. Success in agriculture depends, from among other factors, on the quality of the land and of the seeds. Seed selection is of great concern. Frequent sanctification rites are performed on the good seeds that have been selected for planting, the land, fishing nets, and the ocean. Related to land-blessing rites are those to bring in rains. The purpose of all these rites is to increase productivity, the harvest, and the catch from fishing. But the rites performed in this conjunction go far beyond to cover all aspects of human well-being, including women's fecundity, mending social relations among relatives through reconciliation, warding off diseases and natural calamities, protecting women, men, and children; empowering political leaders, and sanctifying and protecting the exercise of political power (Kibanda, 1997).

Community-strengthening rituals are also performed as required expressions of gratitude for ancestral blessings already received. Every Luba man owes his ancestors the first fruits from his labor and from the marriage of his daughters in repayment for his ability to work and to procreate. The Luba live in extended families of seven generations: Ego's generation, three generations above, and three generations below. Ego's generation's male siblings and cousins owe tributes of the first fruits to their common grandfather for their work power and the ability to procreate. The Luba are primarily agriculturalists. The process of creating wealth in Luba culture begins with the production of an agricultural surplus. The expectation is that this surplus be invested in raising poultry and revenues from poultry raising in turn invested in goat raising. It is also expected that one will have some day accumulated enough revenues from farming and poultry and goat raising combined to pay in bridewealth for a marriage. The belief is that for the prosperity of his undertakings, the achiever must offer a tribute of the first fruit from each stage of the production process—first meal of corn from his fields, first chicken, first goat and first wife acquired with revenues from the sweat of his brow—to the elder who represents the ancestors among the living. At each accomplishment, the elder would make sacrifices to the ancestral spirits asking them to bless the presents, the achiever and all his undertakings. All male descendents of the venerated grandfather partake of the sacrificial meal. The tribute of wife is often symbolic. Generally, after accepting her in tribute, the elder blesses her and appropriates her ritually. He then returns her to the giver thereby fulfilling his own obligation as elder to provide his juniors with wives. The ability to procreate also is a gift from the Creator made available to individual family members by the ancestors. The bridewealth from the marriage of the first daughter must be paid in tribute to the grandfather or his living representative. The occasion is celebrated with a sacrifice of goat to the ancestral spirits and all eligible community members will partake of the sacred meal. The tributes of bridewealth received by the elder from his many juniors are not for him to use as he sees fit. In most cases they are used to procure wives for single relatives, members of the extended family in their order of seniority. The receiving elder would be criticized for unfairness had he to marry a son who is younger than an eligible nephew. He too must pay tributes of first fruits to somebody standing for the ancestors (Mukenge, 1967).

SUMMARY

Divine Creation of the Human Community

God's spiritual creations, including those God involved in the creation of the terrestrial world, were communities rather than sole individuals. In the Mende story, *Mangala*, God, created two pairs of seeds of life, to which He added six more and then placed them all in the womb of the world where they found two preexisting pairs. When Pemba, a male seed, broke the placenta prematurely, he took seven male seeds along. Later on, after the sacrifice and resurrection of *Faro, Mangala* sent him to Earth in an ark in company of the eight female seeds that remained in the celestial womb when Pemba departed with their seven male seed partners. The creation of humans was carried out through the combined mouth of the Nummo *twin*s. The very first ones consisted of seven professionals. In the Yorùbá story, God sent Arch-Divinity *Orìṣà-Nlà* in a mission to fill the preexisting marsh that became Earth in collaboration with the hen and the pigeon while being counseled all the time by Divinity Òrunmìlà. And when the time came to populate the world with humans, *Olódùmarè* sent Divinity *Orèlúéré* in a group of heavenly hosts who became the first human beings on Earth. In the Luba story, *Maweja Nangila* first metamorphosed Self into three Lord Spirits, to whom He later added one more. Afterwards, *Maweja Nangila* created four pairs of superior spirits, each pair comprised of a senior member and a junior member. Then, *Maweja Nangila* made subsequent creations in pairs of senior and junior elements.

The Family Community

As to humans, everywhere across Africa, God creates them man and woman and gave them the mandate to procreate as husbands and wives and populate the world with their progeny of men and women. The African people take marriage and procreation very seriously. Both are preceded by considerable preparations designed to prevent potential threats to marriage stability and to the child's legitimacy, group identity, and material and spiritual well-being. The preparations involve not only the future spouses and parents, but also their respective extended families. Children are taken good care of both as physical beings and returning spirits. Both parents and children are born into biological communities larger than their immediate progenitors. Children's community membership is fostered by means of socialization mechanisms designed to make them valued contributors and responsible fathers and mothers in their adult age. Socialization to this end is a life-long process, but dramatized at major junctions such as birth, initiation, marriage, and death.

The Kinship Community

Kinship communities are based on common descent. They are kept together by pervasive practices of sharing and demonstration of respect for seniority. Also, various rituals are performed which contribute to strengthening the kinship bond both among the living and between the living and the dead: sacred rituals in honor of common ancestors, for instance. Common participation in rituals sometimes takes place at a higher level than the extended family or the clan. Such is often the case with initiation and funerals.

(Endnotes)
1   Gbotokuma, Zekeh S. "Polygyny in Africa: A Male's Post-original Sin or Rejection of the Primeval Monogyny and Affirmation of Sexual Inequality." Quoting "The Revolt Against God." http://www.bu.edu/wcp/Papers/Afri/ AfriGbot. 10 Pages.

2   Countries and their Cultures Forum. ND. "Kikuyu Economy." https://www.everyculture.com/Africa-Middle-East/Kikuyu-Economy.html. Retrieved 6-25-2019.

3   Op Cit.

4   Barnett, Errol. 2013. "Rock Churches of Lalibela, the Jerusalem of Ethiopia." *CNN Travel.* Published 27th June 2013. https://www.cnn.com/travel/article/rock-churches-lalibela-ethiopia/index.html. Retrieved 1-25-2020.

5   Finke, Jens. ND. "Kikuyu Circumcision." From Jens Finkle. *Traditional Music & Cultures of Kenya.* 2000-2003. http://www.bluegecko.org/kenya/tribes/kikuyu/circumcision.htm. Retrieved 3-13-2020.

Chapter 9
A Compassionate Caretaker of Fellow Humans

1. Care for the Household and Hospitality for Guests
2. Care for Children
3. Care for the Sick
4. Care for the Dying

Humans are predestined to live in communities where they share responsibilities and take care of self and each other. This chapter discusses four categories of a community's care beneficiaries: households and their guests, children, the sick, and the dying, as traditionally practiced among different African ethnic groups. Traditional attire, food, and healthcare are extensively described to demonstrate the variety of practices across the African continent, particularly among the Luba of Congo DRC.

1. CARE FOR THE HOUSEHOLD AND HOSPITALITY FOR GUESTS

Regular care for the household consists of housing, clothing, and feeding. Hospitality refers to accommodation, with housing and or food, of travelers in transit or short-term visitors. Hospitality is practiced everywhere in Africa with ethnic variations. Often, relatives who are guests become long-term household members. The illustrations below are taken from the Somalis of Somalia, the Luba of the Congo, DRC, and the Yoruba of Nigeria.

Food and Housing Accommodations for Guests

Both in rural areas and in urban centers, "visitors expect to be invited to eat and the host is obliged to cook more than necessary in case additional guests arrive" (Falola 2001, speaking of Nigeria). Sharing food with passerby neighbors was common in Luba villages. Luba men eat outside in the veranda of a house or in the shade of a *mulemba* tree in an elder's compound. Eating inside is a synonym for stinginess, refusal to share. Eating outside allows for the by-passers to see and eventually join the partakers if they wish to. Often, to encourage them to do so, one of the partakers would yell to by-passers, saying:

> *Maja a Kabuta, mwannyisha wavwa kuja.*
> Eating is a nightjar dance; he who wishes let him join the circle.

A neighbor who is at another's house at meal time and is invited to eat is not expected to simply refuse to eat. That would be equivalent to saying: "Do not eat at my house even if someone invites you to." Eating a little bit and then excusing self would be more acceptable. A related hospitality etiquette prohibits asking a visiting adult relative or friend, at or close to meal time: "Do you want to eat?" Such a question suggests that you do not really want that person to eat. For that reason, the person may say no even if he or she is hungry. A proper approach would be: "Join us; sit over here; the water to wash the hands is right here." Or, if the food is still cooking, "Have a seat, we will be eating soon."

Many traditional houses in Nigeria are rectangular multifamily compounds with large walls and are high enough to prevent neighbors from seeing inside, while allowing light and air to get in. Inside the compound, individual housing units are built around the wall facing a large open internal courtyard. The compound entrance opens into the courtyard. The courtyard is common space where various social and occupational functions are carried out. Yoruba compounds are built with large verandas providing shades for sitting, cooking or relaxing. Many compounds have a reception room for guests designed to prevent guests from entering directly into the courtyard. Among the Hausa, a second reception area—an antechamber—protects further the privacy of the residents, particularly the women who might be working in the courtyard (Falola, 2001).

In Luba villages, in Congo DRC, each wife of a polygamous man has her own house in a determined corner of the compound. Until the 1960s, a respectable head of the household also had a guesthouse (*beesa* or *ndaku*) in the center of the compound. The guesthouse had a sitting area and one or two bedrooms. The sitting area was for welcoming important guests or entertaining locals in bad weather. The room was also used to serve food to visitors. Food prepared specifically for guests is for them alone, not to be shared with members of the host family. The guests may invite some to eat with them, but the latter are expected to turn down the invitation. Special guests, such as in-laws, are welcomed with a whole chicken meal. All the chicken parts must be accounted for; otherwise it was not a chicken, rather only some chicken meat. The leftover pieces were for them to take back home. Stopover travelers were offered hospitality as well. They were served the Luba *nshima* starchy food which is made of corn and cassava flours and served with whatever accompaniment is available (All authentic Luba meals include the *nshima*). Travelers from far away could also seek hospitality at the chief's court. Chiefs generally had several guesthouses. It happened to my brother Ngoyi Kabwina and I in Eastern Kasai, on our way from Tshimenga to FOMULAC Kalenda, past Tielen Saint-Jacques Catholic Mission Station. We sought hospitality at the compound of Chief Kanda Kanda.

A house, as living quarters, has a certain structure. The portable family home of the Somali nomads, *eqal*, is comprised of an atrium, as part of the entryway; and an inner sleeping area. The father and older male children sleep in the men's fire corner. Younger children sleep with the mother in their own fire corner. Older daughters and grandmothers may have their own portable home, though smaller, called *buul*. Male visitors must sleep outside around a fire camp set especially for them. A classic Luba house comprises three sections. First, the bed is always located to the right when entering the house, with the head always turned toward the door. The hearth is always at the foot of the bed in the right corner, away from the entrance. Over the hearth is a stand where items are laid out to dry. This is also where fish and game meat are dried. The left side of the house, opposite the bed, is empty, except for the far left corner, where a jar keeping drinking water is kept. The remaining space is used for sitting on a chair, a stool, a mat, or a goatskin when it is raining outside. It is also used for sleeping quarters for visiting close relatives when separate quarters are not available. Sometimes, out of respect for the guest, the host would give his or her bed to the guest and would sleep on a mat on the floor opposite the bed. A mother who comes to provide maternal care to a daughter in the first three months after giving birth will sleep on the mat, the daughter in her habitual bed. A parent is not permitted to sleep in a daughter's or a son's conjugal bed. Doing so would be a violation in the category of incestuous behaviors. Parents are not allowed to sleep in a son's or a daughter's house as a couple. Worse, it would be an abomination, if they had sex in the house of their son or daughter, married or unmarried. Likewise, it is prohibited for children to have sex in their parents' house.

Clothing

Care for the household includes providing the members with clothing. African people's traditional dress before European influences ranged from the most modest to quite complex. The Igbo of Nigeria and the Luba of the Congo and many others once dressed very simply: short raffia clothes (*madiba*). Initially, both men and women went bare-chested. In some parts of the continent, the *raffia cloth* was an elaborate work of art. Think about the *velour du Kasai* produced by the Kuba people of the Congo. We have described the dress of the Ndebele of southern Africa in connection with their love for corporal decorations. Little girls wore beaded aprons and beaded wraparound skirts. Marriageable young women after initiation, or newlywed without a house of their own built by the husband, wore hoops of twisted grass. The dress of a settled married woman living in her own home built by the husband included a blanket over her shoulders. She also had elaborate dresses and ornaments symbolizing her bond and faithfulness to him. By tradition, a married woman had her head covered with a beaded headband, a knitted cap, or an elaborate beaded headdress in respect for her husband. The principal dress for a Ndebele man consisted of a breast-plate made of an animal skin, decorated with beads around the top, worn hanging from the neck, given to the man by his father at initiation as a symbol of manhood. The others included animal skin bands worn around the head and the ankles and an animal skin around the shoulders to keep warm (Vuk'uzenzele, 2007).[1]

Traditionally, Somali women wore *guntiino*, a long dress knotted on either shoulder and wrapped around the chest and waist, with a fold hanging on the back to be used as a hood. A bright-color camel-thread belt is tied around the waist. The belt for adolescent young women was of particular bright colors terminating in a tassel. In urban centers women wore a long skirt, a blouse, and a shawl on the shoulders. Traditional Somali men wore a white cotton wrapper from the waist to just above the ankles and a top part consisting of another wrapper draped over the shoulder or shaped into a hood. The Yoruba and Hausa of Nigeria have a long tradition of hand-weaving textile cloth making using cotton or silk materials. The dress consisted of *a poncho* called *dashiki* among the Hausa, *buba* among the Yoruba, and *mboubou* in Wolof. The most voluminous *boubou* robe, called *babban-riga*, now omnipresent across Nigeria, is of Hausa origin and was first adopted by the Nupe and the Yoruba. The *Babban-riga* is often worn by kings, chiefs, important merchants and politicians as a mark of prestige. Other hand-woven textile materials from Nigeria include wool blankets and embroidered clothes by the Fulani people, and the wrapper mostly worn in different forms and styles by women: from the chest to above the ankles, around the waist to the calves or below, hanging over the shoulder, or tied around the head. The Fulani practice Islam and generally live by the Islamic code of modesty. They live in different countries—Mali, Nigeria, Cameroon, Chad and Sudan. In general, married men and women wear a long robe. Men wear solid-color large gowns, pants and caps, and wrapped cloth around their head. Women wear wraps and blouses. Nomadic Fulani women wear headdresses rather than the classic Muslim veil. Younger men and women braid their hair and wear headdresses decorated with jewelry (Abdullahi 2001, Falola 2001) (The Heart of Africa. ND. "Fulani Tribe").[2]

Everywhere in Africa, men's apparel has changed more dramatically under the impact of European colonization than women's. In the Congo, the most common women's dress in ancient times consisted of a *raffia* or bead skirt (*civunga*). The torso was generally uncovered. Gradually, the *raffia* or bead skirt was replaced with a wrap worn from the waist down to the ankles. The wrap has remained the distinctive dress of the Congolese woman to date. The wrap (*kikwembe*) is worn with a top made of the same material sewn the African way (*libaya* or *dibaya*) or a western blouse. In rural areas, the wrap is often simply tied at the waist by a cloth belt with the upper edge of the wrap hanging over the belt. On special or festive occasions, the upper part of the wrap is generally rolled over. Sometimes, women wear two wraps rather than one. In this case, the first (*kikwembe*), a longer wrap, hangs over the belt. The second (*liputa, dipupila*), generally a smaller wrap, is worn around the hips and rolled over several times at the waist. The second wrap is not part of a rural woman's typical dress. Slippers, sandals, and thongs are the typical footwear for those who can afford them. Those who cannot, go barefooted. Well-off women, mostly urban, wear more beautiful and more expensive wraps, tops, and shoes. The preferred clothing material for wraps is called wax. The Congo had a wax print textile factory at Maluku, near Kinshasa. Nevertheless, women of distinction prefer imported wax, particularly the one from Holland. It is believed to be of better quality. It preserves its texture and look over a longer period of time and lasts longer. The Congolese woman often substitutes an imported blouse for the wax top. For a more satisfactory dress, she wears a kerchief tied around the head with the ends hanging down in the back. The head kerchief can be of a different material or the same as the other wraps. *La Congolaise moderne* (the modern Congolese woman) enjoys complementing her festive dress with some jewelry, such as a bracelet, a necklace and earrings. However, conspicuous wearing of jewelry is not a common practice among Congolese women (Mukenge, 2002).

Congolese men, just as women, once wore one or two pieces of raffia cloth around the waist. Later, printed material replaced the raffia. Until the 1940s and 1950s, men in some countryside villages dressed in a clothing material (*kikwembe*) wrapped around the hips with the upper end pulled though a belt at the waist and turned over several times to form a role (*cifunda*). The shirt was tucked inside the *kikwembe*. The men's *kikwembe* was comparable to today's most common African women's dress, with the exception that the color was either all white or *nzobazoba*, that is, an alternation of white and blue strips descending vertically. Sometimes, the *kikwembe* was wrapped around the body under the left arm and knotted over the right shoulder. In this form the dress was called *mupaalala*. The *mupaalala* could be worn without a shirt but, since the right side remained open, it was worn with shorts or long pants. The men's *kikwembe*, just like a woman's, descended from the waist to the ankles, and the *mupaalala* from the shoulder to the knees. In the 1950s, long and short pants replaced the *cifunda* completely. The *mupaalala* could still be seen in some regions. Long or short pants were worn with a shirt (*muteelu*). At first, the shirt was mostly a short sleeve-one (*cijika*). Gradually, the long-sleeve shirt (*nshimishi*) became popular. To date, the tie (*nkolu*) and the dress jacket (*nkoci*) are more a part of urban rather than rural attire. Today, as in the past, during ceremonial dances, particularly those executed in the waist, men wear a woman's wrap rolled in *cifunda* around the waist (Mukenge, 2002).

The cases discussed above clearly demonstrate that dress is not exclusively an expression of personal taste. It has always had multiple functions. From among other functions, dress can be an expression of political will imposed by a person of power. During the Mobutu Dictatorship (1965-1997), Congolese men's dress underwent two revolutions. The first revolution came out of China. President Mobutu adopted Chairman Mao Tse-Tung's *abacos* for himself and imposed it on all the citizens as the national dress for men. Ties and jackets were banned. *Abacoses*, imported ready-made or sewn locally with imported material, flooded Kinshasa stores. In fact, local tailors, Congolese and foreigners, became makers of long-sleeve and short-sleeve *abacoses*. However, the *abacos* was too expensive for the ordinary citizen. This condition favored the second revolution, the popularization of the classic multicolored cloth for women, *le wax,* among men. At first, the *wax* became more valued than ever before. Congolese women of higher socio-economic status became unofficial fashion models. Various *wax* materials were imported from Holland. The local factory followed up with imitations. From being exclusively a women's clothing, *le wax* became a men's clothing as well. Wearing *wax* shirts became acceptable to men. Along with the *wax*, men adopted *le boubou*, the Congolese version of the West African *dashiki*. *Boubous* in multicolored *wax* material became part of a man's normal clothing choices. The *wax* and *le boubou* outlived the Mobutu dictatorship. The *abacos* was abandoned. Ties and jackets came back (Mukenge, 2002).

Feeding

Peoples of all cultures adopt diets and develop eating habits which they believe enable them to achieve the life goal of physical strength with plenitude. Each ethnicity has its own notion of what constitutes eating well. Most African diets consist of a starchy food accompanied by some meat, and a variety of vegetable sauces and insects. Variations abound within and across countries as to what starch staple dominates. In Somalia, for instance, rice dishes dominate in the north, spaghetti dishes in the south, and corn or sorghum polenta in rural riverine zones. In Nigeria, yam, cassava, beans, and rice are the leading staples; but of these crops, yam is the king. The Igbo even have solemn celebrations of yam harvest. *Yam* is eaten under several forms: boiled, roasted, fried, or mashed with vegetables and other ingredients. However, in most parts of Nigeria, *amala,* a starch made of yam powder, generally eaten with vegetables and stew, is the most esteemed dish. Yam for *amala* is first dried, pounded, and then converted into powder. Popular also is cassava turned *fufu*, a dumpling made of *garri* powder from grated and roasted cassava. Other popular starches in Nigeria are corn, rice, and beans. Each is consumed in a variety of forms (Falola, 2001).

In Uganda, beans, cassava, corn, groundnuts, millet, plantain and sorghum are the major food crops. Some of the most known traditional African starch dishes in Uganda include *ugali, posho, matoke, and katogo*. *Ugali*, also largely consumed in Kenya and in Katanga and Kivu provinces, in *Congo DRC*, is a paste made from corn flour in northern, southern and eastern Uganda. *Posho* is the name for corn *ugali* in the south. There exists, in the west and northwest, *ugali* made from millet. Cornmeal *posho* is a popular breakfast food. *Matoke* is a dumpling made with boiled or steamed green bananas. *Katogo* is a breakfast meal made with fried plantains. *Matoke* and *ugali* are also popular traditional starch meals in Kenya, Uganda's neighbor. Other Kenyan dominant traditional dishes include *githeri*, a mixture of corn and beans; *pilau*, rice cooked in a flavored broth of meat or vegetables; *mukimo*, mashed green peas, potatoes, corn and pumpkin leaves; *wali wa nazi*, popular along the Indian Ocean, is white rice cooked with grated coconut meat and preferably served with fish, chicken, vegetables, or bean stew coconut rice; and *irio*. Irio, originally a Gikuyu people's staple, is a plate of green peas and potatoes, which is boiled, mashed, and sprinkled with corn kernels, and served side-by-side. It is best appreciated when accompanied by a roasted game meat mixture of mashed potatoes, peas, and corn (Eguda 2017, World Travel Guide ND., Dermand Africa. ND, Migrationology. ND).[3]

In the Congo, *kwanga*, a cassava-based bread, is widespread in the Capital of Kinshasa, Lower-Congo, Bandundu, Equator Province, and part of Eastern Province. *Nshima* or *bidya,* a paste made with corn flour and cassava flour, is the favorite food in Western and Eastern Kasai provinces. In North Sankuru, rice is the king, whereas beans prevail in the Kivu provinces. Plantain is consumed as a starch also. *Lituma*, a plantain cake originated from Eastern Province, has become familiar in Kinshasa as well. The staple meals we have identified across the African continent are not consumed alone. They are always accompanied by other foods—vegetables, meat, fish, and insects or, very often, some combination. Below are some details about *nshima*, the traditional starch of the Luba people who live in Western and Eastern Kasai provinces of Congo DRC, and its accompaniments to illustrate a particular ethnic notion of good eating.

The Nshima Starchy Meal

Food selection, preparation, serving, and eating are reflective of a people's life style. The notions of good food and bad food, nutritious and non-nutritious foods; major staple food and accompanying secondary foods; meals and snacks; all differ from one people to another. They are cultural and relative notions.

Nshima. If a Luba person tells you he or she has eaten well, more likely than not that person had some *nshima*: a paste made of a mixture of corn flour and cassava flour, accompanied with cassava leaves or some other green vegetable and some meat (e.g., chicken, goat, or fish). Actually, for the Luba, 'to eat' is to eat some *nshima*. Hence *nshima*'s other name, *bidya*, from the verb *kudya*, to eat. It is the one food a Luba person thinks about in the first place when it comes to eating. All other starchy food items—beans, rice, sweet potatoes, and plantains—whether accompanied with meat, greens, fish or not, are *midyoko*: snacks and hunger palliatives. The Luba diet is very rich in leafy vegetables. Cassava leaves are the dominant vegetable. Very often, in addition to or in the absence of cassava leaves (*kaleji*), the *nshima* starch will be accompanied with amaranths (*citekuteku*), bitter leaves (*muteeta*), pumpkin leaves (*mudibu*), sweet potato leaves (*cilungalunga*) or beans leaves (*nsanpu*). Quite often, a typical meal will also include some flying insects (*nswa*), or some caterpillars (*meshi*) cooked in a pumpkin seed sauce (*nteta*). Fish, particularly smoked fish, is often cooked in pumpkin seed sauce as well.

The term *nshima* dominates in Lubaland. In other parts of Kasai it is called *bidya*, *byaji*, or *bidyaj*. Elsewhere in the Congo, it has different names too. It is called *fufu* in Bandundu, Equator, Lower Congo provinces and in the city of Kinshasa; and *ugali* in Katanga, Kivu, and Upper Congo provinces. The ideal *nshima* is a balanced mixture of corn flour and cassava flour. Corn is a seasonal crop and often becomes scarce in the dry season, May to August, and before the first rainy-season harvest in December. Cassava may be available throughout the year. In times of scarcity, there is an imbalance in the *nshima* mixture in favor of the cassava flour. A cassava-dominated *nshima* is denigrated in Lubaland as *mulutu*, a gum-like paste.

Nshima preparation begins with the grinding or pounding of dried and hulled corn (*matala*). Corn harvesting, drying, hulling, and grinding or pounding are a woman's tasks. She pounds corn with a pestle in a large wooden mortar while standing and holding the pestle with both hands. She does the grinding in a kneeling position on a large concave stone with a small flat stone or a short pestle held in her both hands. Each time a grinding or pounding operation is completed, she collects the pulverized corn in a large basin (*dilongo*) or a close knit round basket (*cibata*). Cassava preparation for *nshima* begins with unearthing the roots, steeping them for three-to-four days and, when they are soft enough, drying them on a stand built outside the house or on top of the fireplace in the kitchen. Cassava not consumed immediately is kept in the attic of the kitchen where it continues to receive the necessary heat for better conservation from the fireplace. Dried cassava is sliced and pounded in the same way corn is. Cassava dried on top of the fireplace and stored in the attic is scrubbed first to remove the dark dust. In the cities, cassava is not kept in the kitchen attic; storage time is shorter, and the need for scrubbing is minimal. Also, in cities, traditional methods of making flour have been replaced by a small engine-powered corn mill; or else women buy ready-made flour from modern food stores. The last operation before cooking the *nshima* is sifting in order to separate the refined flour from the unfinished parts. To cook the *nshima*, one heats the water first, and then slowly pours a small quantity of corn flour while stirring with a wooden spoon (*mupanji*). When the mix comes back to a boil, cassava flour and more corn flour are added and stirred up to full consistency. The paste thus formed is *nshima*.

Chapter 9
Vegetables and other Accompaniments to Nshima

The Luba people do not have the habit of eating raw vegetables with the exception of eggplants (*njilu*) of which they only grow the small greenish variety. Even then, eating a raw eggplant is sporadic. In general, eggplants are eaten cooked mixed with another vegetable, such as cassava leaves (*kaleji*) or bitter leaves (*muteeta*). After plucking, all vegetables are washed thoroughly before cooking.

Matamba, or kaleji: cassava leaves. After plucking and washing, *matamba* or *kaleji* goes through some intermediate preparatory stages before cooking, including pounding in a mortar and soaking in a pot for about an hour or more. Sometimes cassava leaves are boiled, and then prepared, washed, pounded and cooked without soaking. This is what is called *kaleji ka munsompela*. Cassava leaves and most vegetables are simply seasoned with oil and salt, generally a small quantity of each. Sometimes, cassava leaves are seasoned with some homemade bicarbonate called *binshidimba*. When seasoned in this manner, cassava leaves are called *cimpwendampwenda*. The Luba people are known for loving cassava leaves. The frequency of *matamba* consumption in Luba families is romanticized as a measure of love:

> *Bakuswa peeba bu mwakaswabo matamba, matamba mu lwesu baaka makwabo.*
> Blessed is the one who is loved like *matamba*, more *matamba* are being plucked even while the previous ones are still in the pot.

Citekuteku. This spinach-like green vegetable is probably the most frequently consumed vegetable in Luba families after cassava leaves, *kaleji. Citekuteku*'s plural—*bitekuteku*—and *kaleji*'s plural—*tuleji*—are often employed in the generic sense of greens. Also, sometimes, as an expression of humility a host will invite a guest of honor to eat some *tuleji* or some *bitekuteku* even if neither *kaleji* nor *citekuteku* is being served.

Bowa. Mushrooms are among Luba families' valued vegetables. The Luba people consider mushrooms a little bit more special than other vegetables, perhaps because of the uncertainty of harvesting them. All mushrooms are wild. Noone grows them. They are picked during the rainy season in areas where the grass has been burned. Perhaps also because of meat scarcity, Luba adults sometimes tell children that mushrooms are a kind of meat.

Insects, a major part of the* Luba *diet. Only certain species of ants, grasshoppers, and caterpillars are edible. Two varieties of flying ants, one white (*bintunta, bitenda*) and one brown (*nswa*) are edible. Both develop in mounds: the white variety in slim and cone-shaped mounds (*mitenda, mitunda*; singular *mutenda, mutunda*) and the brown variety in larger, dome-shaped mounds (*bilundu*; singular *cilundu*). The white ants are eaten raw or grilled. Brown ants are eaten broiled, grilled, or dried. A third variety of edible ants (*mankenena*) develops in mounds also but do not fly. They move around in columns and they sting. Their English name is soldiers.

Crickets and Grasshoppers. Only one variety of crickets, *mintuntu* or *myenza*, is edible. They live in individual holes. Sometimes a *muntuntu* (singular of *mintuntu*) will be seen coming out of the hole and going back in continuously. It is nicknamed *muntuntu wa luholoho*, "coming-out-and-going-in" *muntuntu*. Two varieties of grasshoppers, *minkesa* and *malaala* or *mbedi*, are popular in the Luba country. Also famous is the one called *kamanyimanyi*, which is used as an ingredient in the making of some medicine. Hence its nickname *kamanyimanyi mpasu wa bijimba. Mpasu* is CiLuba for grasshopper. *Wa bijimba* means "one to serve as a medicinal ingredient." Ants of the soldier variety, crickets, and grasshoppers are eaten grilled or broiled.

Meshi, Caterpillars. *Meshi* are more valued than other insects. Edible varieties of caterpillars are called *meshi*. The non-edible ones are *biishiishi*. It is repugnant to touch them. One variety of edible caterpillars, *mansamba*, is commercialized throughout the Congo. The Tshikapa region, in Western Kasai, toward the Congo-Angola border, is known for being the *mansamba* cradle. Caterpillars that are native to the Lubaland are known by the names of the trees in which they grow: *meshi a citefu* (*citefu* tree caterpillars), *meshi a mutooci* (*mutooci* tree caterpillars), and *meshi a cifumba* (*cifumba* tree caterpillars). Close to *meshi* are the grubs (*mposa*) that develop in the heart of the palm tree. Also worth mentioning is the variety called *tumpeketa*. They develop in the young grass that grows on the land that has been put to fire. They have two distinctive characteristics: They are very small in size, much smaller than other caterpillars. Also, they constantly move their heads from side to side. Hence the characterization: *tumpeketa kupa mutu* (head-shaking *tumpeketa*).

Munyinyi ne mishipa. Meat and Fish are other natural accompaniments to *nshima*. The Luba raise chickens (*nzolu*) and goats (*mbuji*), but not primarily for meat. Goats are principally for sealing marriage alliances, and chickens for rituals and for entertaining guests of honor—particularly friends and in-laws. Ducks (*mpaatu, mabata*), pigs (*ngu*Luba), and sheep (*mikooko*) are less valued and are raised to a much lower degree. Game is said to have been abundant in the Luba areas a long time ago. It is no longer the case. The Lubaland territory is relatively small, relatively largely-populated, and lacks forests. Commercialized beef is practically absent from Luba villages. In brief, meat is rare in the Luba people's country. People try to compensate with rodents (*mpuku*). But still the need for meat often goes unmet. Consequently, when available, meat is consumed with parsimony (*kulobelela*)—in small portions that can last. It is generally stewed and the juice serves to dip the *nshima* starch in to make it more palatable, softer, and easier to swallow. Even fish is rare in many Luba villages. There are not many rivers running nearby. Some of the few that are available in a one-day walking distance are shark-stricken. The scarcity of both meat and fish has instilled into the Luba the incentive to practice long-distance trade. Dried fish and smoked meat are brought to the area from other Congolese provinces, particularly Katanga, by returning local seasonal traders. Salted fish, *makayabo*, is another import allowing for meeting the challenge of meat scarcity. In villages, fresh fish is eaten stewed most of time and at times grilled. Fish for future consumption is smoked for better preservation.

Nteta. In general, *nteta* means seeds. In this particular case it designates pumpkin seeds, a very valued accompaniment to *nshima*. The seeds are first removed from the fruit by hand or with the help of a spoon and dropped into a basin or a calabash bowl. Next, they are washed, dried, shelled, mixed with fresh tomato and fresh-cut onion and ground into a mortar with a pestle. The product is collected in a basin or a pot and then divided into small quantities that are then picked up and molded into balls with the right hand palm.

In most cases, *nteta* are cooked with dried fish. The fish is rinsed and cooked in water along with *nteta* and seasoned to satisfaction. *Nteta* can also be cooked with *meshi* (caterpillars). Hairy caterpillars or tough-skin caterpillars are burned first and washed before frying and mixing with *nteta* for complete cooking. Depending on the variety and taste, some caterpillar species are dried or coated with flour before cooking whether alone or mixed with *nteta*. Finally, *nteta* can be cooked mixed with meat, goat meat in most cases. The meat for *nteta* is stewed and seasoned with an aromatic herb called *cikota*.

Condiments. The most common cooking style in Luba villages, and the rest of the Congo, is the stew. The juice from cooking greens, fish, or meat serves as sauce for dipping the *nshima* or sprinkling over rice. Tomatoes and onions are grown in the Congo. However, they are more associated with urban life than rural life. They are often absent from some rural areas. Many villagers season their food with a variety of aromatic herbs. The Luba season their meat, especially chicken, with the leaves of the already mentioned aromatic *cikota* herb. Also popular are two herbs close to each other by name and by flavor: i.e., *lwenyi* and *cidibulwenyi*. Like everywhere, the Luba people cook their meat, fish and vegetables with oil (*mafuta*) and salt (*mukela* or *lwepu*). However, they prefer them, particularly cassava leaves (*kaleji, matamba*) with as little salt as possible (*mukela wa kansadinsadi*). Palm oil is practically the only variety known in Luba villages. Even here the use is very parsimonious. The palm leaf was the measurement standard by cooking. The cook would plunge the leaf in the oil calabash or bottle, pull it out, hold it upside down by the stem, and then bring down the oil into the cooking pot by pressing the leaf with two fingers. Congolese ethnic groups differ as to how they spice their food. The Luba use red pepper (*kansanga*) very sparingly, if at all. They prefer sweet green pepper (*ndungu wa mbuji*). Even then, the Luba may go a long time without it, and without missing it.

2. CARING FOR CHILDREN

Procreation is a high value in itself. In the mind of African people, procreation is a supreme value that often supersedes and justifies marriage. Marriage without children is meaningless and very fragile. Marriage for love alone is nonsense, unless there are legitimate attenuating circumstances for not having children. In most traditional African societies, parents give birth to as many children as the mother can possibly conceive, provided that customary rules of proper birth spacing are respected. The Luba people express the primacy of procreation by saying: "*Kulela ki panu*", "to live is above all to procreate." Taking care of children is part of what human procreation means. Humans do not bring forth children to let them fend for themselves early in their life on Earth. Responsible parents take care of their children until the latter can sustain themselves as adults. Children are believed to be returning spirits. Therefore, spiritual cares are an imperative. Otherwise the child's growth and success in life will be compromised. Children's spiritual cares have been discussed in Chapter 1.

There is no need for restating them here. Actually caring for the well-being of the child begins long before conception, as the parents, particularly the mother, try to avoid behaviors, situations and conditions of mind (genetic package transfer) that can jeopardize conception, birthing, or the child's growth, and its full physical, mental and emotional development. They are also concerned about the social rules of legitimacy that might cause the child to be accepted as a full-fledged community member or be rejected instead. Culturally accepted practices to prevent unwanted pregnancy, or to cause wanted pregnancy to occur, are conceived in the best interest of the child and not of either parent. Care for the baby's well-being before conception takes different specific forms during pregnancy, at birth, and after birth.

Care for the Unborn and Newborn Child

Concern with legitimacy. Luba childcare, before birth, begins with the concern for legitimate procreation. Ideally, the mission to procreate is carried out within the framework of a legitimate marriage as defined by the society's custom. For most African societies, this means a marriage involving a transfer of bridewealth from the groom's family to the bride's family. The *CiLuba* word for procreation is *lulelu*. However, this term is mostly used for procreation in marriage and contrasts with *bulelavi*, disorderly birth-giving, applied to childbearing out of wedlock. In this respect, legitimate marriage is an aspect of child care. Parents' attitudes toward pregnancy before and after conceptions are other important aspects of child care. They include the Luba woman's precaution to prevent unwanted pregnancy, longing for conception, and caring for the baby in the womb and after birth.

Preventing unwanted pregnancy. The Luba woman's sexual life plays a key role in preventing unwanted pregnancy. In traditional Africa, sexual intercourse was not directed toward pleasure alone. What justified it most was the hope that it would result in a pregnancy. For this reason, it was discouraged when pregnancy was unwanted, such as before marriage and after giving birth. A Luba girl was considered ripe for marriage at the age of puberty, when she became corpulent and her breasts formed (*mabeela masaba*). Whereas a girl married around 14 to 16 years of age, a boy generally married around twenty or even later. He had to grow further not only physically, but also intellectually and socially. His maturity was measured by his sense of responsibility and ability to provide for his basic needs for food, clothing and housing. He had to start his own field and build his own house before qualifying for marriage (Mukenge, 1967: 36-37). A girl was expected to remain a virgin until marriage. Her first sexual contact with her husband was a test of virginity for her and a test of virility for him. Very often, if the husband was a young man, this contact was his first sexual experience as well. The Luba believe that if a boy becomes sexually active too early, he will become weak. On the first night, the husband was expected to be powerful in order to perform the deflowering of the bride successfully and gently in order to spare her too much pain. Part of the bridewealth paid by the groom's family to the bride's family for the marriage consisted of a goat for the mother (*mbuji wa nyima*), which was designed to reward her for having preserved her daughter's virginity through good moral education. It was a shame for her and the entire family had the girl to be found no longer a virgin.

In some Luba lineages, *Beena Citoolo,* for example, the bride was forced to denounce the man who had taken her virtue away. Her relatives would go to that man's village, capture any goat of their choice, and it would be his and his family's responsibility to compensate the owner (Mukenge, 1967).

Seeking pregnancy. In marriage, everything was done to allow pregnancy to occur. During sexual intercourse, husband and wife had this goal in mind. Practices that could interfere with conception, such as the withdrawal by the husband before ejaculation, were discouraged (Waife, 1978: 8). A woman who pulled off before her partner's ejaculation was said to have rejected both the man and the soul of the child (*mukuja*) that his sperm carries. Even after the two had reached the orgasm, the man was expected to remain inside the woman for a while longer. The woman was not expected to stand up right away and walk away or clean herself immediately. Instead, she had to continue to lie down on her back, still, long enough to allow the spermatozoids (*biluma*) to walk their way through to the egg.

Caring for the Baby in the Womb. During pregnancy, the future mother is first concerned about preventing miscarriage, then about the health of the fetus, and then, toward the end, about having an easy and live delivery. Sexual activity is encouraged in the first months of the pregnancy. The Luba people say that the sperm strengthens the pregnancy. At the same time, parents are concerned about preventing miscarriage. To this effect, the pregnant woman once wore a medicinal belt of lianas around her waist. This action is called *kukanga difu*, to stabilize the pregnancy. Later during pregnancy, the future mother was concerned about the health of the fetus. Around the seventh month, she abstained from sexual activity. She feared that the husband's sperm would blind the baby or sexual activity could precipitate birth. As she tried avoiding premature birth, she also prepared for an easy delivery. To this effect, while waiting for the pregnancy to come to term, she rubbed her belly with a slippery herb called *nsenu*, which was kept in warm water.

Caring for the baby at birth. The health and safety of the baby are major concerns during labor. The mid-wife instructs the mother to put the health and life of the baby above her child-birth pains. Among other things, she must keep her legs apart while pushing the baby toward the birth canal. Immediately following the delivery, the mid-wife picks up the baby, cuts the umbilical cord, and ties a knot at the end of the section still attached to the baby. While doing this, she pays attention to not letting any drop of blood from the umbilical cord fall on the baby's body, particularly the genitals. The Luba believe that if this happens to a baby boy, he will become impotent. She cleanses the baby's body and clears the baby's mouth and throat with a finger. She checks the baby's nostrils and heartbeat to ensure the baby is alive.

Care for the Baby Early After Birth. Of particular importance for the child's general well-being after birth is the mother's abstinence. The traditional Luba mother's abstinence, begun during the latter part of pregnancy, is continued for at least a year after the baby is born. A mother's sexual activity during this period is deemed not to be good for the child's health. Since the baby is breast-fed, the sperm is believed to spoil the milk in the mother's body. The mother also fears becoming pregnant again too soon. Luba society disapproves of the space between two births being too close in time. To minimize the risk, the husband sleeps with his other wives. In the past, new mothers married to monogamous husbands were sent to their parents during the abstinence period. Christianity changed the way the above traditions were lived. Christian missionaries opposed polygamy and discouraged sending Christian wives to their un-baptized parents. Traditional rules of birth spacing came to be constantly violated in Christian families. These violations, the Roman Catholic Church's opposition to abortion and use of contraceptives, and Luba people's own desire for abundant progeny gave rise to large families even in monogamous households.

Physical Care for the Child

Feeding, bedding, and bathing. The baby's diet during the first three months was centered on the mother's milk and on water. When occasionally a chicken was killed, the mother placed drops of the sauce on the baby's tongue. She also mashed little pieces of meat with her fingers and placed them in the child's mouth. The baby's reliance on the mother's milk could pose health problems both for the mother and for the baby. As much as possible, the mother's meals included some meat or fish. However, both meat and fish were scarce in many Luba villages. Mothers of newborn babies were encouraged to cook their cassava leaves—the most popular green vegetable in the region—in a lot of juice and to drink the juice at the end of the meal to increase the milk in their bodies. At three months, porridge made of cassava flour was added to the baby's diet. Cassava contains a lot of starch and does not contribute much to health.

From birth to about the age of three years or so, the Luba child shared the mother's bed. As with feeding, the baby's regular physical needs during the first three months were provided for by the mother. Every morning, by six o'clock, the time adults woke up to go to the fields, she would wake up the baby. It was believed that if two persons sleep in the same bed, the one who arises first would incorporate the strengths of the other person while discharging his or her own weaknesses on the person still sleeping. To protect the child from her own weaknesses, the mother awakes the child when she arises. Thus, they start their day at the same time. The first care is a massage, a sort of morning exercise for the child, in the veranda of the mother's house. The mother sits down on a mat or a stool with her legs extended. She lays the baby on the stomach on her legs. Then, she stretches the baby's legs one by one, and stretches each arm, and massages the back with both hands. After the massage, she offers the baby to *Maweja*, holding it in her both hands with her arms extended toward the rising sun, wishing the child good health, growth, longevity and success throughout life, including becoming parent of many children, males and females alike. Then, she gives the baby a bath, anoints the baby's body with oil, and feeds the baby at the breast.

Maternal Care and Baby Sitting: Kukola and ndeji. During the first three months, the mother is one hundred percent available to her baby. This is made possible by a system of assistance called *kulola* provided by the mother-in-law, a sister, or a sister-in-law. The assistant takes care of the mother's needs. She fetches the water from the spring, gathers the wood for cooking and heating, and prepares her meals. She massages her abdomen with warm water to prevent coagulation of the blood from the birth-giving process still in her body. In the next three months, these voluntary services will no longer be available. The mother will have to do everything by herself. Fortunately, the Luba wisdom anticipated her continued need for assistance. It has instituted a baby-sitting practice called *bundeji*. The baby-sitter, *ndeji*, may be a little sister or an older daughter in most cases. Thus, after the assistance by an adult woman is over, the new mother will carry out by herself all the chores commonly assumed by a woman for the maintenance of the household. While she is involved in her various chores, the *ndeji* takes care of the baby's needs. However, the *ndeji* is more than a simple baby-sitter. She is one of the baby's first socializing agents. As a matter of fact, the term *ndeji* evokes this function. It derives from verb *kuleeja*, to show. The *ndeji* is thus the one who, among other things, will show the baby the world around him.

Thus, in the morning, the mother will wake up the baby and perform all the usual morning preparations. Then, she will entrust the baby to the good care of the *ndeji* and leave for the fields. The *ndeji* will feed the baby with the porridge and clean him when he soils himself. When the mother comes back, she feeds the baby at the breast for a second time before cooking the mid-day meal. After this meal, it will not be too long before it is time for her to start preparations for the evening meal, which is taken around five or six o'clock. From time to time, the mother will have the baby a taste of the adults' food. Very soon, that is, by the seventh month, the porridge stage will pass away. The baby will be given adults' food only and, as in previous periods, fed at the adults' meal times and in-between, whenever he asks for it.

Teaching to sit, stand, and walk. Between the ages of three and six months, the baby will be trained to the sitting position: first, straight on the mother's or babysitter's lap; then, on the ground. To teach the baby the latter position, the mother sits behind the baby holding the latter by the underarms and making sure the baby's back is straight. Later on, the baby will be trained to rest on the palms of his hands with the arms straightened. By the age of five or six months, the baby will have learned to remain seated without the assistance of an adult and will have developed the ability to hold things in his hands while sitting straight on the ground or on someone's lap. The parents will take advantage of the child's ability to sit straight with straightened arms to train him to crawl. To this effect, they would place an attractive object on the ground in front of the child that the latter will attempt to reach. Around the seventh or eighth month, the parents will be ready to train the child to stand on his two feet. Two complementary methods will be used to this end. The parents may plant two sticks in front of the mother's house, not too far apart from each other. Every morning, one of the parents, usually the mother, will place the child up on his feet holding to one stick with the left hand and to the other with the right hand. Once the child has learned how to stand in equilibrium between the two sticks holding on to each with a different hand, it will not be too long before he starts crawling toward the sticks and trying to use them as supports in order to stand up by himself. As to the other method, either parent will stand facing the baby and hold him in a standing position by his two hands. Then, he or she will sing a rhythmic song designed to make the child forget he is being held. The song goes as follows:

Mutenda manamana	Little One Stand up	
Bayaaya batushiya	People are leaving us behind	
Dya Lumingu batumona	Only to see us on Sunday	Ne

madiba kupukupu	Arriving in our noisy raffia clothes.

While singing the song, the parent will momentarily release the baby's hands, but remain close enough to grab him just in case he were to lose his balance. After several sessions, the parent will begin clapping hands during the moments when the child is released and encourage the latter to do the same. When the child has learned to stand up without any support, the parents will pass to the next training stage, notably, walking. Facing the child in upright position, the parent will bend forward with his arms outstretched toward him. As the baby tries to reach the parent's hands, the latter will back off singing the following song:

Enda, enda, enda	Walk, walk, walk
Enda tudya nzolu	Walk so we may eat chickens
Ne bikuka ne bitaala	Both hens and roosters

Indeed, when a baby begins to walk, the happy event is celebrated with a chicken meal. With this song, as with the previous one, the Luba people believe that, being an incarnate spirit, the child really understands the meaning of the song and will respond accordingly, unless for some reason he wants to make the parents suffer.

Weaning, toilet training, and personal hygiene. The next step is weaning. By now, the baby is more than a year old. The parents have decided to cohabitate again. The child must be weaned. The Luba believes that the father's sperm spoils the milk in the mother's body. The milk will interfere with the baby's development if he continues to drink it. Also, it will not be too long before the mother becomes pregnant again, unless there is some cause of sterility. The baby will no longer be allowed to touch the mother's breast. For the first time the mother lets the baby cry and remain on the ground without her running toward him ready to feed him. If the crying for the breast persists after all, the child will experience the displeasure of sucking it after it has been rubbed with pepper. This is certainly very frustrating for the child. It is not unusual to see the child lose weight during the weaning period. The Luba interprets the child's weight loss as the work of the sibling in the womb. They say:

Mwakunyenda ngudi umudya mubidi aau.
The younger sibling is eating up his body.

In the past, as a protection against the jealous fetus, the parents would have the child wear some medicine (*bwanga bwa lwisu*) around his neck. *Lwisu* derives from verb *kwisudila*, to follow up a birth by another. The last stage of weaning comes around the age of three years. By this age, the child already has a little brother or sister. It is time to detach the child from too close contact with the mother. Among other things, the child, rather than sharing the mother's bed, will from now on sleep with older siblings of the same sex. First, the child is taught personal hygiene and control of his bowel movements. The time has now come to teach the child to eliminate at a specific spot in the garden behind the mother's house, *ku diyala*. In the past, the parents would bury the feces at that spot or throw them away in the wilderness surrounding the garden. Today, they throw them into a toilet located in the garden.

This training could last approximately until the age of four. Past this age, the parents would no longer tolerate the servitude of removing the child's wastes. Now, he had to eliminate in the wilderness beyond the garden. Before the imposition of the toilet by the colonial administration, the adults eliminated in the wilderness also. By modesty, they did not want the children to know that they too experienced the same need. They especially did not want the children to be aware of the time they took care of it. To camouflage it, the person would carry an object in his hands to give the impression of going to take care of some business. Even today, adults in Luba villages do not want to be seen going to the toilet for the bowel movement. In general, they use the toilet at night when the children are asleep. In addition to toilet training, the child is taught how to take a bath. This particular type of training is initiated around the age of five years. From now on, the mother will no longer wash the boy. Preferably he will wash himself along with older children at the creek, with their help, as needed.

3. CARING FOR THE SICK

Diseases with Known Treatments

The human body is susceptible to diseases. In addition to feeding the body, care for human life includes treating the sick. Many diseases are endemic to the Luba area. Herbal medicine was practiced universally by individuals who understood well the physiology of the human body, the local population's worldview and psychology, and the world of plants and their healing powers. The treatments consisted of herbs, liquids, concoctions, powders and ashes extracted from tree barks, roots, lianas, stems or leaves. Identified below are the endemic diseases with their known treatment.

Diseases with Known Treatments

diboba and lupusu paleness and anus wound & diarrhea	*kantembela and mbalanga* measles and smallpox
lukunga and nkoyi palate disease/clapping tongue, and babies' epileptic crises	
maci and mapapa earache and hearing impairment	*masungu* cancerous swelling
mutu headache	

Diboba and lupusu. *Diboba*, whose symptoms are paleness, anemia, intestinal worms and a wound at the anus, is treated with a combination of drinkable liquids from roots, hot concoction pressures and the application of powders on the anus wound. *Lupusu* is a babies' disease. A baby with this disease has a small wound at the anus and an endless diarrhea. The disease is treated with ashes from three types of roots burned together: the main root of a banana tree, a piece of fermented cassava, and the soft part of the root of a creeping plant called *keeba ka nyoka*. The ashes are mixed with local salt (*mukela musunsuma*) and put in the wound regularly until the wound is healed.

Kantembela and Mbalanga. These two are epidemic skin eruptions. *Kantembela* is measles. *Mbalanga* is small pox. *Kantembela* is characterized by a kind of rash on the child's body accompanied by fever, dry cough, red watering eyes and, often, diarrhea. The mother rubs the child's chest and nose with oil or some kind of medicinal cream. She puts some water into the child's mouth and treats the cough and the diarrhea. A patient with *mbalanga* is advised to drink hot liquids. Actually, traditionally, there was no treatment for it, except for the wounds after the eruptions had burst. At this point, the patient was washed with white sand and clear water to clean the wounds. After the treatment was applied on the wounds, he or she was advised to sit in a dry and airy location and given or assisted with a spat to chase the flies away.

Lukunga and *nkoyi*. The palate of a child with *lukunga* becomes dry. The baby slaps the tongue against the palate, which produces a sound similar to a monkey's. Hence the disease's full name, *lukunga lwa nkima*, monkey-sounding *lukunga*. The mouth remains open. The baby has diarrhea and also vomits. The soft spot goes deep into the head. The situation is considered very critical, desperate in most cases. The disease is treated with some ashes seasoned with a special salt, *mukela wa mbanda* or *mukela musunsuma*. The ashes are rubbed on the palate. A baby with *nkoyi* experiences an epileptic crisis. When the convulsions are violent, the disease is called *nkoyi wa kabemba* (*kabemba*-like *nkoyi*). *Kabemba* is a bird that has the habit of turning around in the manner of whirlwind before catching a baby chicken. Sometimes, the term *nyunyi*, bird, is used to designate the disease. Other times, the convulsions are not pronounced, but the baby has high fever and swollen feet. In this case, the disease is called *nkoyi wa mapumpa*. *Mapumpa* is a derivative of *kupumpama*, a verb often employed to designate a sick chicken that does not move much; one that rather stays in one place with its head bent down to the ground. A type of treatment for this disease includes a powder extracted from the roots of two different trees, *cifumba* and *mbenga*. The powder is put into a leaf funnel (*lutondu*) and moistened with water. Then, drops of this substance are regularly put into the baby's eyes.

Maci and mapapa. *Maci*, earache, and *mapapa*, hearing impairment, were treated with the skin of certain trees. The stem or the root from which the skin was to be taken was washed first, then peeled and concocted in little water. Liquids from the imbibed concoction were then dropped into the ear through a funnel.

Masungu. These are swellings (*byuja*, singular: *cyuja*) on some part of the body. They may ripen and burst out. Sometimes, a *disungu* (singular of *masungu*) cannot be easily circumscribed. In such a case, the patient is first given a treatment designed to produce this effect. This treatment and that of the resulting wound usually consist of pressuring hot substances on the site of the disease.

Mutu. This term encompasses all kinds of headache. There does exist, however, a particular kind of headache distinguishable by its location: i.e., in the eye. Hence its name: *mutu wa mu dîsu*, which precisely means headache in the eye. It is also called *mutu wa kapanda*. *Kapanda* derives from verb *kupanda*, to split into parts: e.g., to split wood. The victim experiences severe pains in the region around the eye and sensations of the head splitting into halves. I have personal memories of *mutu wa mu dîsu* from my youth. One day, my father informed a man from another village who was passing by and whose name I don't remember about it. He knew a treatment: a shrub called *cikolokosu*. He instructed my father to unearth a *cikolokosu* that was standing at some spot in the garden surrounding the houses. He had the roots washed and the skin removed and ground in a small mortar. Then, he had the concoction collected in a funnel and some water poured over it. Finally, he had some drops administered into my nostrils. I have not experienced the same kind of headache ever since.

Diseases with Particular Cultural Interpretations

Some diseases are the object of certain cultural beliefs and interpretations. Such is the case with nine diseases from Katanga-Tshitenge's nomenclature.

Diseases with Particular Cultural Interpretations

| *binyoka* | *cibota* | *ciseki* | *muzakalu* |
| rheumatism | paleness | epilepsy | shaking |

| *munana* | *nkoyi* | *nsudi* | *nteta* |
| swelling belly | children's epilepsy | leprosy | furuncle |

nyima
Backache

Binyoka and *nyima*. *Binyoka* designates all kinds of rheumatism. A person with this disease has swollen legs, especially in times of humidity, and has difficulty moving them. His walk and the movement of his legs evoke those of a goat. For this reason, the disease is also called *bikonu*, paws. *Binyoka* is incurable. It can only be alleviated from time to time by massaging the body with hot water and particular herbs. It is believed that the individuals who walk on the water and herbs used to treat *binyoka* will catch the disease. *Nyima* is CiLuba for *back*. It also designates *backache*. This condition is common place in Lubaland. This should surprise no one. The Luba are agriculturalists and the dominant instrument of labor is the short-handle hoe. To cultivate with a hoe, one has to lean forward to be able to reach the ground. People with supernatural powers are capable of causing the individuals they dislike to catch the disease. Also, one can catch the disease by walking on the substances used to treat a patient with the disease. In fact, most treatment consists of moving the pain from the body of a particular patient to some location where someone else will catch it. This form of treatment is called *kutentula*, to relocate. This is how the spread of the disease was culturally explained.

Cibota. Literally, *cibota* means banana. A person with this disease becomes pale and weak. He is continuously sick and anemic. The disease only attacks men. Not any man though. The Luba believes that the disease is caused to a man by his wife's infidelity, especially if she shares with him presents made to her by her lover or purchased with money provided by her lover. Healing is not possible unless the wife avows her misconduct or a diviner denounces her.

***Ciseki* and *muzakalu*.** Ciseki is epilepsy. The Luba people have no cure for it. They believe that if the patient breaks wind during the seizure, the persons around him will catch the disease. Therefore when the crisis occurs, the attendants position the victim's head in the way they think it should be and then disperse. The term *muzakalu* derives from verb *kuzakala*: to shake, to tremble. It is used interchangeably with its synonym, *lukanku*, a derivative of verb *kukanka*, which also means to shake. A person suffering from *lukanku* has shaking hands and legs. The Luba once believed that the disease victimizes individuals who eat their in-laws' leftover food (parents in-law or sons in-law).

***Kasheeleela*.** This is a form of anemia found among newborn babies. It is often fatal. The victim becomes very skinny and does not grow. Hence the name *kasheeleela*, which designates a piece of wood that has burned and reduced to its smallest dimensions. The Luba people attribute the illness to malevolent actions of witches.

***Munana* and *nsudi*.** *Munana* is characterized by the swelling of the belly. There is no treatment for it. It is believed to be very contagious. Therefore, victims are put in quarantine. When they die, rather than being given proper funeral and internment, their remains are instead laid across a pit dug on top of a natural mound somewhere in the wilderness. *Nsudi* is leprosy. The disease is considered a curse. It starts with an irregularly shaped stain on any part of the body. Over time, the stains multiply and become wounds. Later on, the limbs begin to fall off. People have deep fear of the disease and of the patient. Individuals who die of leprosy are not given proper funeral or internment to prevent their reincarnation. Their remains are disposed of by abandoning them in the wilderness laid across a pit dug on top of a mound.

***Nkoyi* and *nteta*.** *Nkoyi*, is epilepsy among infants. A mother who maintains contacts with the mother of a child suffering from *nkoyi* exposes her own child to becoming victim of the disease. One particular type of contact to be avoided is helping the mother of a child sick of *nkoyi* where there are discharge loads from her head. *Nteta* is characterized by the swelling of a part of the body. The origin may be a furuncle. *Nteta* may also be caused by the presence of a strange object in the body, such as a thorn. A deep wound left by such an object, if not properly treated, can cause *nteta* too. People believe that individuals with evil powers can cause it as well. Thieves can catch it by stealing produce to which the owner has attached or sprinkled special substances, precisely for the purpose of teaching the eventual thief a lesson. Produce is plucked by hand. Consequently, *nteta* from stealing produce attacks the hands most of the time.

That certain diseases are surrounded with particular cultural beliefs is not limited to the Luba. Among the Phende, for instance, it is believed that a woman who touches certain men's initiation masks, or walks on the soil of the initiation site, or else eats of the food reserved for the initiates, will be hit with unending issue of blood, infertility, delivery complications, or serial miscarriages. Similarly, an initiate who violates certain initiation prescriptions or prohibitions will experience bloody urination or penis swelling (Mudiji, 1989).

Chapter 9
Other Common Endemic Diseases

The nomenclature of diseases that are endemic to Kasai, including the Luba region, includes more than diseases that have known treatments and those associated with particular cultural beliefs. Thirteen more, uncategorized by any common particularity, can be mentioned.

Other Common Endemic Diseases

| *bufofu* | *cikupi* | *kamina bidya* | *kamunda* |
| blindness | scabies | epiglottis | hernia |

| *lubunga* | *mfwenka* | *mputa wa* Lubangu | |
| sleeping disease | chest cough | cancerous wound on the skin | |

| *mukoko* or *ditunguka* | *mukooko* | *mukupa* or *ditombo* | |
| impotence | whitening of the skin | madness | |

| *munda* | *nshingu wa mboma* | *tuneka* | |
| stomachache | goiter | paralysis | |

Bufofu. This is blindness. The Luba tries to treat it, but they have no cure for it.

Cikupi is the name of a skin disease characterized by the presence of small, but itching, stains on the body of the victim. The patient is inclined to scratch the itching stains, which has the unfortunate effect of spreading the disease. This disease also affects goats and other animals. *Cikupi* is CiLuba for scabies.

Kamina-bidya. This disease is characterized by the infection of the epiglottis. The victim has difficulty swallowing the starch *nshima*. Hence the disease's compound name *kamina*, a derivative of *kumina*, to swallow, and *bidya*, another name for starch *nshima*.

Kamunda, hernia, sometimes results in the enlargement of one testicle. Such a testicle evokes the image of a jug of a hunting bag full of game meats. In this stage, the disease is called *mulondo*, jug, or *nsapu*, hunting bag.

Lubunga. This term derives from verb *kubungila*, to doze. The patient dozes frequently. It is also called *disama dya tulu*, precisely, sleeping disease. Today, the disease is no longer as epidemic and fatal as it was until the early twentieth century.

Mfwenka, also called **disama dya lukoso**, or else *nkosolo wa cyadi,* chest cough, is characteristic of individuals who suffer from asthma or tuberculosis. As tuberculosis, the disease is sometimes called just *cyadi*, chest.

Mputa wa Lubangu. *Mputa* is Ciluba for wound or wounds. *Mputa wa* Lubangu is a special type of wound. Its main characteristic is that it does not heal. It is symptomatic of cancer.

Mukoko. According to Katanga-Tshitenge (1968), this term is a synonym for *ditunguka*, impotence, presumably preferred to the latter in order to keep children unaware of the true nature of the disease. A sexually impotent person is called *mutungu* or *muntu mutunguka*. The three terms—*ditunguka, muntu mutunguka,* and *mutungu*—are derivatives of verb *kutunguka,* which signify the falling of corn grains off the ear. The sexually impotent is thus likened with a corn ear that has lost all its grains. Such a corn ear no longer has the power to reproduce itself. Neither does the impotent man.

Mukooko is a skin disease. Its victim loses the blackness or dark-brown color of his skin. The skin becomes whitish or yellowish. In most cases, the disease attacks the hands, the arms, and the neck.

Mukupa is a synonym for *ditombo* or *ditomboka*. The latter two terms derive from the verb *kutomboka,* to become mad, insane. The Luba people have no treatment for the insane. All they can do is to immobilize him when he has become a public danger. This they once did by putting a huge cast around the insane person's leg. This action is called *kwela cyobo. Cyobo* is cast.

Munda is the tem for stomachache. It may be *munda mwa cinyengu,* torn stomach, colic; *munda mwa dyupa,* also called *munda mwa kasulu,* running stomach, hence diarrhea; or worse, *munda mashi,* dysentery.

Nshingu wa mboma, also called *cidipiku*, is goiter. A person with this disease will experience enlargement of the front of his neck in the form of a calabash.

Tuneka, paralysis, mostly attacks the legs. The victim is unable to walk.

4. CARING FOR THE DYING

In Luba villages, when the dying journey becomes irreversible, relatives gather around the dying person to assist him or her during transition. Traditionally, assistance consists of social readjustments, physical cares, and spiritual cares.

Readjusting Social Relations at the Time of Death

Imminent death. When all the attempts to save a person's life have failed and death has become imminent, the relatives' concern shifts toward clearing the way, securing a peaceful transition, and readjusting social relations between the departing and the family: both the living family and the ancestors. The following readjustments are discussed in that order: confession, reconciliation, the farewell and last will, the agony, expiation, and conjugal intimacy termination (Ngindu, 1969).

Confession: When death appears imminent, all adult relatives present gather around the dying person under the leadership of the elder. Usually a discussion is engaged about what might be the cause of the sickness and the imminent death. This is the time for self-examination and public confession. The presiding elder goes first, recalling one by one all the disputes he might have had with the dying person. If he has ever uttered a curse on him, he must retract it. If, for some reason, he has kept rancor against him, he must avow it. After the elder, the other family members do the same in their decreasing order of seniority. The dying person does the same when his turn comes. The Luba word for this action is *ditonda*, a derivative of the verb *kutonda*, to avow, to confess.

Reconciliation: If, during confession, someone recalls a dispute that the dying person had with a family member, and if one of the two had or still has a grudge against the other, the person in question will be brought in. The two will confess themselves to each other publicly, restating and retracting all evil words, all words of hatred they have uttered against each other. The Luba calls this action of restating and retracting one's words *kwakululula meeyi* (to speak one's words over). Following the retraction, the two parties will be invited to drink water from the same cup (*kunwa cibalu*). Then a chicken or a goat will be killed and all members of the assembly will partake of this meal of reconciliation. After the above requirements have been taken care of, the presiding elder speaks again, this time saying: We have heard all the confessions, if the wrong doings that have been confessed are the cause of this sickness, then let the sick be healed and live in peace. This part of the ritual is called *kwakwila mubeedi* (to speak for the sick). It is required in all cases of critical illnesses, including those of children. But, if after all, the sick person dies anyway, the Luba will believe that the other party was not sincere in his confession, or that the true cause of the sickness and the death is yet to be discovered.

Farewell and last will: The Luba like for a dying person to leave his last words to his beloved ones. For a Luba, there is no more miserable fate than dying away from any family member that one can speak to in one's last moments. Instant death is disliked for this reason. Of the victim of sudden death, the Luba say: *mmufwa ki mmulaya*: he died without saying farewell. Instant death does not allow one to speak one's last words. That is probably why it is generally interpreted as an intentionally inflicted act of an evildoer, or a prompt punishment of the dead by the ancestors for grave offenses committed against the family. Some examples include adultery of a wife, incest committed by the dying person, or refusal by him to pay the required tributes of the first (bridewealth) from his daughters' marriages to the entitled elder who has an ancestral claim over them.

In the farewell, the dying blesses his children and gives them his last advisement, exhorting them to love one another, *kunangangana,* and to be mindful of one another, *kuvulukangana*; and, especially, to keep ancestral traditions (*kulama mikenji ya bankambwa*). He invites the sons to take good care of their sisters. He warns the wife against betraying his memory with any dishonorable conduct. He requests that whoever inherits her treats her well. Generally, such a request is reserved for a wife who has lived an exemplary life. Very often the dying designates the heir and custodian of his children. Generally, the designee inherits the widow as well. To ensure that his sons will get married, he assigns them in advance the bridewealth that will come from their sister's marriages or reminds them of the assignments already made. He tells his family who his debtors and creditors are, the nature of the respective obligations and the circumstances in which they were contracted. Preferably, he pays all his debts before dying. The farewell of a dying woman is very simple: goodbye to her children, exhortation of the older ones to take good care of the younger ones, and exhortation of all to love and to be mindful of one another.

The agony and expiration: At the very first signs of agony, little children are taken out of the house in which the dying person lies. They are not allowed to see a person dying. In particular, children should not watch their father or mother expire. The reason is to spare them from having nightmares or fixations. Sometimes, little children wear a line of dark color on their forehead designed to prevent them from seeing the ghost of the deceased person. Among some Luba lineages, only special title children wear the charcoal line. Sometimes, in addition to the charcoal line ritual, called *kulaaba dikala*, the children who have been in contact with a dead person are treated to a chicken meal known as *nzolu wa bu manji*. The concept of *manji* is explained below. Death occurs when the principle of life (*moyo*) separates itself from the human body (*mubidi*). At this point, the dying person breathes his or her last, *kukuula moyo*, and the family members present explode in lamentations.

Conjugal intimacy termination: Soon after the death of a man is confirmed, his wife takes her top off and wears a diaper of a clothing material firmly tightened between her legs. The Luba name for this diaper is *mukaya*. Over it the widow wears a piece of material hanging in the front and another in the back. Each is called *lubondya* or *didiba*. In the past, the *mbondya* (plural of *lubondya*) were the only clothes that she wore over the diaper. Today, she wears a long clothing material wrapped around her legs and tied in the waist. The diaper is designed to prevent the ghost (*mukishi*) of the dead man from penetrating into his wife's uterus (*kubwela munda mwa mukajende*) and taking residence therein. Fundamentally, the wearing of the diaper symbolizes the termination of conjugal intimacy between the deceased husband and his widow. To this same effect, an ad hoc witch doctor carves a wooden horn (*lusengu lwa muci*) and fills it with a substance made out of the leaves of an aromatic plant called *lwenyi*. The smell of this plant is supposed to discard the ghost of the dead from his widow and thus prevent it from harassing her.

Physical Cares for the Departing

Taking care of the body: Physical cares for the dying include cares for the body, preparing the body for burial, and the burial itself. The Luba resent dying in solitude, away from the family. Such a misfortune is called *kufwila mu cisuku*, to die in the wilderness. Some of the services that the family renders to a dying person are closing the eyes and the mouth, changing the position of the body from time to time, and relaxing his arms and legs. While his head rests, facing up, on a wreath, the wife—the senior wife if the deceased is polygamous—carries the bust across her lap while the lower part of the body lies on a mat. When she is tired, generally after several hours, the whole body is then laid on the mat. The mourners sit on both sides to facilitate cooperation in performing the task of turning the body periodically side to side. Therefore, the concern of a person who has no relatives living nearby is: Who will take care of my body? Who will turn me over when I die? (*Meme mufwa nganyi wankudimuna?*). I will spoil lying on one side (*Meema mufwa ne mbola luseka*) (Ngindu, 1969).

Preparing the body for burial: The preparation of the body for the burial takes place behind the house. The wife, or the senior wife, plus two men give the deceased man his last washing. They shave his forehead, cut his nails and give him a bath of cold water from the river. They then anoint him with oil, dress him in his nicest clothes, and adorn him with necklaces of pearls. In the past, they would also place some pearls in his mouth or his right hand to travel with. He will have to pay KALONGO, the mystical ferryman who carries the spirits of the departing in a boat across the dark waters of the mysterious vast river that separates the world of the living from the invisible land of the departed (Ngindu, 1969). A woman's body is prepared in similar manner by her sisters, co-wives, or sisters-in-law in the presence of the husband. Her clothing includes a head scarf in addition to her other nice clothes. Grandchildren prepare the bodies of their grandparents if the latter no longer have any living brothers or sisters. The washing of the body is carried out in absolute silence as a mark of respect for the dead. Following this, the body is wrapped in a white shroud and then put in a coffin or simply in mats. At this point, the crowd explodes in loud lamentations. The moment of the last separation has come since the burial takes place the very day of the death, or the next morning if the death has occurred in the evening or during the night. The inability to prevent decomposition is probably the reason behind the hasty internment.

Burial: The Luba bury (*kujika*) most of their dead people in the garden that surrounds the houses in the homestead where they have lived. They also bury adult men in their reception house (*beesa, ndaku*), which is very often the central house in the homestead. In the latter event, the house is destroyed at the end of the mourning period because mortuary houses are believed to be contaminated with death. The most common burial place for a child is in the front porch (*lutanda*) of the mother's house. Following the washing and clothing, the crowd moves toward the burial place in cries. As soon as the body reaches the grave site the lamentations stop momentarily. While everybody stands still, two, three, or four people deposit the body in the grave. One of them goes down to the bottom of the grave to arrange the body in the niche and untie the departed person's belt. A tied belt would interfere with his movements in the journey toward the land of the spirits (*ku bajangi*), thus binding his ghost to the tomb. Had this to happen, he would come back to terrify the living.

Farewell address to the dead at internment: At internment, the elder members of the extended family who are present address the dead person in their declining order of seniority, deploring his departure, proclaiming their innocence regarding the cause of his death, and exhorting the dead to take revenge of anyone who might have betrayed him. Generally, the widow speaks also, deploring her husband's death and the fact that he leaves her alone with the children. She asks him to look over the children and exhorts him to take her life if she is responsible for his death. An adult relative present who refuses to address the dead in these terms declares himself, by this fact, having had a hand in the person's death. Why would an innocent person be afraid to take a public oath?

The walk back from the grave: To avoid bringing the spirit of the dead back to the living space of the humans, burial participants are required to walk together from the grave site directly to a river for a purification bath. The men go to one place, and the women to a different one. The sisters of the deceased walk the widow to the river. After the bath, the widow changes clothes. She abandons by the river the clothes that she wore while in contact with the deceased husband (Mpyana-Yenga, 1975). When the bathing is over, the participants return to the house of mourning by a different route, one that has not been contaminated by their previous contact with the dead. Before dispersing the persons who buried the dead, particularly those who dug the grave and deposited the body therein, the relatives of the dead treat them to a chicken meal called *nzolu wa cîna* (chicken for digging the grave).

The vigil: In general, the vigil (*kulaala pa mbelu*) lasts a week or two after the burial. During this entire period, the men sleep outside around a fireplace set for the circumstance in the front of the house wherein the person died. The women sleep inside the house. Sometimes a shelter of palm branches is erected in the front porch for additional mourners to sleep in. The relatives of the deceased have their heads completely shaved as a sign of distress. All family members are expected to take part in the mourning ceremonies. Some of these ceremonies involve singing and dancing to the sounds of drums and tom-toms. Refusing to partake in these activities is equivalent to rejecting the dead person:

Kubenga myombo	To stay away from the sticks
Nkubenga cyondo	And the drums
Nkubenga ne mufu mwina	Is to reject the dead himself.

The pivotal role of the widow: Day and night the mourners are entertained with food, beverages, and music. However, the widow is the central figure in the mourning ceremonies. It is then that she is expected to show her continued love for her deceased husband and deep desolation for his death. She laments at sunset and sundown. She laments accompanying whoever else laments. She laments with a bowed head and her eyes down. In the past, she would have her body covered with ashes. She speaks little. She gives up all corporal cares including taking a complete bath. During several months, the widow is tainted with her husband's death. She participates in it. She is a taboo person and lives in semi-isolation (Ngindu 1969, quoting Th. Theuws 1960).

Dispersal of mourners: One week (sometimes more) after the death, on the day of the week when the person died, but now more and more on a Sunday or a market day, the mourning is adjourned. This day is called *dituku dya kutangalaja madilu* (day of mourning adjournment). Both the eve and the day of adjournment are very festive: people sing, dance, eat, drink, and fire guns. On that day also, the mortuary house is swept for the first time since death occurred, and the dirt is burned. If a shelter was built in the front porch, it is torn down and burned along with the dirt. This ritual is called *kwosha nsaasa*, to burn down the shelter (Weydert, 1938).

Closure: For a child, the mourning period actually ends with the adjournment as just described. For an adult, the dispersal of the mourners is not the last stage in the succession of death-related events. The real closure comes about a year later. In the past, it was only then that the widow had her first complete bath since her husband's death. Symbolically the event is called *kwowa mâyi*, to take a bath. It was also then that she started wearing her nice clothes again. Presently, these two rituals are performed at an intermediate date. The event then is called *kwela dibaya* (to wear the blouse). *Dibaya* is the top of a woman's clothing set. *Kwela* means to throw over one's body, to wear.

Definite conjugal status termination: At the final closure of the mourning ceremonies, that is at the *kowa mâyi*, the widow finally frees herself from her deceased husband's ghost. The bath and the wearing of fine clothing are designed to mark the reaching of this final milestone. However, the most significant event on that night, which actualizes the definite rupture of her marriage with him, is her estrangement by having a sexual intercourse with another man. Ritually, she must perform this act with a relative of the deceased husband designated by the family council. The ritual act of copulation takes place late at night behind the house of the deceased husband or, preferably, outside of the village, at the intersection of roads. After this ritual, the widow can no longer reenter the house in which she lived (Ngindu, 1969).

Spiritual Cares for the Departing

Part of the cares for the dying and many funeral rites are expressions of the belief that the person continues to live beyond death. For instance, the Luba likes for a dying person to speak his last words to the beloved ones. For a Luba man or woman, there is no more miserable fate than dying away from any family member that one can speak to in one's last moments. They abhor instant death since it does not allow one to speak one's last words. That is probably why it is generally interpreted as an intentionally-inflicted act of an evildoer, or a prompt punishment of the dead by the ancestors for grave offenses committed against the family. A person who dies by such a punishment will not be welcomed enthusiastically into the subterranean community of the ancestors. If rejected, he may become an errant ghost who terrifies the living. In the eulogy and the final address at the time of internment, each departing person is reminded that if his death is an ancestral punishment for some wrongdoing on his part, he only has himself to blame and will have to defend himself before the ancestors' council.

Several other practices speak to the continuation of the departing person's life after death. When someone expires, his or her principle of life, *moyo*, becomes a ghost, *mukishi*. By separating itself from the body, the *mukishi*, especially that of an adult man, husband, and father, turns into a *manji*. This term designates a person who has taken someone's life violently, such as in a battle or war. To live in peace and be accepted into the community of his peers, the *mukishi* needs expiation. The expiation rite, called *kutenteka*, is officiated by another *manji* such as a person whose fetishes are believed to have killed a sorcerer or an enemy. Before the officiator and the audience, the son of the deceased performs a war dance called *kusempela*, or *kufuuna*, with a sword in his right hand, menacing to behead anyone who would challenge him. This part of the ritual is designed to reassure the dead, the hero, that the son who survives him can defend his (father's) title of *manji*. Then, in front of the dead, the officiator beheads a chicken that he and the other *manji* present prepare, cook and eat on the spot, of course with *nshima*, the staple food. To the son of the deceased, the officiator gives the heart or the liver of the chicken on a portion of *nshima* after dipping the latter in the sauce. If the son is still too young to eat with the adults, the officiator places some *nshima* with some meat from the chicken on it on the child's fontanel (*lubombo* or *mbuyangala*) (Ngindu, 1969: 90). The preparation of the body for burial includes adorning the dead person with necklaces of pearls. In the past, they would also place some pearls in his mouth or his right hand to travel with. He would have to pay *KALONGO*, the mystical ferryman who carries the spirits of the departing in a boat across the dark waters of the mysterious vast river that separates the world of the living from the invisible land of the departed (Ngindu, 1969).

SUMMARY

Caring for self and loved ones is a natural penchant. African peoples across the continent build various kinds of houses to shelter self and the household from bad weather and environmental threats and to offer hospitality to eventual guests, including long-term visiting relatives. They develop differential clothing styles for men, women, boys, and girls, which change with life circumstances and the passing of time. To preserve life, humans produce or buy food which they cook in various forms and serve and eat in a variety of ways. Caring for one's children begins before conception and even before marriage as future parents, particularly mothers, avoid kinds of behaviors that can compromise their ability to conceive and/or give birth to healthy children. They provide for the child's material needs as well as for their spiritual needs commensurate with the kind of returning spirit the child is. The care for a child includes training into adult roles on a regular basis with special emphasis at life junctions such as adolescence, marriage, birth giving, and death. This chapter also shared disease treatment systems that peoples all over Africa have developed, including herbal medicines by traditional practitioners and spiritual healing practices. This is followed by social, physical and spiritual cares for the dying. Social cares consist of restoring broken relationships with relatives, including mutual confession of wrong doings and reconciliation. At death, during the time before burial, and at internment, religious rituals are performed to secure the departing person's fruitful journey and joyous acceptance into the ancestors' village.

(Endnotes)

1   Vuk'uzenzele. 2007. "Ndebele Traditional Dress." Capetown, South Africa: Government Communications. https://www.vukuzenzele.gov.za/ndebele-traditional-dress. Retrieved 5-14-2019.

2   The Heart of Africa. ND. "Fulani Tribe." https://theheartofafricafulanitribe.weebly.com/food and-clothing.html. Retrieved 6-3-2019.

3   Eguda, Omachona. 2017. "Celebrating African Cuisine: 10 Delicious Ugandan Dishes." *OMENKA Magazine,* July 25, 2017. https://www.omenkaonline.com/celebrating-african-cuisine-10-delicious-ugandan-dishes/.

World Travel Guide. "Uganda Food and Drink." https://www.worldtravelguide.net/guides/africa/uganda/food-and-drink/. Retrieved 6-6-2019.

Dermand Africa. ND. "Check out Uganda's Most Popular Foods." https://www.demandafrica.com/food/check-out-ugandas-most-popular-foods/. Retrieved 3-16-2020.

Migrationology. ND. "Kenyan Food Overview: 20 of Kenya's Best Dishes." https://migrationology.com/kenyan-food/. Retieved 3-16-2020.

Chapter 10
A Freedom Seeker and Nation Builder

1. Legitimate Access to Community's Resources and Political Power
2. Levels of Political Organization in Pre-colonial Africa
3. The Search for Territorial Autonomy
4. Models of National Unity Building

1. LEGITIMATE ACCESS TO COMMUNITY'S RESOURCES AND POLITICAL POWER

Right of Access to the Resources of the Environment

In all creation stories, God has granted human communities collective ownership rights over the resources of their environment: land, rivers, forests, fauna and flora. To recall one example, in the creation story of the Gikuyu of Kenya, *Ngai,* God, took the Gikuyu's ancestor to the top of Mount Kenya from where He showed him the country's bounty that was going to be his descendants' as a gift from Him, the Most High. The country had abundant varieties of plants, animals, rivers, plains, and meandering hills. All in it was beautiful and splendid and was for them to use judiciously to meet the needs of all the members (Mbiti 1970, Idowu 1994, Jefferson and Skinner 1990). The right to the resources primarily means the right to food. Food is essential to life and physical integrity. Right to food includes free access to hunting, fishing, and gathering grounds, and even extends to the common practice of sharing household food with visitors. Similarly, African land tenure systems guarantee access to land not only to clan members, but also to non-members with permission. Freedom of access to resources includes the freedom of movement and frequenting of public places. Luba people's ethics prohibits setting barriers on roads to keep some people from using them or blocking access to the market place. The road belongs to everyone. Among to Luba, the marketplace belongs to the village community, is regulated by chief's appointees, and is open to everybody, from within or from without. Traditionally, lands, forests, rivers, roads are inalienable communal property. They could not be the object of a commercial transaction. Neither did they fit the notion of being vulnerable to theft (Kalanda, 1992).

Divine Origin of Power and Authority

Some acts of Creation suggest that God wanted some individuals to exercise functions of leadership and authority. To complete the creation of the earth, *Olódùmarè*, God in Yorùbá religion, sent Arch-Divinity *Orìshà-nlá* at the head of a delegation, which included the hen and the pigeon as his assistants. As *Orìsà-nlá* threw the soil on the marshy land, the hen and the pigeon spread it over until the marsh became dry land. When the earth was ready for occupation, *Olódùmarè* charged Divinity *Orèlúéré* to lead a party of heavenly hosts who became the first inhabitants of the earth (Idowu, 1994). The Mande of Mali claim descent from Keita, the legendary founder of the Mali Empire. They recognize a hierarchy of divinities operating under the overall authority of God Creator *Mongala*. Standing in first place was *Faro*, the celestial seed to whom *Mongala* gave the form of twin fish representing *Faro*'s strength and life, and body, respectively. *Faro* was sacrificed by *Mongala* in reparation of incest committed by *Pemba*, *Mongala*'s previous celestial seed. *Mongala* had *Faro* cut into 60 pieces and ordered for the pieces to be scattered all over the Earth where they became trees. Then, *Mongala* resurrected *Faro* in a human form, transformed the celestial placenta in which *Faro* was conceived into an ark and sent *Foro* to Earth on top of the ark along with eight original ancestors of humans from the same placenta as *Faro*, accompanied with animals and plants. The ark lands on *Mountain Kouroula* in *Keita*'s birthplace region. *Sourakata*—ancestor of the bards, royal genealogist griots—brought *Faro*'s sacrificed skull to Earth. *Faro* became distributor of *Mongala*'s divine blessings through other divinities. To *Simboumba Tangnagati*, he gave the first 30 words and the eight females seeds from God's clavicles, making him responsible for the seeds, the rain, and speech. *Kanisimbi*, one of the receivers of seeds from *Simboumba Tangnagati*, was the first human ancestor. He planted some of the seeds in the form of cardinal points replicating God's four clavicles. The plants were: *fani berere* at the east of the field; *fani ba* at the west end; the small millet *saño* at the north end; rice, *malo*, at the south end; and corn, *kaba*, in the center, where he had previously built a shrine (Dietrerlene, 1955). In the Luba story, Creator *Maweja Nangila*, The Eternal and Omnipotent One, is the Eldest and Most High Spirit, *Mvidi Mukulu*. To create the universe and all that exists in it, material and immaterial, He first metamorphosed Himself into three Superiors Spirits: Himself *Maweja Nangila*, and two Lord Spirits who share his divinity and power to the highest level. He placed the one who appeared first to his right to assist him in the capacity of First Born Son and the second to his left to assume the position of Senior Lady. Thereafter, God created another Lord Spirit in the capacity of Emissary. There thus came to exist four Lord Spirits: The Creator, The First-Born Son, The First Lady, and the Emissary Spirit. The four Lord Spirits share the title of *Maweja*. They are: (1) *Maweja Nangila*, The Creator, (2) *Maweja wa Cyama*, the Son, (3) *Maweja Cyama*, the First Lady, and (4) Mulopo Maweja, the Emissary Spirit. Thereafter, *Maweja Nangila* created eight spirits, four seniors and four juniors:

Four Senior Spirits	*Four Junior Spirits*
Nkimba	Lumanya
Mule Mwedi	Mwadyamvita
Mushikuluje	Cyela-Mpungi
Muntu-Lufu	Kadya-Bilumbu

(Mudimbe 1991, Kalanda 1992).

Connections to the Spirits of the Founding Fathers

In pre-colonial Africa, gaining access to functions of chief or king was often contingent upon proper descent and legitimate investiture. Kingship and chieftainship were regarded as divine functions, kings and chiefs as entitled descendents of God's chosen ones to rule. As a power holder, the African chief or king becomes the direct depositary and heir of the powers of the leading ancestor, spirit of the founding father of the group, including his prerogatives and charges over the land and the subjects. He is also connected to other eminent ancestors through a special cult as leaders among the departed (Mudiji 1997). The illustrations below are drawn from the Yorùbá, the Kuba, the Silluk, and the Luba, respectively.

On Earth, leaders who are believed to be incarnate spirits are at the top of the power hierarchy. In ancient Egypt, gods were believed to incarnate in natural objects, animals and humans. God *Horus* was incarnated in the sun and in the pharaoh. Consequently, the king was man, god, and sun at the same time. *Horus* was a major divinity in Egyptian religion. An outgoing king passed the title of god *Horus* to his successor (Frankford, 2000: 10). Thus, through coronation, each incoming pharaoh acquired the divinity, powers, and name of *Horus* as well as special powers from the insignia he received (David, 2002). *Woot*, the founder of the *Kuba* dynasty, was considered the earthly equivalent of *Mboom*, God. *Mboom* created nine primordial animals prior to the appearance of man. *Woot*, the first man on earth, gave birth to nine children. *Woot*'s descendants perpetuated his divine right to rule over the Kuba society. Likewise, Yorùbá monarchs claim divine origin from divinity *Odùdúwà* who is credited with the founding of the sacred city of Ifè-Ifè in execution of a mandate from Creator *Olódùmarè*, head of the Yorùbá pantheon. *Odùdúwà,* in whom resided all authority, religious and secular, is believed to have dispatched his sons to establish other cities, where they reigned as priest-kings and presided over cult rituals. In this manner, *Ifè*'s ruling dynasty extended its authority over *Yorùbáland*. Deriving his status from *Odùdúwà*—original ancestor and priest-king of *Ile-Ifè*—the king of *Ile Ifè* is considered by most Yorùbá people as the father and spiritual leader of all the *Yorùbá* People. The *Oba* "king" of Benin was also believed to be a sacred monarch and a living deity. He was the intermediary and the earthly counterpart of other deities and divine forces: e.g., the deity *Olokun*, Lord of the Waters, who gives wealth and children. The *Oba* was held responsible for the well-being (physical and spiritual health) of his people and the continuity of the state. All throughout the year, he performed rites inside the palace to benefit his people. Yearly, at the *Ugie Erha Oba* festival held in honor of his ancestors, the *Oba* offered sacrifices to the ancestors to make the world safe from the destructive actions of lesser spirits and witches. The Shilluk case is similar. The Shilluk live in South Sudan. The Shilluk king, *Reth*, must be a descendent of *Nyikang*, the mystical founder of the monarchy, of whom he is an incarnation. Particular members of the monarchy have the exclusive authority to perform certain rituals that have beneficial effects on all citizens. The Ashanti Queen Mother is believed to be the daughter of the moon, whereas the king is the son of the sun. Her *kra*, soul, is animated by the sun. When she dies her *kra*, spirit, unites with the *kra* of the sun. Thus the *kra* of the Queen mother, the *kra* of the King, son of the Sun, and the *kra* of the sun become one. The Queen mother and the king are thus deified. As another example, Luba society is divided into chiefdoms, large and small, each tracing descent from an immigrant from the *Luba Empire* in the *Kabongo* region, in *Congo's Northern Katanga Province*. Political power in each chiefdom is divided between the power-takers' descendants of the founder by his senior wife and the power-givers' descendants of the founder by his other wives. Non-descendants participate in the governance on personal merit or as representatives of their clans in the chief's council (Zahan in Olupona 2000; Idowu 1994; Kaplan in Olupona 2000; Komba, 1997, quoting OL.V. Thomas and LUNEAU).

Proper Investiture Rituals

The investiture is a series of ceremonies through which a contender to the throne is turned into a chief or king. Actual access to power is not always determined by the conventional rule of heredity even where proper descent is required. Personal merit as a high executive officer or military hero from within, or conquest by an outsider warrior can propel a commoner to the throne. However, in general, to function as an effective chief or king, even a usurper seeks legitimization through proper investiture rituals. The rituals must be officiated by the appropriate authority for the function. Investiture rituals confer spiritual powers and induct the chief or king into fellowship with the spirits of the founding fathers and past rulers. Thereby, the chief becomes a spiritual mediator of the ancestors to his people and, along with the ancestors, a spiritual protector of the people and the land. A single case will suffice at this point: a Hema chief's investiture. The Hema live in northeastern Congo DRC and northwestern Uganda. The Hema society is politically divided into chiefdoms, large and small. Investiture rituals are officiated by authorities from designated clans. An aspiring *Omukama*, Chief, who is not a member of the *Bito* clan, had to be invested by a power giver from the *Mubito* clan, a sub-group of the *Bito*. A candidate from the *Baggere* clan had to seek investiture from an authority from the *Kaiba* clan.

The investiture process begins with the candidate, surrounded by the dignitaries of the chiefdom, moving to a particular location. Chiefs from particular Hema clans have to seek investiture in Bunyoro, whereas others, such as the Maguru, have to go to Lake Mobutu (Albert) first before heading to Bunyoro. Their ancestors lived in these locations. At the lake, four notables from the Maguru chiefdom and a notable from the Kaiba clan participate in the ceremonies. The Kaiba dignitary is the officiant power giver. The candidate is surrounded by all the dignitaries from his chiefdom. At the very start, a ram and a bull—the latter known for having reproduced a large drove—are let go free to be abandoned alive by the lake. The *Omukama* in the making, seated in a boat, is given a ride on the lake by the four dignitaries and the officiant. At the exit from the lake, the king in the making is led into an ad hoc shrine where he is invested with spiritual powers, thereby becoming the mediator of the ancestral spirits to his people. From here, the chief and his suite return to the chiefdom headquarters. A big feast, dances, and songs are organized for the populace. The king enters his house and comes back out dressed in chiefly attire: a large *ficus* robe, a leopard skin, and a hat of woven palms ornamented with leopard teeth, shells, and feathers. The officiant rubs the chief's face with a powder extracted from a tree known for bringing prosperity to its users. He does so while pronouncing the following words: "Today we invest you *Omukama*." Then, four times, he would order the *Omukama*: "Sit down here!" while each time alternatively sitting him on and lifting him off the chiefly stool. Thereafter he would bestow upon the seated chief other insignia of power, notably: pearls for the neck, an iron arrow, and a leopard skin to cover the chiefly stool. This would conclude the major part of the Hema investiture process (Lobho, 1980).

2. LEVELS OF POLITICAL ORGANIZATION IN PRE-COLONIAL AFRICA

African societies had reached different levels of political autonomy before European domination. They were organized, from the simplest to the most complex, in bands, lineages, chiefdoms, kingdoms, and empires. The section below highlights examples of these pre-colonial political entities, many with strong democratic and gender-inclusive systems, and it provides critical knowledge for current generations.

Bands, Lineages, and Chiefdoms

Band communities were composed of a limited number of nuclear families. Their cooperative arrangements were temporary and task specific. The Mbuti of the Congo, the Kung of the Kalahari Desert are examples of band societies. Lineages are localized communities composed of extended families whose members trace descent from a known common ancestor. Lineages are often lower descent levels of a clan. The Ambum, who live in the Bandundu-Kwilu region of the Congo DRC, are organized in lineages. The clan is a descent group whose members can no longer trace the descent lines connecting them to a common ancestor. Nonetheless, they maintain among themselves a high sense of community based on common cultural traits, such as language, a totemic name (family emblem) and taboos—including prohibition of intermarriage. Matrilineal clans among the Kongo of Congo and Angola are in this category. The ancestor and the ancestor's link to the living descendents are mythical. Chiefdoms are permanent political entities based on kinship, which have a deep hierarchical structure, incorporating several lineage levels. The Bakwa-Kalonji Chiefdom, among the Luba of Kasai is a good example. Several intermediate lineage levels separate the maximal lineage (*cisamba*) from the minimal lineage (*dîku dya dilolo*) (Sangpam 1994, Vansina 1965, Mukenge 1967).

Kingdoms

Kingdoms were composed of chiefdoms united on bases other than common descent. The bases for kingdom national unity could be marriage alliances, pacts or patron-client relationships. Political autonomy could be preserved by establishing marriage alliances with potential enemies (Vansina 1968, Davis 1981); (The Editors of Encyclopedia Britannica. ND).[1] The Kingdom of Bunyoro was a centralized state comprised of a hierarchy of chiefdoms superheated by four chiefdoms, each forming a distinct administrative district of the kingdom. The king, *Mukama*, was the highest authority. The village was the base unit. Altogether there were about 150 villages in Bunyoro. The kingdom was founded by Hema invaders who superimposed themselves over the indigenous Iru. The Hema were in turn superseded by the Bito latecomer Nilotic invaders (Beattie, 1961). The Kanyok are another example of a kingdom. They are culturally related to the first Bantu immigrants who settled in the Upemba Lake region along with the Luba and who remained there after such other groups as the Lund, the Pende and the Chokwe left by 1000 BC. The Kanyok power structure reflected the earlier preeminence of matrilineality. For instance, important political functions were entrusted to maternal uncles. Such was the case with the *Mwnanga*, authority responsible for war and village security; *Kalul*, one overseeing judicial, financial, and marriage palavers; *Kanahumbi*: entrusted with the lineage's movable property and transfer of inheritance; and *Shingahemb*: responsible for religious services to the ancestors. Some other important functions were assumed by women. For example, *Inmwan*, literally mother of the chief, was a chief's generation elder sister who assumed the position known elsewhere as queen mother. She performed important religious ceremonies connecting the living and the ancestors and was considered the consecrated replacement of the mother of the legendary founder of the Kanyok Dynasty. *Inabanz*, another important female function, was the maternal aunt or sister of the chief who oversaw the chief's court. The Kanyok Kingdom was founded by Shimat-a-Citend at Mulundu and later consolidated by Kabw-a-Shimat after defeating rival chiefs. Kabw's son, Ciband-a-Kabw, reinvigorated the Kingdom after long periods of uncertainty and integrated several centers of influence such as Ditu and Museng through alliances and conquests (Yoder, 1992).

Clientages

Clientages often involved control over land by one group and some form of serfdom by another. The Tutsi-Hutu relationship in 19th century Rwanda under the centralized government of King Rwabugiri assumed this form to an extent. Hutu commoners increasingly became dependent on members of the Tutsi nobility for access both to land and to cattle. The Hutu are primarily agriculturalists. Many lost their lands to the king's loyalists. The Tutsi have always controlled cattle. Both Tutsi and Hutu marry by exchanging cattle for the bride. Thus, Hutu clients became dependent on their Tutsi patrons both for livelihood and for marriage. A variant clientage system existed in the neighboring Burundi. Here, the social fabric was more complex. The Tutsi ruling minority was comprised of Banyaruguru (people from above) enjoying a higher social status and the Hima, a small nobility that overtly opposed monarchy in the 1960s. Both within Tutsi and Hutu patrilineages, there existed social cleavages based on the perceived quality of families. The individuals were ranked as being from very good families, good families, families that were neither good nor bad, and bad families. But the most underlying inequality differentiation was between clients in need of protection and a patron with enough wealth (cows and land) and influence to provide such protection. Clients reciprocated in services and in kind gifts. Historically, this exchange relationship was based on mutual loyalty and affection rather than coercion. It operated as "the normative frame of reference for the institutionalization of political ties" (Lemarchand, 1995: 12). It became deliberately exploitative in the 1960s when the Tutsi ruling minority began expropriating Hutu lands, thereby fostering upon hundreds of Hutu a permanent inferiority status of landlessness without independent sources of livelihood (Newburry 1988, Lemarchand 1995).

Empires

Empires were political entities born out of conquest and composed of unrelated kingdoms. The Mali Empire (1300-1500) is a case in point. The empire came into existence when the Mandinka warrior Sundiata Keita, a member of the Malenke subgroup and leader of the small kingdom of Kangaba, conquered and unified the competing kingdoms that had resulted from the fall of ancient Ghana Kingdom. Sundaiata ruled from 1235 to 1260. His successors, the most famous of whom was Mansa Musa, expanded the empire to its greatest limits, stretching far beyond Timbuktu and Gao to the East, Walata to the North, and Takrur to the west. Law, order and safety reigned throughout the empire. The empire reached high levels of prosperity. Its rulers became known and respected everywhere as great leaders of a great empire. They converted to Islam and made the required pilgrimage to Mecca, but they did not force their people into Islam. The forms of political organization identified here for illustration had in common a high degree of democracy, although the bands alone were egalitarian. At the same time the social organization of non-egalitarian political societies appear to have functioned simultaneously as an incubator of forces of unity and conflict (Davidson1991, Vansina 1965).

Shaka's Zulu **Nation** is another African empire of historical significance. The Zulu were one of the more than 200 *Nguni* clans that lived in the Natal region of South Africa. A combination of factors concurred to the formation of the Zulu Kingdom: the advance of the white settlers and population growth, were key. As a consequence, conflicts for grazing lands became more frequent among Nguni clans. Age-group circumcision required long periods of seclusion. To better prepare the youth for the fight, the leaders substituted regiment training for circumcision ceremonies. The regiments were formed across the clans and organized in age-sets. Each was identified by a name and assigned to a royal household. Cross-clan regiments resulted in the formation of three kingdoms: *Mthethwa* led by Dingiswayo, *Ngwane* (later *Swazi*) by Sabhuza and *Ndwandwe* by Zwide. Shaka was born out of wedlock to a young boy, Senzagakona, and a young girl, Nandi. Senzangakona later married Nandi and became chief of a small clan called Zulu. But Shaka continued to suffer from being an unwanted child. He developed remarkable athletic skills and joined one of Dingiswayo's regiments. A courageous and natural leader, he became an innovator commander, training his regiments in new techniques and developing their loyalty to him directly. He had his soldiers run barefooted and received continuous training in fighting and discipline as a standing army. He replaced the long throwing spear with a short stabbing assegai. Tactically, he favored the pincer movement which resembles the position and form of *buffalo* wings. To implement this tactic, the two wings advance outwardly while the center moves backward so as to encircle the enemy and finish him up with the assegai after he would have thrown his spear (Davis 1991; Omer-Cooper 1994, July 1992).

Conflict for territory first broke between Sabhuza and Zwide, which Zwide won. Sabhuza relocated to the north in what later became Swaziland. Zwide later won a war against the Mthethwa in which their leader Dingiswayo perished. Shaka's unit was the only one that remained intact when Dingiswayo was killed. Shaka's army confronted Zwide's in several forms: stopping their advance, retreating to isolate them and exhaust them, and pursuing them as they were trying to go back. The crushing battle for Zwide took place in 1826. Afterwards, the Zulu extended their power much further north through a serried of annual campaigns, defeating ethnic groups one after another. The latter had three choices: join Shaka, continue to fight, or migrate to distant lands as refugees, in a movement called the *Mfecane* in South African history (Davis 1981, Omer-Cooper 1994, July 1992).

3. THE SEARCH FOR TERRITORIAL AUTONOMY

Segmentation

Failed Rules of Rotation: Initially in Lubaland, it was expected that the chiefdom throne will circulate among the sons of the chiefdom founder by his senior wife from the oldest downwardly. Thus, the first son was to be replaced by the second in seniority, and so on. With the passing of time, the descendents of each son became a distinct lineage within the chiefdom. The power was supposed to circulate among these lineages in their decreasing order of seniority. To fight the tendency toward monopolization, a ten-year limit came to be established. Also, provisions were made for the contender to the throne to be known the very day a new chief was sworn in. As a part of the inauguration process, the new chief was required to select his *Lwaba*, his preferred successor, from among the many contenders. By definition, the chosen *Lwaba* had to be a member of a political segment other than the chief's own. However, with the passing of time, rotation became problematic due to numerical multiplication of contenders, to the tendency of some lineages to keep the power longer, and to the process of segmentation.

Segmentation: Through segmentation, disputes between brothers over power led an initially one lineage to split into two rival lineages, separate and autonomous from each other, each competing for the chiefdom throne along with other eligible candidates from several other lineages. The power became plutocratic, with candidates striving to outdo each other in amounts of wealth paid to the incumbent chief and to power-giving notables. The power to install chiefs into office was supposed to circulate as well. The circulation became difficult to implement and the power-giving prerogative ended up being monopolized by a few lineages, mostly the *Ntite* lineage. It is suspected that some individuals might have obtained power through conquest rather than normal rotation. In some cases, segmentation led to the split of the chiefdom into totally autonomous political entities. The most known case is that of the split of the *Bakwa Kalonji* between *Kalonji ka Cibanda* and *Kalonji ka Mukuna*, also called *Kalonji ka Mpuka* and *Kalonji ka Tshimanga*, respectively. The split came about when Kabula-Mpuka seceded from the *Bakwa-Kalonji* chiefdom following a power conflict between him and his older brother Cimanga Lwasambuta who was the incumbent. There is also the case of the *Bakwa-Kashila* and *Bak'Odila* caused by the separation of Lutumba Odila from the original *Bakwa Kashila* in reaction against the incumbent Ngandu Kashila, his brother (Ngandu 2004: 41). Another example comes from the Lozi Kingdom. Here, Mwanambinji, King Mboo's younger brother, solved a dispute with the king by founding himself a smaller kingdom within the kingdom (Vansina, 1968).

Segmentation caused the original chiefdom to weaken. The situation became worse under Belgian colonial rule as the colonial administration often favored candidates who were most submissive to them whether they were traditionally qualified to rule or not. In this connection, let us mention a contemporary case of segmentation—*the South-Kasai Autonomous State* (1960-1963). At Congo's independence (1960), there was one Kasai Province with its capital city at Kananga, former Luluabourg. In 1959-1960, the Luba living in Kananga and the surrounding regions were expelled from there during an ethnic conflict, to their native land in what is now Eastern Kasai. Their leaders also failed to secure the political positions they had hoped for in the national government of the Congo. They withdrew to their homeland and attempted to form a state of their own, The *South-Kasai Autonomous State*. The Congolese Government fought it and it was finally incorporated into the *Eastern Kasai Province*. Its capital city Mbuji-Mayi, became the capital of the new larger province. Kananga continued to be the capital city but of Western Kasai only. As another example, in the southeastern part of Congo, the Katanga secession was an even greater threat to Congo's integrity in the 1960s.

Indirect Rule

From the bottom up, territorial autonomy among the Luba of Kasai begins at the *lubanza*, homestead level. The man, husband and father, is the highest authority, followed by the senior wife. The other wives, if any, and the children come thereafter in that order. The man and his children are by birth right members of a particular *dîku* descent level whose members trace descent from a common ancestor. Traditionally, they would reside on the lands bequeathed by this ancestor, which are collectively owned by all his descendents. On these lands, they were free to settle and cultivate anywhere, except on parts already occupied by others. The man's authority over his homestead extends over his fields. There is nobody above him to tell him how to conduct business in them, let alone to keep him from doing so.

The land belonging to a particular *dîku* is the collective property of its members. Non-members must receive permission from the elders to build or farm on it. Traditionally, land is inalienable. Individuals can use it. The product of their labor is theirs, but the land remains the collective property of the *dîku* as a whole. A particular *dîku* is one among many *mêku* (plural of *dîku*) tracing descent from a common founding father of a higher-level descent group encompassing them: the *cifuku*. The chief of *cifuku* is a member of a particular *dîku* and does not own or control other *mêku's* lands. Within the *cifuku*, each *dîku* is autonomous vis-à-vis other *mêku*. The only obligation befalling it from above was acollection of in-kind itemscorn, cassava,chicken—organized at occasions to pay as a tribute to the chief of *cisamba*, the most encompassing territorial and political entity in the land, of which the *cifuku* is a segment. Each *cisamba*, large or small, is an autonomous chiefdom with no other traditional authority superseding it. The *cisamba* chief exercises power and authority—legislative, administrative, and judiciary—over the entire chiefdom. His prerogatives included ordering collects of in-kind tributes, collective fishing by creek damming and fish asphyxiation, and hunting by fire setting. He was entitled to one half of any large game killed within the boundaries of the chiefdom and part of the fish captured in collective fishing operations. Since Belgian colonization, however, the traditional chieftaincy has been emptied of its power and authority. In many cases, the power of the incumbent in large chiefdoms has been pulverized through balkanization. Long before Congo's independence (1960), the chief had become a simple agent of the colonial administration. Since then, he has been further marginalized and is simply being passed by.

The practice of indirect rule in Kasai goes back to the founding of the Luba Empire by the *Songye Nkongolo Mwamba* in the sixteenth century. Where this principle existed, local authorities continued to be designated and to function according to their own indigenous rules. King's or chief's messengers were sent periodically to the provinces to collect tributes, in-kind taxes consisting of goods produced locally. King Ngoi Sanza of the Luba Empire is recorded as having divided his own kingdom into numerous autonomous chiefdoms (Vansina, 1968: 75).

Wherever in central and southern Africa the Luba Empire extended its influence, this principle of indirect rule was introduced. Around 1600, Ilunga Cibinda, a Luba Empire prince, took it to what later became the Lunda Empire. Both in the Luba and in the Lunda empires, the food for the king and his entourage came from tributes, that is, in-kind taxes, paid by subordinate chiefs. Each local chief discharged his tax responsibilities with the kind of goods his subjects produced. In the Luba Empire, militarized expeditions of chief's traveling messengers called *kakwata* were sent to the provinces of the empire to collect taxes and communicate the king's messages to local chiefs. *Kakwata* expeditions were absent from the king's own homeland. They were more frequently conducted in provinces close to the capital, and traveled once a year to outer-chiefdom provinces. This meant that outer provinces could conduct their business as they saw fit all-year long without interferences from the king. Also, in the Lunda Empire, when a chief expanded his political power over a new territory, the local chieftain's relationship to the land remained unchanged. The local chief and his people would continue to be *mwaantaangaand*, land owners, whereas the new comers, including their leader, regardless of their political positions, would be *cilool*, tenants. From the Lunda Empire, members of the royal family spread the indirect rule principle to the kingdoms of Kasanji *and* Lwena (Vansina, 1968: 81-84).

External Politics

Self-Exile: Segmentation applies mostly to territorial divisions evolving within the same polity. There are cases where a disgruntled political contender would satisfy his ambition for political autonomy by exiling himself to a foreign land and founding a new polity there, over which he would exercise sovereign power. Cibinda Ilunga's departure from the Luba Empire and founding of the Lunda Empire is a case in point. After Cibinda Ilunga became king of Lunda and Princess Rweej became his queen, her discontented twin brothers, Kinguri and Cinyama, self-exiled themselves and founded the kingdoms of Kasanji and Lwena, respectively (Vansina 1968).

National Rise against External Threats: Autonomy could also be preserved by mobilizing citizens for the purpose of warding off some external menace: natural or human. The need for protection against external threats seems to have been the force that prompted the formation of states. Cheik Anta Diop (1991) names, from among other cases, the mobilization of civilians in ancient Egypt to counteract the potential damages from the floodings of the Nile River, and later during the reign of Thurmose III (1470 B.C.), to fight the Hyksos invaders; the rise of ancient Nubians under Queen Kandaka (Candace) against the armies of Julius Caesar; and the Mossi against the emperors of Mali and Songhai.

Marriage Alliance with Potential External Enemies: An African marriage unites not only the two spouses, but also the two family communities from which they originate. Political autonomy can be preserved by establishing marriage alliances with potential enemies. The practice is quite widespread among kingly or chiefly families. Sometime after Nkongolo founded the Luba Empire, the noble man Ilunga Mbili (*Mbidi* in Ciluba*)*, who intended to establish peaceful relationships with him, married his two sisters, Bulanda and Mabela. As already pointed out, upon migrating to what later became the Lunda Empire, Cibinda Ilunga married Queen Rweej of *the* Lunda (Vansina 1968, 78). In West Africa, the Kingdom of Benin was founded by Oranyan, also called Oraniyan, an immigrant from Ife, the Yorùbá holy city of origin, who married the daughter of a local chief. Their son Ewaka became the first official king *of Benin* (https://www.zyama.com. African States. Retrieved 7/18/2011). The *Bakwa-Kalonji*, the largest chiefdom among the Luba of Kasai, refer to themselves as *baana ba Kabedi' a Ilunga*, descendents of Kabedi'a Ilunga, a contracted form for Kabedi-wa-Ilunga. Kabedi was a Kanyok princess that Cimanga Lwasambuta, the founding ancestor of the *Bakwa- Kalonji*, married.

Alliance Pacts: There are also cases where neighboring clans or chiefdoms would form a federation to ward off a common menace. In such cases, Luba chiefdoms would establish a pact between them, named *bujilanga*. *Bujilanga* derives from the verb *kujila* to renounce, to abstain. It is an engagement by the contractors to abstain from any act of malice that would hurt a cosigner or any member of his group. Generally, an animal was sacrificed. Sometimes, when the threatening calamity was deemed very destructive, a human being was sacrificed to give an aura of solemnity. The most commonly known historical case of human sacrifice among the Luba of Kasai is that of Ciyamba, a woman reportedly purchased from a local marketplace and sacrificed in order to prevent her sacrificers from betraying one another and to compel them to unite against all external attackers of any contracting member of the pact. Ciyamba would have been buried alive on the side of the road, with her legs broken and her bust above the ground. With her hand extended to the by-passers, asking for food, she remained in that position until death came. Ciyamba's sacrificial place is said to have been somewhere around Lake Mabika, in the Mpyana Chiefdom (Mukenge, 1967). To memorialize this great event, the contracting lineages (*bisamba*), all located in the present Gandajika Territory, adopted a collective identity: that of *Baluba Ciyamba*, meaning Luba people of the Ciyamba branch. Nowadays, there is no unanimity as to which chiefdoms participated in the *Ciyamba pact*. The most commonly cited are *Beena Kaseki, Beena Manda, Beena Mpyana,* and *Beena Nsona*. There have been other human sacrifices in the history of the Luba of Eastern Kasai, all with female sacrifices. The *Beena Lwanga, Beena Kanyaka, Beena Kanyiki, Beena Kanangila, Beena Lulamba*, and *Beena Mbala* sacrificed a woman by the name of Nzeba. Other cases include the *Bakwa Sumba* and *Beena Ciswaka (Bakwa Kalonji)* who sacrificed a woman called Ntumba; whereas *Bakwa Tembwe, Beena Mbulanga, Beena Kanyiki, Beena Cimenga* and *Beena*

Chapter 10

Kaluma sacrificed Cyanda wa Mulondo (Mpoyi Mwadyamvita (1987). In all these cases of human sacrifices, the purpose was to create a kinship-like solidarity among the contracting groups (Kalanda, 1992), whereby preventing internal complicity that would have slowed down the process of warding off whatever external threat there was. The oral tradition relates that the sacrifice of *Ciyamba* was prompted by the invasion of Lubaland by Songye warriors loyal to Chief Ngongo Lutete, one of the slave trader leaders under the authority of the infamous *Typo-Tip*.

4. MODELS OF NATIONAL UNITY BUILDING

The Asante Model of Integrated Political Directorates and Rallying Nationalistic Symbols: The Ashanti kingdom (Late 16th and Early 17th Centuries) became a powerful confederacy after Ashanti leaders, beginning with King Osei Tutu, conquered other Akan kingdoms of *Akwamu*, Bono, and Denkiyira. They formed a political directorate composed of the best from the united kingdoms:

1. A Constitution based on the Ashanti institution of the Golden Stool (royal throne)
2. The most respected and practiced religious ideals and political structures, which consisted of: (a) the divine right kingship; (b) the leadership of Asantehene the King; priest, magician and spiritual counselor *Okomfo Anokye*; the queen mother, royal family members from the conquered kingdoms); (c) and the symbols of the royal stool from the sky, as practiced by the Ashanti Kingdom.
3. The most dignified rules, etiquettes, and fashions of the court from Bono.
4. The best military organization and traditions from Akwamu (each state in the union was responsible for a unit in the army).
5. The king of the most central, most prosperous, and most powerful city (Kumasi) as the nation's highest sacred religious and political authority.
6. A council of advisors representing the other states in the union.
7. A skilled administrative leadership appointed on merit rather than heredity.
8. The first specialized ministry of finance to be brought into existence.
9. An ad hoc position of *Adamfo* (Friend) to represent outlying districts of the empire at the royal court in Kumasi (Osae et al 1973; Collins 1997; Davidson 1977).

The Kuba Model of Direct and Multi-Level Representative Democracy and Ethnic Economic Specialization: The Kingdom of Kuba (16th-20th centuries) was founded by a federation of eighteen groups of immigrants called *Bushongs*. The country was divided into provinces headed by ethnic chiefs. Political participation was actualized through hierarchy of representative councils: village council, ward council, town council, provincial council, and central state council. Initially, Kuba villages were residential communities of particular clans. Clan elders formed the village council which assumed state functions. With the passing of time, increasing immigrations transformed many villages into large towns. Clans in these urban areas became wards, that is, sections of the town. Residents of each ward sent their elder to represent them in the town council. The village headman, the ward-clan elder, and the town chief presided over their respective councils and represented the latter in the provincial council. The provincial council was headed by the chief of the entire ethnic group, the paramount chief. At all levels, ethnic representation was equal regardless of the numerical importance of the population. In addition to equal representation, the *Bushong* elevated the best cultural contributions of the various ethnic groups composing the kingdom to national culture status. Thus, cultural practices such as dances, arts, agriculture, and house building, in which particular ethnic groups excelled, were promoted as Kuba dances, Kuba arts, Kuba farming etc. The *Bushongs* themselves were expert boat makers, fishermen and hunters. Thanks to state encouragements, these activities along with those practiced by others such as cloth-making and iron smith crafts, experienced high levels of prosperity—with the exception of those practiced by a few ethnic groups, such as agriculture. Standing above the provincial councils, was the central state council. At the beginning, the Kuba King was elected for a four-year term. Later on, the term was extended to ten years. Both men and women were eligible. Membership in this highest council, however, was reserved for the paramount chiefs of the original eighteen founding groups of the kingdom. They formed the highest ruling body in the kingdom called *Bushon*g. The *Bushong* alone elected the king. The other ethnic groups, labelled as strangers for being late comers, were excluded from participating in the highest political function of the kingdom (Williams 1987; Vansina 1968).

The Lunda Model of Minimal Territorial Control, Positional Succession and Perpetual Kinship: Chibinda Ilunga, a discontented candidate to kingship in the Luba Empire, migrated to the South, conquering Lunda chiefdoms and uniting them into what came to be known as the Lunda Empire. He brought along the organizing principles of the Luba Empire. Both in the Luba Empire and in the Lunda Empire, the food for the king and his entourage, came from tributes (in-kind taxes) paid by subordinate chiefs. Each local chief discharged his tax responsibilities with the kinds of goods produced by his subjects. Apart from paying the annual tributes, distant provinces could conduct their business as they pleased. Lunda leaders invented two inseparable mechanisms to foster loyalty to the king: positional succession and perpetual kinship. Whoever took the political position of *Mwant Yaav*, King, automatically inherited the kinship status and relations of the preceding *Mwant Yaav*. He and his relatives became forever relatives of the previous king's kinsmen with the same mutual rights and obligations. Conquered local chiefs were kept in their traditional position and given the title of *Mwant-a-Ngaand* (Owner of the Land). Newcomer groups were given the purely political title of *Cilool* (sub-chief) (Vansina, 1968).

The Zulu Model of Cross-Ethnic Militarization, Centralization and Loyalism: Shaka built the Zulu nation on the work of unification begun by Dingiswayo, consisting of turning initiation age-sets from various clans into a military regiment, assigning them a unifying name, and stationing them in the royal household standing army. Shaka inspired them to build loyalty to him, to the regiment and to the Zulu nation. Hundreds of small clans came to be united into a great nation with one language and a common military history. Defeated clan chiefs became King Shaka's vassals and had to provide military support for the king. The king was expected to be responsive to the needs of his people, to be strong and to rule with justice and generosity. He performed religious ceremonies on behalf of his people. The clans that made up the Zulu nation maintained their individuality and continued to operate according to their customs. In some cases, Shaka replaced customary chiefs with appointees loyal to him. The army, consisting of the youth from all over the country, was stationed in several barracks in the central region of the kingdom. Personal discipline, loyalty to Shaka, and Zulu nationalism were the guiding principles for all. He initiated a system of centralized bureaucracy composed of corps of appointed administrators directly accountable to him. Shaka forged a Zulu nation that survived him and continued to operate as an independent country until 1887, when it was conquered by white colonizers. The spirit of unity he created among the Zulu people lived on even much longer (Davis 1981, Omer-Cooper 1994, July 1992).

The Luba Kasai Model of Corporate Lineages' Complementary Roles and Rotational Succession; and Shared Governance: Three operational rules regulated the exercise of state power among the *Luba* of Kasai: (1) corporate lineages' complementary roles; (2) rotational succession; and (3) shared governance (Mukenge 1967, Kanyinda-Lusanga 1974).

Corporate Lineages' Complementary Roles: The Luba society in Eastern Kasai is made up of autonomous chiefdoms, large and small, founded by immigrants from the 16th-to-19th centuries Luba Empire, which was located in what is now Northern Katanga region. Each chiefdom is comprised of a hierarchy of lineages claiming descent from a common founder. The chiefdom is the maximal, highest lineage. The power of the state in each chiefdom is divided among two categories of corporate lineages at the rank of sub-chiefdom: The power takers and the power givers. The power takers (*bakalenga*) are descendents of the chiefdom founder by his senior wife. Traditionally, only they are eligible to provide chiefs who rule over the chiefdom. The power givers (*babiloolo*) are the descendents of the chiefdom founder by his other legitimate wives. Only they can confer a contender the legitimacy and authority to exercise the functions of chief. No chief can be considered a legitimate ruler until he has been installed into power by a legitimate member of an authorized power-giver sub-chiefdom (Mukenge, 1967). Power in both categories belongs to corporate lineages at the sub-chiefdom rank. Only their legitimate members can qualify.

Corporate Lineage Rotational Succession: Initially it was expected that the chiefdom throne would circulate among the sons of the chiefdom founder by his senior wife from the oldest downwardly. Thus, the first son was to be replaced by the second in seniority, and so on. With the passing of time, the descendents of each son became a distinct lineage within the chiefdom. The power was then supposed to circulate among these lineages in their decreasing order of seniority. To fight the tendency toward monopolization, a ten-year limit came to be established. Also, provisions were made for the contender to the throne (*lwaba*) to be known the very day a new chief was sworn in. As a part of the inauguration process, the new chief was required to select his *Lwaba*, his preferred successor from among many contenders. By definition, the chosen *Lwaba* had to be a member of a political segment other than the chief's own. However, with the passing of time, rotation became problematic due to numerical multiplication of contenders, to the tendency of some lineages to keep the power longer, and to the process of segmentation. Through segmentation, disputes between brothers over power led to one lineage splitting into two rival lineages. These lineages were separate and autonomous from each other, each competing for the chiefdom throne along with other eligible candidates from several other lineages. The power became plutocratic, with candidates striving to outdo each other in quantities of wealth paid to the incumbent chief and to power-giving notables. The situation became worse under Belgian colonial rule as the colonial administration often favored candidates who were most submissive to them whether they were traditionally qualified to rule or not. The power to install chiefs into office was supposed to circulate as well. The circulation became difficult to implement and the power-giving prerogative ended up being monopolized by a few lineages, mostly the *Ntite* lineage. It is suspected that some individuals might have obtained power through conquest rather than normal rotation. They might have been legitimized after the fact.

Shared Governance: The requirement for power sharing in the Luba political system is not limited to the distribution and rotation among power-taking and power-giving corporate lineages. It extends to governance and is more inclusive in this respect. Here the shared governance principle applies to the exercise of the chief's powers. In addition to senior lineages traceable to the founder's senior wife, and junior lineages descended from his other legitimate wives, some chiefdoms have lineages of original inhabitants called *basangana*, which means those found there, that is, original landowners who have been assimilated into the Luba ethnic nomenclature. The *basangana* are not included in the political competition described above. Also not included are some groups considered as *biikadi*, literally "those who have come to be with us", that is, asylum-seeker late-comer clients. Where they exist, the *basangana* and the *biikadi*, both numerically insignificant minorities, do not have reserved functions. They do, however, participate in the chief's council as cabinet members on individual merit or as sub-chiefs representing their respective constituencies. The chiefdom, the highest level of political authority in the Luba traditional system, is governed by an executive council including the chief, a cabinet of appointed functionaries, notables representing title-holding corporate lineages, and sub-chiefs representing the chiefdom's major political segments, sub-chiefdoms (*bifuku*).

Kings' Rituals of Political Integration

***Chiefs and Kings as Unity Builders*:** More than a secular authority, the African chief or king is the symbol of group unity and a personification of its essential values. Being endowed with mystical powers tied into his physical body, the chief or king becomes a sacred being and, when exercised in this capacity, his power becomes sacred as well (Dimandja, 1997, quoting Evans-Pritchard and Fortes 1940, and de Heusc 1989). The king's vitality was an expression of the state of well-being of the nation, including the fertility of the soil, the quantity of the harvest and the health of the people and the cattle, from among other aspects of life affected by his state of well-being (Diop, 1974).

The Yorùbá Oba: The traditional Yorùbá society was organized in city-states surrounded by farmlands ruled over by chiefs. Ile-Ife, the mother city of creation, is believed to have been founded by two mystical spirits from Heaven, *Oduduwa* and

Obatala. Ododuwa became the first king of the Yorùbá people. His children founded the seven Yorùbá kingdoms of *Owu, Sabe, Popo, Ila, Benin, Ketu,* and *Oyo.* Ile-Ife was densely populated. Courtyards were sacred places. Sometimes one large courtyard was reserved for religious ceremonies designed to accommodate a large population. Shrines to deities were built all throughout the city from the center to the periphery. With the passing of time, Oyo, a tributary state believed to have been founded by Oduduwa's son, Oranmyan, came to supersede Ile-Ife in military might and political influence (Davidson 1997, Osae et al 1973, Poynor 2001). Periodically, the *Oba* of Oyo performed religious ceremonies for the well-being of the population. Another example, the Oba of Benin was believed to be a sacred king and a living deity. He was the intermediary and the earthly counterpart of other deities and divine forces, such as Deity *Olokun,* Lord of the Waters, who gives wealth and children. The *Oba* was held responsible for the well-being (physical and spiritual health) of his people and the continuity of the state. All throughout the year, he performed rites inside the palace to benefit his people. Yearly, at the *Ugie Erha Oba Festival* held in honor of his ancestors, the *Oba* offered sacrifices to the ancestors to make the world safe from the destructive actions of lesser spirits and witches (Kaplan, in Olupona, 2000).

The Swazi King: In Swaziland, the king is the central figure in the *Ncuala* annual ritual. The *Ncuala* is set apart as a sacred period of three weeks during which public rituals are performed. All social groups of the kingdom, from the Queen Mother to the commoner, participate in assigned functions appropriate for their respective social statuses. Although performed during the king's youth, the ritual reaches its highest point at the king's passage to full manhood, that is, when he officially marries his ritual wife. The ritual is carried out in two periods: in two days of Little *Ncuala,* and six days of Big *Ncuala.* These are separated by days of sacred songs and dances performed throughout the kingdom. Wrong timing of the ritual is feared as potentially disastrous for the kingdom. Therefore, the Little *Ncuala* always begins at the sun's southern summer solstice and dark moon, and the Big *Ncuala* at the full moon. The most significant event during the Big *Ncuala* is the killing of a special black bull, selected by the king by striking it with a rod doctored for fertility and potency. The youth finish the killing. The killing of the bull is expected to fortify the king. Parts of the bull's carcass are used for the king's medicine and the remainder is offered to the ancestors (Kuper, 1986).

Political Integration through Queen Mothers' Royal Functions

Queen mothers, mothers of kings, sometimes aunts or sisters, rule along the kings. They are generally very much respected for their wisdom, political actions, and extensive knowledge of traditions and genealogies. They play several major political integration roles in the management of the affairs of the kingdom, such as: advising the king on major political policies, active participation in matters of succession to the throne, assuming administrative functions parallel or complementary to those of the king, and organizing national unity-building ceremonies. Highlighted below are queen mothers' roles which contributed to the continuity of the kingship and integrity of African kingdoms.

Advisement, Collaboration, and Substitution*:* Idia, a 15th century queen mother in the kingdom of Benin, was appointed queen mother by her son Esigie whom she had helped defeat his rival brother Arhuaran in the succession race following the death of their father Oba Ozolua. She had also taken a significant part in delivering a major part of the country taken away by the Igala neighbors during the chaos caused by the civil war between the two brothers. She was thus very instrumental in preserving both the continuity of the kingship and the integrity of the kingdom. Queen Mother Idia's importance for the kingship and the kingdom was so great that she had her effigy engraved in an ivory pendant mask worn by kings in protective religious ceremonies. In Benin tradition, the firstborn son was raised to become king and that was the mother's responsibility—a very instrumental role for the continuity of the kingship, especially when the son was the king's only son. Similarly, Queen Mother Erelu Kuti of the Kingdom of Lagos contributed to the continuity of kingship: both by serving as regent when the stool of the king was vacant, and by blessing the king during coronation. In Juaben, among the Asante, the queen mother, the biological mother, was the major adviser to the chief in all matters. She was very knowledgeable in matters of succession to the stool of the chiefdom and was vested with the authority to nominate eligible candidates to the elders of the royal family, and to king-maker elders and sub-chiefs. In former Dahomey (today's Benin), the *Kpojito*, queen mother of the Fon people, was an influential member of the kingdom's great council and commander of an exclusively women's special military unit called *The Amazons*, in addition to day-to-day administrative tasks. In the ancient Kingdom of Kush, *Kandaka, Queen Mother*, was very famous amongst title holders. She shared both lay and priestly royal functions of the king. In Yorùbáland, the queen mother participates in the coronation of the new king by blessing him before his installation (Bortolot 2003, Wikipedia. ND. "Queen Mothers (Africa)").[2]

Parallel Administrations: The Lozi queen mother, in Zambia, and her brother, the king, rule from two separate administrative capitals, each over a different part of the country and with different advisers, different local chiefs, and different armies. In Ashanti, the *Asantehemmaah*, Queen Mother, oversees matters of women's welfare and of conflict between men and women, appoints the directors to the women's court, and sees to it that all queen mothers are available in cases of domestic affairs and others involving women. All cases must have a hearing. The queen mother holds weekly formal court meetings. Each session is attended by authorized elders whose task is to listen and interrogate the litigants. The verdict is reached by consensus in the absence of the queen mother. Sometimes the *Asantehemmaah*, Queen Mother, hears and rules. In 1988, to enhance the power and political influence of queen mothers in society, Ashanti queen mothers formed *The Ashanti Queen Mother Association*, with leaders from across the Ashanti region. Under the Ghanaian constitution, queen mothers can become chiefs. The Ghanaian Parliament includes The National House of Chiefs, and the number of queen mothers who become recognized chiefs keep growing. In Yorùbáland, a category of women titled *Iyalode* oversee women's affairs in kingdoms across the country and represent women in the councils of the king. Among the Bashi of Congo DRC, the queen mother controlled almost half the land of the kingdom while ruling the kingdom until the son became of age to assume the functions of king (Geography. ND. "African Queens and Queen Mothers"; Wikipedia. ND. "Queen Mothers (Africa)").[3]

Chapter 10

National Festivals: In the 1940s, under the rule of the Swazi King Sobhuza II, a tradition was introduced in Swaziland (*Eswatini*) that consisted of annual ceremonies held at the Swazi Queen Mother's residence. The participants were unmarried young women from chiefdoms across the Kingdom. They were placed in age regiments where they underwent virginity tests. Those found pregnant had their parents charged with a fine of a cow. The practice was justified as a strategy for preserving girls' chastity, providing services to the royal family, and promoting solidarity among women through working, dancing and singing together during the festival. The night following their arrival at the Queen Mother's residence, the young women would disperse to the surrounding areas and work together in regiments cutting tall reeds. The next night they would tie the reeds into bundles and bring them to the Queen Mother's residence to be used to repair holes in the fence surrounding the royal village. Together in regiments, they would rest, wash, and prepare the costumes and the ornaments for the festival. On the festival day, the young women would parade dancing and singing in front of the royal family, dignitaries, and spectators. Thereafter, groups from selected villages, joined by king's daughters and royal princesses, would be taken to the center of the field where they would execute special dances. *The Swazi reed dance* tradition was adopted by King Goodwill Zwelithini of the Zulu in 1991 as a means to curb the spread of HIV by encouraging young women to remain virgins. Here the annual dance takes place in a royal kraal called *Nongoma*. The participants, dressed in special attire in colors reflective of their status (i.e., virgin or not a virgin; betrothed or not-betrothed) dance for the King, each carrying a long reed on her head which she deposits in front of the king. In Zululand, the girls participate in a slow-motion procession carrying reeds on their heads. The procession and the whole festival are led by the chief Zulu princess (Wikipedia. ND. "Umhlanga ceremony").[4]

Elders' Sacred Status and Moral Authority in Stateless Societies

In stateless societies, the elders hold the authority to rule. They derive their sacred status from the belief that the more one grows in age, the more sacred one becomes. The old ones become mediators between humans and the beings beyond. After their death, the respect due to them is transformed into ancestral cults. Among the Kikuyu of Kenya, the *Athuri*, elders, are the spokespersons for the community. They are the wisest members of the community. They receive direct communication from *Ngai*, God, who instructs them, perhaps during sleep. They are the highest authorities on interpreting divine messages, explaining the significance of social institutions and natural phenomenato the members of the community. The Karimonyong of Uganda are divided into age-sets. The lower sets owe respect to higher ones. Respect for elders is the greatest of values held by the people. This is backed by the belief that calamities come from failure to respect elders. It is believed that elders are closer to God than the others and so they are the ones who bless and perform the rituals. They are near to the ancestors in that they belong to the past, which belongs to the ancestors. The Nandi of Kenya have two parallel powers: the elders and the *orkoivot*. The leader of the elders, *poiyot*, has a key role in discussions, where he introduces matters and takes decisions in the name of the group. The *orkoiyot* is the senior member of a lineage which is the heir of the power of divination. His person is sacred—his name is not carried lightly on the lips. He does not take part in the discussions but is indispensable for deliberations. All major community activities require his consent. He performs rites to ensure success of enterprises, causing rain to fall at the right time. The *orkoiyot* is the representative of God whose uniqueness, control over nature, otherness, and power of the final say in discussions is embodied in his person. Of great importance across many African communities, the power of the ancestors is seen in the elders. Elders and religious persons are embodiments of the ancestors (Komba 1997, quoting J.P.; Carruthers 1995, Colleyn 1988).

SUMMARY

In several African creation stories, political authority is of divine creation. For example, the Yorùbá pantheon is hierarchical. Creator *Olódùmarè* is above all other gods. *Olódùmarè* is the head of the government; the *òrìṣàs* are his appointed ministers. From among the *Orìṣàs,* Arch-Divinity *Orìṣà-nlá* supersedes the others. At least twice *Olódùmarè* appointed *Orìṣà-nlá* to lead a delegation including himself, the hen and the pigeon, to transform a preexisting marshy land into a dry habitable land, the Earth. When Earth was solid enough to support the human population, the fauna and the flora, *Olódùmarè* charged Divinity *Orèlúéré* to lead the party of heavenly hosts who would become the first human inhabitants. Among the Mande of Mali, *Mangala* (God) resurrected *Faro* Seed from the purifying sacrificial death He had put him to, sent him as the leader of an ark to purify the incestuous earth of the impetuous *Pemba* Seed, and to plant more productive seeds of life. Leaders, by virtue of this mandate from God, occupy positions of authority. *Maweja Nangila*, God of the Luba, first created Lord Spirits who share his divine powers at the highest level. He then created great spirits in hierarchies of seniors and juniors, with juniors expected to recognize and pay respect to the authority of the seniors. African societies have developed various kinds of political systems, some more complex than others. They include task-specific and temporary bands, descent-based corporate lineages, clans and chiefdoms; kingdoms made up of unrelated chiefdoms, and empires established by conquest and subordination of once independent kingdoms. Of note, African nations have applied varied strategies to foster nationalism. For example: 1) the *Asante model* of integrated political directorate of nationalistic symbolism; 2) the *Kuba model* of direct and representative democracy and economic specialization drawing on ethnic strengths; 3) the *Lunda model* of minimal political control over constitutive chiefdoms, positional succession and perpetual kinship; 4) the *Shaka's Zulu Nation's model* of cross-ethnic militarization, centralization, and personal loyalism; and 5) the *Luba Kasai model* of corporate lineage, complementary roles and rotational succession, and shared governance. Also discussed in this study were cases of unification by royal rituals performed for the well-being of the nation and the people (e.g., the Yorùbá Oba, and Swazi King), political unification deriving from respect for the elders' sacred status and moral authority (e.g., the Karimonyongo of Uganda, Kikuyu and Nandi of Kenya), and political integration through the queen mothers' royal functions (e.g., the Ashanti, Yorùbá, Swazi, Zulu, and others).

Chapter 10

(Endnotes)

1	The Editors of Encyclopedia Britannica. ND. "Sobhuza I, King of Eswatini." https://www.britannica.com/biography/Sobhuza-I. Retrieved 3-14-2020.

2	Bortolot, Alexander Ives. 2003. "Women Leaders in African History: Idia, First Queen Mother of Benin." *THE MET Heilbrnn Timeline of History.* October 2003.

https://www.metmuseum.org/toah/hd/pwmn_3/hd_pwmn_3.htm. Retrieved 5-6-2020.

Wikipedia. ND. "Queen Mothers (Africa)." https://en.wikipedia.org/wiki/Queen_mothers_(Africa), Retrieved 5-8-2020.

3	Geography. ND. "Queens and Queen Mothers." https://geography.name/queens-and-queen-mothers/. Retrieved 5-8-2020.

Wikipedia. ND. "Queen Mothers (Africa)." https://en.wikipedia.org/wiki/Queen_mothers_(Africa), Retrieved 5-8-2020.

4	Wilipedia. ND. "Umhlanga (ceremony)." https://en.wikipedia.org/wiki/Umhlanga_(ceremony). Retrieved 5-5-2020.

PART FOUR

A PARTNER WITH NATURE IN MEETING HUMAN NEEDS

Chapter 11. A Steward of Community's Natural Resources
Chapter 12: An Explorer and Civilization Builder

Chapter II
A Steward of Community's Natural Resources

1. Sacred Mutual Stewardship of Humans and Natural Species
2. Common Patterns of Judicious Resource Exploitation
3. Animal Raising and Care
4. Care for Domesticated Plants

God wanted human beings on Earth to live well and to be healthy and full of energy. At creation, God made the world hospitable to human life and filled it with plants and animals for human consumption and comfort. In the Abaluyia story, "God created man so the sun would have someone for whom to shine." He created "plants, animals, and birds to provide food for man." *Olódùmarè,* God of the Yorubá people, took several steps to make earth habitable. He first had the preexisting marshy land solidified by having Divinity *Orishà-nlà* drop loose soil on top of it and the hen and the pigeon spread it all around. Having had the chameleon inspect the land twice, *Olódùmarè* sent *Orishà-nlà* back to earth, this time in company of Counselor Divinity *Òrunmìlà,* along with a palm tree to provide drink (wine), oil (seeds), food (kernels), and other trees valued for their sap (drink). He also created lagoons and rain as sources of water. *Olódùmarè* sent back the hen and the pigeon, this time with the mission to multiply and serve as continuous sources of meat for humans. In the creation story of the Gikuyu of Kenya, as indicated previously, *Ngai* (God) took the Gikuyu's ancestor to the top of Mount Kenya from where he showed him the country's bounty that was going to be his and his descendants' as a gift from Him, the Most High. The country had abundant varieties of plants, animals, rivers, plains, and meandering hills. All in it was beautiful and splendid. One particular message is clear here: the resources of the natural environment are sacred, and they are there to be used judiciously to meet human needs in the framework of the community. They are not just there, unassigned to anyone, waiting for some giant, or a select few, to come, seize them, and dispose of them at will. This chapter examines African peoples' patterns of responsible stewardship as it regards land and related resources, animal raising, and domesticated plants (Mbiti 1970, Idowu 1994, Jefferson and Skinner 1990). It offers detailed descriptions of traditional farming methods, indigenous crops, animals, and food production.

1. SACRED MUTUAL STEWARDSHIP OF HUMANS AND NATURAL SPECIES

Before creating humans, God made sure there would be life-sustaining resources available: land, water, animals, and plants, in addition to the sun and other heavenly bodies; and air, rain, and other atmospheric elements. Throughout the centuries, African peoples have developed attitudes and established practices enabling them to use the resources of their environment in efficient ways that allow them to satisfy their needs while also preserving the resources. The role of religious beliefs, attitudes and rituals in the interaction of humans with natural species can be seen, for instance, in the practice of traditional medicine, in Gikuyu people's interaction with the physical environment, and in *Woyo* seed blessing ceremonies, all three discussed below in that order.

Traditional African Medicine

African medicine is natural. It draws heavily on healing plants which grow all over Africa and are easily accessible. They grow in all imaginable ecological settings. In Ethiopia, for instance, medicinal plants are found in:

> deciduous bushland, dry bushland, wetlands, dry sandy plains, forest floors, dried river courses, stream banks, cultivated irrigated land, home gardens, road sides, river banks, floodplains, steep bare mountain slopes, rocky slopes, open grassland, fallow fields, woodland, forest margins, and shrub lands (Moges and Moges 2019).[1]

Traditional medicine is practiced quite extensively in some African countries. For example, as many as 90% of the population in Sudan and 70% in Ghana depend on herbal medicine for their health needs. In Ghana, Mali, Zambia and Nigeria 60% of children with high fever are treated with herbal medicine first (Abdullahi 2011, Karar and Kuhnert 2017).[2]

Some plants are associated with one healing power, others with two or three, and still others with a long list of healing functions. For instance, three plants growing in Sudan are identified with a long list of healing functions each.

> *Tabaldi* (*Aloe sankitana*): Fruit and leaves used for diarrhea, amoebic dysentery, skin diseases, constipation, fever, tonsillitis, hemorrhoids and inflamed colon

> *Damesisa* (*Amdrosia maritima*): Herb and seeds used to treat diarrhea, pneumonia, vitiligo, psoriasis, cardiovascular disorders, mild obstruction of the respiratory tract in asthma

> *Um galgil* (*Belanites aegiptiaca*) - Herb Tree: The whole plant, fruit, and seeds used to treat malaria, intestinal worms, itchy skin, insect bites, bronchitis, yellow fever, syphilis, and epilepsy (Khider, 2018).[3]

African traditional medicine is faith-based. First there is the belief that sickness and death come from God. But the actual sickness or death of particular individual, at particular time, in a particular location, may be precipitated by another powerful force than God. It is in the nature of God's creations, including humans, to die. God has predestined humans to be born, grow and die in old age. When an old person dies, usually there are no suspicions of an immediate cause that might have precipitated his or her death. But death at any other age, particularly at a young age, is generally attributed to some intervening force: 1) an envious or hater witch, a parental curse, an ancestral punishment for wrongdoing to a family member; 2) or else a punishment by the ancestral spirits or fetishes (spiritual powers encased in an object) of a stranger the victim has wronged in some significant way. Traditional medicine is collaborative in that it is delivered by knowledgeable experts endowed with distinct healing powers from divine creation working on the same case: 1) the diviner who conducts the diagnostic; 2) the seer who, through mystical revelation, can perceive the invisible—past, future, or in a distant location; 3) the priest who ministers through counseling, prayers, incantations, or sacrifices to the spirits, or provides other spiritual therapies; 4) the medicine man or woman who applies herbal treatment in various forms; and 5) the midwife who coaches, administers massages and medicine to facilitate delivery, who identifies and announces what kind of spirit the newborn baby is, and treats the new mother with warm baths to prevent blood coagulation. Some of these health providers assume several of these functions in combination.

African traditional medicine is community-based and holistic. All of these health provider experts are members of the community, imbibed in its culture including religious beliefs and practices, and knowledgeable of the family situations, living conditions, and psychological concerns of the potential clients. The health services they provide are holistic in that, thanks to the collaboration among these experts, the treatment addresses the patient's physical, spiritual, and psychological needs for healing at the same time. In addition, traditional medicine is not a private transaction between the provider and the patient. Instead, all operations—e.g., consultations with the diviner or the seer, prayers by the priest, the administration of herbal medicines, and exorcisms to remove sorcery or evil spirits—are conducted in the compound of an elder before an audience.

Gikuyu's Sacred Attitudes toward Nature

In the conception of the Gikuyu people, there is an element of divine presence and sacredness in all of God's creations, notably: heavenly bodies such as the sun, the moon, and the stars; phenomena like thunder and lightning, eclipses of the sun and the moon, clouds, rain, wind, and storms; earth formations such as mountains and rocks; and living species like forests, trees, and animals. All are manifestations of the presence of the Creator. For this reason, elements of the natural environment, even inanimate ones like mountains and rocks, were approached with an attitude of reverence. Such conception and attitude are shared and encourage environmental preservation practices all across Africa. As a manifestation of the Creator's presence and a sacred abode of the ancestors, the forest served as a hidden place for sacred rituals and refuge against enemy invaders and raiders. It was also a weather regulator in that tall mountain forest trees attracted rains, thereby influencing the formation of rivers, season changes, and food production. The forest is home to all species of trees. All trees were treated with reverence as their nature dictated. There were trees for house building, for food, and for medicine. Some trees were identified as poisonous. Small trees at the periphery of the forest were designated for making small tools such as walking sticks, farming sticks, or clubs. Above all were trees classified as sacred, two trees in particular: *Mukuyu* (fig tree) and a tree locally known as *Muu*. These trees served as shrines under which religious sacrifices were made to ancestors. In these manners, the forest was central to the physical and spiritual life of the Gikuyu people. Due to this centrality, the forest was equated with the human heart in Gikuyu proverbs and wisdom parlance.

Everyone was expected to tend to trees, valleys, hills, and rivers as a natural stewardship duty. The elders took upon themselves the duty to instruct young people on the importance of environment preservation using all effective powerful cultural tools of communication: "stories, riddles, slogans, tales, poetry, commentaries, proverbs, sayings and songs." *Mukuyu, the sycamore tree*, is Gikuyu people's major totemic sacred tree. They mystically and ritually identify themselves with it. They are not allowed to cut it or harm it in any other manner. For example, setting fire to the forest, sexual acts, and acts of violence in the forest were prohibited. Violations were sanctioned with cleansing rituals and animal sacrifices (sheep). Reverence for the *Sycamore tree* is extended to its counterpart totemic animals. Totemic plants and animals are classified as relatives and allies. Leopard (*Ngari*) and Elephant (*Njogu*) fall into this category. Persons given these names are expected to exhibit their character, such as strength for the elephant and courage for the leopard. Water (rivers and streams) was the object of reverence as a natural gift from God and as a symbol of life. Efforts were made to keep away from water anything considered as polluting (such as defecation). The role of nature in everyday life was manifest in farming. It was customary for the Gikuyu people to plant trees in the fields to provide shade for the plants and serve as wind breakers. Use of composts of plant remains, cow dung and urine, and chicken droppings as fertilizers was a normal practice as well. Rubbish and refuse were properly disposed of in ad-hoc pits and then applied to plants in gardens by the houses or in distant fields to increase fertility. Mixed cropping (different compatible plants in the same field) and proper rotation of mutually enriching plants were practiced regularly to increase the yield. Fallowing was a constant practice. It allowed for soil regeneration during the years of rest, thereby preventing permanent soil exhaustion. Underlying all the above actions, cautions, and precautions was a strong belief that if land is destroyed the community will be destroyed (Gathogo 2013, op. cit).[4]

Woyo Seed Blessing Ceremonies

The *Woyo* people live on the Atlantic shores of Congo-Kinshasa and the Enclave of Cabinda. The Woyo people are agriculturalists, but also fish for their livelihood. Success in agriculture depends, from among other factors, on the quality of the land and of the seeds. Seed selection is of great concern to the Woyo people. The Woyo perform sanctification rites on the good seeds that have been selected for planting, on the land, on fishing nets, and on the ocean. Related to land-blessing rites are those to bring in rains. The purpose of all these rites is to increase productivity, the harvest, and the catch from fishing. But the rites performed in this conjunction go far beyond to cover all aspects of human well-being, including women's fecundity, mending social relations among relatives through reconciliation, warding off diseases and natural calamities, protecting women, men, and children, empowering political leaders, and sanctifying and protecting the exercise of political power (Kibanda, 1997).

Seed-blessing rites are an integral part of rituals to the Spirit of the Land performed annually in mid-October. The planting time is announced by natural events including cold wind from the ocean, considered by the Woyo people as the home of the spirits who are responsible for the rain, the fecundity of the soil, and fish abundance. In preparation for the seed-blessing rites, participating clans are investigated to make sure violations of taboo observances are repaired. Families of violators must be purified by the priest for them to qualify for participating in the ritual. Some of the rituals are:

> *Consecration of sacred objects to be used for blessing the seeds and the sea.
>
> *The blessing of the sea along the Atlantic Ocean from the mouth to the upper limit of the original village, *Mwanda*.
>
> *Brooding: meditation by the main priest, while lying on his stomach, designed to increase the catch during ocean fishing parties.
>
> *Immolating a goat at the ancestral altar, partaking of the sacred meals on the next day, and visit to the altar to see if the spirits have accepted the sacrifice, a promise of abundance. Sacrifice acceptance by the spirits and the ancestors is confirmed if ants have eaten pieces of flesh off the goat bones (Kibanda, 1997).

The formal rituals involve prayers soliciting blessings from *Buunzi, the Spirit of the Land*, who is the spirit of the original founder of Woyo clans. The prayers include the following petitions:

> *Cleansing the hearts of the officiates so they may become the sacred vessels through which blessings from *the Spirit of the Land* are transmitted to the people.
>
> *Cleansing the roads and the village, thus protecting them from serpent bites and wild animal attacks.
>
> *Blessing the seeds so they may bring forth abundant harvest and prevent sicknesses.
>
> *Bringing abundant rains that will deliver the village from drought, make crops grow fast, increase the harvest, and wash away scourges.
>
> *Blessing and sanctifying persons who have violated taboos so they may experience happiness.
>
> *Enhancing the health of the youth who will soon undergo initiation and the families that will be reunited in acts of reconciliation.
>
> *Blessing the livestock and the game.
>
> *Warding off misfortunes and lightning.

*Blessing all the instruments of work: hoes, machetes, tools for climbing up palm trees, and fishing nets and other fishing accessories.

*Blessing the chief's instruments of power: sculpted ivory ornaments, sculpted cane, hat, and the command sword.

*Conferring to the chief the power to strengthen women and men, to heal infected wounds, to stop or ward off violent winds, small pox, and other disasters (Kibanda, 1997).

2. COMMON PATTERNS OF JUDICIOUS RESOURCE EXPLOITATION

Selected Land Tenure Systems

The Kongo: In the Kongo system land is owned by matrilineages and was inalienable, that is, it could not be bought or sold. Selling community land was equated with pronouncing a death sentence on the community. The owner matrilineage could grant land use rights to members or non-members. The harvest belonged to the grantee but the land remained the undivided property of the grantor, that is, the clan as whole. After the death of the grantee, the land and fruit trees growing on it, houses and fields return to community ownership and become part of the community's ancestral heritage (*fwa-dia-kânda*). Clan land did not belong to the chief. The latter was a manager not landlord or a sovereign proprietor. There existed no land that did not belong to any community. Neither was there abandoned land. Unused lands were reserved for future use or were farm lands temporarily left in fallow to allow planting soil to regenerate (Fu-Kiau, 2001).

The Igbo: Land accessibility rules and land use patterns of the Igbo people are complex. In principle land belongs to the lineage, is accessible to every member, and is inalienable. The Igbo are patrilineal. Sons inherit the land of their fathers. Daughters marry out and live in the lands of their husbands. In practice, the system makes provisions for strangers, married women, and other landless to have access to land. For instance, one can acquire temporary access to land as a generosity from a friend or in exchange for a symbolic gift of kola. A loaner can acquire usufructuary rights in a piece of land as long as the loan has not been repaid. In some communities, access to office requires payment of a fee for the land associated with the office. Village lands are exploited in blocks in a designated section of the communal land. Fallowing is universal but the duration is shorter where the density of the population is high. Land clearing is done by men with machetes and hoes. It is a common practice to have tree tops lopped by expert climbers rather than felling the whole tree. The leaves are left on the ground to dry and are then burned and used as fertilizer. In the past, when there was not enough rain for planting, appeal was made to the mystical rainmakers. Intercropping was used to discourage erosion. In this system, three or more crops with different maturity terms are planted in the same field at particular intervals (Uchendu, 1965).

The Luba: The Luba society is divided into autonomous chiefdoms, big and small. Each chiefdom consists of a hierarchy of residential lineages tracing descent from a common ancestor who is the chiefdom founder. *Lubanza*, homestead, the baseline, is the unit of production and reproduction. The level one above the *Lubanza compound* is *Beena Muntu*, extended family—a group of individual families, monogamous and polygamous—united by shared obligations to common ancestors, including ritual sacrifices and payment and redistribution of tributes of the first fruits. Next up is *Dîku*, principally characterized by collective ownership of land. Traditionally, a *dîku* member, individual or family, was free to reside, cultivate, hunt, or fish anywhere without having to ask anybody's permission. The products belonged to him or her, except for the half of any big game which was owed to the chief. The land used to these ends continued to belong to the clan. This ownership was inalienable. Crop rotation, shifting cultivation, and fallow were common practices. Planting was done on platforms or mounds and, for some crops, such as cassava and sweet potato, in trenches between platforms. Land clearing, tilling, and weeding were done with the hoe; pruning with the machete; and tree felling with the ax. Seeding on mounds or on platforms was done with the hoe or the heel, and distribution of cassava seeds was done with the hoe as well. Most harvesting was done by hand. Cassava and sweet potato were unearthed with the hoe. Crops for conservation were dried and then stored in the granary in sealed baskets or in calabashes. Corn was dried in shells and stored tightly next to each other to prevent mice from penetrating between them.

Hunting and Gathering Practices

Hunting Large Game: Large game is scarce in Lubaland. There are practically no forests in the Luba country. Where there exist river banks, they are used for cultivation during the dry season, when nothing grows in the savannah. The Luba farm in the river banks by felling the trees, unearthing the grass with a hoe and setting them on fire. Apparently this method of cultivation has accentuated the pre-existing scarcity of forests in the area, thus reducing further an important natural habitat for game. The same method of farming is practiced in savannah fields during the rainy seasons, September to December and February to May. Even without implicating this method of farming specifically, human usage of land, whether for farming, settling, or hunting, chases the game away. However, the most detrimental practice insofar as the survival of game is concerned is hunting by fire setting. To practice this form of hunting, men set fire all around a large area suspected to house abundant game. They then move behind the fire closely, picking up the small game killed by the blaze or the smoke, but essentially readying themselves to compete with their spears, javelins, and bows and arrows for the large game that will be trying to escape from the blazing fire. While men are doing this, women and children follow at a distance picking up the rodents that the fire has burnt to death and digging out those that have managed to hide in holes. When the encircled area has been consumed by the fire and the game in it killed, the men join the women and the children in picking up burnt birds and small animals.

Where there still exist some large games, the hunter recognizes the location of each species thanks to his knowledge of their habits and habitat. He identifies their cries and footprints. He knows the styles of their pathways and the magnitude of devastations they cause to the plants or the crops (Bamuinikile 1975, quoting Albert Bouillon 1954).

Chapter 11

Other than by fire setting, the Luba hunt by stalking, digging pits, hounding, and setting traps. Stalking (*kuzomba*) is generally practiced individually. The animal is shot with a powder gun. Hunting by pit digging (*kumbula majimba*) is practiced individually also. An animal entrapped in the pit is killed with spears (*mafuma*) or javelins (*misongolo*). Hounding (*kutua buluwa*) is practiced in a party. At the beginning, the dogs (*mbwa*) are leashed, each hunter holding his as they track the animal's smell. Once the game is identified physically, the hunter releases the dog(s) and both begin to chase the animal. Since dogs are faster runners than men, they wear bells (*ndibu*, singular: *ludibu*) around their waist so that their location and direction may be identified at every moment. A game killed in a collective hunt belongs to the killer or to the owner of the killing dog, but must be shared with the other members of the hunting party according to traditional rules of sharing, after the parts due the chief, generally half of the animal or so, have been separated.

Trapping Rodents: Rodents are more available than the large game. Trap setting is the most common method of capturing them. It can be the work of an isolated individual or of a hunting party. In individual trap-setting, called *kuteya misubula*, the hunter simply sets the trap in the pathway or near the hole. The bait is always the kind of food the animal is known to cherish. A collective hunt by trap setting begins by identifying the passage of the rodent. Then a trap in the form of a conic net is set on the rodent's pathway with its back toward the rodent's abode. The hunt takes place when the animals are sensed to be out in the neighborhood of the abode. Starting from a point believed to be behind the animals, the members of the hunting team advance in a row, making noise with their voices, and beating the bushy grass and the shrubs with clubs. This particular operation is called *kusaala*, battue (beaten). Its purpose is to frighten the animal and to drive it into the trap as it tries to rush toward the hole. Once in the trap, the captive has little room to move around and escape. It will not be long before a member of the hunting team approaches and kills it with a club.

A last worth-mentioning form of hunting rodents consists of digging into the mounds where they live. It takes place in a clear land after the grass has been set on fire. It is practiced collectively in most instances.

Gathering Insects/Ants: For the most part, gathering consists of capturing certain species of insects and caterpillars. Insects occupy an important place in Luba diet. Only certain species of insects are edible. Two species of edible insects are flying ants: one white, *bintuta*, and one brown, *nswa*. The two varieties grow in different types of mounds: slimmer and cone-shaped mounds (*mitenda*) for the white ants; larger, round, and sometimes dome-shaped mounds (*bilundu*) for the brown ants. The white ants are associated with the month of October. They are captured by digging into the mound and by dislodging them from the mound's womb. This double operation is performed at a time when the ants are mature and fattened enough to be a tasty food, but before the wings become strong enough for the ants to fly out of the mounds on their own.

The brown ants are captured at the times they swarm out of the mound. These times are known in advance from experience. From experience, also, Luba adults know the side of the mound where the ants will come out. In preparation, they clear the grass on the lower part of the mound on that particular side and dig a large pit at the foot of the mound. Behind the pit, they light a candle made of a waxy substance called *kamonya*.

The ants come out at night during the months of November and December. Generally, as soon as they exit from the mound, they fly in the direction of the moon as they are attracted to the moon light. The strategy for catching them in large quantities consists in positioning the pit and the candle in such a manner that the ants do not see the moon and are attracted to the candle light instead. As they move toward the candle light, they fall into the pit.

A third variety of edible ants is not winged. They develop in the cone-shaped mounds like the white ants and are captured in the same manner. Unlike the former varieties, however, these ants sting. The upper part of their bodies is reddish and crust-like. The lower part is minuscule and soft. The Luba name for this variety of ants is *mankenena*. They are called "soldiers" in English.

Catching Crickets and Grasshoppers: Other categories of edible insects include crickets and grasshoppers. The edible variety of crickets (*mintuntu*, singular: *muntuntu*) is brown. Also called *myenza* (singular: *mwenza*), these insects live in individual small holes in the ground. They are captured by digging. At certain periods of the year, the crickets come out of the holes by themselves, and are easily captured. The Luba word for grasshoppers is *mpasu*. One important variety of edible grasshoppers is called *minkesa* (singular: *munkesa*). They live in a sort of tall and bushy grass called *masela* (singular: *disela*). In hot days, the *minkesa* produce a sound by rubbing their long folded legs against the wings. The other *minkesa* respond to this sound by moving in its direction. Young people, teenage boys in particular, capture the *minkesa* along the roads by using a similar strategy. The captor imitates the sound and, as the *munkesa* approaches, he tends a long and strong straw in its direction and tries to get the *munkesa* to hold on to the head of the straw. Prior to tending the straw to the grasshopper, the captor rubs its head against his underarms. The sweat in the underarm has a salt-like taste that the grasshopper is supposed to enjoy. As the *munkesa* sucks the salt from the head of the straw, the captor slowly pulls the straw out of the tall bushy grass and delicately hits the grasshopper to the ground on the road so that it is killed without being smashed. A second popular variety of grasshoppers is called *mbedi* or *malaala*. This variety is green and slimmer than the *minkesa*. But it has more fat and better taste. The *mbedi* grow in the young grass that grows in the land that has been set to fire. Children capture them, along with other varieties of grasshoppers, by walking or running after them. They catch them with their hands or hit them with a *cibeetu*, a palm branch terminating in a sort of fly-swatter made of its own palms.

Collecting Caterpillars: As with insects, only certain varieties of caterpillars are edible. Edible caterpillars are called *mêshi* (singular: *dîshi*). Non-edible caterpillars= name is *biishiishi* (singular: *ciishiishi*). The majority of edible caterpillars grow in trees and are identified by the names of their host trees. These are: (1) *mutooci* tree caterpillars (*mêshi a mutooci*), *cifumba* tree caterpillars (*mêshi a cifumba*), and (3) *citefu* tree caterpillars (*mêshi a citefu*). The three varieties are gathered locally. A fourth variety, also of local origin, consists of the already mentioned grubs (*mposa*) that grow in the heart of the palm tree.

A fifth variety of caterpillars consumed by the Luba is *mêshi a mansamba*. This variety is commercialized throughout the Congo. It is imported into Lubaland and other parts of the Congo from the Tshikapa area, in the Western Kasai Province. The last species of edible caterpillars grow, not in a tree, but rather in the young grass that grows in a land.

A Sample of Fishing Traditions

Fishing in the Niger Delta: The rivers and lakes of the Niger Delta in Mali are prolific producers of fish both for the Mali domestic market and for export to other West African countries. The seasonal floods of the Niger River, its main tributary (*Bani*) and smaller feeders, and the lakes drive flocks of fish away from the water bed and make fishing impracticable. When the water recesses, fish return to the beds and are easily accessible. These are the periods of abundant catches and intensive fishing activities. The seasonal nature of fishing activities has turned Niger Delta fishermen into *transhumants* who live in temporary fishing camps by the rivers during the water-recess and high productivity months, and return to their permanent villages during the water-rise and low-catch periods. Two ethnic groups—the Bozos and the Somonos—are said to have dominated the fishing industry in Mali since time immemorial. Boating is their classic mode of transportation to and from both fishing grounds and marketing stations. The extended family is the basic unit of production and nucleus of the fishing industry's organizational apparatus. Malian fishermen in the Niger Delta make a wide range of fishing implements, such as (1) surrounding nets which are set into the water vertically to surround a whole school of pelagic fish, (2) throw or cast nets – circular nets which are thrown into the water and hauled back with the caught fish, (3) hand nets designed to scoop fish near the surface, and (4) dip nets, hand nets with a long handle used to scoop fish or crabs. Fishermen in other parts of the Niger Delta use some more complex fishing systems including stakes erected in fences, enclosures of woven mats constructed in heart form, raffia screens, traps with sliding gates, and a trigger with a bundle of grasses attached, designed to keep the gate open (Dyenye and Olopade 2017, Abowei and Hart 2008, Kanare ND).[5]

Fishing in Uganda: *Uganda* is endowed with several lakes and rivers replete with countless fish and other water life species. Traditional fishing gear consisted of spears, arrows, and fish-pots. Nowadays, most fishing is carried out using small wooden boats propelled by oars: long poles with a broad blade at one end. An increasing number of boats are being equipped with a petrol engine. Fish poisoning with local herbs was practiced in shallow water of rivers, lakes and swamps. Gillnets are made out of cotton, hemp, or flax. The Japanese have introduced nylon gillnets. Eastern Lake Albert in Uganda is known for its prolific reserves of *muziri,* small fish (silver fish), also called *mukene* in the Alur language. Fishing is done during the night by casting and collecting gillnets off boats while managing lamps to cast the light. With lamps placed at the top of the boat, the fishermen paddle offshore to scoop out the fish from the water using landing nets called *kitambi kya muziri. Muziri* fishermen usually work in teams in order to be able to control an engine boat with one or two boats attached to it (Wikipedia. ND., "Fishing in Uganda").[6]

Fishing in Lubaland: Four major rivers run in parallel, South to North, across Lubaland. These are: *Lubilanji* (at the Eastern border), *Luilu* and *Mbuji-Mayi* (in the middle), and *Lubi* (at the Western border). These rivers have very few tributaries in the

Luba area. A few small lakes also exist in the region. People living along these waters practice fishing where access is not handicapped by leech-infected swamps and where the hope for some significant catches supersedes the risks of being driven away by the torrent or attacked by sharks. Most of the Lubaland is dry. Even drinking water is scarce. People must walk dozens of miles before reaching the next creek or river. Because of the long distances between the villages and the waters, fishing is a time consuming activity for most people. As such it pales in importance with agriculture, Luba people's number one source of subsistence. For this same reason, fishing is practiced more frequently during the dry season, May to August, when agricultural activities are reduced. Furthermore, during the rainy season, September to December inclusively, and February to April, frequent heavy rains render the rivers so high that they overflow onto bordering marshes or dry lands, making fishing impracticable in large part.

The Luba practice different types of fishing, individually or collectively. Generally, angling from a hand-manned canoe (*bwatu*) requires the cooperation of at least two persons so that there is always somebody to control the canoe while the other is busy with a heavy fish, for instance. Fishing with a net in high waters requires even more people because of greater possibility for heavy catches and greater risks for capsizing. Fishing by setting traps in creeks is usually practiced individually. All these forms of fishing are practiced by men. The only form practiced by women is collective in nature. It takes place in the heart of the dry season, when the creeks are at their lowest. Women dam the creek, intoxicate the fish with a substance called *bubawu* made out of certain wild leaves, and catch the fish as they float over the water. Downstream the dam, the women also erect makeshift fences of wood and stones around spots of water, bail them out with a wooden bowl, *luupu*, and capture the entrapped fish.

Adult Luba in their sixties speak of the old days when rivers and creeks in Lubaland were overpopulated with fish, and when people who lived along these waters used to eat fish like greens. If that is true, then things have changed because even fish is scarce nowadays in the Luba country. Most fish consumed locally is dry fish imported from distant regions. It is possible that the pre-existing fish reserves have been exhausted from mere overuse or because of the method of intoxication which perhaps kills the young fish and the eggs.

3. ANIMAL RAISING AND CARE

Domesticated animals play various roles in the lives of African peoples across the continent. They provide meat, milk, wool, leather, skins, horn, fat, and the dung. Fowls supply meat, eggs, and feathers. Cattle, sheep and goats often serve as religious sacrifices, bridewealth goods, and payment for political bids. Cattle, goats, and sheep dominate in the sub-Saharan landscape. Goats and sheep prevail in arid zones, cattle in semi-arid zones, and in sub-humid zones where livestock is generally mixed with farming (Otte and Chilonda, 2002).[7]

Chapter 11

Animal Raising in Ancient Egypt

Cattle, goat, and sheep were being raised all throughout Ancient Egypt's history: Old Kingdom, Middle Kingdom, New Kingdom, and Late Period. Sheep were farm animals. Functionally, three categories of domesticated animals could be identified in Ancient Egypt: pets, sacrificial gifts to the gods, and cult symbols in the temples. Pets included cats, dogs, monkeys, gazelles, and birds. Sacrificial gift animals were specially bred to be offered to the gods. For example, at Tuna el-Gebel, ibises and baboons were reared and buried in honor of *Thoth*, the god of Hermopolis (city). Cult symbol animals were regarded as incarnations of the gods. The *Apis* bulls of Memphis were incarnations of *Ptah*. Rams were identified with *Amun*, the patron god of the city of Thebes. The Egyptians raised a number of cattle varieties, but the horned African breed ox was preferred for sacrifices to the gods. There were special farms for fattening oxen and bulls destined for sacrifice to the gods. The cattle were cared for by herders who tended them during the day and slept by them at night to protect them from theft. Ancient Egyptians raised horses as well. Horses were possessions of prestige for the wealthy who used them for hunting and pulling chariots in ceremonial manifestations and in battles. Horses were kept in special stables, given prestigious names, and fed with the best fodder. Venerated animals were given special burials, mummified, adorned with jewelry, and placed in special tombs in the temple or in the animal cemetery (Dunn. ND, Facts and Details. 2018).[8]

Cattle in Africa

Early records point to the domestication of cattle in Kenya, East Africa, about 15,000 years ago and the *Zebu*, or *Bos Indicus* breed in particular, during the first millennium BC. Cattle were domesticated both in the pre-desertification Sahara Pastoral Period, 7,000 years ago. *Sanga* is the term used in Southern Africa for a breed of cattle known for having originated in the Ethiopia-Somalia region by 1,600 BC. In West Africa, cattle first appeared in Niger during this very period. At the time, hornet goat was being raised in Algeria and Nubia. Between 6,000 and 5,000, cattle were being raised in Mali. The Bororo-Fulani of northern Nigeria raise goats, sheep and cattle. They move their cattle from one area to another searching good grazing land and thereby also avoiding tsetse fly-infested areas where the animals can get infected with *trypanosomiasis*. The herders who live around Lake Chad, periodically set the grass to fire to generate green pasture. Many African societies—e.g., the Masai, the Swazi, the Tutsi of Rwanda, and the Bashi of the Congo—raise and value cattle above any other domestic animal. Cattle procure a sense of worth to the owner, and are a great source of prestige and pride. The Maasai of Kenya live for cattle and think cattle live for them. They have appointed the most valiant age-set (the *Morani*) to the function of protectors of society and cattle. The high value of cattle and the imperative to protect cattle dictates the layout of Ndebele villages in southern Africa. Cattle belonging to individual villagers are housed in a common kraal built in the center of the village and surrounded by the houses on all sides. The owners take their herds to different locations during the day for pasturing and bring them back to the common kraal in the evening. *Nguni* cattle, generally multicolored, are the dominant indigenous breed in Southern Africa. They belong to the *Bos Taurus* (humpless) and *Bos Indicus* (humped) breeds. Long time victimized by systematic South African government policies of banishment and forced cross-breeding with imported breeds, the *Nguni* cattle breed has only survived thanks to its high fertility, adaptability to local vegetation and climate, as well as resistance to diseases. Now, the very government is trying to propagate it for these qualities (Namibian 2016, Bester et al. ND).[9]

The Hema Extensive Cattle Care System

The Hema people who live in Eastern Congo take care of their cattle not only physically, but spiritually as well. Every Hema-owned cattle drove has a guardian spirit. The drove belongs to the clan. Preferably the bull for the drove should have the color consecrated to the clan's protector spirit. The bull cannot be sold. It will die of old age or will be killed on the tomb of the clan leader if the latter dies first. The bull, head of the drove, is ritually identified with the clan leader, just as the drove is identified with the clan. Daily care for the cattle begins early in the morning with an assembly at the entrance of the kraal around a dung fire made for the purpose of warming up the animals, while the fume helps chase the flies away. This is the time for milking the cows and is specifically the men's responsibility. Precautions are always taken not to milk the cows exhaustively. Calves are better fed through sucking. The women burn some special herbs in the milk containers to give the milk some special flavor. The morning milk is the family's breakfast. The remaining is kept to be added to the evening milk and stored for next day consumption. Toward the end of the morning hours, when the grass dries enough, the cattle are taken to pastures. At some point, they will be led to the water, rested and then brought back to the pastures where they will stay until evening comes. Back to the kraal, they are taken all way to the center around a big fire. Evening milking will take place here. The fire burns all night long. The security house by the entrance remains open permanently. The guards who stay there hardly sleep. They are required to remain watchful at all times. Cattle owners are expected to remain attentive to cattle diseases to be able to promptly intervene when needed. The high importance of cattle in the lives of the Hema is manifest in their detailed knowledge of each individual cattle and extensive classification systems of cattle based on the form of their horns, sex, age category, fur color, reproductive age stage, and more (Ruhigwa, 1975).

Table 9a: *Elaborate Cow Naming System of the Hema People of the Congo and Uganda*

Naming Classification Based on the Form of the Horns, Sex and Age			
Form of the Horn\Sex and Age	Bull or Bull Calf	Heifer	Cow
Hornless Animal	*Rusomi*	*Kasomi*	*Nsomi*
Animal with outward curved horns	*Rutagura*	*Katagura*	*Ntagura*
Animal with inward curved horns	*Rukome*	*Kakoke*	*Nkome*

Animal with downward curved horns	Rutenga	Katenga	Matenga
Animal with enforced horns	Rusimbamu	Kasimbamu	Nsimbamu
Animal with evaded horns	Rwanzara	Kanzara	Nyanzara
Animal with straight horns	Rwemereza	Kemereza	Nyemereza

Table 9b: *Elaborate Cow Naming System of the Hema People of the Congo and Uganda (Continued)*

Categories Based on Number and Size of fur Color			
Color\Sex and Age Category	Bull or Bull Calf *Enumi*	Heifer *Enyama*	Cow *Ejigiga*
Two small spots	Rubamba	Kabamba	Ibamba
Two large or medium spots	Ruyenze	Kayenze	Mayenze
Most of the robe is one color	Ruhuga	Kahuga	Mpuga
White robe with small light-brown spots	Ruhura	Kahura	Mpura
White robe with small dark-brown spots	Rubaya	Kabaya	Mbaya
Black, Red, or Brown with a single yellowish spot	Rubibi	Kbibi	Mbibi
Multiple-spot fur	Rutimba	Katimba	Ntimba

Adapted from Ruhigwa 1975 (Many more term-specific categories of cows with multicolor fur are not included in the above two-table nomenclature).

Goat and Sheep Rearing

Farming food crops and raising goats and sheep were in high esteem in the Gikuyu society, Kenya. The Gikuyu people, rich and poor, lived in round houses. The poor had small fields and one or two animals. The rich had large fields and large flocks. Both took good care of their animals, which were housed in stables. The poor constructed their stables in a corner inside their homes, while the rich built theirs outside at the outskirt of the courtyard. The stables were round just as the homes but built of wood with an elevated floor above the ground. The rich practiced two feeding methods for their goats and sheep. Female animals were pastured on hilltops where plenty of grass was available. The males were stall-fed at home with sweet potato vines brought by the women of the house from the family fields. The female animals were raised primarily for reproduction, the males for slaughter and meat sale and consumption. Stall feeding began at weaning and could last up to two years before slaughter. Feeding the animals well for fattening before slaughter was such a preoccupation that at times the owners seemed to place the growing of sweet potato vines for the animals above cultivation of maize and millet for human consumption (Watt, 1942).

The Oklahoma State University's Department of Animal Science identifies seven goat breeds as indigenous to Africa. These are: *Benadir, Somalian, Boer, Nigerian Dwarf, Nubian, Pygmy,* and *Sahelian,* The *Benadir* breed is found in southern Somalia. It is used both for meat and milk. Another Somali goat breed, also found in Djibouti and northeast Kenya, is known under different names—*Abgal, Boran, Galla* and *Ogaden*, from among others. It is raised primarily for meat, but is also praised for its milk production, and its resistance to drought, gastrointestinal parasites, and infectious diseases. It is easy to maintain since it can feed on grains, hay, garden and kitchen scraps and any type of vegetation. The *Boer* goat, found in South Africa, is an improved breed made of a mixture of indigenous African breeds with elements from Europe, India, and Angora/Ankara, Turkey. It is above all a source of meat but produces milk as well. The indigenous breeds, collectively called *veld goats*, consist of several regional sub-breeds. *Nguni* goats, the most widespread, also called *Mbuzi*, are reported to have lived in South Africa since the later Stone Age (1million to 6000 years ago). The *mbuzi* are an important source of meat, milk, hair and skins. They also have an important cultural significance as sacrificial animals in Zulu traditional ceremonies. The Xhosa *Lop-ear goat* breed dominates in Eastern Cape. They represent all color patterns: uniform solid, speckled, spotted, flowery and marble. The speckled Northern Cape goat breed was once taken to Namibia, thereby escaping the South African miscegenation. The white color dominates all over the body covered with red, red-brow, and black spots and strips. The *Kunene goat* breed, also called *Kaokoland*, is found in the Namibia Kunene region. This breed is multicolored, adapted to hash climate, and often moves around with the nomadic Himba people. *Mbuzi* and other *Veld goats* are fed naturally by walking them to areas where grass, shrubs, and plants are available. (Reddy 2018, Louw ND., Arca del Gusto ND.).[10]

Originally used for meat and milk, the *Nubian goat* breed has been turned into a primarily dairy producer. Its milk is flavorful and has high butterfat content. For these reasons, the breed is highly sought after for cheese production. The breed is adaptable to heat, capable of breeding all year long, and very social and ostentatiously affectionate for humans. The *Nigerian West African Dwarf Goat* ranks higher than other goat breeds in many respects: i.e., its resistance to trypanosome and some parasitic intestinal infections, high milk-production capacity, and higher butterfat content. These qualities make it the ideal supplier of raw materials for making cheese and soap. The *Pygmy goat*, an evolved branch of the *Nigerian Dwarf goat*, abounded in the Cameroon valley. They are friendly, hardy, adaptable to all climates, and a good source of milk. They are very active, feed on greens and grains, and need fresh water, shade, and warm shelter. The *Sahelian Goat*, indigenous to West Africa also, is found in Mauritania, Mali, Niger and Chad, and is adapted to the region's arid, dry and desert conditions. Usually of white, white-black, or white-brown color, this goat breed is known by some other names, such as *Fulani, Peul,* and *West African long-legged goat*. It is primarily raised for meat and skin production (Holms ND, Chiejina and Behnke 2011, Roys Farm ND, That's Farming 2018).[11]

Chapter 11
Sheep in Africa

West Africa is home to several varieties of sheep breeds, including the *West African Dwarf sheep*, the *wool sheep*, the *Peulh* breeds, the *Moorish* breeds, and the *Senegal's ladoum sheep*. The *West African Dwarf sheep* dominates in several West and Central African countries, notably Senegal, Chad, Cameroon, Gabon, and the Republic of the Congo (Congo Brazzaville). It is primarily raised for meat. Generally half-black and half-white colored, the breed does have some totally black sub-species, *the Kirdi* species in particular. The *dwarf sheep* are small in size and have short legs. Rams (males) are horned; ewes (females) may or may not have horns. The breed offers the advantages of being trypanosome tolerant and adapted to humid, sub-humid and savannah climates. The *Wool Sheep,* of which the *Mali macina sheep* are a variety, are large, produce little milk and meat, but are suppliers of coarse wool, which is used in making blankets. Two of the *Peulh breeds* are the *Toronquee* and the *Djalonquee* varieties. The *Toronquee* breed sheep are large, black and white colored, and produce a lot of meat and milk. *Djalonquee*, a smaller, short-legged variety of the *Peulh* black and white sheep, produce a large quantity of meat. The *Moorish sheep breed* is represented in West Africa by the *Nar*, the *Touabir* and the *Targui* varieties. *Nar*, a coarse-hair variety of the *Moorish breed,* is used for crossing with *Astrakhan* sheep to make fur. *Touabir*, another coarse-hair variety of *Moorish* sheep, are large, black and white, and good meat producers. The *Targui*, another good meat producer sub-breed of the *Moorish* sheep, have long hair, long legs, and can walk long distances in search of grass. The *Senegal's ladoum* sheep are huge, without wool, pretty, and highly commercialized. Expert sellers have extensive knowledge of the breeds, their distinguishing appearance traits and their countries of origin: local, Mauritania, Niger, and others. An improved variety of a traditional *touabir sheep, ladoums* are preferred over other breeds for their height, ability to put on the pounds, and for their delicious meat. They are competitively sought after as status symbols. Separate, more prestigious, stables are sometimes built for *ladoums* away from the stables for ordinary sheep. Rich sheep owners have several stables of *landoums*, some located on top of apartment buildings. The status of *landoum* sheep owners is elevated to the highest levels during the Muslim religious festival of *Tabaski,* generally known as *Eid-Adha*, which is celebrated in Muslim countries to mark the end of *the haj* and in commemoration of Abram's willingness to sacrifice his only son Isaac to God. The sacrificial animal can be a goat, sheep, camel, or cow. In Senegal, *Tabaski* is a day festival dominated by ostentatious consumption and distribution of sheep meat. Reportedly, hundreds of thousands of sheep are sacrificed and ostentatiously consumed. These sheep are so badly in demand at the coming of *Tabaski* and the risks of sheep loss so high that owners spend nights awake, watching over their precious animals. To reduce the risk of sheep reserve depletion at the approach of *Tabaski*, the Senegalese government suspends taxes on sheep imports. (The Economist 2019, Humanity Development Library.2.0. ND, Lewis 2014, Sobhani 2016).[12]

4. CARE FOR DOMESTICATED PLANTS

Domestication of Food Crop Plants

Crop domestication in Africa goes way back to ancient times. Apparently, as early as 6,000 BC, barley and sorghum were being grown in Nubia, Central Sudan. Subsequently, other crops were cultivated in Ethiopia, the Niger bend, the Sahel region, Gambia, and along the Zambezi River. Included were *Guinea corn, bulrush millet,* and *fonio, yam, palm oil tree, dry rice, gourds, melons* and *beans*. Worth mentioning also are *teff* and *enset,* which are found in Ethiopia only. World Watch Institute lists the following crop plants as indigenous to Africa[13]:

Food Crop Plants Indigenous to Africa

1. African eggplant
2. Bambara bean
3. Cowpea
4. Dika
5. Egusi
6. Enset
7. Miracle melon
8. Finger millet
9. Fonio
10. Lablab
11. Locust bean
12. Marama
13. Marula
14. Monkey orange
15. Moringa
16. Pigeon pea
17. Potato
18. Safou
19. Sorgum

Some indigenous crops have been replaced by transplants. A spice called *grains of paradise*, the Bambara ground nuts, and African rice are good examples. Transplanted crops to Africa are of two origins: Asia and the Americas.

African Crop Plants of Foreign Origin

Crops of Asian origin:
banana plantain Asian rice taro eddo cocoyam mango
lime bread fruit sugar cane, black pepper ginger

Crops originating from the Americas:
amaranth avocado beans cacao cassava corn
guava Okra papaya peanuts peppers pineapple
potato squash sunflower sweet potato tomato
(Encyclopedia Britannica. ND)[14]

Care for Particular Crops Grown in Lubaland

Care of Corn: Corn and cassava are by far the major food crops grown in the Luba region. Their importance in the production system was superseded only by cotton, a colonial imposition. In the 1950s and 1960s, Luba adults indicated at that time that corn was introduced into their area through contacts with the *Chokwe*, but could not say when. One thing is certain, however, when the *Bia-Franqui Expedition* reached the Luba territory in 1891, the cultivation of corn had become an established practice. Corn is cultivated in all seasons. However, the best seasons are *Mvul'a Mbedi,* First

Rains (September to December) and *Mvula ya Nshisha*, Second Rains (February to end April). During these two seasons, corn is cultivated in gardens around the houses and, especially, in the fields of the plain some kilometers away from the village. During the dry season (early May to end-August), the plain is too dry to enable any crops to grow in it. Riverbanks, which still contain sufficient humidity, are then used as an alternative planting site.

Traditionally, corn was planted on mounds of earth erected all throughout the field. With the institution of the *paysannat system*, it came to be grown on the platforms required by the colonial administration for planting cotton. To plant corn the traditional way, the farmer made a pocket with his right heel on the top of the mound or the sole, dropped four grains into the pocket, and used his toes to cover the pocket with soil. There was only one pocket per mound. On soles, pockets were placed two steps apart. Sorghum, *mamvwa* or *tumbumba,* was planted in the same manner. Maintenance of cornfields involves weeding and protecting the grains and the plants from predators. Corn is weeded in the same manner cotton was: once by hand when the young plants first sprout and, then, three times with the hoe. Corn is the target of three types of predators: ants, birds and wild animals, and small cattle, notably goats and sheep. The farmer protects his plants in various ways: by using traps to catch rats and birds, sending children to the fields to frighten the birds, and setting smoking fire in the field in the hope that it will frighten the birds. To protect the plants against animals, he once built a hut in the field and spent nights in it, awake most of the times, to be able to chase the animals out whenever they would come.

Corn is harvested three and a half months after planting, that is, in January for First Rains corn, which is planted in September, and in May for Second Rains corn planted in early February. These two months are dry and sunny, which in fact accelerates the drying process. In colonial times, dry-season, riverbank corn was harvested in September if planted in June, or in October-November if planted later because of overwhelming cotton demands. Harvesting is a woman's duty. Upon harvesting, good quality corn ears are carried home in their shells properly arranged in a *cisaka*, a close-knit basket nailed to a firm wooden base. At home, corn is dried under surveillance. Husked ears are spread out against one another on the ground in front of the house, while someone, working or just relaxing in the verandah, watches over to keep caprines and fowls away. Dried corn is arranged and stored in a granary called *diyeba*. The strategy is to arrange the corn ears so closely that it is difficult for rats to run between them. Abandoning this traditional mode of storing corn, the colonial administration imposed added new system called *gardiennat* custody in the *paysannat* (peasantry) zones. Here, after harvesting and drying operations, the farmers took some of best ears of corn or husks of peanuts to a community storage built in the courtyard of the village chief to be conserved for the following planting season. Only selected grains resulting from experimental breeding at the stations of *the Institut National d'Etudes Agronomiques au Congo* (INEAC) were permissible into *gardiennat* (Beguin, 1965).

Cares for cassava. The Luba once grew several cassava varieties. All varieties stayed in the soil eighteen months to two years or more. All could grow on any kind of soil, but with different levels of productivity. Most of them exhibit some degree of bitterness. Practically all have disappeared. In the 1970s, the last survivals (*ditadi* and *ndundu*) could still be seen here and there. Where it still existed, *ndundu* was only planted around the fields as border markers. Its bitter leaves were occasionally consumed in times of vegetable scarcity. Neither its roots, nor those of other traditional varieties, were consumed anymore. Three cassava varieties—*kalaadi, mumbunda,* and *kanzenze*—are of more recent introduction. Missionaries who grew the latter two in their gardens probably introduced them to the area. Both were sweet. Nevertheless, they were disappearing to the benefit of *kalaadi*, the most recent of all varieties, which is more bitter than the other two, but supported by the colonial administration as part of the so-called educational crops (Mukenge, 1967). The following description applies principally to the latter variety.

Prior to the introduction of cotton and the imposition of the soles, cassava was planted on a flat ground. Following these two innovations, cassava came to be planted between the soles. In general, cassava is not grown first in a new field. It is planted in cornfields at a time that the corn has grown tall enough not to be suffocated by it. Cassava is planted by propagation. Prior to planting, the cultivator brings bundles of cassava stems to the field, breaks them into pieces of about two decimeters long and places them on the ground, one by one, two if they are of very small size, two steps apart. Then, with a hoe, he makes a little hole into the ground at the place where each piece has been deposited and buries the latter in it.

Cassava plants have three major enemies: fire, cattle, and wild swine. The danger of fire is not big when the plants are still young because during this period cassava is associated with other crops—particularly corn, beans and peanuts—which have to be weeded at specific stages. But by the time cassava approaches maturity, it is by itself in the field. It is then that tall and dry grasses become a real danger. Not only does the fire destroy the stems and the leaves, it also spoils the roots. In the event of such a misfortune, one would have to wait at least a year for the roots to become edible again. As a preventive method, people weed their cassava field frequently and are always ready to run to the field and fight an eventual fire. Cattle eat cassava leaves, thus undermining the chances for an abundant crop. They break mature stems, thereby rendering cassava no good for immediate consumption. Therefore, it is imperative to protect cassava against goats and sheep. Protective methods are the same as for corn: keeping the animals leashed and splattering their wastes over the plants. Swine, both domestic and wild, can devastate cassava fields. They unearth and eat the roots. Therefore, pressure is exerted upon owners of pigs to keep them in stables and feed them rather than letting them wander around fending for food.

It takes cassava two years or more to mature. Here again, harvesting is a woman's task. After unearthing the tubers, the woman piles them up at some place in the field, usually under a tree if there is one. Then, she peels them and takes them to the water for steeping (*kwela mu mâyi*). A creek is a choice place for this operation. The immersed cassava remains in water for a number of days, at least two, sometimes up to eight, depending on the variety. When the tubers have softened enough, they are taken out of the water and dried to the sun by the creek on thick grass, in the field on branches, or at home on a kind of stand called *cisasa*. If there is no sun, cassava will be dried on a stand built in the kitchen above the fireplace. Sometimes, especially during the dry season, cassava is not steeped. In this alternative, the harvester, after peeling the tubers, splits them longitudinally into two or more pieces and spreads them in the field, on an improvised stand made of branches, or takes them home to dry. Cassava can also be stored in the attic for future consumption.

Care of beans. Beans and groundnuts are next to corn and cassava in terms of the amount of care they receive during their growing stage and the importance they have in the diet and trade. Beans also fertilize the soil and by covering the ground, they enable the soil to resist erosion and protect the field by suffocating the weeds. Three varieties of beans prevailed in Luba society: red, green, and white. The white variety, *nkunda ya nzengu*, has the largest grains and takes longer to cook and to digest than the other two varieties. The green variety, *nkunda ya kambululu,* has the smallest grains and takes longer to cook than red beans, but cooks faster than the white variety. The green variety and the red variety, *nkunda ya cibalabala*, are considered by the Luba as traditional to their region.

Beans are grown during both rainy seasons: September-December and February-May. They are generally seeded in cornfields at the time corn is weeded. The mode of seeding is the same as for millet. The field is prepared first. Then, the grains are broadcasted over a portion of the field. From there, the planter goes over the area superficially turning up the soil in order to cover the grains. Beans are weeded first by hand two weeks after planting, then with a small hoe (*kakasu ka kahamba*) two weeks after that, and finally with a hoe after the husks have already formed. Mature beans are the prey of birds. Children must be sent to the field to frighten them. For a more permanent effect, scare crows (*bifweta*, singular: *cifweta*) must be placed throughout the field or at least in the four corners.

Beans are harvested when the husks become yellow. However, not all of the husks in a field become yellow at the same time. Therefore, the harvest takes place in at least two rounds. First-season beans are harvested in January and second-season beans in May. Each member of the harvesting party has a small basket (*kabondo*) or a calabash bowl (*citonga*) to put the beans. They then pour the contents into a centrally placed large basket called *mutenga*, *cisaka*, or *cibata*. If the common basket is full and the harvesters still have time, they start another. In the end, they carry the baskets home on their heads. From there, the beans are spread on a clean spot in the courtyard to enable complete drying. For good conservation, beans are husked first. Husking (*dishiipula*) is done little-by-little by women when they have time. They do it by pounding the husks in a mortar. The result of the pounding process is poured into a basket of the *cibata* type. The *cibata* is then shaken in order to separate the husks from the grains. The grains are placed into a dry calabash (*cibungu*) and kept in the granary of the storehouse.

Care of groundnuts. The Luba grow two major types of groundnuts. One type, called *nyimu*, has round nuts and only one seed per pod. The other type, *tumbela* or *tubindi*, often has more than one seed per pod. The growing of *tumbela* was supported by the colonial administration. The *nyimu* did not enjoy similar support. Thus, *nyimu* were not grown on a large scale. What follows concerns the *tumbela*.[8] The *tumbela* are what Americans call peanuts and are grown in the savanna during the September-December rainy season. Before independence, INEAC (*Institut National d'Etudes Agronomiques au Congo*) introduced a selected white variety of *tumbela* into the *paysannat* zones. Peanuts of this variety were locally nicknamed *yangambi*: they were probably first experimented with at the *INEAC* station at Yangambi in Northeastern Congo. In 1968, C.F.D.T. (*La Companie Française pour le Développement des Fibrers Textiles*) introduced a new red variety, which looked just like the old variety, *nkasa*. The soil for planting peanuts must first be mellowed with a hoe. Planting takes place immediately after heavy rains, that is, when enough water has penetrated the ground. Peanuts are planted in lines. The farmer protects peanuts against ravagers by the same methods as for protecting corn, notably, by setting traps, making loud noises and maintaining a smoking fire in the field. The weeding pattern is the same as for beans, and happens in several rounds as well.

Peanuts are harvested when the leaves become yellow and begin to dry and fall. Both men and women harvest peanuts. Children help separate the peanuts, while women take the peanuts home to dry in the sun. When peanuts are dry enough to be put away, they are kept in close-knit *mitenga* on wooden beams, horizontally arranged on the floor of the storehouse. Prior to storing, the *mitenga* are covered, at the top, with the leaves of a tree called *mujiwu*, or those of another tree by the name of *munkala*. The top and the borders of the *mitenga* are then cemented with rammed earth similar to that used to cover the walls of houses.

Examples of Thorough Care for Special Food Crop Plants

Three systems of care for domesticated plants stand out in Africa. These are: care for *millet* in West and East Africa, care for *teff* in Ethiopia, and care for *native rice* in Casamance Senegal.

Millet: *Millets* are small-grain cereals. There exist nine species of millets worldwide of which four are indigenous to Africa. Of the four, one—*Teff*—only exists in Ethiopia. The other three—*fonio, black fonio*, and *guinea millet*—are unique to West Africa. Two species are also widespread in Africa—*pearl millet and finger millet*—and are of foreign origin. *Pearl millet* has come to dominate 76% of the African market. Together, the six species provide 40% of the world's production. *Finger millet* dominates in East and Southern Africa. Millets are valued for their adaptability to semi-arid territories of the Sahel, dry mid-highlands of Ethiopia, and the fringes of the Kalahari Desert. Most of all, millets are very rich in nutrients. They have high levels of quality protein, ash, calcium, iron and zinc. These nutritional qualities make millet highly recommended for infants, lactating mothers, the elderly, and convalescents. Millet producing countries in West Africa are (in order of importance) Nigeria, Niger, Burkina Faso, Mali, and Senegal. Millet producers in East and Southern Africa are Ethiopia, Sudan, Uganda, Kenya, Zimbabwe, Zambia, Malawi, Madagascar, Rwanda, and Burundi. Millet production is a long process. It begins with seed selection, by separating the seeds from peduncles and other possible mixtures. Then, good healthy seeds are separated from bad, unhealthy seeds. Separation is done by winnowing or by placing the seeds in a salt solution. The good heavy seeds drop to the bottom of the vase; the bad ones remain afloat on the surface. Next, the good seeds are rinsed with clean water to remove excess salt and then are dried in the sun. Seed preparation for planting ends with picking up the pebbles from the seeds by hand. The land must be prepared also. Land clearing and tilling are done by hoeing or oxen plowing. Nowadays some use tractors. The best time for planting is at the first rainfalls of the season. Planting is done on platforms or in furrows between platforms. In either case, the soil must be smoothed. This is done with a hand-manned cutlass or by drilling in furrows if an oxen plow or tractor is used. Millet is mostly produced intercropped with one, two, or more other crop plants: such as sorghum, peanuts, cowpeas, or cassava. Intercropping may be done in relay-cropping or double-cropping sequences. In relay-cropping, two or more different plants are sown side-by-side in the same field, at different time intervals, during the same planting season. Double cropping is planting in rotation in the same field. In any case, individual plants must be optimally spaced from each other. Other than proper preparation and planting, normal plant growth requires timely weeding. Optimally, millet is weeded two to three weeks after sprouting, and two weeks thereafter. Millet is a fast growing plant, and is ready for harvesting two to four months after planting. Timely harvesting prevents seed breaking and grain loss. Harvesting is followed by drying in the sun or indoors above the home fire. Just a little after the drying process is the time for threshing for conservation. Sometimes grains for conservation are mixed with ash before storing. Vigilance is required all throughout the millet production-conservation process in order to detect eventual attacks by worms, flies, or grasshoppers and to promptly intervene (Obilana, A B. ND. FAOSTAT. 2019).[15]

Teff: *Teff* is a tiny-seed, grass like cereal plant. The Ethiopians have farmed *teff* since ancient times (apparently since 4000-1000 BCE) and it remains the people's main livelihood. There are three major varieties of *teff*: white, brown, and mixture of white and brown. In Ethiopia, *teff* grows practically everywhere, but most significantly in Oromia and Amhara (over 80%); more particularly in the midland and, to a lesser extent, in lowland regions. Production in the highlands is marginal. *Teff* farming is the enterprise of the entire family. Men, women, and children participate in it along gender lines. At all stages of the production process, *teff* farming is carried out with a wide range of traditional tools and equipment adapted to the nature of the task at hand and environmental conditions. Most of the preparative activities are carried out by men. Men are responsible for plowing, thinning, cutting, and planting. Plowing is generally done using a pair of oxen. Plowing and thinning are repeated several times before seeding. *Teff* cutting is done with an iron sickle. Men also do the winnowing: first, they separate the threshed *teff* grains from the rough straw; then, with the help of some wooden tools, they blow stranger materials and broken seeds off of healthy seeds. Thereafter, women clean the seeds. Women will work on the seeds again before seeding by men. The most common method of sowing *teff* is casting the seeds by hand on a flat ground. Women come thereafter to cover the sowed seeds with acacia thorns, especially on rainless days, thereby sheltering the seeds from birds and other predators. To a lesser extent, row planting is practiced in lieu of casting. Grains are sowed in specific quantities at fixed intervals. This method economizes on the number of grains actually invested and ensures their equal distribution throughout the field. For greater productivity and better quality product, it is customary to grow teff in rotation following particular crops, notably: onions, beans, chickpeas, and lentils, respectively. These crops harbor and nurture the microbes that enhance soil fertility. After planting by men, *teff* production falls to the women. The first major step is weeding. Weeds reduce *teff* productivity and have to be removed. *Teff* farming and production is Ethiopia's major source of livelihood, and in some parts of the country, the entire family is mobilized to do *teff* weeding. Traditionally weeding is done by hand. But increasingly chemicals are being used instead. However, reportedly, farmers prefer weeding by hand over using herbicides since the latter are life threatening to weed microbes, to human health, and to the environment. Proper weeding allows *teff* to grow normally to maturity and harvest time. Threshing is the next step and begins with preparing the ground by digging out the vegetation and smoothing the ground. The most practiced traditional method of threshing is animal trampling. After threshing comes the drying of the straws over several months. The piling is done in such a manner that the panicles are sheltered inside the pile against the rain, birds, and rats. Traditional teff storage was meant to last several years in conditions that minimized attacks by weevils or fungi, insects, or pets. Storages consisted of above ground silos looking like small houses. These storage units were made of wood, mud, teff straw, and wood bark fibers. In some parts of the country, the storage was built inside the farmer's residential house. Presently, the majority of farmers use plastic sacks for storage. Women's *teff*-related jobs do not stop at storage. *Teff*-food preparations, such as grinding or taking *teff* grains to milling plants, are carried out by women; so is the baking of *injera*, the Ethiopian *teff* bread and the accompanying meat or vegetables. *Injera* and other *teff* products are praised for their high nutritional and medicinal value. *Teff* contains no gluten and is rich in proteins and minerals such as magnesium and iron, among others. *Teff* grains for sale are packaged and taken to the marketplace. Packaging in plastic sacks—also a family activity—is now preferred over traditional packaging because it better prevents water penetration (Gizaw, Tsegay et al. 2018; Fikadu, Wedu, et al 2019).[16]

Native Rice: *Rice* is grown as the main staple crop in many countries of the *West African coast*. Reportedly, there only exist two species of rice in the world: the African species (*Oryza glaberrima*) and the Asian species (*Oryza sativa*). The African species—cultivated by the Jola people in the Niger bend region of Mali for approximately 3000 years—spread to Senegal's Casamance region, to the swampy regions of Gambia, and Guinea Bissau. Everywhere it was cultivated in vast fields, was central to the diet, and was sold in large quantities in local marketplaces. African rice has been almost completely replaced by the Asian rice introduced by the Portuguese by the 16th century. Apparently, its seeds scatter more easily, the grain is more difficult to mill, and the yields are lower. Unfortunately, to the eye of the consumer, these disadvantages shadow its benefits, such as being more resistant to diseases and pests and more tolerant of iron toxicity and severe climates. Also, it grows to maturity faster. By this it is a more promising response to Africa's chronic food insecurity. Rice is a rainy season-planting crop. It is sowed in water. The Jola are counted among the most skilled rice growers in West Africa. In the Casamance region of southwest Senegal, Jola men and women farm rice with mastery in various ecological settings: on hills, in flooding valleys, and in river channels. They have developed special technologies allowing them, for example, to:
- dyke flooding water with earth to keep the sprouted rice in water
- furrow flooded rice parcels with shovels made of long wooden handles and large iron blades

- bundle parcels to collect and retain rainwater or fresh water from uphill springs
- make cuts through rice bundles to distribute water to various rice fields
- carve deep fields, surround fields with walls, and build sturdy dykes to keep marshy toxic water off the fields
- use hand knives to harvest mature crops
- spread large quantities of manure over the fields during the dry season to fertilize the soil before planting time (Linares 2009, 2002).[17]

SUMMARY

In Africa, land and the resources of the natural environment are the patrimony of ethnic communities as bequeathed by their ancestors. Community members have the right to use them freely under the supervision and guidance of the elders and the chiefs. The products of their labor—farming, hunting, gathering, or fishing—belong to them, but can also be shared under accepted rules. Land, forests, trees, and rivers are sacred abodes of the spirits and sources of livelihood for the community, including providing remedies for preventing and treating ailments and diseases. Some trees and animals are treated with reverence as totems, such as the Gikuyu people's reverence for the sycamore tree. In Ancient Egypt, venerated animals were given special burials, mummified, adorned with jewelry, and placed in special tombs in the temple or in the animal cemetery.

Farming, hunting, and fishing may take various forms. But all extractive activities are expected to be judicious, decent, moral, and non-destructive. Many are preceded or followed by cleansing or expiatory rituals. Of great importance, traditional land tenure systems vary, but allow inalienable rights to the community. Traditional African practices had respected systems for farming, and also intermittent periods for the land to rest and be conserved for future generations.

Africans raise all kinds of animals and fowl. However, cattle, goats, and sheep dominate the scene, with cattle being the most prestigious. Some breeds in each of these three categories are indigenous to Africa, and are adapted to the continent's varying climates and terrains. For instance, Nguni cattle in Southern Africa have only survived thanks to its high fertility, adaptability to local vegetation and climate, as well as resistance to diseases. Across many African countries, cattle ownership confers the highest social status, and cattle are preferred payments for marriage alliances and political offices.

Among non-cattle raisers, goats and sheep are symbols of wealth and sources of prestige. According to regional customs, goats are most valued for reproduction, marriage payments, slaughter at festive occasions, or to sell for meat. Indigenous African goats—e.g., the Somali *Abgal*—are reckoned for resistance to drought, gastrointestinal parasites, and infectious diseases. Some sheep breeds are preferred sacrificial animals. Others, such as the Senegalese landoum, are in high demand for being status symbols and wanted for conspicuous consumption during religious festivals.

Conscientious stewardship of domesticated plants is manifest in the particular care for successful growing of millets, including the Ethiopian *teff*, and native rice species. Millets are valued for their adaptability to the semi-arid territories of the Sahel, dry mid-highlands of Ethiopia, and the fringes of the Kalahari Desert. Growing *teff* involves a long list of tedious tasks performed by entire families using traditional tools and equipment. *Teff* has no gluten and is rich in nutritional proteins and minerals.

The Jola people of the Niger River bend, in Mali, and the Casamance region of Senegal, have been growing native rice for many generations. They have continued to grow African rice even after the latter has been considerably displaced by the Asian variety. Native rice is more resistant to diseases and pests and more tolerant of iron toxicity, severe climates, and variations in water depth. Also, it grows to maturity faster. For these reasons, it is a more promising response to Africa's chronic food insecurity. Taken together, this chapter offers a close review of African traditional land management and food production practices that demonstrate a reverence for the natural resources provided by the Creator, as well as a broad diversity of practices and applications.

(Endnotes)

1   Moges, Admasu and Yohannes Moges. 2019. "Ethiopian Common Medicinal Plants: Their Parts and Uses in Traditional Medicine–Ecology and Quality Control." Published November 27, 2019 https://www.intechopen.com/books/plant-science-structure-anatomy-and-physiology-in-plants-cultured-in-vivo-and-in-vitro/ethiopian-common-medicinal-plants-their-parts-and-uses-in-traditional-medicine-ecology-and-quality-c. Retrieved 7-7-2020.

2   Abdullahi, Ali Azazeem. 2011. "Trends and Challenges of Traditional Medicine in Africa." *African Journal of Traditional, Complementary and Alternative Medicines: AJCAM.* Published online 2011, Jul.3. https://www.ncbi.nlm.nih.gov/pmc/articles/PMC3252714/. 7-9-2020.

Karar, Mohamed and Nocolai Kuhnert. 2017. "Herbal drug from Sudan: Traditional uses and phytoconstituents." *Pharmacognosy Reviews* (Vol.11, Issue 22). July-December 2017. https://go.gale.com/ps/anonymous?id=GALE%7CA506270691&sid=googleScholar&v=2.1&it=r&linkaccess=abs&issn=09737847&p=H.

3   Khider, Tarig O. 2018. "A Look at Some Medicinal Plants from Sudan-Mini Review." *Journal of Advanced Pharmacy Research* 25-10-2018 .https://aprh.journals.ekb.eg/article_18046_6ca7a88ef1ccd5173ebe4622b79c8a70.pdf. Retrieve 7-9-2020.

4   Gathogo, Julius. 2013. "Environmental management and African indigenous resources: echoes from Mutira Mission, Kenya 1920-2012)." In Studia Historiae Ecclesiasticae vol. 39/2.33-56 Pretoria: The Church History Society of South Africa). Online Version: https://en.wikipedia.org/wiki/Kikuyu_people#Origin. Retrieved 5-28-2016.

5   Dyenye, Henry Eyina and Alaba Olopade Olopade. 2017. "A review of Fishing Methods and Gears in Niger Delta Nigeria". *Journal of Natural Sciences Research.* Vol. 7, No 6, 2017. https://pdfs.semanticscholar.org/0379/f85cfce63d80d8f62dd29d9a04f5698b0238.pdf. Retrieved 7-19-2019.

Abowei, Jasper and Aduabobo Ibituru Hart. 2008. "Artisanal Fisheries Characteristics of Fresh Water Reaches of Lower Nun River, Niger Delta, Nigeria." https://www.researchgate.net/publication/27796853_Artisanal_Fisheries_Characteristics_of_the_FreshWater_Reaches_of_Lower_Nun_River_Niger_Delta_Nigeria. Retrieved 3-11-2020.

Kanare, A. ND. "Session VI – Technologie des Pêches Telles qu'Appliquée aux Pêches Continentales: Collecte, Traitement et Commercialisation du Poisson en Plaines Inondables." http://www.fao.org/3/AC673B/AC673B10.htm. Retrieved 6-17-2020.

6 Wikipedia. ND. "Fishing in Uganda".https://en.wikipedia.org/wiki/Fishing_in_Uganda. Retrieved 6-17-2020.

7 Otte, M.J. and P Chilonda: 2002. "Cattle and small ruminant production systems in sub-Saharan Africa: A Systematic Review." Rome: FAO Agriculture Department. http://www.fao.org/3/a-y4176e.pdf. Retrieved 3-16-2020.

8 Dunn, Jimmy. ND. "Cattle, the Most Useful Animal of Ancient Egypt." http://www.touregypt.net/featurestories/cattle.htm. Retrieved 12-10-2019.

Facts and Details. 2018. "Livestock and Domesticated Animals in Ancient Egypt." Updated September 2018. http://factsanddetails.com/world/cat56/sub404/entry-6155.html. Retrieved 3-16-2020.

9 Namibian 2016. "Know your Cattle: Nguni Cattle." *News – Agriculture* 2016, 10-17. Page No 17. https://www.namibian.com.na/157001/archive-read/Know-your-cattle--The-Nguni-cattle. Retrieved 3-16-2020.

Bester, Jenny, et al.ND.,L.E. Matjuda, J.M. RUs, and H.J. Fourie. ND. "The Nguni: A Case Study." Irene, South Africa: Animal Improvement Institute. http://www.fao.org/3/y3970e04.htm. Retrieved 3-16-2020.

10 Reddy. 2018. "Somali Goat Characteristics, Profile, and Facts." GOAT FARMING. September 12, 2018. https://www.goatfarming.in/somali-goat-characteristics-profile. Retrieved 3-17-2020.

Louw, Marinda. ND. "Indigenous Goat Farming in South Africa." *Slow Food Foundation for Biodiversity.* http://southafrica.co.za/indigenous-goat-farming-in-south-africa.html. Retrieved 3-17-2020.

Arca del Gusto. ND. "Nguni Goat." *Slow Food Foundation.* https://www.fondazioneslowfood.com/en/ark-of-taste-slow-food/nguni-goat/. Retrieved 3-1-2020.

11 Holmes, Tori. ND. "Everything you need to Know about the Nubian Goat." https://www.wideopenpets.com/everything-you-need-to-know-about-the-nubian-goat/. Retrieved 5-28-2019.

Chiejina, Samuel N. and Jerzy M. Behnke. 2011. "The Unique Resistance and Resilience of the Nigerian West African Dwarf Goat to Gastrointestinal Nematode Infections." *Parasite Vectors. 2011, 4:12. Published Online 2011, Feb3. http://www.ncbi.nlm.nih.gov/pmc/articles/PMC3042002/).* Retrieved 6-22-2016.

Roy's Farm. ND. "African Pygmy Goat Information with Picture." https://www.roysfarm.com/african-pygmy-goat/. Retrieved 3-1-2020.

That's Farming. 2018. "Going for Goats – the Sahelian Goat." 12-22-2018. https://www.thatsfarming.com/news/goat-sahelian-goat. Retrieved 5-31-2019.

12 The Economist. 2019. "Why people in Senegal pay a fortune for fancy sheep". Printed *Edition/Middle East and Africa.* Dakar May 16th 2019. https://www.economist.com/middle-east-and-africa/2019/05/16/why-people-in-senegal-pay-a-fortune-for-fancy-sheep. Retrieved 3-18-2020.

Humanity Development Library.2.0. ND. "Sheep and Goat Breeding." http://www.nzdl.org/gsdlmod?e=d-00000-00---off-0hdl--00-0----0-10-0---0---0direct-10---4-------0-1l--11-en-50---20-about---00-0-1-00-0--4----0-0-11-10-0utfZz-8-10&cl=CL1.16&d=HASH014f85dc05de37bfc936774b&gt=2. Retrieved 3 18-2020.

Lewis, Jori. 2014. "Senegal's Shepherds TABASKI." *Saudi ARAMCO World*. Current Issue. January/February 2014. https://archive.aramcoworld.com/issue/201401/senegal.s.shepherds.of.tabaski.htm. Rertrieved 3-18-2020.

Sobhani, Delena. 2016. "Counting Sheep in Senegal." *Berkley Center for Religion, Peace & World Affairs*. September 19, 2016. https://berkleycenter.georgetown.edu/posts/counting-sheep-in-senegal. Retrieved 3-18-2020.

13   World Watch Institute. 2011. "Africa's Indigenous Crops." State of the World, January 2011. http:/https://www.doc-developpement-durable.org/file/Fertilisation-des-Terres-et-des-Sols/agroforestrie/principes/Africa-s-Indigenous-Crops.pdf. Retrieved 5-1-2020.

14   Encyclopedia Britannica. ND. "18 Food Crops Developed in the Americas." Written by Melissa Pertruzello. https://www.britannica.com/list/18-food-crops-developed-in-the-americas. Retrieved 5-2-2020.

15   Obilana, A B. ND. "Overview: Importance of Millets in Africa." *ICRISAT*. Nairobi, Kenya. http://afripro.org.uk/papers/Paper02Obilana.pdf. Retrieved 6-19-2020.

FAOSTAT. 2019. "Geographic Distribution of Millet in Africa." Updated 8th July 2019. https://www.infonet-biovision.org/PlantHealth/Crops/Millet. Retrieved 6-20-2020.

16   Gizaw, Birhanu, Zerihun Tsegay, Genene Tefera, Endegena Aynalem, Endeshaw Abatneh, and Getasew Amsalu. 2018. "Traditional Knowledge on Teff (Eragrostistef) Farming Practice and Role of Crop Rotation to Enrich Plant Growth Promoting Microbes for Soil Fertility in Eastern Showa, Ethiopia." *Agricultural Research & Technology: open Access Journal*. Published June 22, 2018. https://juniperpublishers.com/artoaj/pdf/ARTEOAJ.MS.ID.556001.pdf. Retrieved 6-19-2020.

Fikadu, Asmiro Abeje; Tsega Desalegn Wedu, and Endalew Abebe Derseh, et al. 2019. "Review of Economics of Teff in Ethiopia." *Crimson Publishers*. Published April 19, 2019. https://crimsonpublishers.com/oabb/pdf/OABB.000542.pdf. Retrieved 6-24-2020.

17   Linares, Olga F. 2009. "From past to future agricultural expertise in Africa: Jola women of Senegal expand market-gardening." PNAS. https://www.pnas.org/content/106/50/21074. Retrieved 6-24-2020.

Linares, Olga F. 2002. "African rice (Oryza glaberrima): History and future potential." *PNAS* December 10, 2002, 99 (25). https://www.pnas.org/content/99/25/16360#:~:text=Native%20to%20sub%2DSaharan%20Africa,The%20two%20strains%20of%20O. Retrieved 6-19-2020.

Chapter 12
An Explorer and Transformer of Spaces and Civilization Builder

1. Precursors to Humans
2. The First Peoples
3. Migrant Settlers
4. Long-Distance Traders

The human being has a strong propensity toward migrating to unknown spaces, settling down there, and building communities of fellow men and women. As described by some African creation stories, the creation of Earth was a move into the unknown by divinities commissioned by God. Some legendary ancestors are portrayed as having migrated to some previously unknown land that became the birthplace of their descendants. Others are said to have directed their progeny to migrate to some unforeseen distant environments where they would multiply and prosper. The *Hominids Proto-Humans* migrated from their cradle in East Africa to the entire continent, then to Asia and to Europe. Likewise, the first human beings to colonize Planet Earth spread from East Africa, not only to the Nile Valley and West, Central, and Southern Africa, but also to Asia, Oceania, Australia, and even to the Americas. From their homeland in the Upper-Nile, sedentary Nubians moved northwardly, exploring and colonizing the land along the Nile River, establishing communities, and eventually organizing them into two major kingdoms. Finally, they united the two kingdoms into a single Egyptian nation. From the Nile Valley, some Nubians headed to West Africa while others, identified in the literature as Ethiopians, penetrated into Asia through Arabia, Mesopotamia, Elam (present Iran), and made their way to Indus Valley. In later times, Bantu migrants from West Africa crossed the Equatorial Rainforest and spread all over sub-Equatorial Africa. For their part, the Nilotes left their homeland in what is today South Sudan to invade the Great Lakes countries of East Africa and superimpose their civilization of the cattle and the spear over the pre-existing Bantu civilization of the hoe, the ax and the machete. This chapter elaborates on these movements and their impact on societies within Africa and outside the continent. Section 1 is devoted to the precursors to humans, notably: divinities legendary ancestors, and the hominids. *The First Peoples in Africa* and the *First Peoples* of *African* descent in *Asia, Oceania* and the *Americas* will be discussed in Section 2. Section 3 expands on the spreaders of *African* civilizations, these are: the *Nubians/Ethiopians* (the builders of the home-grown empires of the Western Sudan), the *Bantu*, and the *Nilotes*. Finally, Section 4 examines long-distance traders by water and by land. We are only dealing with *Africans* in the continent and peoples of African descent in Near and *Far Asia, Oceania,* and the *Americas* as illustrations of the points we are trying to make: human propensity toward migrating to unknown wild spaces and transforming them into human communities with particular lifestyles. Our sole purpose is to summarize the relevant existing information about the above-mentioned categories of actors for the benefit of the general reader. It is not our intent to engage in expansive scholarly analyses. Neither do we have any pretense of being exhaustive on any particular group or topic.

1. **PRECURSORS TO HUMANS**

This section examines original migratory movements and changes brought about by divinities and legendary ancestors in Africa, and the Hominids in Africa, Asia and Europe. Here and elsewhere in this chapter, the highlight is on migratory moves to unknown environments and ensuing cultural adaptation/transformation patterns. The goal is simply to substantiate, with the facts at hand, the human penchant toward venturing into spaces beyond the horizon and subsequently developing new societies and cultures in previously unknown lands.

Divinities and Legendary Ancestors

Divinities: Humans' orientation toward exploration of unknown spaces was inherent in divine creation. To create Earth, Creator *Olódùmarè* of the Yorùbá people sent Arch-Divinity *Òrìsà-nlá* with a bucket of loose soil to fill a marshy land that *Òrìsà-nlá* had never seen before. His was a discovery trip with a transformation mandate. *Òrìsà-nlá* was equipped with a bucket filled with loose soil and accompanied by the hen and the pigeon to help spread the soil over the wet marsh in order to turn it into a dry land, Planet Earth. On a second trip, *Olódùmarè* sent Òrìsà-nlá with palm trees to plant as a regular source of food, drink, and clothing. When the Earth was dry enough and equipped to sustain living species, *Olódùmarè* dispatched Divinity *Orelúerè* at the head of a delegation of heavenly residents to become the first inhabitants of the Earth. *Orelúerè* and his delegation landed in a location where they had not been before, and by their landing there, became the sacred city of *Ile Ife*—the mythical origin city of the Yorùbá people. On Earth, *Orelúerè* became an incarnate ancestor and guardian of marriage and domestic morality. From the Dogon people of Mali, we learn that creation began with the forming of a world mother egg—by Amma (the Creator)—filled with pairs of male and female seeds. *Pemba,* one of the male seeds, exited from the egg on a piece of eggshell that became the first Earth. *Pemba* transformed parts of the Earth into fields by planting male seeds he had brought along. The egg of the creation of the world was the placenta in which life first formed. Since the piece of the placenta (eggshell) that became Earth was that of *Pemba*'s own mother egg, his fertilizing it was an incestuous act. This impinged on the fertility of the field and the growth of the plants, resulting in stunted harvest. In the meantime, to repair *Pemba*'s wrongdoings, *Amma*, the Creator, sacrificed *Faso*, one of the male seeds that remained in the egg of creation after *Pemba*'s impromptu departure. He cut him into pieces and scattered them all over the Earth. Afterwards, *Amma* resurrected *Faso* and sent him at the head of an ark to the incestuous land that the mischievous *Pemba* had caused to exist. In pursuing this mission, *Faso* was going into the unknown and, once there, he transformed the land by replacing *Pemba*'s infertile fields and seeds with more fertile ones, thereby purifying Earth as well. There are elements of venturing into the unknown in one of ancient Egypt's creation stories. In the beginning there were the infinite primordial waters (*Nu*). God *Atum-Re* emerged from the waters, thereby self-creating. *Atum-Re* settled on a location on the waters which became the *Benben Mound* of Creation. *Atum-Re* begat *Shu* and *Tefnut* by the power of his will and his word. *Atum-Re* sent *Shu* and *Tefnut* on a mission to establish the world. It took them too long before returning. In the meantime, *Atum-Re* became very concerned about their survival. Believing they were lost, he removed his eye and sent it searching for them. The eye found them and returned with them to *Benben*. *Atum-Re* was so glad for their return that he cried with joy, his tears dropped onto the fertile earth of the *Benben Mound* and turned into human beings, men and women. At least three moves by the divinities involved in this story are ventures into the unknown. Firstly, there is no indication that *Atum-Re* had planned ahead where in the infinite waters he would settle. Secondly, neither was the world *Shu* and *Tefnut* explored known to them in any manner. Thirdly, the eye searching for *Shu* and Tefnut was not told where specifically to go (Idowu 1994, Dieterlene 1955, Mark 2016).[1]

Legendary ancestors were explorers who did not know where they were going until they got there. Following creation, the ancestors of the Kung people were living underneath the Earth with Creator, *Kaang*. *Kaang*, then, ordered the Kung ancestor to climb up to the surface through a hole. Of course, the ancestor did not know what the surface of the earth would be like. His move was an adventure into the unknown. As another example, the Creator of the Luba mandated *Ngoyi* and *Pemba*, the first couple, to procreate and send their children along the rivers with the mission to reproduce and multiply. The story does not say if, when, and how the descendants would actually fulfill this mission. What is clear, however, is that this would be for them a discovery mission into the unknown. *Odùduwa*, the legendary ancestor of the Yorùbá, is reported to have been the leader of a migrant band of the Yorùbá people who came to Ile Ife from somewhere else. Thanks to his strong personality and influence, he conquered more land, established himself as a powerful king, and came to be acknowledged as the father of all the Yorùbá people. The Shilluk of southern Sudan practice divine kingship. Shilluk kings claim descent from a legendary ancestor named *Nyikang*, believed to have instituted the Shilluk kingship in the west bank of the White Nile—present homeland of the Shilluk people—having migrated to the area from somewhere else. This is another example of moving to the unknown. The Shilluk king was elected and invested as *Waqlimi*, a royal title meaning *Son of the Great God*. In this capacity, the king was believed to function as *Nyikang's* medium and expected to govern with equity and practice justice for all. Had the king to break the rule—such as becoming tyrannical in his exercise of power—he would thereby desecrate the king's status of "Son of the Great God" and "King of heaven and Earth," and was to be killed and his progeny excluded from royal succession (Roach 2008, Mudimbe 1991, Idowu 1994, Jackson 1990).

The Hominids

Hominids are proto-humans whose evolution culminated in *Homo Sapiens Sapiens*, the current humankind species. The first hominid remains and tools to ever exist on Earth have been discovered in several parts of *Africa*, with much greater concentration in Eastern Africa, from South Africa to Ethiopia through Tanzania, Zambia, and Kenya. They are classified in a sequence as shown below (Stein and Rowe 1989, Hublin 1999):

> 1. ***Australopithecus***: existed 3.8 to 1.4 million years ago; found in Taung, South Africa; Olduvai Gorge, Tanzania; Lake Turkana, Kenya/Ethiopia; Hadar, Ethiopia; and Laetoli, Tanzania.
>
> **2. *Homo Habilis*** (skilled man) lived 2 to 1.5 million years ago; found in Olduvai Gorge, Tanzania; and Lake Turkana, Ethiopia.
>
> 3. ***Homo Erectus*** (or *Homo Ergaster*): 1.8 million to 300,000 years ago; found in South Africa, Olduvai Gorge, Koobi Fora and Lake Turkana, in Kenya.
>
> 4. ***Homo Heidelbergensis***: 700,000 to 200,000 years ago; found in Elandesfontein, South Africa; Broken Hill, Zambia; Lake Ndutu, Tanzania; and Bodo, Ethiopia.
>
> 5. ***Homo Sapiens:*** 80,000 to 35,000 years ago; found in Lake Laetoli, Tanzania; Broken Hill, in Zambia; and Saldanha, South Africa.
>
> 6. ***Homo Sapiens Sapiens:*** appeared 140,000 to 15,000 years ago; found in Klasies River, South Africa; Boscop, South Africa; Fish Hook, South Africa; and Gamble's Cave, Kenya.

Elsewhere in *Africa*, Hominid fossils and tools have been found in *Chad* (*Australopithecus Afarensis*), in the *Sahara Desert in Mali* (*Homo Sapiens Sapiens*), in *Gibraltar, Morocco* (*Homo Sapiens*); and in *Ternifine, Algeria* (*Homo Erectus*). The Hominids in these parts of Africa were migrants from Eastern Africa. Some recent research suggests that *Homo Sapiens Sapiens* may have appeared in the same time period in *Eastern Africa* and, with some noticeable differences, in other regions of *Africa*, here as descendants of migrant *Homo Sapiens* from *Eastern Africa* (Groeneveld 2017).[2]

Outside Africa, hominid fossils and tools have been found in Europe, the Near East and the Far East. There are three natural easy crossings the Hominids might have taken to step out of the continent of Africa into Eurasia. These are: The Strait of Bab-el-Mandeb between Djibouti and Yemen, the Sinai Peninsula, in Lower Egypt, and the Strait of Gibraltar between Morocco and southern Spain. Hominid remains found outside Africa include (Stein and Rowe 1989):

> 1. **Homo Erectus:** Found in the Cocacus region of the Republic of Georgia (Homo Erectus Georgicus); in Java, Indonesia (Homo Erectus Javanean); and at Zoukoudian, near Beijing, China (the Peking Man).
>
> 2. **Homo Neanderthalensis:** All across Europe, and ***Denisovans*** in Asia.

3. ***Homo Heidelbergensis:*** In Mauer, Germany; Sima de los Huesos, Spain.

   4. **Homo Sapiens:** In Apidina Cave in southern Greece; in Jebel Qafzeh Cave, near Nazareth, in Israel; in the Nefud Desert, Saudi Arabia; in Niah Cave, in Borneo, Indonesia; between the Black Sea and the Caspian Sea, in North Asia; and in Yunnan Province, China (the *Yuamau Man*).

It thus appears that, in continuous movements, from Southern and Eastern Africa through Nubia, some hominids traveled eastward through the land that later became Aksum and now Ethiopia, while others kept heading northward through what later became Upper Egypt and Lower Egypt. From here, some turned east, others west. The hominids were hunters and foragers. They developed and perfected the art of making tools of stone for foraging and hunting, which enabled them to live sufficiently, to adapt to varying environments and climates, and to spread all over the world. In other words, it was in the nature of the Hominids to migrate to distant unknown spaces and develop a *modus vivendi* there.

2. THE FIRST PEOPLES

Today's dominant populations in Africa and in countries of Asia, Oceania, Europe, and the Americas, are immigrants who superimposed themselves on pre-existing *Homo Sapiens Sapiens* indigenous groups: generally short in stature, less than 5 feet tall. Some of these original human inhabitants of Earth have been absorbed through intermarriage or decimated. Many subsist as subjugated numerical and political minorities. However, even these marginalized first occupant minorities had come from afar as explorers of unknown spaces, and had developed lifestyles and other patterns of adaptation to the physical environment of their newfound countries. In Asia, India has a plethora of indigenous peoples, including the Andamanese, who are of African origin. In the Philippines, major indigenous tribal groups live in the northern and southern regions. Others are scattered across the islands. The Aetas, classified as *Negritos*, a pejorative appellation for Black people, live in the Central Luzon Region, north of Manila, the Philippine's capital. In Thailand, most indigenous peoples live in northern mountains, including ten groups officially identified as *Chao Khao*, "Hill Tribes," and are considered *non-Thai*. A few live in the south, including the Mani, one of the Orang Asli groups collectively called *Negritos*. In Malaysia, there are the Senoi, the Semangs and the Proto-Malay. The Senoi and the Semangs are believed to have separated from a past common trunk. Europe has its share of indigenous peoples, such as the Picts of England, the Fins of Finland, and the Sami of Finland and Sweden. So does the Arctic, including Canada. Here lived the Dorset and the Tunits, whom both completely disappeared years ago. Their lands have been recolonized by the Inuits—previously known as Eskimos—and by the Norse people and others. The indigenous people in Continental North America include the builders of the Cochise Culture in New Mexico and of the Mogollon Culture in Arizona, as well as the Mound Builders in Ohio, Illinois, Indiana, and Missouri. In Mexico's Sierra Madre Mountain Range, are found the Huichol Indians; a hybrid between an original indigenous ethnic group and European immigrants, on the one hand, and the Purépecha indigenous Mexicans of the State of

Chapter 12

Michoacan. In the Caribbean, the Taino, a branch of the Arawak people, are said to have been the first inhabitants of the Bahamas, Cuba, Jamaica, Hispaniola (Dominican Republic and Haiti), and Puerto-Rico. To close the list, it is worth mentioning three groups from South America, notably: the Canari of Ecuador who built the city of Guapondlig, later replaced with the Incan city of Tomipamba, and much later with the Spanish colonial city of Cuenca; the Quechua who live along the Andean mountains of Peru, and the Aymara of Bolivia who developed the states of Colla, Luppaca, and Cana in the Andes. The historical primacy of *First Peoples* in today's lands of the living on Earth is thus an observable worldwide phenomenon. The illustrations below, however, are limited to *First Peoples in Africa* and *First Peoples* who are descendants of Black African immigrants to Asia, Oceania, and the Americas.

The First Peoples in Africa

In Africa, the first occupants of the land, across the continent, are known under various names: some pejorative, others neutral. Twa, Nu, Kung, Khoi, and San are perhaps the most neutral terms. It is known that these *Homo Sapiens Sapiens*, just as the *Hominids* who preceded them, originated from eastern and southeastern Africa. Their presence elsewhere implies long journeys of exploration. Some must have moved westward below the *Equatorial Rainforest*; others northward to Nubia and Egypt; and still others from there to West Africa across the grassland that later became the Sahara Desert. Briefly presented below are: Sahara and Kalahari Deserts' rock painters, the Anu of ancient Egypt, and an identification of contemporary first peoples who live in different parts of Africa.

Desert Rock Painters: Impressive rock paintings and engravings, dated back to the time when the present Sahara and Kalahari deserts were savanna lands, have been found across these arid domains. The oldest ones, 10,000-7,000 BC, in North Africa, feature humans hunting a kind of ox known as *Babalus Antiquus* and other large animals such as elephants and rhinoceroses. Other discoveries, dating around 9,500-7,000 BC, consisting of humans with round heads, have been found in Algeria. The most recent human figures include the so called "The Hair Dresser," in the Sahel (4,000 BC, human figures with body paintings in Chad's Ennedi Mountains and human figures in Niger's Air Mountains (2,500 BC). There are also paintings and engravings of domesticated animals, the most recent ones portraying *cows* – The Bovidian or Pastoral Period (7000-4000 BC), *horses* – The Horse Period (3,000-2,000 BC), and *camels* – The Camel Period (2000 BC). Rock paintings have been discovered in a Namibian cave. The largest collection exists in Drakensberg Mountains in Southern Africa, particularly South Africa and Botswana, is home to thousands of rock paintings and engravings left behind in caves and on rock shelters by the ancestors of the San (Bushmen) people. Some motifs are abstract, others depict human, animal, or even half-human half-animal motifs. A rock at Tsodilo, Botwana, features a red eland bull, a rare animal that could be closely seen only by the San people who lived in the same environment at the time. The same rock carries the picture of a motionless female giraffe and several images of other animals as well as handprints covered with red blood standing for the artist's signature. Some San motifs were metaphors. For example, the running blood and milk of a bull killed during a trance-dance symbolizes the rain that will be brought down by the spiritual powers of the dance-trance rituals. Five rock sites in South Africa have been developed as touristic destinations. Bushman's Kloof, by Cederberg Mountain, in Western Cape, houses over 2,500 rock paintings and engravings. The Clanwilliam Living Landscape Project regularly conducts workshops on San culture and tours to rock sites. Kamberg Rock Art Center, in KwaZulu-Natal, oversees over 40,000 San Bushman rock art paintings in and around Ukhahlamba-Derankesberg Park. Famous rock paintings are also found at Wildebeest Kuil Rock Art Center, in Northern Cape. Some engravings in this zone portray spiritual healing meditation scenes and rain dances. At the Drankesberg Rock Art, in southern Cape, rock painting sites include the open-air Bushman Cave Museum located in the Giant's Castle Reserve. Another cave, outside the museum, has over 500 rock paintings. The oldest rock engravings (77,000 years of age) and the oldest rock paintings (73,000 years) are found in Blombos Cave in the southern Cape (Salomon 2005, Wilcox 1984, Coulson 1999, Discover Africa, 2017, British Museum ND).[3]

The Anu of Ancient Egypt: In Ancient Egypt, the indigenous first occupants of the land were called *Twa* or *Anu*. Their gods, such as *Ptah* and *Bes*, were pictured as dwarf gods. Whereas some Egyptian gods were regional, *Ptah*, patron god of *Memphis*, along with *Re, Osiris*, and *Amun*, were venerated throughout the Egyptian territory and history. *Ptah* was not an ordinary god. He was the Supreme Creator of all that exists, including the gods. God *Bes* was very active in human lives: scaring away demons, playing drums or other musical instruments at life events, comforting and supporting women during childbirth, and boys at circumcision ceremonies. Egyptian *Twa* (*Nu*) were well respected as bearers of celestial gifts and are credited with having laid down the foundations for ancient Egyptian civilization to build on (Diop, 1974). Many *Anu* people worked for the king and were buried in secondary tombs surrounding royal tombs. Egyptian *Anu* also practiced agriculture, cattle raising, and jewelry making and dealing. They introduced writing (David ND, Diop 1974).

Contemporary First Peoples in Africa: From the Nile Valley, some *Anu* groups migrated to West Africa. Those who settled in the land from the Nile Valley to Mali are known as Twa aka Anu. A branch of the Twa aka Anu, the Tellen, lived in the Bandiagara Escarpment (sandstone cliff) in Mali, between the 11th and 16th centuries AD and were later invaded by the Dogons. Several first people groups live in the Congo Basin under various regional names, including Mbuti or Bambuti, in the Ituri Forest; Babinga, in the forest west of the Ubangi River; Batwa or Twa, south of the Congo River; and Batwa, in the Lake Kivu region in the Congo, Rwanda, and Burundi. Elsewhere in Central Africa, Twa populations are found in Central African Republic (the Aka), in Gabon (the Aka), and in Cameroon (the Baka and the Gyeli). Southern Africa is the homeland of the Khoi/San (Bushmen). Reportedly, these first indigenous populations have diversified in this manner from a common ancestor some 2,800 years ago. Also, wherever they live, the first peoples have proven to possess vast knowledge of the physical environment: the terrain, animal species, their respective characters and social behaviors; plants, their nutritional value, and healing properties (Verdu, 2012).[4]

Chapter 12
African First Peoples in Asia and Oceania

First Peoples of African descent are found in Asia, in Oceania, and the Americas. From among them are the Africoid Arabians, the Andamanese of India, the Aetas of the Philippines, the Mani of Thailand, and the Semangs of Malaysia.

The Africoid Arabians: Today's Black people of Arabia are racially identified as *Africoid Arabians* or *Afrabians*. Early in human history, Arabia was a black empire, the Adite Empire, named after *Ad*, claimed in mythology to be the grandson of *Ham*; the latter is identified in the Bible as ancestor of the Blacks. *Ad* is believed to have come from the northeast. After his death, he was replaced in power by his sons *Shadid* and *Shedad* successively. *Shedad* expanded the empire over the entire Arabia and Iraq, prompting Canaanite migration to Syria and the shepherd invasion of Egypt. The empire was destroyed in the 18th century BC, by the Jectanides, an amalgamation of white invader tribes who had come to settle among the Adites. To avoid complete onslaught, the Adites scattered throughout the country, including the Hadramout Mountains, in southern Arabia, today Yemen. Some even crossed the Red Sea through the Strait of Babel Mandeb and settled in Ethiopia, then Aksum. Later, the remaining Adites in Arabia regrouped and retook control over the country. This is known as the second Adite Empire. The Jectanides were absorbed in the black population, and only survived through their mixed-race progeny (Jectanides and Adites). It has been suggested that the Arabs are descendants of this mixed-race progeny. The Adites are acknowledged by their descendants, their Kushite and Canaanite neighbors, and in the Koran as having been great architects and builders of magnificent palaces. Their high achievements in construction and religion were comparable to those of the Babylonians (Diop 1974, Donnely 1882). [5]

The Andamanese of India: Numerous ethnic groups of African descent, identified as indigenous tribes, are scattered all over India. The Andamanese are the indigenous Black people who live on India's Andaman and Nicobar Islands, in the southeastern part of the Bay of Bengal. Following the colonization of the region by the British, and later by the Indian Government, the Andamanese were forced into slavery, including being the prey of international piracy by Malay, Burmese, Chinese, and European slave dealers; in addition to being given as tribute payments to kings. They are almost completely wiped out by diseases, violence, and forced displacements from productive lands and resources to the most inhospitable and poor environments where they survive on wild game, fish, and plants. Only 700 Andamanese survive today, distributed into four territorial groups as follows: the Sentinelese (70), the Onges (100), the Great Andamanese (50), and the Jarawas (470) (Joseph 2018). Officially, Indian Blacks are classified in the Constitution as "Scheduled Tribes." Some have, more than others, mixed with latecomer immigrants of different races. Some have migrated from mainland Asia into the Philippines, Thailand, and Indonesia, about 30,000 ago, during the last glacial period, walking over land bridges brought to the surface by the dropping of the sea level. Later migrations were by water (Survival 2005). [6]

The Aetas of the Philippines: The Aetas of the Philippines, the Semang of Malaya, and the Mani of Thailand are some of the living first peoples in these parts of the world. The three groups are ethnically related and collectively identified as *Negritos,* to stress their blackness. The Aetas are mostly found in the Central Luzon Region, north of Manila, which is the Philippines' capital. They are described as having dark to dark-brown skin, with curly hair, and usually below five feet tall. They worship the *Supreme Being* and believe in the existence of nature spirits who, along with God, control the natural environment and the living species in it. Although primarily known as hunters and gatherers who live in temporary homes made of sticks, they are knowledgeable in herbal medicine and very skilled in cloth weaving, planting, arts, and instrumental music. Chronic victims of forced displacement and marginalization, they live in permanent poverty. In addition, for thousands of years, the Aetas lived near Mount Pinatubo, in Zambales (in Central Luzon Region) and were devastated when the volcano irrupted in 1991. Some of the survivors moved to the city and are influenced by Philippino culture, are married to Philippino spouses, and sending their children to school (Valdeavilla ND).[7]

The Mani of Thailand: The Mani are recognized as the original *Homo Sapiens Sapiens* from Africa to settle in Thailand—just as the Andamanese are in India, the Aetas in the Philippines, and the Semangs in Malaysia. The name *Mani* belongs to the South-East Asia's Mon-Khmer language family, of which Mon and Khmer are the most important languages in the region. Mani is only one of the names by which the dominant majority in Thailand designates people of African descent. Whereas *Mani* means human being, the other names are racial insults. However, their ancestors are credited with playing a pivotal role in the development of trade in South East Asia more than a thousand years ago, which contributed to the rising of principalities such as Mon kingdoms and Siam (Thailand), Malay Empire, the Shampa (in Cambodia and Vietnam), and the Khmer empires. In addition to being middlemen, the Forest People (Mani) contributed products of the forest such as precious resins, dyes, woods, medicines and animal products. Upon occupying the region, *the Thai* enslaved the Mani and caused many to die from mistreatment, exploitation, and excessive tribute extraction practices. The predicament of the Mani people was exasperated in the 20th Century, when the Thai Government deprived them of land rights and citizenship and forcibly relocated them to inhospitable lands, such as swamp forests and mountains, where they survive on products of hunting, fishing and gathering. As a result of relocation, many Mani came to live in the Banthad Mountain Chain, in southern Thailand. These mountains were the battle ground of Thailand Government troops and the insurgents during the 1970s. The Mani were caught in the crossfire. Additionally, their camps were the targets of bombings by government troops who suspected them of being susceptible of allying themselves with the insurgents against the government. The Mani were almost completely wiped out. Only 300 survive today. In some areas, the Mani have organized in defense of their rights to life and to the land, and have led the government to develop eco-tourism there, while those in other parts of the country continue to be completely ignored (Rattanakrajangsri et al. ND).[8]

The Semangs of Malaysia: The Semangs are one of the three ethnic groups in Malaysia who are classified as *Orang Asli* (original peoples, first peoples). The other two are the Senoi and the Proto-Malay. The three groups are believed to have diverged from each other some 200 to 300 generations ago. The Semangs, now the smallest numerically, were the first occupants of the land. They settled in Penisular Malaysia before anybody else. They are described as dark-skinned and having curly hair. Their primary source of subsistence is hunting and gathering. The Sonoi, the largest in numbers, are believed to be a hybrid race of Negritos and some East Asian ethnicities. They are described as having wavy hair and representing a range of skin colors. They practice hunting and gathering as well as trade. Proto-Malay (Aboriginal Maly) groups, second in numbers among *the Orang Asli*, are believed to have come to Thailand from central Asia through Indo China, reaching Thailand by sea in 2000 BC, long after the Semangs. They settled in the coastal areas practicing fishing supplemented with agriculture. In pre-Malayan times, the Semangs and other *Orang Asli* (First Peoples) played a significant role in regional development as middlemen traders as well as providers of forest products. Throughout *Malaysia*'s history, *the Semangs* have suffered land expropriations, exploitation as debt-slaves, and relocation to inhospitable remote areas—notably the mountains of Northern and Central Thailand. Traditionally, they live in temporary bamboo houses. Nowadays, some live in government–imposed resettlement villages. The Semangs are considered in danger of disappearing physically, culturally, and linguistically—some sub-groups more so than others. Reportedly, their population has declined to 2.6 percent of its initial number (Masron et al. ND).[9]

The Aboriginals and the Torres Strait Islanders of Australia

Australia is home to hundreds of *Black First People* groups speaking diverse languages. They came from Asia through the islands of Malaysia, Singapore, Burnei, East Timor, Indonesia, and the Philippines. They carry different local names, such as Anangu, in South-West and Central Australia; Koorie, in New South Wales and Victoria; Murrie, in Queensland; Nunga, in extreme Southwest; Noongai, in Southwest Wales; and Palawa in the southern Tasmania Island. Collectively, they are identified as Aboriginals if they live in mainland Australia, and Torres Strait Islanders, if they are from Torres Strait Islands, to the North. There is no agreement as to how long they have lived these areas. The undisputable fact is that they are the first *Homo Sapiens Sapiens* to have occupied the region. Existing evidence shows that they once developed a vibrant culture, which practiced agriculture and aquaculture, in addition to hunting and gathering; each group maintaining close relationship with their land and assuming effective custody over their country. They view spirituality and ancestral traditions as essential elements of their being. However, the fate of these indigenous peoples changed drastically under the establishment of British colonial rule following Lieutenant James Cook's 1770 historic landing on the east coast of Australia. Indigenous populations were up to 90% decimated in a short period of time—due to being victims of new diseases (e.g., smallpox, measles, and influenza) brought along by exiled British convicts; rapes of women and girls, which spread venereal diseases; rampage killings, direct violent conflicts, and massive land expropriations. Demographically, the indigenous people in Australia today (208,500 persons) represent 3% of the population, with a greater concentration in New South Wales and in the Northern Territory. A third lives in cities, the majority in remote areas. Until 1960, Aboriginal and Torres Strait Islander peoples were constitutionally excluded from official population statistics. Since 1971, they have been incorporated in census to obtain better knowledge of their demographics, notably: their perceived faster growing population, particularly among children, since the latter automatically include children of mixed parentage (aboriginal and non-aboriginal).

Black First Peoples in the Americas

The *Australoids*: Early migrants to the Americas are designated as *Australoids* because of their immediate geographic origin from *Australia* and ethnic and cultural proximity to Black peoples who colonized Australia 60,000 years ago. The *Australoids'* presence in the Americas has been documented through archeological finds, such as *Pedra Furada*, a 32,000-year-old large painted rock in the State of Piaui, Northeastern Brazil; and an arrow point embedded in a horse toe and a clay fireplace. The latter is respectively dated back to 24,000 and 36,000 years ago, which was found in a cave in southern New Mexico, USA. Other than the Black people of Australia, the *Australoids* are genetically related to the Black people in south Arabia and Iraq, to the Mundas and Kolarians of East-Central India, and to the Vedas of Srilanka. The *Australoids* are believed to have entered the Americas through Bering Isthmus, Alaska, and the Yukon Territory in northwest Canada. Bering Isthmus is the central part of Beringia, the land and maritime area between the Lena River in Russia and the Mackenzie River in Canada. From there, the *Australoids* gradually moved to southern parts of North America. Their movements seem to have been facilitated by a series of ridges (rocks) resulting from the erosion of ice at the end of the Wisconsin Glaciation Period about 10,000 years ago. Early Australoid sites have been found in southern California, southwestern Colorado, southern Arizona, and the Texas Gulf Coast. Those in South America include Punin and Poltacalo, in Ecuador, and Logoa Santa, in eastern Brazil. Punin is the name of an Ecuadorian village where the skull of an *Australoid* woman was discovered in 1934 (Rashidi, 1992).

The Asiatic Negroids: These are descendants of Black African migrants to Asia who later came to northern America from southern and eastern Asia some 15 millennia ago. They moved further south taking advantage of a corridor-like walkway along the eastern foothills of the Rocky Mountains created by the eastern recession of the Keewatin ice sheet which once covered the west of Canada. Their vestiges include industries of pointed stone projectiles, first discovered near Clovis and Folsom, two archeological sites in New Mexico. *Clovis* and *Folsom projectile points* were attached—through a central groove called a flute—to wooden spear shafts ending in a split. Dating back to the *Paleoindian Period* (between 13,000 and 6,000 B.C.E.), these archeological artifacts, also designated as *Paleoindian projectile points*, have been found across North America, and even in South America, in Venezuela, for instance, often in proximity of mammoth or bison bones. Folsom artifacts are admired for their outstanding artistic and technological quality (Rashidi 1992, Crow Canyon Archeological Center 2011, 2014).[10]

3. MIGRANT SETTLERS

The most significant transformative and improvement changes to the world we live in have come into existence as the results of the works of *Homo Sapiens Sapiens* migrant groups who have deliberately moved from their original homes to unknown distant spaces in search of a better life. As in the previous topics, our interest is in those who emanated from Africa and who either settled in different parts of the continent or moved out to other continents. Four groups are discussed in this study: The *Nubians*, the *Ethiopians* (the builders of the home-grown empires of the Western Sudan), the *Bantu*, and the *Nilotes*. Unlike these groups, others explored foreign lands within or outside Africa not to stay and make a living there, but rather to establish business networks and thereby improve living conditions at home. Illustrations in this category come from traders by water—such as the ancient Egyptians, the Phoenicians and the Somalis; and from traders by land—notably the Twaregs between North Africa and Sub-Saharan Africa; the Dyula across several countries in West Africa; and the long-distance traders who established trading networks between the ancient kingdoms of Mapungubwe and Zimbabwe in continental southern Africa and East African trading cities.

The Nubians

Just as eastern Africa—from Ethiopia to South Africa—is the cradle of the humankind, so is Nubia the birthplace of African civilizations. The historical Nubia covered the country along the Nile River, called the Middle Nile, which coincides with present day northern Sudan and southern Egypt. Nubian groups moved gradually to Lower Egypt following the Nile River. Some of the early northward movements came from Abyssinia (Ethiopia) to Sennar, on the Blue Nile, in Sudan. In another northward movement from Nubia, the Anu descended slowly down the Nile and founded the cities of Esneh, Erment, Qouch, and Holiopolis. Also attributed to them are the beginning of agriculture (by 4000 BCE), irrigation, dam building, sciences, arts, writing, and many elements of Egyptian religion. By 3500 BCE, the Nubians formed the first political states, following up with the unification of Egypt around 3200 BCE, all leading to the development and flourishing of the Nile Valley civilization. Thus, the Egyptians of Lower Egypt (North) looked up to Upper Egypt (South) as their motherland, whereas those of Upper Egypt traced their descent from much further south, notably Nubia (Diop, 1974).

Nubia owed its early development to the invention of iron weapons and tools. Their pointed spearheads enabled them to defeat groups that were still relying on stone tools. From the Middle Nile and the Unified Egypt, Nubian groups gradually moved westward across the grassland that later became the Sahara Desert, and settled in what are today West Africa and North Africa. An early Egyptian agricultural development, *the Tasian Culture*, penetrated into *West Africa* during *the Makalian Phase* (11,000 years ago). In those days, the *Sahara* was wet grassland with large lakes and several rivers. The *Tasian Culture* first developed in Upper Egypt during the pre-dynastic period. The adjective *Tasian* comes from Deir Tasa, a location on the East bank of the Nile River. Early cultivation of emmer wheat and barley took place here and nearby, along with the herding of sheep and goats. An improved posterior phase of the *Tasian Culture* in the same area is known as the *Badarian Culture*, distinguishable by its pottery with a black top, combs and spoons of ivory, geometric slate palettes, female figurines, and copper and stone beads. The latter development seems to have occurred in the aftermath of the Sahara desiccation, which facilitated the repopulation of Egypt with fugitives from the west and southwest. The Libyans who later took over power in Egypt after 950 BC were an outgrowth of this and subsequent movements. From the Sahara, some fugitives headed southward to Western Sudan, today's West Africa, bringing along the cultivation of sorghum, rice, yams and melons from Upper Egypt. The *Badarian Culture* planted the seeds for the *Amratian Culture* to emerge. The latter, dating to about 3600 BCE, also originated from Upper Egypt and was concentrated around Al-Amirah, near modern Abydos. Its agricultural achievements were comparable to those of the Badarian period. Their pottery was dominated by dark-red burnished wares and red wares with a black top. Occasionally, the pots were decorated with designs of human or animal figures in a white slip. Other important finds include an early drawing of the pharaoh's red crown, mace heads in a disk shape, and artistic vases of stone and carvings of ivory (Davidson 1991, The Editors of Encyclopedia Britannica ND. "Amratian Culture").[11]

The civilization that started in Nubia and flourished in Egypt spread to other parts of Africa with various degrees of adaptation. Some of the transfers included stone buildings such as temples, pyramids, tombs, towers, mummification and walls surrounding public squares; metallurgical products, such as jewels, knives, arrowheads, and spearheads; and hieroglyphic writing, such as that found around a baobab tree in Senegal, *Njoya* in Cameroon, and *Vai* in Sierra Leone. In their historical legends, West African peoples, such the Yorùbá of Nigeria and the Dogon of Mali, point to the Great Water (Nile River), to the East, as their land of origin. The Fang of Gabon and Cameroon point to the same area (Northeast). There are many other cultural remnants of Nubian migrations to West Africa in ancient times. To mention a few: 1) the ox-tail once carried by Egyptian pharaohs and priests is now part of Nigerian religious leaders' attire at ceremonies and official functions; 2) The kings' practice of human sacrifices in ancient Dahomey was reminiscent of Egyptian pharaohs' human sacrifices to the gods. Some hair styles, once practiced in ancient Egypt, were found across Africa: e.g., artificial hair arranged in layers or tiers, special hairdo worn by Senegalese girls (the *djimbi*) or married women (the *djéré*). It was a custom among the Dogon to wear a bonnet similar to the bonnet-like crown once worn by the pharaoh of Upper Egypt. Other Egyptian remnants among the Dogon include the god-serpent, ceremonial dances in the dark, ritual man-eating, the calendar, measurements, knowledge of astronomy, physiology, and star constellations—including the Sirius star system. In brief, the Nubians, early in their history, set out to explore the unknown world—both near and far beyond what their eyes could see—and transformed it in many ways. Secondary and tertiary migrations were common. Thus, the Dogon of the Bandiagara Escarpment (a 500 meter-tall and 150 kilometer-long sandstone cliff) would say that their ancestors came from East, while referring to the Mande region as their actual land of origin. The Bantu migrated from the Benue region between Nigeria and Cameroon and first settled just south of the Equatorial Rainforest. From here, some pushed further south while others headed toward the Great Lakes region to the northeast. The Nilotic Luo are recorded to have moved from the Upper Nile in Sudan to Ethiopia, then from Ethiopia to northern Uganda, and finally from there to the Kenya's Nyanza Province near Lake Victoria (Diop 1974, Davidson 1991, 1969; Shillington 1993).

Chapter 12

The Ethiopians

Ethiopians (people with burnt faces), was the appellation given Black people by ancient Greek writers. In Africa, the Ethiopians lived in Nubia, Libya, and Egypt. Libya was the name given to the region west of Egypt. In addition to being traders by land and navigators by sea, the Ethiopians developed a similar civilization in the different parts of the world where they lived. Their civilization included mummification, irrigation, cattle raising, dam building, large cities, stone monuments, writing systems, use of metal tools, and two-story houses with a sewage system. This civilization flourished in the 3rd millennium BC. Below is a short survey of Ethiopian groups outside Africa: i.e., the Sabaians of southern Arabia, the Sumerians of the valleys of Tiger and Euphrates, the Elamites of Khuzistan in what is today Iran, and the Harappans and their Dravidian descendants in the Indus Valley (Jackson 1990; Rashidi 2002, 1992).

The Sabaians: In Southern Arabia, the Adites, original Black people of southern Arabia, joined the Ethiopians (Kushites) who had come there earlier from Axum across the Red Sea and established a colony of farmers and cattle raisers in a land praised for its fertility. Over time, the region came to be known as Saba (or Sheba), and its inhabitants as Sabaians. These people culturally integrated with the Ethiopians (Kushites) in Aksum. The Kushite people in both locations shared numerous customs, including circumcision, similar social hierarchies, and a dam-building tradition. Their common religious practices included invocation prayers to the seven planets (Neptune, *Saturn*, *Jupiter*, *Sun*, *Venus*, *Mercury*, and *Moon*), seven daily prayers while facing North, 30 day fasting, sacred springs and stones, and deification of famous ancestors. Economically, both the Sabaians and the Aksumites were skilled farmers who practiced terraced and irrigated agriculture in the mountains (Hadmout in Sheba; and Tigre and Amhara, in Aksum), and extensive farming in the valleys. In Aksum, farming consisted of hoe cultivation of *ensete* in the southern region and grain crop plowing in the North. The crops included the native *teff* and imported wheat, barley, and millet. Additionally, the two countries' economy was further characterized by ongoing intense commercial exchanges and involvement in regional trading networks with Somalia, Kenya and Tanzania. From Saba, the *Aksumites* brought iron spearheads and axes, glass, and wheat. In exchange, they sold ivory, tortoise shells, cinnamon, and rhinoceros' horns. Sabaian traders also successfully positioned themselves as intermediaries between the people of Aksum and traders from Persia and India in trading exotic product for African ivory. Finally, Saba-Aksum integration was linguistic as well. The original inhabitants of Aksum spoke Cushitic languages. They intermarried with the Sabaians. Out of long interactions between Sabaian and Cushitic languages, there developed a hybrid language, Ge'ez, which became the mother of the Amharic language spoken in Ethiopia today. The vestiges of Kushite civilization in Southern Arabia, Saba, include inscriptions, writing systems and Amhara and Galla languages (Diop 1974, Davidson 1991, July 1992, Shillington 1993).

The Sumerians: In the valley of Euphrates, in Mesopotamia, the first civilization, established by Ethiopian migrants called Sumerians, flourished during the third millennium BC. The Sumerians were characterized in inscriptions as blackheads, or black-faced people, beardless, and with shaven heads. Their myths and legends pointed to Kush as their land of origin. The Bible (in *Genesis*) attributes the founding of Sumer (*Shinar*) to Nimrod from Kush. The Sumerian epic—The Epic of Gilgamesh—praises its hero Father *Enlil* as "King of the Blacks." The Sumerians evoked god *Anu* of Upper Egypt as their god as well (Rashidi 1990, quoting Cheikh Anta Diop). The Sumerian society was organized in city-states, which later consolidated into kingdoms. One such kingdom was Ur, which existed until 440 BCE. Ur's III Dynasty is celebrated for the greatness of its leaders, its expansive geographical growth, agricultural accomplishments, and wealth. It fell to multiple external assaults and vanished by 1700 BCE (Diop 1974; Rashidi 1990, 2002).

The Elamites: These were the inhabitants of Elam, former name of modern era Iran. Elam was made of three states at the time: Anshan, Awan, and Shimaski. The first Elamites were Sumerian migrants. It is known that the Sumerians were Ethiopian Blacks. Susa, in the lowlands of Khuzestan, was Elam's cultural center. In the early years (Proto-Elamite Period: 3200-2700 BCE), power in Elam often alternated between Sumerian kings in Mesopotamia and domestic Elamite rulers, with Khuzestan often alternatively annexed and broken off. Mesopotamian cultural influences in Elam were growing greater and greater, and reaching far beyond Khuzestan. The Sumerian King Enmebaragesi of Kish, in Mesopotamia, conquered Elam during the Old Elamite period (2700-1500 BCE), thereby inaugurating three long dynasties of Sumerian rule over Elam. The Sumerian Elamites left behind such marks of civilization as the artistic and sculptural artifacts excavated at Susa (residence and capital city of the celebrated Black warrior king *Memnon*), an epic poem of *King Memnon* entitled *Ethiopia*, and temples and royal tombs that the Assyrian king Ashurbanipal desecrated and pillaged in 640 BC. Elamite kings were pictured on urns found in tombs at Susa as Black noblemen carrying insignia of power such as a golden spear. Elamite artifacts, which were similar to those produced in their original motherland, the Nile Valley, included arrow heads, stone implements, mace heads, metal mirrors, pottery forms, and more. The Elamites venerated a large pantheon of deities, including many identical to Sumerian and Akkadian gods in Mesopotamia. Several temples were dedicated to Mesopotamian gods. Some divinities were officially identified in royal inscriptions. Elam succumbed to destructive policies during the Assyrian occupation (911-609 BCE) (Rashidi 1990, 2002; Wikipedia ND, Elam ND).[12]

The Harappans and Dravidians: The appellation *Harappans* comes from Harrapa, a location in the Punjab State of India. The Harappans were the Ethiopians who developed the first civilization in the Indus Valley (2200-1700 BCE). Their civilization included the preeminence of mother goddess in Harappan cities, cultivation of cotton, and domestication of chicken. The Harappans built the historic city of Mohenjo-Daro (whose meaning is Mound of the Dead) in what is today Sindh Province, in Pakistan. The descendants of the Harappans who migrated from the Indus Valley into the interior south of India are known as Dravidians. Two Dravidian groups, the Dasas and the Dasyus, are remembered for their incessant fight against the nomadic Aryan invaders. They were finally conquered by the Aryans and reduced to the status of slaves under the name of *Sudras*. From the Indus Valley, the Dravidians have preserved the cult of the mother goddess, invoked to ward off the evil spirits, contagious diseases, and epidemics. The appellation *Amma* given to mother goddess in southern India's villages is the same one among the Dogon people of Mali with these same functions, as well as similar altar building and sacrifice making practices. The Dravidians were kingdom builders. Pandya, one such a kingdom, in the southernmost in India, was famous for its largest city of Madurai with its literary academies—including Tamil Sangam, its learned scholars, and its literary productions. Another kingdom, Chola (N.E. of Pandya), was a bastion of maritime powers and a trading partner of Persia, Arabia, China and Ceylon. Dravidian descendants who penetrated further into India's interior to escape Aryan encroachments came to be classified as *Untouchables*, along with Aryan-Dravidian mixed races. They are rejected and mistreated as intrinsically impure and polluted across generations and subjected to inhumane conditions, denied land, education, and normal jobs. Current generations of Untouchables have renamed themselves Dalits, organized, and engaged in the fight for human rights and human dignity (Rashidi 1990, 2002).

The Builders of Home-Grown Empires of the Western Sudan

Western Sudan, Modern West Africa, was endowed with diverse natural resources that the inhabitants sought to exploit for human development and society building. This included fertile lands for crop farming made possible by the seasonal flooding of the Niger and the Senegal rivers, the two rivers for long distance water transportation and trade, prolific fisheries all along the rivers, and diverse mineral reserves in strategic locations. The Soninke people took advantage of these opportunities to build the Kingdom (Empire) of Ghana (700-1200 AD). Capitalizing on these very resources and the developments achieved by Ghana, the Malinke built an even larger empire, the Mali Empire (1300-1500 AD), which, in turn, was followed along the same paths by the Songhay Empire (1350-1600 AD). Kanem Bornu, to the east, and the Akan states in the forest to the southwest, putting to use the resources from their immediate environment and from afar, built bustling societies as well. All these empires, as we will see, were homegrown, in the sense that they were the works of particular local ethnic groups slowly growing beyond the boundaries of their own lands into the territories of their neighbors and annexing them through intense wars or gradually through mutual-defense or peaceful coexistence treaties.

The Soninke People and the Building of the Kingdom of Ghana: The Soninke, a sub-group of the Mandinka people, lived to the southwest of the West African savanna, by the sources of the Senegal and Niger rivers, between Mauritania and Mali. Their country was called Wagadu. The name Ghana, which originally meant *Chief*, was one of the titles of Mandinka kings. The country was very rich in gold. *Kaya Maghan*, another king's title, meant *Lord of Gold*. Soninke artists were very skilled iron workers. They made strong iron tools for farming in the savannah and fishing on the Niger River. They also made weapons of war, particularly spears. Their homeland was situated between the gold fields of Takrur and Bambuk to the south and important Sahara trade roads to the north. Berber merchants of the Sahara Desert brought trade goods from the north, especially salt from Taghazi mines, in the desert, to exchange for gold from the south. The Soninke people took advantage of their technical knowledge, and their strategic location to control the trade, acting as intermediaries and imposing taxes on transactions. The traders from the north who obeyed the laws of the land and paid the required taxes enjoyed safety and hospitality. Gradually, the Soninke extended political control over their neighbors through conquests, marriage alliances, and peace treaties. The Ghana Empire weakened under the impact of repeated raids by the Berber herders who lived in Awdaghust, a settlement just north of the Soninke. With the expansion of Islam, Awdaghust became a Muslim community. Ghana's leaders accepted Islam, but they did not force their people to convert. In 1020 A.D., Berber groups of Western Sahara united into a movement called the Almoravids. In a jihad war against the Black people of Ghana, the Almoravids captured Awdaghust in 1054; continued to harass Ghana and eventually destroyed the capital Kumbi Saleh in 1076 AD. Thereafter, they forced everyone to pay tribute to their leader, at the time Abu Bakr, imposed an additional poll tax on non-Muslims, and finally cut off Ghana's access to the gold mines of Bambuk and Takrur. Politically and economically weakened, the empire lost control over the provinces. The provinces engaged in a destructive war to attain hegemony over the empire. Two groups emerged over the other: The Soso Kingdom of Tegrur, led by Sumanguru, and the Mandinka, under the leadership of Sundiata Keita. Keita won, recaptured the lost provinces and reunited them in a new political formation: The Mali Empire (Davidson 1991, 1977; Osae et al. 1973).

The Malinke and the Building of the Mali Empire: The Malinke, a subgroup of the Mandika people, under leadership from the small kingdom of Kangaba, spearheaded the formation and development of the Mali Empire. The founder, Sundiata Keita, ruled from 1235 to 1260, first from Jeriba, and later from Niani, as capital city. Sundiata's successors converted to Islam and made the compulsory trip to Mecca, but did not force their people into Islam. The most famous from among his successors, Mansa Kankan Musa, expanded the empire to its greatest limits: from Timbuktu and Gao to the east, Walata to the north, and Takrur to the west. Law, order, and safety reigned throughout the empire, which gave security and freedom of movement to Dyula (Wangara) traders and others. They traveled freely because belonging to Islam gave them unity and strength. Musa appointed government officials to look after the forests and fisheries on the Niger River. He put others in charge of agriculture and finance. The empire reached high levels of prosperity. Mali's rulers became known and respected everywhere as great leaders of a great empire. Mansa Musa wanted to be known worldwide as the greatest Black Muslim leader in Western Sudan. He accommodated Muslims with Muslim courts of law. His triumphant trip to Mecca in 1324 brought him worldwide fame. He traveled through Cairo and made lavish gifts of gold, which upset Cairo markets for years after his visit. He established Mali's embassies in Egypt and Morocco and brought scholars from Morocco and Egypt to Timbuktu. One of them was As-Saheli, who designed mosques in Timbuktu and Gao and built a palace for the emperor. Other scholars came on their own from North Africa and Egypt. The Koran grew in importance and served as a Constitution. Wealth and glories of Mali's emperors and their entourage inspired greed and rivalries among the leaders of the provinces. Some provinces, such as Gao, rebelled against the emperor by refusing to pay taxes. Mismanagement played a part in the decline, especially after the skillful governments of Mansa Musa. At the example of Gao, the leaders of Tagrur and their Wolof neighbors declared their independence as well. Mali's enemies from the south intensified harassments of governors and garrisons.

Mali's fame and reputation eventually vanished (Osae et al. 1973).

From Sorko Fishermen's Communities to the Songhay Empire: The Songhay Empire was an outgrowth of small communities of fishermen who lived along the middle Niger, southwest of Gao. By the 8th century AD, the Sorko had become experts in hunting the hippopotamus by canoe. Before long, they began to expand their influence over neighboring groups by trading along the Niger River. They established trading villages along the river from which they extended their control over inland villages. By the 9th century, they united the communities in the area into one kingdom, Songhay, with Kukiya as the capital. The Songhay established strong trading relations with Muslims at Gao, a relay trading station for gold from Bambuk with merchants from abroad. By the 11th century, Songhay rulers converted to Islam and Gao became the capital city. In the 14th century, the Mali Empire extended its control over Gao and other western parts of Songhay. But in the 15th century, as the Mali Empire was getting weaker, Songhay was gaining in commercial and military strength. By 1500, Songhay leaders had conquered Mali and replaced it with a new state called Songhay under the leadership of Sunni Suleyman Dandy, followed, after 35 years of rule, by Sunni Ali and then Askiya Muhammad the Great. Sunni Ali successively fought against the Mossi, the Dogon, and the Fulani. He expelled the Twaregs from Timbuktu and conquered some of their settlements in the desert. To the south, he conquered Jenne, an important commercial center and noted market for gold and kola. Sunni Ali drowned while returning from his last military campaign against the Fulani. His son replaced him on the throne. The Muslims in Songhay were dissatisfied with Sunni Ali's expulsion of Muslims out of Timbuktu, his occupation of Timbuktu, and refusal to force his people to convert to Islam. They ousted his son and appointed as king of the Songhay a proven Muslim faithful, Muhammad Ture, who became Askiya Muhammad the Great and founder of the Askiya Dynasty of the Songhay rulers. He pursued the expansion of the empire in the name of *jihad*. He appeased the Muslim world, traveled to Mecca, and had the *Caliph of Egypt* appoint him *Caliph of the Sudan*. He revived Timbuktu, but in confrontation with the Twaregs, he conquered Air and Taghaza in the Sahara Desert. Askiya obtained the revenues to run the empire from trade, produce from royal farms, and tributes and taxes from the provinces. He replaced traditional chiefs with appointed governors. The Songhay Empire declined due to several factors, namely: greed, corruption, and mismanagement; lack of mechanisms other than force to assimilate convert groups, secession of tributary states, and provocation by hostile Muslim states to the north and European-connected states to the west. The *coup de grace* came from the 1591 Moroccan invasion (Shillington 1993, Davidson 1991, Collins 1997).

The Akan Forest States: To the southwest of Western Sudan, sat in the forest three Akan States: Bono, Akwamu, and Ashanti. Their founding fathers had come in several migration waves from the Sudanese savannah to the north in the late 12th or early 13th century AD. The first of the Akan states was Bono, founded in 1295, and lasted until 1740. The migrants who originally came from the bent of the Niger River eventually settled at Bono-Mansu, about 100 miles north of Kumasi in modern Ghana. They developed a thriving economy that included trade with Mali and Songhay, the exploitation of local gold reserves, the fabrication of jewelry and artifacts used in elaborate ceremonies for the chieftaincy, and trade in tools, utensils, and other household items. The Bono administration used standard weights to measure the gold dust that served as currency. Akwamu was a federation whose member states derived their economic prosperity from trading in gold from the region of Birim Abuakwa on the Birim River. They were the first to raise an expansive empire with an impressively organized administrative bureaucracy. Their conquest of Ga and the capital Accra in 1677 opened access to the Atlantic Ocean and enabled Akwamu to trade with the Europeans and acquire firearms. With more arms, the King, called the *Akwamuhene*, was able to expand the territory of Akwamu eastward across the Volta River. The size of the empire at its peak made it difficult to govern. The empire was also a drain on economic, military, and administrative resources. In 1733, the Akim, longstanding enemies, defeated Akwamu in collaboration with its dissatisfied subject states. Subsequently, other states sought their independence, eventually reducing Akwamu to an insignificant principality.

A leader, Osei Tutu, left Akwamu for Ashanti to replace his uncle in power. The Ashanti resided at the confluence of Pra and Ofin rivers. From here, some Ashanti groups moved northward and established settlements in the lands around today's city of Kumasi. During the 17th century, they began to unite under the leadership of the Oyoko clan to gain control of two important trade routes with Western Sudan that passed through this area; but they were too weak vis-à-vis the dominant Denkyira clans. Things began to change with the return of Osei Tutu to Ashantiland following the collapse of Akwamu. He assumed power and turned the Ashanti into a powerful confederacy with Kumasi as its capital. Kumasi became an important political, commercial, and religious center. Osei Tutu's mentor, Okomfo Anokye, a priest and magician, helped bring from the sky the royal stool that became the symbol of national unity. The Stool represented all spiritual and political powers of the Ashanti people. All the Ashanti owed loyalty to the Stool and the Asantehene, His Majesty the King. When the Ashanti defeated Bono, they brought members of the royal family to Kumasi. The newcomers taught the Ashanti rulers how to organize the court, and rule with pomp and dignity. Bono goldsmiths and other artisans taken to Kumasi taught their Ashanti counterparts the skills that are today considered typically Ashanti. When Osei Tutu came from Akwamu, he brought Akwamu military organization and traditions with him. This, combined with the acquisition of European firearms, allowed the Ashanti to finally subdue the Denkyira. Subsequently, Ashanti control reached all the way to the Atlantic coast. It became the strongest, most successful, and most enduring of all Akan states (Collins 1997, Davidson 1977).

The Nomadic Kanembu People and the Making of the Kanem-Bornu Empire: Initially, Kanem was a settlement of the nomadic Kanembu people located at Njimi, north of Lake Chad, who became permanent residents. Njimi became a terminal station of several international long-distance trade routes to Nubia and Egypt through Darfur, to the east; and to Libya and Tunisia, through Bilima Oasis and the settlement of Air to the north. All kinds of goods from eastern Guinea in today's southern Nigeria were transacted here. Around 700 AD, the Kanembu founded the Kanem kingdom, with Njimi as its capital, under King Sef of Saif. In 850 AD, the Sefawa Family came to power, thereby inaugurating the Sefawa Dynasty that lasted over 800 years. Kanem incorporated the territories west and east of Lake Chad. Kanem kings wore the title of *Mai*. In 1086, Mai Hume adopted Islam as his own religion and religion of the

Chapter 12

court. During the reign of Mai Dunama Dibbelemi (1221-1259), Kanem expanded considerably, extending its control over the northern trade road up to Fezza, in southern Tunisia; and over Adamawa and Bornu, west; and Kano and Wadai, east of Lake Chad. In the 14th century AD, Kanem experienced considerable political turmoil caused by internal conflicts and external assaults, resulting in Mai Umar Idrismi being forced by the Bulala to move the Kanembu people from Njimi to Bornu, west of Lake Chad. In 1460, a new capital city, Ngazargamu, was built and fortified. However, instability continued. In the 16th century, Mai Idris Katakarmabe reconquered and reinstated the capital Njimi, making him King of Kanem, again, in addition to being King of Bornu. The two states united under his authority as Kanem-Bornu Empire. By now, the Kanem-Bornu Empire extended from southern Tunisia and southern Libya (north); much of Chad (east), eastern Niger (west); and northeastern Nigeria and northern Cameroon (southwest). The Sefawa Dynasty was at its highest power ever. Decline came during the 17th century and total dissolution in the 19th century (Davidson 1977, World Civilization ND. "African Civilizations").[13]

The Bantu Migrants

Bantu Migrations: The greatest majority of African peoples south of the Equator are Bantu. These are peoples whose languages belong to the large group known as *Bantu* languages. The Bantu are reported to have come to this area in waves of migrations. First, during the second millennium BC, immigrants from the Benue region in eastern Nigeria and western Cameroon crossed the Equatorial Rainforest to settle in the savannah just south of the forest. Second, during the first millennium BC, migrant groups from here went further south, along the lower Congo River, to as far down as Angola and Namibia. Third, during the latter part of the first millennium BC and the early part of the first millennium AD, the migratory movement proceeded northeastward toward the Great Lakes region in East Africa. There were also localized migrations in small groups, such as the Embu (around 1425AD) and the Kikuyu who moved from the borderlines of modern Somalia and Kenya, to central and western Kenya, respectively, around 1425 and 1545 AD. Finally, at a later period, *Bantu* groups spread quickly from the Great Lakes region southward all the way to South Africa. It is believed that the Karanga who built Great Zimbabwe arrived in the latter wave (Davidson 1991, Spear 1994, July 1992).

Documenting Bantu Migration and Spread: From studying common words, ethnolinguists have suggested that the first Bantu language speakers to live in the Congo Basin were fishermen and root cultivators. They had words for goats, oil palm, yams, paddles and dugout canoes, fishtraps, and fishhooks, from among others. But they did not have words for bananas, grains, cattle herding, and iron work. The word "iron" has over 50 roots in Bantu languages. This suggests that the languages had already largely differentiated when iron was introduced. In the Savannah, the Bantu learned the terms for grains such as millet and sorghum, and for cattle herding from Cushitic languages where millet and sorghum farming and cattle herding had been practiced for centuries, along with irrigation and fertilization. The Bantu generally lived in large villages and practiced a mixed economy of itinerant agriculture, poultry and goat rearing, and metalworking. Three factors contributed to the multiplication and spread of the Bantu. First, the adoption of the iron technology gave them greater mastery over the environment and increased food supply. Second, the availability of food surplus allowed for the development of specialists in other fields, such as mining and blacksmithing, to take place. Third, the introduction of the banana, a high nutritional-value crop from Asia, produced a healthier population (Spear 1994, Davidson 1991).

The Luba and the Spread of Bantu Culture: The Katanga region, in the present-day Democratic Republic of the Congo, DRC, played a major role in the spreading of Bantu culture in central and southern Africa. Two thousand years ago, it nurtured the Bantu language speakers who became carriers of Bantu civilization to other parts of the sub-continent. In the first millennium AD, Katanga gave birth, near Lake Kisale, to some of the early and most advanced copper mining and smelting states of their kind. Lake Kisale's flourishing fishing and mining industries, and dynamic states in fertile and well-watered grasslands, stimulated population growth, which in turn, created the need for a more centralized state, which Nkongolo Mwamba provided with the founding of the Luba Kingdom near Lake Boa, at about 1400 AD. By its state formation strategies, conception of kingship, and governing principles, the Luba Kingdom, now an empire, later influenced the creation and sustainability of many similar states in southern Congo, Uganda, Rwanda, Burundi, Malawi, Zambia, Zimbabwe, and the Congo-Angola area (Davidson, 1991).

The Bantu Builders of the Kingdoms of the Savannah: The founders of the kingdoms of the savannah are portrayed as immigrants who came from somewhere else as explorers of the places where they established political formations. The Balopwe who, under the leadership of Nkongolo Mwamba, founded the Luba Kingdom—which later expanded into the Luba Empire—were immigrants from distant Songye territories who came to the region around Lake Boya as explorers of unknown territories. Later, in the 16th Century, after the Luba Empire had been consolidated, Chibinda Ilunga, a disgruntled contender to the throne, migrated to the South, conquered and consolidated Lunda chiefdoms into the Lunda Empire. After Chibinda Ilunga became king of Lunda and the Lunda Princess Rweej became his queen, her discontented twin brothers, Kinguri and Cinyama, self-exiled themselves to foreign lands where they founded the kingdoms of Kasanji and Lwena, respectively. The Chokwe of Angola claim that they are descendants of migrants who moved to their current location in protest against Princess Rueej when the latter gave her sacred royal bracelet to Chibinda Ilunga when they married. In the 14th century AD, Wene, also called Nimi a Lukeni, migrated with a group of followers from the *Boma* area, in present Lower Congo Province, Democratic Republic of the Congo, southward into the lands of the Ambundu and the Ambwela peoples where he founded the Kingdom of Kongo around the present city of San Salvador, Angola. At the borderline of the savannah, in Maindombe, sat the Kingdom of Bolia whose founders are claimed to have come to the area in the 15th century as immigrants from Bondombe, somewhere southwest of Boende, in the tropical forest. The Tyo people, once organized in a Kingdom in the Maindombe region also, attribute their origin to some immigrants who would have come in serial movements from outside the area. Further up the Kasai River, the Bushong founders of the Kuba Kingdom attribute their origin to Woot, an immigrant from somewhere along

Chapter 12

the Congo River (Visona et al. 2001; Vansina 1964, 1968).

The Nilote Conquerors

In many parts of East Africa, the Bantu were later invaded and gradually subjugated by groups of cattle raisers from what is now South Sudan, in search of better pasturing lands and climate conditions. This included the Kalenjin and the Luo of Kenya and, later, the Maasai of Kenya and Tanzania; the Tutsi of Rwanda, Burundi, Uganda, and Tanzania; and the Hema (Hima) of Uganda, Rwanda, and the Democratic Republic of the Congo. Initial Nilotic migrations, in about 500-1000 AD, were local—from the plains of Equatoria and Bahr-al-Ghazal, in South Sudan, to the bank of Upper Nile and its tributaries: the White Nile and the Blue Nile. These movements were prompted by growing demographic pressures above the carrying capacity of the land. Some Nilotic groups, such as the Dinka, the Nuer and the Shilluk, stayed in the original homeland. The Shilluk are more sedentary agriculturalists. The Dinka and the Nuer are more nomadic or transhumant pastoralists. The Nilotes are recorded as having migrated to Kenya in three historically distant waves: (1) Cushitic-language speaking groups, between the second and the first millennia BC, or even before; (2) relatively small groups of cattle herders, perhaps the Kalenjin from among them, around 500 BC; and (3) massive waves of nomad pastoralists, 500 years ago. The Luo are believed to have begun their migratory journey somewhere between 1300 and 1400 AD by expanding from their Upper Nile cradle in Sudan to southwestern Ethiopia where they are known as Anoka. Their economy in Ethiopia consisted of fishing, farming, mining and hunting. From Ethiopia, armed groups of Luo men, women, children, and livestock moved southward to northern Uganda. Their descendants here are known as Acholi, Lango, and Alur, from among others. From northern Uganda, some Luo groups pushed further south into Kenya, to the present Nyanza Province on the banks of Lake Victoria. They adopted the farming and large-kingdom traditions of their Bantu host societies, while promoting pastoral living wherever they could. They came to live primarily off fishing, farming and pastoral herding. They achieved political dominance in the area by overthrowing the ruling Chwezi king. Thanks to their numerical and political dominance, the Luo were able to keep their culture and language intact. Today, they are largely represented in all modern intellectual and skilled occupations. Nilotic conquerors established long-lasting dynasties, such as the *Bito* (a branch of the Luo) who ruled over Bunyoro in Uganda; the Hima kingdom of Ankole, in Uganda also; and the *Bami* (kings, singular *mwami*) in Rwanda and Burundi. These societies gradually became asymmetrical, with the newcomer cattle raisers on top and the pre-existing farming *Bantu* groups at the bottom. In Rwanda, the system became *a clientage,* with *the* Tutsi ruling class monopolizing political power, cattle ownership, and land ownership. Most Hutus had to carry out some service to a Tutsi master in order to have access to cows for marriage and land for growing food to feed their families. In Ankole, in a similar system, Iru farmers fed the cattle of their Hima masters and performed other duties for them for compensation (Davidson 1969, 1991, Newbury 1988, Shillington 1993).

An Explorer and Transformer of Spaces and Civilization Builder

4. LONG-DISTANCE TRADERS

Traders by Water

The Egyptians: Ancient Egyptians invented technologies and developed knowledge enabling them to see into the unknown. This includes a 24-hour sun clock to count the time, the observation of the changing movements and constellations of the stars to determine one's location in time and in space, the North Star to tell the direction, and both the constellations and the fluctuating floods of the Nile to demarcate the seasons. Egypt was strategically situated and developed major commercial harbors at the intersection of three major navigable channels: the Nile; the Suez Gulf, the Red Sea, and the Indian Ocean, and the Mediterranean Sea. The Nile River contributed to the development of Egypt, among other things, as an important channel of imports from Nubia: e.g., construction materials. All transportations of people and goods from Nubia to the Delta were made by boats and ships on the Nile River. Reportedly, Egyptian boats, such as those found painted on vases and murals dating back to around 6,000 BC, are among the earliest boats in history. The oldest excavated ship remnants were made around 3000 BC. The boats were first made of papyrus reeds and, later, of wood. The papyrus grew along the Nile River, while the wood came from Nubia and Lebanon. The original papyrus boats could be dissembled and carried in pieces over dry land and reassembled once back to water. Most Egyptian ships were intended for trade on the Nile and in the Mediterranean Sea (Wikipedia. ND. Ancient Egyptian Trade, Gilbert 2008).[14]

Expeditions of boats traveled regularly up and down the Nile River. From the river, caravans of donkeys penetrated further south into the Sudan or into Eastern Desert. Egyptian boats would come back from Nubia bringing gold, ebony, ivory, and precious stones, incense, animal skins, and many wild animals that the pharaohs wanted to domesticate. It is reported that during the reign of the last pharaoh of the Old Kingdom, an expedition came from Nubia with 300 donkeys loaded with spoils and exotic goods, including elephant tusks and incense. Egypt was also involved in maritime trading networks with Asia through the Suez Gulf, the Red Sea, and the Indian Ocean; and with the Near East and Southern Europe and North Africa, through the Mediterranean Sea. The land of Punt (in modern Somalia) housed major trading ports connecting Egypt to Eastern Africa through the Red Sea, to the Near East through the Persian Gulf, and to Asia through the Indian Ocean. Opone (*Pwene* or *Pwenet*), perhaps the most important port city in Puntland, traded with Egypt over many centuries as supplier of spices, myrrh, frankincense, and gum, from among other trade items. The land bordering the Gulf of Aqaba (at the northern tip of the Red Sea) was a major producer of these goods. The historical expedition of Queen Hatshepsut, a 15th Century BCE pharaoh of Egypt (Eighteenth Dynasty), to Puntland in 1493 BCE, was motivated by her desire to facilitate trade between the Gulf of Aqaba and Puntland and to procure myrrh and frankincense mortuary goods for Karnak (temple on the east bank of the Nile in Thebes, today Luxor). All was paid for in gold from Nubia. Myrrh was also the *raison d'être* of at least two earlier royal expeditions to Punt, one by King Sahure (Fifth Dynasty, 25th Century BCE) who brought along malachite and green gold as well. The other expedition was led by Hen Anu, an officer of Pharaoh Mentuhotep (around 1950 BCE). Several more expeditions to Puntland were made by Queen Hatshepsut's successors, including Thutmoses III around 1479-1478 BCE. Other Red Sea trading centers in those ancient times included Menouthias Island, in East Africa (presumably Pemba Island, or Mafia Island (or Zanzibar), and Rhapta, in Azania (South Africa). On the Mediterranean Sea, Egypt traded with Phoenicia (Lebanon), Turkey, and Greece. Turkey and Greece supplied olive oil and wine, whereas Phoenicia was a major supplier of much needed timber (cedar tree) for boat construction and other carpentry usages. In pursuit of these interests, Egyptian presence in Phoenicia was considerable even as early as the Old Kingdom, around 2575 BCE. Other than commercial ships, Egypt produced galleys, ships of war also used to protect commercial boats from piracy. There were also ships owned by religious temples. Thus, militarily empowered, the Egyptians conquered and exercised direct rule over Nubia for 500 years. (Shillington 1993, Wikipedia ND. "Ancient Egyptian Navy," Gilbert 2008, OER Service World Civilization ND).[15]

During the Late Period (1100-400 BCE), Egypt became so weak that it was occupied by a series of foreign powers: e.g., the Lybians (21st Dynasty), the Kushites or Ethiopians (Dynasty 25th, around 746 to 653 BCE), the Assyrians (between Dynasty 25th and 26th), and the Persians (26th). King Piye of Nubia conquered Egypt around 727 BCE, thereby creating the 25th Dynasty. During the 25th Dynasty, the Kushites ruled over Egypt for more than 70 years. Egypt experienced considerable prosperity, particularly during the reign of King Taharqa. Egyptian religion, arts, and architecture flourished once again. The Kushites were driven out by the Assyrians. During the Assyrian war of occupation against the Kushites, Egyptian trade through the Red Sea and the Indian Ocean suffered considerable setbacks, which compelled the Kushite rulers of Egypt to intensify the Mediterranean trade by Egyptian and Phoenician fleets and expand it to north of the Atlantic in search of metal supplies needed for military equipment (Van Sertima, 1976).

The Phoenicians: The Phoenicians were descendants of a people from the land of Punt (today's Somalia) who settled in Canaan, a land believed to have included parts of today's Israel, Palestine, Lebanon, and parts of Syria and Jordan.[16] The Bible identifies the Canaanites as brothers of Kush and Mizrain (Egypt). In other terms, they were Blacks of Nile Valley origin. All Canaanite experiences – military, commercial, religious – were tainted with Kemetic (Egyptian) presence. For instance, the Phoenician religious mythical god of wisdom, Taout, was the Egyptian god Thoth. The Phoenicians were the first people to invent the bireme, a relatively high-speed military ship (galley) consisting of long vessels, long before the 6th Century BCE. As career sea-navigators operating from what is today Lebanon, the Phoenicians established a chain of trading cities around the Mediterranean Sea between 1200 and 900 BCE. From South to North, some of the Phoenician port cities along the Mediterranean Sea included Tyre, Sarepta, and Sidon. These three cities, and others, were connected with one another along the shore while others, such as Leptis and Dougga, served as links with interior West Africa through the intermediation of Berber traders. One of the Phoenician Mediterranean cities, Carthage, dating back to the 9th Century BCE, became the most famous of all. Carthage was located at the site of modern-day Tunis, capital city of Tunisia. Over the years, the Phoenicians at Carthage, by now identified as Carthaginians, became trading partners with local Berbers for food in exchange for iron-work goods. By 400 BCE, the Carthaginians expanded their maritime exploration travels to the West African coast of the Atlantic Ocean, pushing as far down as Cerne, on the coast of modern-day Mauritania. Carthage's prosperity ignited the envy of the Romans, who led a series of three wars, the Punic Wars, to destroy Carthage at all costs. On the Carthage side, the wars were commanded by Hannibal Barca, who won the first two, but lost the third. Carthage was defeated and completely burned down by the Romans in 146 BCE (Rachidi 1990, Shillington 1993).

The Somalis: The Somali people have a long history of powerful seaport trading cities and seafaring international trade networks. Both of Somaliland's shores—the Gulf of Aden, to the north, and the Indian Ocean, to the east—were strewn with port cities of various sizes. In ancient times, Somalia was called the Kingdom of Punt and traded with Egypt through the Red Sea, with the Middle East and Persia through the Persian Gulf, and with East Africa and Asia through the Indian Ocean. Below are selective samples of Somalia's major historical seaport trading cities, foreign trading partners, and maritime trade goods. To begin with, throughout the centuries, different port cities came to prominence in Somaliland's maritime trade. Such was the case with:

Opone, Mossiylon, Malao, and Mundus in ancient times;

Berbera, on the shore of the Gulf of Aden (in the north), and Mogadishu, on the shore of the Indian Ocean (deep in the south), in the 18th and the 19th centuries;

Hobyo, Kiswayo, and Zeila, in the Middle Age; and

Eyl, Las Khorey, and Qandala, in early Modern Era. (Wikipedia.ND. "Maritime History of Somalia").[17]

Some of Somaliland's major trading partners throughout human history are presented in Table 10.

Table 10: *Somalia's International Trading Partners across the Centuries*

Historical Periods	International Maritime Trading Networks
In Ancient Egyptian time (3100 - 30 BCE) (Somalia the called Kingdom of Punt).	*The Egyptians, the Phoenicians, the Babylonians, and the Mycenaeans (Mainland Greece).*
During the Classical Era (8th century BCE - 6th century AD).	India, Greece, and Rome
In the Middle Ages (476 - 1450 AD) and the early Modern Era (1500AD - 1800 AD)	Egypt, Arabia, Persia, China, Venitia, and Portugal.
During the period of imperial hegemony over Somalia (1891 - 1960).	The Far East, Europe and the Americas (often along with British and other European ships).

(Adapted fromWikipedia.ND."Maritime History of Somalia").[18]

Chapter 12

In ancient times, frankincense, myrrh, spices, and gum were in high demand. Several of Somaliland's seaports were major distribution centers. For centuries, Somalis also imported and distributed cinnamon from China, India, and Ceylon (the Island of Sri Lanka, in the Indian Ocean, southeast of India). In the 16th century, Mogadishu came to prominence in the exchange of fabrics and spices from India for gold, wax, and ivory from East Africa, the port city of Kilwa in particular. Mogadishu itself was a major cloth weaver and exporter of its Benaadir cloth to Egypt and Syria. Mogadishu and other Somaliland seaport cities served as transit stops for merchants from China, India and East Africa in route to and from Egypt. In the 18th and the 19th centuries, Berbera, on the shore of the Gulf of Aden, was Somaliland's most pre-eminent trading seaport and maintained intense commercial relations with the Egyptians, the Phoenicians, the Babylonians, the Persians and many other nations. It was a major exporter of a vast range of goods from the interior, including livestock, frankincense, myrrh, gold, ivory, ostrich feathers, gum, and more. For a long time, the Somali Ajuran Sultanate dominated the seafaring trade with Arabia and India. In early 19th century, during the Gobroom Dynasty, Somaliland became a major exporter of home-grown agricultural products to Arabian markets (Wikipedia. ND. "History of Somalia").[19]

Thus, Somaliland was rich, prosperous, and internationally renowned among nations in the ancient world. But time and again, the Somali people have had to defend themselves against aggressors from near and far, envious of the strategic location and prosperity of Somali coastal cities and the country. Such was the case in the 16th century AD with Ethiopian Christian expeditions against Somali Muslims, and the control by the Sharifs of Yemen's Mocha seaport city over Saylac, and Berbera coastal cities on the Gulf of Aden. In the 17th century, Somaliland was the target of attacks by Ottoman Turks and Portuguese penetration into coastal cities, except Mogadishu. The 18th century brought about repeated depredations by the Portuguese, as well as the Yemeni Sharifs of Mukha's rule over Northern Somaliland. In the 19th century, the Sultanate of Oman, in the Arabian Peninsula, extended his rule over the Benaadir Coast on the Indian Ocean (Wikipedia ND. "History of Somalia").[20]

As seen in the above cases, assaults on Somalilalnd were the works of individual powers each operating alone. The 19th century brought about a new era in the history of the Somali people, an era of imperialist conspiracies by several nations operating in concert. The first conspiracy was the split of Somaliland into five separate colonial possessions (1891-1960): British Somaliland (north central), French Somaliland (east and southeast), Italian Somaliland (south), Ethiopian Somaliland (the Ogaden), and the Northern Frontier District (NFD) of Kenya. In the 20th century, as African countries were becoming politically liberated from colonial rules, the colonizers conspired to only release British Somaliland, Italian Somaliland, and French Somaliland, while withholding Ethiopian Somaliland and the Northern Frontier District (NFD) of Kenya. The three regions united into an independent democratic Somalia Republic (1960-1969). Then came Mohamed Siad Barre's power takeover in a military coup supported by both the United States and the Soviet Union (1969), followed by his unsuccessful wars against Ethiopia and Kenya in an attempt to recuperate the parts of Somaliland that were arbitrarily given to these countries in the imperialist scheme. Not unexpectedly, the former colonizers stood by Ethiopia and Kenya, joined by the Soviet Union in the case of Ethiopia. Muhamed Siad Barre's dictatorial, oppressive and divisive policies balkanized the Somali Republic into marginalized and inter-fighting clans. He lost popular support. For an unrevealed reason, he gave a large part the Somali Republic in concessions to American corporations. Ever since that time, America has waged aggression wars and organized proxy wars by African nations against the Somalis at home and pursued those in refuge in Yemen. At some point, at least six African countries had troops in Somalia fighting to protect American interests. These were: Uganda, Djibouti, Burundi, Kenya, Sierra Leone, and Ethiopia. We don't know how many there are currently. Today, the Somali people live in extreme poverty and permanent hunger. The once dynamic trading and sailing waters are now overpopulated by heavy-leaden large cargo ships carrying tons of oil from the Middle East, as well as large fishing vessels from powerful countries. The only maritime activities associated with the Somali people are piracy attacks on foreign fishing vessels by dislodged Somali refugees defending themselves from Yemen.

Traders by Land

The Twaregs and the Trans-Saharan Trade: The economies of Western Sudan (West Africa) and North Africa in ancient times were integrated through several points of encounter. Timbuktu was one of those centers. Timbuktu had a trading avocation from its very beginning due to its location. It was the place where Tuareg nomads would come to Western Sudan during the rainy season to leave their goods and return into the desert during drought. Timbuktu is located at the bend of the Niger River, which is also the highest meeting point of the river and the Sahara Desert. Timbuktu was a major commercial center where Tuareg and Arab traders from the north traded regularly with Songhay, Wangara, and Fulani merchants from Western Sudan, exchanging salt from Taghaza in the Sahara Desert brought in by camel caravans for gold from Wangara/Takrur between the Senegal and Niger rivers, which were brought in by canoes. In the 13th century, with the founding of the University of Sankore, Timbuktu became a major center of Islamic training and scholarship. Books written by both Arab and Western Sudan scholars became an additional major trading item. They were sold and taught in the mosques of the University of Sankore and others across the city. Timbuktu, and Gao to its east, were connected to North Africa by a direct trading route descending from Sijilmasa, in Morocco. Other routes went to Audaghust and to Wangara/Takrur, in ancient Ghana from Sajilmasa. To the east, a trading route from Tripoli, in Libya, descended directly to Kano, in Hausaland, with a branch going to Kanem Bornu by Lake Chad. There was also a route from Cairo, in Egypt, going to Gao, in Songhay, through Ghart, in the Sahara, and Tadmakka, just north of Gao. Through these trading networks, West Africa was connected with the major cities in North Africa, notably, Marrakesh and Fez in Morocco, Tlemcen and Algiers in Algeria, Carthage and later Tunis in Tunisia, Tripoli and Liptis in Libya, and Cairo in Egypt. Another route linked the Nile River to a major salt mine at Lake Chad and to other cities further to the west (Collins 1990, July 1992, Shillington 1993, Timbuktuheritage.org. ND).[21]

Dyula Ethnic Networks and Economic Integration of Western Sudan: Since the early years of the Ghana Empire, the Mandinka traders of Mali, known as Dyula or

Wangara, operated as a vital link between gold-producing forest lands and the entire Western Sudan and North Africa. As early as the 14th century, they organized in small companies of traveling merchants connecting all the parts of West Africa. They dealt mainly in gold and kola nuts. They had the advantage of a common language and generations of experience in long-distance trade. They endowed themselves with a permanent merchant leader called *Dyulamansa*, chief of the Dyula. By recognizing one leader, the Dyula enhanced their organizational efficiency. Unity and organizational efficiency enabled them to found market towns, cities, and even states. Political integration in the Mali Empire and implantation of Islam reinforced the Dyula ethnic unity and provided additional protection and security. Under Mansa Musa, Mali's power stretched far past Timbuktu and Gao to the east, Walata to the north, and Takrur to the west. Law, order and safety reigned throughout the empire. The Mali empire reached the highest levels of prosperity. Mali's leaders became recognized everywhere as great leaders of a great country. With the implantation of Islam, Islamic laws relating to administration of justice, the inheritance of property and the improvement of market organization became the base for building larger states and markets. West Africans adopted techniques for long-distance trade that developed through Islam. The system of credit and exchange and currency standards enhanced the systematic and orderly transfer of goods between diverse groups. For instance, the Almoravid *dinar*, called *mitcal*, became the standard in long-distance transactions in some parts of West Africa (Davidson 1991, 1977; Williams 1987).

Mapungubwe, The Historical Zimbabwe, and East African Trading Cities: Mapungubwe, the large southern African kingdom (1220 - 1300) that preceded Zimbabwe, was located near the confluence of the Limpopo and Shashe rivers and commercially connected to East African harbor cities through the Limpopo River and, through them, to Arabia, China and India. The people of Mapungubwe are reported to have been both raisers of cattle, sheep, and goats, and farmers of millet, sorghum, and cotton. Their exports included salt, cattle, fish, gold, iron, ivory, wood, and various other items. Zimbabwe, a state founded by the Karanga, a subgroup of the Shona people, extended over the Mashonaland plateau and adjacent lowlands between the Zambezi and the Limpopo rivers. The country was also referred to as *Mwene Mutapa*, the title name of its king. Zimbabwe's economic strength came from cattle raising, farming, and long-distance trade with the Indian Ocean coastal cities of Sofala and Kilwa. Kilwa served as the major entrepôt, while Sofala was the major port of export of gold and ivory amber, pearls, and copper from Mwene Mutapa. Cotton cloth imported from India, and porcelain from China, traveled from Kilwa, Mombasa and Malindi (two other trading east coastal cities) to Sofala. There was no goldfield in Zimbabwe. Gold was mined in *The Leopard's Kopje* near the modern city of Bulawayo. Zimbabwe kings controlled gold/copper mining and smelting economies of the time, particularly exportation nexuses. They used the wealth they accumulated to build some 150 stone buildings; the most impressive of all was housed in Great Zimbabwe, built around 1300 AD. Some of the buildings, such as the acropolis, date back to the 11th century (1000) AD. Others were newer (18th century). Such was the case with the elliptical enclosure, the adjacent embankment, and a conical tower in the valley below the acropolis (South African History Online ND,[22] Collins 1994, Motley 1969, July 1992).

An Explorer and Transformer of Spaces and Civilization Builder

SUMMARY

This chapter provides an expansive review of divine notions of political development, and continues to tell the story of the earliest humans in Africa, and their spread to other continents, with their specific contributions. Divinities commissioned by God ventured into the unknown to participate in the creation of the Earth. Legendary ancestors came from somewhere to the once unknown locations which became the birthplaces of their human descendants. These actions by God's highest-ranking mediator spirits prefigure migratory movements by future inhabitants of the Earth to unknown territories which they would transform into living spaces carrying special marks. The Hominids, Proto-Humans, were the actual pacesetters. Created in Eastern Africa, they moved out to various spaces and left the marks of their stone technologies; not only elsewhere in Africa, but also in the Middle East, Asia, Polynesia, and Europe. Likewise, *Homo Sapiens Sapiens* moved out of East Africa to become the First Peoples, first human occupants of the land, in other parts of Africa (the Twa, the Anu, the San, for example), in Asia (the Andamanese), and Oceania (the Aeta, the Mani, and the Semangs), and in America (the Australoids, and the Asiatic Negroids). Generally short in stature—and primarily living off hunting, gathering, and fishing even, where they practice other occupations—*the First Peoples*, wherever they survive, have become marginalized numerical and political minorities. This chapter subsequently relates the story of Africa's greatest civilizations: i.e., Nubia and the Nile Valley Civilizations. Nubia, in the Middle Nile region, is the cradle of African civilizations. The Nubians moved gradually northward, building communities on both banks of the Nile River, over time consolidating these communities into kingdoms that ultimately formed a single nation: i.e., Kemet, currently known as Egypt. They developed an unprecedented civilization, the Nile Valley Civilization, and created a society governed on the basis of the laws of science, religious beliefs and worldviews, and internalized human values of justice, fairness and equity. The Nubians spread from the Nile Valley to West Africa, carrying along such marks of their civilization as the Yorùbá pantheon and religious rituals; the Dogon people's astrology and rituals; the cultivation of sorghum, rice, yams and melons; metallurgical products, such as jewels, knives, arrowheads, and spearheads; and hieroglyphic writing, such as those found around a baobab tree in Senegal, in Njoya, Cameroon, and in Vai, Sierra Leone.

African people from the Nile Valley who developed civilizations in South Arabia (the Africoid Arabians), in Canaan (the Phoenicians), in Mesopotamia (the Sumerians), and in the Indus Valley (the Harappans and the Dravidians) were collectively identified by the Ancient Greeks as Ethiopians. While occupying these lands, the Ethiopians built state societies, cities, and monumental houses of worship, and developed irrigated agriculture and writing systems, from among other accomplishments. The Bantu who migrated from the Benue region in eastern Nigeria and western Cameroon, crossed the Equatorial Rainforest, and spread all over Africa below the Equator along with their civilization of state building, hierarchal government structures, iron and copper technology, itinerant cultivation by the hoe, the ax and the machete, and livestock raising. Nilotic groups from South Sudan migrated to the Great Lakes Region of East Africa and subjugated their Bantu predecessors by the power of the spear and consolidated their domination by integrating cattle raising and land farming. Ultimately, the story of Africa is one of peoples, kingdoms, and nation-states that left a mark across many continents and were the predecessors for early technology, trade, and knowledge.

(Endnotes)

1   Dieterlene, Germaine. 1955. "Mythe et organisation sociale au Soudan français." *Journal des Africanistes/Année1955/25/pp 39-76*. https://www.persee.fr/doc/jafr_0037-9166_1955_num_25_1_1873. Retrieved 4-30-2018.

Mark, Joshua J. 2016. "Gods & Goddesses of Ancient Egypt – A Brief History." *Ancient History Encyclopedia*. https://www.ancient.eu/article/884/gods--goddesses-of-ancient-Egypt---a-brief-history/ Retrieved 1-16-2020.

2   Groeneveld, Emma. 2017. "Homo Sapiens - Ancient History." https://www.ancient.eu/Homo_Sapiens/. Retrieved 3-18-2020.

3   Solomon, Anne. 2005. "Rock Art in Southern Africa." *Scientific American, 175. The Sciences. January 1, 2005*. https://www.scientificamerican.com/article/rock-art-in-southern-africa-2005-01/. Retrieved 3-12-2020.

Wilcox, A. R. ND. *The Rock Art of Africa*. Rutledge Library Editions – Archeology. https://books.google.com/books?id=qilKDwAAQBAJ&pg=PA197&lpg=PA197&dq=Dorothea+Bleek+1933+Rock+Painting&source=bl&ots=7EFMK2Xgb5&sig=ACfU3U1z8jdNg-NKobKqjitvsXFn6uqtGA&hl=en&sa=X&. Retrieved 3-12-2020.

Discoverafrica. 2017. "Five destinations to view rock paintings in South Africa." February 27, 2017. https://www.discoverafrica.com/blog/five-destinations-to-view-rock-paintings-in-south-africa/. Retrieved 5-13-2019.

The British Museum. ND. "African Art – Introduction to rock art in northern Africa." https://africanrockart.britishmuseum.org/regional_introduction/rock-art-in-northern-africa/#:~:text=A%20possibly%20concurrent%2. Retrieved 2-2-2021

British Museum. ND. "African Rock Art: Niger." https://africanrockart.britishmuseum.org/country/niger/. Retrieved 2-2-2021

4   Verdu, Paul. 2012. "Perspectives de la génétique humaine sur l'origine de la diversité de populations des pygmées d'Afrique Centrale." *Journal des Africanistes 82-1/2,2012. pp. 53-71.* https://journals.openedition.org/africanistes/4269?lang=en. Retrieved 10-2019.

5   Donnely, Ignatius. 1882. "The mythologies of the Old World: A Recollection of Atlantis. Chapter 1. Traditions of Atlantis." https://www.sacred-texts.com/atl/ataw/ataw401.htm. Retrieved 3-23-2020.

6   Survival 2005. "Background on the Tribes of Andaman Nicobar Islands." January 6, 2005. https://www.survivalinternational.org/news/175. Retrieved 1-17-2020.

7   Valdeavilla, Ronica. ND. "The Aeta: The First Philippine People." https://theculturetrip.com/asia/philippines/articles/the-aeta-the-first-philippine people/. Retrieved 11-13-2019.

8   Rattanakrajangsri, Kittisak, Thapat Maneerat and Macus Cochester. ND. "The Mani People

of Thailand on the Agricultural Frontier." https://www.forestpeoples.org/sites/fpp/files/private/publication/2013/12/conflict-or-consent-chapter-11-mani-people-thailand-agricultural-frontier.pdf. Retrieved 11-15-2019.

9   Masron, Tarmiji, Fugimaki Masami, and Norhasimah Ismail. ND. "Orfang Asli in Peninsular Malaysia: Population, Spatial Distribution and Socio-Economic Condition." http://www.ritsumei.ac.jp/acd/re/k-rsc/hss/book/pdf/vol06_07.pdf. Retrieved 11-17-2019.

10   Crow Canyon Archeological Center. 2011, 2014. "Peoples of the Mesa Verde Region." https://www.crowcanyon.org/EducationProducts/peoples_mesaverde/paleoindianartifacts.asp. Retrieved 11-5-2020.

11   The Editors of Encyclopedia Britannica. ND. "Amratian culture." https://www.britannica.com/topic/Amratian-culture. Retrieved 11-4-2019.

12   Wikipedia. ND. "Elam." https://en.wikipedia.org/wiki/Elam. Retrieved 3-24-2020.

Elam. ND. "vi. Elamite Religion." http://www.iranicaonline.org/articles/elam-vi. Retrieved 3-24-2020.

13   World Civilization. ND. "Chapter 11, African Civilizations." *OER Services.* https://courses.lumenlearning.com/suny-hccc-worldcivilization/chapter/bornu-empire/. Retrieved 3-31-2020.

14   Wikipedia. ND. "Ancient Egyptian Trade." https://en.wikipedia.org/wiki/Ancient_Egyptian_trade. Retrieved 3-24-2020.

Gilbert, Gregory P. 2008. "Ancient Egyptian Sea Power and The Origin of Maritime Forces." *Foundations of International Thinking on Sea Power.* No 1. Australia: Sea Power Center. https://www.navy.gov.au/sites/default/files/documents/IntSP_1_Ancient_EgyptSP.pdf. Retrieved 3-25 2020.

15   Wikipedia. ND. Ancient Egyptian Navy." https://en.wikipedia.org/wiki/Ancient_Egyptian_navy. Retrieved 3-25-2020.

Gilbert, Gregory P. 2008. *"Ancient Egyptian Sea Power and The Origin of Maritime Forces." Foundations of International Thinking on Sea Power.* No 1. Australia: Sea Power Center. https://www.navy.gov.au/sites/default/files/documents/IntSP_1_Ancient_EgyptSP.pdf. Retrieved 3-25 2020.

OER Service World Civilization. ND. "Ch. 11 African Civilization – Nubia." https://courses.lumenlearning.com/suny-hccc-worldcivilization/chapter/nubia/. Retrieved 3-25-2020.

16   Mark, Joshua J. 2018. "Canaan." https://www.ancient.eu/canaan/. Retrieved 1-29-2021.

The University of Pennsylvania Museum of Archeology and Anthropology. 1999. "Canaan and Ancient Israel." https://www.penn.museum/sites/canaan/LandandTime.html#:~:text=The%20land%20known%20as%20Canaan,portions%20of%20Syria%20an. Retrieved 1-29-2021.

17   Wikipedia. ND. "Maritime History of Somalia." https://en.wikipedia.org/wiki/Maritime_history_of_Somalia. Retrieved 4-2-2020.

18   Wikipedia. ND. "Maritime History of Somalia." https://en.wikipedia.org/wiki/Maritime_history_of_Somalia. Retrieved 4-2-2020.

Wikipedia. ND. "History of Somalia." https://en.wikipedia.org/wiki/History_of_Somalia. Retrieved 4-7-2020.

Chapter 12

19Wikipedia. ND. "Maritime History of Somalia." https://en.wikipedia.org/wiki/Maritime_history_of_Somalia. Retrieved 4-2-2020.

20Wikipedia. ND. "History of Somalia." https://en.wikipedia.org/wiki/History_of_Somalia. Retrieved 4-7-2020.

21Timbuktuheritage.org. "History of Timbuktu – A Multicultural African Legacy." http://www.timbuktuheritage.org/timhistory.html. Retrieved 3-26-2020.

22South African History Online. ND. "Kingdoms of Southern Africa: Mapungubwe." https://www.sahistory.org.za/article/kingdoms-southern-africa-mapungubwe. Retrieved 3-26-2020.

World Civilization. ND. "Chapter 11, African Civilizations." *OER Services*. https://courses.lumenlearning.com/suny-hccc-worldcivilization/chapter/bornu-empire/. Retrieved 3-31-2020.

Conclusion

Muntu wa Nzambi: The African Human as God's Special Creation

The purpose of this book was to single out elements from African creation stories, belief systems and cultural practices which characterize the human being as what God wanted the human to be from Creation; in other words, to draw a portrait of human at human's best. The goal has been reached by elaborating on 12 key attributes per chapter. As a distinct entity which is a direct product of divine Creation, the book presents the African concepts of human as: (1) a spiritual being in a physical body; (2) a moving body full of vitality; (3) a speech master; and (4) a creative mind. As an active agent, human is always involved in networks of interaction with other living entities. In interaction with the spirits, human is: (5) a firm believer in God and (6) a fervent devotee of the spirits. Wherever human appears, he lives in communities of other humans where he is in constant interaction in such capacities as: (7) an ethic-bound community member, (8) a family-kinship community builder, (9) a compassionate caretaker of fellow humans, and (10) a freedom seeker and nation builder. Human's interaction with the spirits and with fellow humans extends to and impacts human's interaction with the natural environment. Here human manifests self as: (11) a steward of the community's natural resources, and (12) an explorer of unknown living spaces and a civilization builder. In summary, the book describes how Africans conceptualize their role on Earth, and how this belief stems from their understanding of God's plan for His creation. In writing this book, the author relates the multiple and important contributions of African peoples and civilizations to the foundation and fabric of world history and contemporary life.

1. A Spiritual Being in a Physical Body

This is the human in its original state of being upon freshly emanating from divine creation. African worldview purports that human is God's own spirit infused through the creation process into the human body. God's spirit permeates and animates the body. It survives physical death and lives eternally among the ancestors in closer proximity to God, yet is still among the living in an invisible form. Within the human body, God's spirit, the vital force, coexists with a cluster of other innate forces which contribute to the shaping of a person's full self, personality, and destiny. In addition, through Creation the human being was endowed with mystical powers such as revealed knowledge of future or long-past events, and the ability to mystically carry out superhuman acts capable of altering the fate of another person for better or worse. Although most people lost their powers when the original relationship between the Creator and God's creations on

Conclusion

Earth was altered, a few individuals continue to be born with such powers. Human's special gifts from creation include the call to spiritualization while living on Earth, immortality of the spirit, and reincarnation after death. Through trance during religious ceremonies, human can incorporate a spirit and serve as the medium through which the spirit communicates with the audience. Through ordination to priesthood or investiture to the chiefdom or kingdom stool, the candidate can be elevated to the spiritual rank of past incumbents, become their equal, and incorporate their spiritual powers to bless and protect the community. Finally, as reincarnations of the spirits of departed relatives through conception and birth, newborn babies are welcomed and treated as spiritual beings and befriended to make them feel wanted, thereby keeping them from getting dissatisfied with life on Earth and returning to their origins.

2. A Moving Body Full of Vitality

African worldviews state that the inner divine spirit and cognate spiritual forces permeate the human body. In association with the constantly moving biological systems and vital organs, they invigorate the body and keep it in constant motion. Human life is maintained by these biological systems and vital organs animated by constant flows of breath, blood, and hormones. The human body structure is made of flexible junctures allowing for motion in all directions, rhythmic dances, and songs. When the internal organs, the bone structure and the skin envelope operate optimally, the human body can execute performance tasks requiring strength and endurance, such as farming and sports. An apt body is mounted with agile hands capable of carrying out varied manual tasks requiring dexterity, including making a wide range of useful tools and producing various utilitarian and decorative products. Taken together, the African worldview celebrates that God's creation has resulted in a human of many talents and capabilities.

3. A Speech Master

Human beings are created with the ability to integrate ideas and articulate them in various forms of speech. The chapter describes traditional customs related to learning to speak and learning the norms of one's community. African children develop language articulation skills by challenging each other in games involving word-syllable inversions, counting rhymes, and riddles and enigmas. Adults take pride in articulating personal names with various meanings attached such as, status titles, respect for totemic animals or plants, or praises for personal accomplishments. Advice about the facts of life is often given using proverbs embodying ancestral wisdom nurtured generation after generation. Public speaking often takes the form of call and response to engage the audience and sustain their attention and interest. Narratives involving animal stories and legends are other classical forms of articulated speech. Important teachings are often delivered in songs. Epics of heroic figures, ethnic pride, memorials, and social critiques are often expressed in songs.

4. A Creative Mind

Growing out of the original incarnate divine essence is a vibrant character endowed with multiple vital talents and mental aptitudes. This includes the intellectual capacities to: 1) conceive and express ideas in articulate language, as already explained; 2) observe, understand and gain functional knowledge of the milieu and its natural and social resources; 3) memorize, store and reenact significant past events and stories of heroic figures; 4) gain insights, discern nuances, and adjust individual behaviors to varying situations; and 5) create mental images and transform them into physical actions and or objects.

5. A Believer in God

Authentic Africans believe in God's eternal existence, omnipresence, omniscience, and omnipotence. God has no beginning and no end. God existed, exists and will always exist and is present everywhere. God also has the power to do anything imaginable and His powers supersede all other powers—be they of the divinities, ancestors, witches or most powerful animals. Their powers come from God. God's powers are inherent in God's divine nature. The extent of God's power is manifest in everything He has created and made possible. God is the Almighty Creator of the universe and all that exist in it: spiritual or physical. This chapter describes the creation of various categories of beings and their relationship to one another. God first created the Lord Spirits who share God's nature and powers to the highest level, then the planets and the elements, and then the inhabitants of Earth with humans at the very end. The creation of humans always involved some form of infusion of God's breath of life. Not only is the God of the Africans the Supreme Being and Creator, God is also the Generous Provider. God created the terrestrial world as a suitable place for humans to subsist and grow, and He equipped Africa with immense resources for humans to draw on to live abundantly and prosper.

6. A Fervent Devotee of the Spirits

In African religious thought, it is as if God created the entire universe for the benefit of the human being. God appointed some of God's highest-ranking spiritual creations, divinities, to be humans' protectors and immediate providers. A few select divinities assisted God in the creation process. The majority of divinities served and still serve as God's ministers in the governance of the terrestrial world. God also entrusted the humans to the daily care of the ancestors acting as God's mediators and family elders. There also exist natural spirits created by God and who also assume protective roles among the living. The general attitude of the African people toward the protective spirits—God, divinities, ancestors and nature spirits—is one of devotion expressed through prayers, offerings, sexual observances, and taboos.

7. An Ethic-bound Community Member

The human being is born into a community that is regulated by binding moral principles. The chapter describes in great detail the norms which dictate human behavior and convey personal responsibility. This knowledge is important to appreciate African beliefs before the arrival of Europeans. The most universal principles include prohibitions such as attempting to take someone's life, assault, denying someone food, slander, or humiliating an elder, refusing to pay the tributes of the first fruits, breaking the incest taboo, taking someone's wife, sexually abusing a child, taking someone's property, and denying someone access to public spaces. Transgressions call for sanctions, social as well as spiritual. Sanctions include repairing the wrong that was committed and paying fines for the restoration of the broken social order.

8. A Family-Kinship Community Builder

In addition to being born into a community, the human being is called to become a community builder. The chapter relates how the African worldview has expectations of the individual to the building up of his family. The family community is built through marriage and procreation. The African marriage is an alliance between families sealed through the payment of the bridewealth by the groom's family to the bride's family, and maintained by the carrying out of gender roles according to the prevailing custom. Constructive procreation entails taking care of the child's physical and spiritual needs and socialization of the child into expected adult roles. The book describes one's responsibilities to the extended family and clan. Individuals contribute to the building of the kinship community by carrying out reciprocal responsibilities, including pervasive sharing practices, participating in collective religious obligations and rituals to common ancestors or divinities, and contracting loyalty pacts with potential enemies.

9. A Compassionate Caretaker of Fellow Humans

To live one must learn how to care for self. However, the African man or woman is born with an instinct to care for others as well, which is reinforced by society in all aspects of life. The chapter describes how household organization and practices enable family members to fulfill their role and to care for others. Housing and feeding for the household are made available with potential guests in mind. There is a high value placed on parental care for children, which is seen as a natural necessity. African mothers care for their children even before marriage, then at conception, during pregnancy, at birth, and during the child's many growing years. The book also describes how African people care for the sick—the types of medicinal treatments, the consultation with the diviner to discover hidden causes, and with seers for revealed knowledge and mystical confrontation of witches and other evil forces. Africans believe that care for the dying includes restoration of broken relations through reconciliation with family members, and moral confrontation at internment to face the ancestral judgment awaiting them if their death was a punishment for some wrongdoing, and purification rites.

Conclusion

10. A Freedom Seeker and Nation Builder

Human beings live in communities and satisfy their survival needs with the resources of their environment. According to African worldview, free access to such resources is a basic human right. Traditional African communities have established mechanisms guaranteeing this right in relation to land, forests, rivers and other natural waters, as well as hunting, gathering and fishing grounds. The book describes these norms, as well as the rules for access to political power. In traditional Africa, prior to European intervention, political autonomy was sought and practiced at various levels of authority. In principle, power rotated among the descendants of the founding fathers according to established rules. Disregard for the rule of rotation often led to segmentation, while migration resulted in building independent nations in foreign lands. The chapter describes how a variety of nations sought territorial autonomy through mobilizing the citizens or establishing marriage alliances or peace pacts with leaders of enemy clans or countries. Of particular importance, the chapter relates political systems that fostered national unity: i.e., 1) integrated political directorate leaders of once rival nations (the Ashanti model), 2) local participatory and multi-level representative democracy (the Kuba model), 3) royal religious rituals (the Yoruba and the Swazi models), 4) incorporating the new king and his family into the kinship networks of the departing king (the Lunda model), 5) shared governance (the Luba Kasai model), and 6) cross-ethnic militarization, centralized authority (the Shaka-Zulu model).

11. A Steward of Community's Natural Resources

Human and nature are intertwined since Creation and demonstrate how God created land, animals, forests, rain, rivers, and water life—with the human being in mind. In some creation stories God explicitly entrusted the environment and its resources to humans for judicious use and mutual protection. Following Creation, humans and animals lived in conviviality and mutual support. The mandate of mutual support and protection is perpetuated through religious beliefs regarding the healing power of the plants and other of God's creations on Earth, and attitudes of reverence and patterns of sacred interaction with totems. The chapter also describes the rationale of domestication of animals such as sheep, goats, and cattle—for livelihood, status building, sacrifices and trade at local markets and regional long-distance trading networks. The chapter shares a wealth of knowledge on key crops across Africa and traditional production techniques that value land-preservation and caretaking. African farmers have developed sustainable practices and technologies adapted to the nature of the plant, the ecology, climate, and seasonal variations.

12. An Explorer and Transformer of Spaces and Civilization Builder

In some African stories, the creation of Earth was an adventure into the unknown by God's messenger great spirits. After life on Earth had been established, the Hominids left their birthplace in Eastern Africa to migrate to the rest of the continent. Some pushed further out into Europe; others moved into the Middle East; others migrated into southern Arabia and journeyed all way to Far Asia. Everywhere they have left marks of gradually perfecting stone technologies to better exploit the resources of changing environments. The Hominids are now extinct. The First Peoples, who were the first Homo Sapiens Sapiens who occupied the earth in a more permanent manner, also originated from Eastern Africa and spread over the continent. In Africa, they are known as Twa, Pygmies, Nu, Sam, Khoi and many other names. This study was limited to Africans and descendants of African migrants. The chapter relates a rich and complex history of the rise and evolution of African civilizations. Just as the Hominids and the First Peoples, large scale movements of civilization builders originated in Nubia, moved from their native homeland around the confluent of White Nile and Blue Nile to explore, colonize, and develop Kemet, today known as Egypt. The civilizations they developed in Nubia, Kemet, and Axum are known as Nile Valley civilizations. Black people from the Nile Valley, who migrated across the Red Sea into Asia, are known as Ethiopians, and built civilizations in southern Arabia, Mesopotamia, Elam (present-day Iran), and the Indus Valley. Nile Valley civilizations were very complex: consisting of great kingdoms, large cities, impressive architectural monuments, a major religion with a hierarchical pantheon of divinities, and advanced sciences of the Earth and the sky. In far West Africa, descendants of Nubian immigrants built home-grown kingdoms and empires known as classical African civilizations of the Western Sudan: the Soninke in Ghana, the Malinke in Mali, the Sorko fishermen in Songhay, the Asante in Ashanti, and the nomadic Kanembu in Kanem-Bornu. Emerging at the southern fringe of the Equatorial Rain Forest, Bantu migrants from Benue, between Cameroon and Nigeria, established farming economies dominated by the technology of the hoe, the ax and the machete. Taking advantage of immense mineral reserves, they developed tools and implements, enabling them to spread over Central, Southern, and Eastern Africa, establishing villages, hierarchical political systems, and trading networks. In East Africa, latecomer migrant Nilotes from southern Sudan, adopted Bantus' farming systems and, taking advantage of their traditional civilization of the cattle and the spear, established political apparatuses supplanting the Bantu. Rather than through settlements, African peoples throughout the centuries and across continents contributed to civilization building by establishing major networks of long-distance trade by land (Tuaregs, Dyula, Kingdom of Zimbabwe) or by water (Egyptians, Phoenicians, Somalis). The details in the book are important and informative for students and scholars of pre-colonial African history, religion, and culture.

CITED ACADEMIC BIBLIOGRAPHY

Abdullahi, Mohamed Diriye. 2001. *Culture and Customs of Somalia.* Westport, Connecticut: Greenwood Press.
Abraham, W. E. 1974. *The Mind of Africa.* Chicago: The University of Chicago Press.
Ayoade, John A., H.I. Ibrahim and H.Y. Ibrahim. 2009. "Analysis of women involvement in livestock production in Lafia area of Nasarawa State, Nigeria." *Livestock Research for Rural Development*, 21, (12) 2009. https://lrrd.cipav.org.co/lrrd21/12/ayoa21220.htm. Retrieved 6-22-2019.
Atal *sa* Angang, Dosithée. 1997. «Conception Africaine de la Vie, de La Mort et de l'Au-Dela.» Centres d'Etudes des Religions Africaines, 1997, in *Religions Traditionnelles Africaine et Projet de Société.* Kinshasa : Facultés Catholiques de Kinshasa. Pp. 365-398.
Atal, sa Anyang. 1990. "Adresse de Bienvenue du Professeur Atal sa Anyang, Doyen de la Faculté de Théologie Catholique de Kinshasa." In *L'Afrique et ses Formes de Vie Spirituelle.* Kinshasa: Facultés Catholiques de Kinshasa. Pp. 9-12.
Atal, sa Anyang. 1997. "Religions Traditionnelles, Cultures et Sociétés." In *Religions Traditionnelles Africaines et Projet de Société.* Kinshasa: Facultés Catholiques de Kinshasa. Pp. 23-28.
Awolalu, Joseph Omosade. 1991. "The Encounter between African Traditional Religion and Other Religions in Nigeria." In Olupona, Jacob K., Editor, 1991, *African Traditional Religion in Contemporary Society.* St. Paul, Minnesota: Paragon House. Pp.111-118.
Awolalu, Joseph Omosade. "Background on the Tribes of Andaman & Nicobar Islands." *Survival* 2005.
https://www.survivalinternational.org/news/175. Retrieved 7-10-2019.
Balolebwami, Alphonse M. 1997. "Les Rites d'Intronisation du Mwâmi chez les Bashi." *Cahiers des Religions Africaines.* Vol.31 no 61-62, 1997. pp. 123-133.
Bamuinikile, Mudiasa. 1975. *Le Bukole et son Impact sur la Societé Luba.* Lubumbashi Université Nationale du Zaire, Mémoire.
Bascom, William. 1969. *The Yoruba of Southwest Nigeria.* New York: Holt, Rinehart and Winston.
Batukezanga, Zamenga. «Le jeu favori," Section of "Souvenirs du village." In *Littératures francophones d'Afrique centrale*, éd Jean-Louis Joubert (Paris: Nathan, 1999, 210.)
Beach, D. N. "The Rise of the Zimbabwe State.» In Robert O. Collins, Ed. 1994. *Problems in African History : The Precolonial Centuries.* Second Printing. New York and Princeton: Markus Wiener Publishing, Inc. Pp. 127-134.
Beguin, Hubert. 1960. *La mise en valeur agricole du Sud-Est du Kasai: Essai de Géographie Agricole et de Géographie Agraire et ses Possibilités d'Applications Pratiques.* Bruxelles.
Beguin, Hubert. 1965. «Espoirs, Bilan et Leçons d'un Paysannat au Congo.» *Tiers-Monde*, Tome 6, No 24, Octobre-Décembre, 1965: 891-913.
Ben-Jochannan. 1991. *African Origin of the Major Western Religions.* Baltimore: Black Classic Press.
Benneman, Walter I., Jr., O. Yarian and Alan M. Olson. 1982. *The Seeing Eye: Hermeneutical Phenomenology in the Study of Religion.* University Park and London: The Pennsylvania State University Press.
Bimwenyi, O. Kweshi. 1983. "Dieu dans La Théologie Africaine.» *Bulletin de Théologie Africaine.* Vol. V, no 9, janvier-juin 1983. pp. 85-91.
Bockie, Simon. 1993. *Death and the Invisible Powers: The World of Kongo Belief.* Bloomington and Indianapolis: University of Indiana Press.
Bohannan, Paul. 1966. *Social Anthropology.* Holt, Rinehart and Winston, Inc.
Bourdillon, M.F.C. 2000. "Witchcraft and Society." In Olupona, Jacob K., Editor, 2000, *African Spirituality: Forms, Meanings, and Expressions.* The Crossroads Publishing Company. pp. 176-197. New York.
Bozongwana, Rev. Wallace. 1983. "Ndebele Religion and Customs."
https://www.inkundla.net/net/imbali/child/20Birth/20and/20After.php, 11/12/2008

Bibliography

Brincard, Marie-Thérèse, Editor. 1983. *The Art of Metal in Africa.* The African-American Institute. New York.

Carlton, K.S. 1968. *Social Theory and African Tribal Organization.* Urbana, London: University of Illinois Press.

Carruthers, Jacob Hudson, Sr. 1995. *MDW NTR Divine Speech: A Historiographical Reflection of African Deep Thought from the Time of the Pharaohs to the Present.* London: Karnak House.

Centre d'Etudes des Religions Africaines. Editor. 1990. *L'Afrique et ses Formes de Vie Spirituelle.* Kinshasa: Facultés Catholiques de Kinshasa.

Chernoff, John M. 2000. "Spiritual Foundations of Dagbamba Religion and Culture." In Olupona, Jacob K., Editor, 2000, *African Spirituality : Forms, Meanings and Expressions.* New York: The Crossroad Publishing Company. Pp. 257-274.

Collins, Robert O. 1990. "Western and Central Sudan." In Collins, Robert O. Ed. 1990. *Western African History.* Princeton: Markus Wiener Publishers. Pp. 2-21.

Colleyn, J.P. 1988. Eléments d'Anthropologie Sociale et Culturelle. Bruxelles: Editions de l'Université de Bruxelles. P 156. Retrieved 10-22-2019.

Coulson, David. 1999 "Ancient Art of the Sahara." *National Geographic.vol195, no6, June 1999.* Pp. 98-119.

Crapo, Richly H. 1987. *Cultural Anthropology: Understanding Ourselves & Others.* The Duskin Publishing Group, Inc.

Criaule, Marcel and Germaine Dieterlen. 1965. "The Dogon." In Ford, Daryll, Editor. 1965. *African Worlds: Studies in the Cosmological Ideas and Social Values of African Peoples."* London: Oxford University Press.

Cuypers, J.B. 1965. "Les Bantous Interlacustres du Kivu." In Vansina. *Introduction à L'Ethnographie du Congo.* Kinshasa, Kisangani, Lubumbashi: Editions Universitaires du Congo.

Danfulani, Umar Habila Dadem. 2000. "Pa Divination: Ritual Performance and Symbolism among the Ngas, Mupun, and Mwaghavul of the Jos Plateau, Nigeria." In Olupona, Jacob K, Editor, 2000, *African Spirituality: Forms, Meanings, and Expressions.* New York: The Crossroad Publishing Company. pp. 87-111.

David, Rosalie. ND. *Religion and Magic in Ancient Egypt.* Penguin Books.

Davidson, Basil. 1991. *Africa in History: Themes and Outlines.* New York: Macmillan Publishing Company.

Davidson, Basil. 1977. *A history of Africa 1000-18000.* New York: Longman.

Davidson, Basil. 1969. *The African Genius: An Introduction to African Social and Cultural History.* Boston: Little, Brown and Company.

Davis, N.E. 1981. *A History of South Africa.* London: Longman.

Demolin, Didier. 1990. "Music and Dance in Northeastern Zaire, Part I: The Social Organization of Mangbetu Music." In *African Reflections: Art from Northeastern Zaire.* Eds. E. Schildkrout and C.A Keim. Seattle: University of Washington Press, 1990.

De Plaen, Guy. 1968: «Le Rôle social de la magie et de la sorcellerie chez les Bayansi.» *Cahiers Economiques et Sociaux.* Vol. VI, no 2. Kinshasa, Congo: IRES. 203-235.

Diallo, A. 2000. "Status of Fish Stock in Senegal." In Abban, E.K. et al (Eds). *Biodiversity and sustainable use of fish in the coastal zone.* Dakar: Centre de Recherches Oceanologiques de Dakar-Thiaroye. Pp 38-40.

Dieterlene, Germaine 1975. *Conversations with Ogotemmeli: An Introduction To Dogon Religious Ideas By Marcel Griaule, Germaine Dieterlene (Introduction).* Oxford University Press. USA.

Dieterlen, Germaine. 1957. "The Mande Creation Myth." *Africa,* Volume 27, Issue 2, April 1957, pp 124-138.

Dieterlene, G. 1955. « Mythe et organisation sociale au Soudan français.» *Journal des Africanistes/ Année 1955 /25 / pp 39-76* https://www.persee.fr/doc/jafr_0037-9166 1955_num_25_1_1873. Retrieved 4/30/2018.

Dimandja, Elu'a Kondo. 1997. "Légitimation du Pouvoir (avec applications a l'histoire politique du Zaire) ». *Cahiers des Religions Africaines.* Vol.31, no 6162, 1997. Pp. 65-81.

Bibliography

Diocèse de Mbuji-Mayi. 1997. « Mvita myela Baluba-Lubilanji kudi bukwa bisamba ». *Ecce Ancilla Domini* ,Special, Numero 2. Mbuji-Mayi, Notre Dame de Fatima : Coeur Immaculé de Marie:11-12.

Diop, Cheik Anta. 1991. *Civilization or Barbarism: an Authentic Anthropology.* Brooklyn, New York: Lawrence Hill Books.

Diop, Cheik Anta. 1974. *The African Origin of Civilization: Myth or Reality.* Chicago, Illinois: Lawrence Hill Books.

Dopamu, P. Ade. 1993. "Traditional Medicine with Particular Reference to the Yoruba of Western Nigeria." In Thomas-Emeagwali, Gloria, Editor. 1993. *African Systems of Science, Technology & Art: The Nigerian Experience.* London: Karnack House.

Ekechukwu, A. 1983. "The Problem of Suffering in Igbo Traditional Religion." *Bulletin of African Theology.* Kinshasa: Société Missionnaire Saint- Paul. Pp. 51-64.

El-Baz, Faroouk. 1988. « Finding a Pharaoh's Funeral Bark ». *National Geographic.* Vol. 173, NO 4. April 198. Pp. 514-533.Encyclopedia. 2019. "Mound Builders".

Faik-Nzuji, Clementine. 1967. *Essai de Méthodologie pour l'Etude des Proverbes Luba du Kasai.* Kinshasa: Ecole Normale Moyenne du Sacré-Cœur, Mémoire.

Faik-Nzuji, Clementine. 1974. *Kasala, Chant Héroïque des Luba.* Lubumbashi: Presses Universitaires du Zaïre.

Falola, Toyin. 2001. *Culture and Customs of Nigeria.* Westport, Connecticut: Greenwood Press.

Ferraro, Gary. 1992. *Cultural Anthropology. An Applied Perspective.* West Publishing Company.

Fikadu, Asmiro Abeje; Tsega Desalegn Wedu, and Endalew Abebe Derseh, et al. 2019. "Review of Economics of Teff in Ethiopia."*Crimson Publishers.* Published April 19, 2019. https://crimsonpublishers.com/oabb/pdf/OABB.000542.pdf. Retrieved 6-24-2020.

Flam, Jack D. "Signs and Symbols in Traditional Metal Art of the Western Sudan." In Brincard, Marie-Thérèse, Editor. 1983. New York: The African-American Institute. Pp. 19-30.

Frankfort, Henri. 2000. *Ancient Egyptian Religion: An Interpretation.* Mineola, New York: Dover Publications, INC.

Frobenius, Leo. 1983. « Lungononyo et Nkashama.» in *Mythes et Contes Populaires des Riverains du Kasai.* Bonn: Inter Nationes.

Brobenius, Leo. 1983. Aux Pays des défunts. » in *Mythes et Contes Populaires des Riverains du Kasai.* Bonn: Inter Nationes.

Fu-Kiau, Kimbwandende Kia Bunseki. 2001. *African Cosmology of the Bântu-Kongo: Principles of Life & Living.* Brooklyn, New York: Athelia Henrietta Press.

Fu-Kiau, Kimbwandènde kia Bunseki. 1991. *Self-Healing Power and Therapy: Old teaching from Africa.* New York: Vantage Press.

Fu-Kiau, K. Kia Bunseki. 1985. *The Mbongi: An African Political Institution.* Nyangwe, Zaire; Roxbury, MA: Omenana.

Gathogo, Julius. 2013. "Environmental management and African indigenous resources: echoes from Mutira Mission, Kenya 1920-2012)." In *Studia Historiae Ecclesiasticae* vol. 39/2.33-56 Pretoria: The Church History Society of South Africa). Online Version: https://en.wikipedia.org/wiki/Kikuyu_people#Origin Retrieved 5-28-2016.

Gizaw, Birhanu, Zerihun Tsegay, Genene Tefera, Endegena Aynalem, Endeshaw Abatneh, and Getasew Amsalu. 2018. "Traditional Knowledge on Teff (Eragrostistef) Farming Practice and Role of Crop Rotation to Enrich Plant Growth Promoting Microbes for Soil Fertility in Eastern Showa, Ethiopia". *Agricultural Research & Technology: open Access Journal.* Published June22, 2018. https://juniperpublishers.com/artoaj/pdf/ARTEOAJ.MS.ID.556001.pdf. Retrieved 6-19-2020.

Gore, Rick. 1991. « Ramses the Great ». National Geographic 179 (April): 2-31.

Gravrand, R.P. Henry cs.sp. 1990. « La Prière et la Spiritualité Africaines, Sources de Spiritualité et de Prière Chrétienne.» *Cahiers de Religions Africaines*, vol.24, n 47, janvier-juillet 1990 (137-153).

Gyekye, Kwame, "Ancestorship and Tradition." In Mario Beatty, Editor, 2001, *History of Africa and the Diaspora (AFR 201).* Acton, MA: Tapestry Press, Ltd. Pp. 63-65.

Hilliard. Constance B. 1998. "Ancient Mali: The Foretelling of the Great Sundiata's Birth." In

Bibliography

Constance B Hilliard. 1998. *Intellectual Traditions of Pre-Colonial Africa.* Pp 298-305. Boston: McGaw Hill.

Hublin, Jean-Jacques. 1999. *Archeology Magazine Archive.* Volume 52, Number 4, JulyAugust 1999. Reprinted in Beatty, Marion. 2001. History of Africa and The Diaspora (AFR 201).Pp. 92-96. Acton, MA: Tapestry Press, Ltd.

Idowu, Bolaji. 1994. *Olódùmarè: God in Yoruba Belief.* Brooklyn, New York: A&B Books Publishers.

Jackson, John J. 1990. *Introduction to African Civilizations.* New York: Carol Publishing Group.

Jahn, Janheinz. 1961. *Muntu the new African Culture.* New York: Grove Press, Inc.

Jefferson, Margo and Elliott P. Skinner. 1991. *Roots of Time: A Portrait of African Life and Culture.* Trenton, New Jersey: African World Press, Inc.

Jell-Bahlsen, Sabine. 2000. "The Lake Goddess, Uhammiri/Ogbuide: The Female Side of the Universe in Igbo Cosmology." In Olupona, Jacob K., Editor, 2000, *African Spirituality: Forms, Meanings and Expressions.* New York: The Crossroad Publishing Company. Pp. 38-41.

Jiddawi, Narriman Saley and Marcus C. Ohman. 2002. "Marine Fisheries in Tanzania." Abstract. *Ambio A Journal of the Human Environment.*31(7-8):518-527 . December 2002.

Jiddawi, Narriman Saley and Marcus C. Ohman. 2002. "Marine Fisheries in Tanzania." Abstract. *Ambio A Journal of the Human Environment.*31(7-8):518-527 . December 2002.

July, Robert W. 1992. *A History of the African People.* Fourth Edition. Prospect Heights, Illinois: Waverland Press.

Kabasele Lumbala, F. 2005. *Ndi Muluba.* Louvain-la-Neuve. Editions Panubula.

Kalanda, Mabika. 1992. *La Revelation du Tiakani.* Kinshasa: Lask.

Kalanda, A. 1959. *Baluba et Lulua: Une ethnie à la recherche d'un nouvel équilibre.* Bruxelles: Editions de Remarques Congolaises.

Kalu, Ogbu U. 2000. "Ancestral Spirituality and Society in Africa." In Olupona, Jacob K., Editor, 2000, *African Spirituality: Forms, Meanings and Expressions.* New York: The Crossroad Publishing Company. Pp. 54-84.

Kanyinda-Lusanga, M.T.M. 1974. *Les Institutions Socio-Politiques Traditionnelles et les Institutions Politiques Modernes au Zaire: Le cas de la société luba du Kasai.* Louvain: Université Catholique de Louvain, Dissertation doctorale.

Kanyinda-Lusanga, Theodore. 1968. *Pouvoir Traditionnel et Institutions Politiques Modernes chez les Baluba du Sud-Kasai.* Kinshasa: Université Lovanium, Mémoire, Kanyinda, Lusanga et Guy Malengreau. *Continuité et Discontinuité de l'Action Administrative dans l'Organisation Territoriale du Zaire.* Kinshasa: Centre Interdisciplinaire d'Etudes et de Documentation Politique (CIEDOP), 1985.

Kaplan, Flora Edouwaye S. 2000. "Some Thought on Ideology, Beliefs, and Sacred Kingship among the Edo (Benin) People of Nigeria." In Olupona, Jacob K., Editor, 2000, *African Spirituality: Forms, Meanings and Expressions.* New York: The Crossroad Publishing Company. Pp. 114-151.

Katanga-Tshitenge, Joseph D. 1969. *Grandes Périodes Educatives chez les Baluba.* Kinshasa: Editions IMPRIDECO.

Kenyatta, Jomo. « Marriage System ». Reprinted in Skinner, Elliott P., Editor, 1973. *Peoples and Cultures of Africa.* Garden City, New York: The Doubleday/Natural History Press. Pp. 280-296.

Kenyatta, Jomo. 1938. *Facing Mount Kenya by Jomo Kenyatta.* London: Secker and Warburg.

Kibanda, Matungila. 1997. "Le Rite Woyo Bénédiction des Récoltes (Mwamwa) Comme Act de Célébration d'un Ordre Economique Social et Ecologique ». *Cahiers des Religions Africaines.* Vol. 31, no 61-62, 1997, 185-205.

Komba, Paul Nzinga. 1997. "Continuity and Discontinuity in the religious Role of African Political Systems." *Cahiers des Religions Africaines.* Vol. 31, no 61-62, 1997, 105-119.

Konneh, Augustine. 1996. *Religion, Commerce, and the Integration of the Mandingo in Liberia.* Lanham, MD: University Press of America.

Krige, E. J. 1936. "The Military Organization of the Zulu." In Skinner, P., Editor. 1973. *Peoples and*

Bibliography

Cultures of Africa. Garden City, New York: Natural History Press. Pp. 483-502

Kuper, Hilda. 1986. *The Swazi: A South African Kingdom.* Second Edition. New York: Holt, Rinehart and Winston.

Levi-Strauss, Claude 1958. *Anthropologie Structurale.* Paris: Plon.

Levi-Strauss, Claude 1949. *Les Structures Elémentaires de la Parenté.* Paris: Presses Universitaires de France.

Lumor, Francis. 2009. *Significance of Animal Symbolism among the Akans-of AKyem Abuakwa Traditional Area.* Kumasi, Ghana: Kwame Nkrumah University of Science and Technology. College of Art and Social Sciences B.A. (Hons.) Publishing Studies http://ir.knust.edu.gh/bitstream/123456789/374/1/fulltxt.pdf. Retrieved 1-5-2020.

Lufuluabo, Fr. Mizeka. 1977. *L'Anti-Sorcier Face à la Science.* Mbujimayi: Editions Franciscaines.

Lufuluabo, François. 1961. *Vers une Théodicée Bantue.* Mechliniae: Documents et Recherches.

Lumor, Francis. 2009. *Significance of Animal Symbolism among the Akans-of AKyem Abuakwa Traditional Area.* Kumasi, Ghana: Kwame Nkrumah University of Science and Technology. College of Art and Social Sciences B.A. (Hons.) Publishing Studies http://dspace.knust.edu.gh/bitstream/123456789/374/1/fulltxt.pdf. Retrieved 2-23-2020.

MacGaffey, Wyatt. 2000. « Art and Spirituality ». In Olupona, Editor. 2000. *African Spirituality: Forms, Meanings and Expressions.* The Crossroad Publishing Company, 223-256.

Magesa, Laurenti. 1997. *African Religion: The Moral Traditions of Abundant Life.* Maryknoll, New York: ORBIS BOOKS.

Mair, L. 1970. *Primitive Government.* Baltimore: Penguin Books.

Malengreau, Guy. 1985. «Cours de Politique Indigène». In Kanyinda-Lusanga and Guy Malengreau. *Continuité et Discontinuité de l'Action Administrative dans l'Organisation Territoriale du Zaire.* Kinshasa: Centre Interdisciplinaire d'Etudes et de Documentation Politiques (CIEDOP): 90-282.

Matungila, Kibanda 1997. "Le Rite Woyo de Bénédiction des Récoltes (Mwamwa) comme Act de Célébration d'un ordre Economique Social et Ecologique». In Centre d'Etudes des Religions Africaines, 1997, *Religions Traditionnelles Africaines et Projet de Société.* Kinshasa: Facultés Catholiques de Kinshasa. Pp. 185-205.

Mbiti, John, S. 1991. "Flowers in the Garden: The Role of Women in African Religion." In Olupona, Jacob K., Editor, 1991, *African Traditional Religions in Contemporary Society.* St. Paul, Minnesota. Pp. 59-72.

Mbiti, Joseph S. 1970. *African Religions and Philosophy.* Garden City, New York: Anchor Books, Doubleday & Company, Inc.

Mbiti, John. ND. "General Manifestations of African Religiosity." An Exploratory Paper at the meeting of the Standing Committee on The Contribution of Africa to the Religious Heritage of the World. http://www.afrikaworld.net/afrel/mbiti.htm. Retrieved 8/8/2007

Middleton, John. 1965. *The Lugbara of Uganda.* New York: Holt, Rinehart and Winston.

Millard, Candice. 2001. "Keepers of the Faith: The Living Legacy of Aksum." *National Geographic*, July 2001:100-125.

Miller, Peter. 1988. « Riddle of the Pyramid Boats ». *National Geographic.* Vol. 173, No 4, April 1988. Pp. 534-550.

Morlighem, H. et T. Fourche. 1973. *Une Bible Noire.* Bruxelles: Max Arnold.

Motley, Mary Penick. 1969. *Africa : Its Empires, Nations, and People.* Detroit: Wayne State University Press.

Mpyana-Yenga. 1975. *Intronisation et Funerailles des Chefs dans l'Entité Ciyamba.* Lubumbashi: Université Nationale du Zaire, Mémoire.

Mudiji, Malamba Gilombe. 1989. *Le langage des Masques Africains: Etudes des formes et fonctions symboliques des Mbuya des Phende.* Kinshasa: Facultés Catholiques de Kinshasa. Mudiji, Théodore Malamba, « Liens du Pouvoir au Sol ». *Cahiers des Religions Africaines.* Vol. 31, no 61-62, 1997, 31-45.

Mudimbe, V. Y. 1991. *Parables & Fable: Exegesis, Textuality, and Politics in Central Africa.*

Bibliography

Madison: The University of Wisconsin Press.

Mufuta, Kabembe.1990. « Croyances Traditionnelles et Pratiques Spirituelles». In Centre d'Etudes des Religions Africaines. 1990. *L'Afrique et ses Formes de Vie Spirituelle*. Op Cit. Pp. 173-192.

Mufuta, Kabemba. 1974. "Littérature Orale et Authenticité (II)". *Revue Jiwe*. Lubumbashi, Zaire : MPR/UNAZA, 55-75.

Mufuta Kabemba (Patrice). 1969. *Le chant kasalà des Luba*. Paris: Julliard, Collection : Les classiques africains.

Mukenge, Tshilemalema. 2002. *Culture and Customs of the Congo*. Westport, Connecticut: Greenwood Press.

Mukenge, Léonard. 1967. «Croyances Religieuses et Structures Socio-Familiales en Société Luba Bwena Muntu, Bakishi, Milambu». *Cahiers Economiques et Sociaux*, V, 1. Kinshasa: Institut de Recherches Economiques et Sociales (IRES), 3-95.

Mulago, Vincent. 1991. "Traditional African Religion and Christianity". In Jacob K. Olupona, Editor, *Traditional African Religions in Contemporary Society*. St Paul Minnesota: Paragon House. Pp. 119-134. Pp. 120-121.

Mulago, gwa Cikala Musharhamina. 1973. *La Religion Traditionnelle des Bantu et leur Vision du Monde*. Kinshasa: Presses Universitaires du Zaire.

Neimark, Philip John.1993. *The Way of the Orisa*. San Francisco: Harper San Francisco.

Newbury, Catharine. 1988. *The Cohesion of Oppression: Clientship and Ethnicity in Rwanda, 1860-1960*. New York: Columbia University Press.

Ngandu, Wa Kalonji. 2002. *Tuntuntu Ntuntu*. Baton Rouge, Louisiana: Nkashama Ngandu Pius.

Ngindu, A. 1969. "Propos et problèmes concernant le culte des morts chez les baluba du Kasai," *Cahiers des Religions Africaines*. Kinshasa: Facultés Catholiques, III, 5.

Niangoran-Bouah, Georges. 1991. "The Talking Drum: A Traditional African Instrument of Liturgy and Mediation with the Sacred." In Olupona, Jacob K. 1991. *African Traditional Religions in Contemporary Society*. St. Paul Minnesota: Paragon House. Pp. 81-92 .

Nyon, Mgr. B. 1990. « Apport et Originalité de la Spiritualité Africaine ». *Cahiers des Religions Africaines*. Vol. 24, n 47, janvier-juillet 1990, 127-135 (129.

Nzongola, Ntalaja. 1975. *Urban Administration in Zaire: A Study of Kananga. 1971-73*. Madison: University of Wisconsin, Doctoral Dissertation.

Nzuji Madiya (Clémentine). 1974. *Kasala: chant héroïque luba*. Kinshasa: Presses Universitaires du Zaire.

Obeng, Pashington 2000. "Asante Catholicism: an African Appropriation of the Roman Catholic Religion." In Olupona, Jacob K., Editor, 2000, *African Spirituality: Forms, Meanings and Expressions*. New York: The Crossroad Publishing Company. Pp. 372-400.

Okeja, Uchenna. 2016. *Mbiti and Current Issues in African Philosophy*. The Journal of Traditions & Beliefs: Vol.2, Article 5. Oklahoma State University Board of Regents 1994. http://afs.okstate.edu/breeds/region/f-africa.html. Retrieved 5-25-2019.

Oklahoma State University Department of Animal Science. 1997. "Livestock Breeds Originating from Africa." *OSU's Breeds of Livestock* - African Breeds. http://afs.okstate.edu/breeds/. Retrieved 5-1-2020.

Olupona, Jacob K., Editor. 2000. *African Spirituality: Forms, Meanings and Expressions*. New York: The Crossroad Publishing Company.

Olupona, Jacob K. "Introduction." In Olupona, Jacob K., Editor, 2000, *African Spirituality: Forms, Meanings and* Expressions. New York: The Crossroad Publishing Company. Pp. xv-xxxvi.

Olupona, Jacob K., Editor. 1991. *African Traditional Religion in Contemporary Society*. St. Paul, Minnesota: Paragon House.

Olupona, Jacob K., "Major Issues in the Study f African Traditional Religion". In Olupona, Jacob K., Editor. 1991. *African Traditional Religion in Contemporary Society*. St. Paul, Minnesota: Paragon House. 25-33.

Omer-Cooper, J.D. 1994. "The Zulu Aftermath." In Collins, Robert O. Editor. 1994. *Problems in African History: The Pre-colonial Centuries*. New York: Marcus Wiener Publishing, Inc.

Bibliography

Omoyajowo, Joseph Akinyele. 1991. "The Role of Women in African Traditional Religion." In Olupano, Jacob K. Ed., *African Traditional Religions in Contemporary Society.* St. Paul Minnesota: Parogon House, 1991,73-80.

Oosthuizen, G. C. 2000. "The Task of African Traditional Religion in the Church's Dilemma in South Africa." In Olupona, Jacob. K., Editor, 2000, *African Spirituality: Forms, Meanings and* Expressions. New York: The Crossroad Publishing Company. Pp. 277-283.

Oosthuizen, Gerhardus Cornelis. 1991. "The Place of Traditional Religion in Contemporary South Africa." In Olupona, Jacob K., Editor, 1991, *African Traditional Religion in Contemporary Society*. St. Paul, Minnesota: Paragon House. Pp. 35-50.

Osae, T.A., S.N. Nwabara, and A.T.O. Odunsi. 1973. *A History of West Africa: A.D. 1000 to the Present.* New York: Hall and Wang.

Otte, MJ, and P Chilonda: 2002. "Cattle and small ruminant production systems in sub-Saharan Africa: A Systematic Review." Rome: FAO Agriculture Department. http://www.fao.org/3/a-y4176e.pdf. Retrieved 3-16-2020

Parsons, Talcott. 1951. *The Social System*, New York: Free Press.

Presley, Cora Ann. 2018. *Kikuyu Women, the Mau Mau Rebellion and Social Change in Kenya.* New York: Routledge.

Rashidi, Runoco. 2002. "Africa in Early Asian Civilizations: A Historical Overview." In Rashidi 2002. *African Presence in Early Asia.* New Brunswick (USA) and London (UK): Transaction Publishers. Pp. 21-58.

Rashidi, Runoko. 1992. *Introduction to African Classical Civilizations.* London: Karnak House.

Ray, Benjamin C. 2000. "African Shrines as Channels of Communication." In Olupona, Jacob K., Editor, 2000, *African Spirituality: Forms, Meanings and Expressions.* New York: The Crossroad Publishing Company. Pp. 26-37.

Ray, Benjamin C. 2000. *African Religions: Symbol, Ritual, and Continuity.* Second Edition. Upper Sadder River, New Jersey: Prentice Hall.

Reefe, Thomas Q. 1981. *The Rainbow and the Kings.* Berkeley: The University of California Press.

Roach, John. 2008. "Massive Genetic Study Supports 'Out of Africa' Theory." National Geographic News, February 21, 2008.

Roberts, Mary Polly Nooter. 2011. "Memory and Identity at the Threshold in Gregory Maqoma's Beautiful Me." *African Arts*; Winter 2011, 44,4; Pro Quest p.76.

Runoko. Editor. 2002. *African Presence in Early Asia.* New Brunswick (U.S.A.) and London (UK): Transaction Publishers. Pp. 21-58.

Sangpam, N. S. 1994. *Pseudocapitalism and the Overpoliticized State.* Brookfield, VT: Ashgate.

Sanon, Mgr A.T. 1990. "Religion et Spiritualité Africaine: La Quête Spirituelle de l'Humanité Africaine ». *Cahiers des Religions Africaines*, vol. 24, n. 47, janvier-juillet 1990, 37-54.

Shillington, Kevin. 1993. *History of Africa.* London: The Macmillan Press LTD.

Silverberg, Robert. 1969. "..and the Mound Builders Vanished from the Earth". *American Heritage Magazine.* Volume 20, Issue 4.

Simmons, William S. 1971. *Eyes of the Night: Witchcraft among a Senegalese People*. Boston: Little, Brown and Company.

Skinner, Elliott P. Editor. 1973. *Peoples and Cultures of Africa.* Garden City, New York: The Doubleday/Natural History Press.

Sobhani, Delena. 2016. "Counting Sheep in Senegal." *Berkley Center for Religion, Peace & World Affairs*. September 19, 2016. https://berkleycenter.georgetown.edu/posts/counting-sheep-in-senegal. Retrieved 3-18-2020.

Soyinka, Wole. 1971. *La dance de la fôret.* Oswald: Honfleur.

Spear, Thomas. 1994. "Bantu Migrations" Excerpts from Spear, Thomas. 1981. *Kenya's Past.* Essex: Longman. Pp. 29-33. Reprinted in Collins, Robert O., ed. *Problems in African History: The Precolonial Centuries.* New York and Princeton: Markus Wiener Publishing, Inc. Pp. 95-99.

Stein, Philip L. and Bruce M. Rowe. 1989. *Physical Anthropology.* Fourth Edition. New York: McCraw-Hill Book Company.

Bibliography

Sturtevant, William. 1964. "Studies in Ethnoscience." American Anthropologist. 66 (3) part 2: 99-131.

Tempels, Placide, R. P. 1965. *La Philosophie Bantoue*. Paris: Présence Africaine.

The Economist. 2019. "Why people in Senegal pay a fortune for fancy sheep." Printed Edition/Middle East and Africa. Dakar May 16th 2019.

The National Earth Science Teachers Association. nd. "Inuit Culture, Traditions, and History." *Windows to the Universe*.
https://www.windows2universe.orgearth/polarinuitculture.Html.

Theuws, Th. 1960. "Naître et mourir dans le ritual luba. » *Zaire* XIV.

Thomas, L.V. and Luneau, R. 1976. *La terre africaine et ses religions*. Paris: Librairie Larousse.

Tissières, Hélène. 1998. « Memory: Luba Art and the Making of History «Exhibition Review. *Research in African Literatures: Spring 1998: 29, 1: ProQuest page 237. Exhibition curated by Mary Nooter Roberts.*

Tshibanda-Mbwebwe, Christian. 1971. *L'Influence du Paysannat sur les Structures Socio-Economiques Traditionnelles du Village Nsona-Shabanza*. Kinshasa: Université Nationale du Zaire, Mémoire.

Tshibangu, Tshishiku, Mgr. 1993. *Diba dia Kuleja Dikima ne Ditekemena Dijima Bwa Matuku Acivwavwa*. Mbuji-Mayi: Cilowa.

Twinomugisha, Charles "Compare Traditional Religion of Baganda People and Current Religions in Uganda." Article posted 12/18/2008.

Uchendu, Victor C. 1965. *The Igbo of Southeast Nigeria*. New York: Holt, Rinehart and Winston.

Uzukwu, E. Elochukwu. 1990. « Igbo Spirituality as Revealed through Igbo Prayers ». In Centre d'Etudes des Religions Africaines. 1990. OP. Cit. Pp. 155-172.

Van Caeneghem, R. 1956. *La notion de Dieu chez les Baluba du Kasai*. Bruxelles : Académie Royale des Sciences d'Outre Mer. Reprint and New Preface by Munkamba Kadiata Nzemba.

Van Wing, J. 1959. *Etudes Bakongo*, 2e éd. Bruxelles: Desclée De Brouwer. Extracts. In Mulago 1973. Op. Cit. Pp. 31-41, 87-92.

Vansina, Jan. 1965. *Introduction a l'Ethnographie du Congo*. Kinshasa: Editions Universitaires du Congo.

Vansina, Jan. 1966. *Kingdoms of the Savana*. Madison: The University of Wisconsin Press.

Vansina, Jan. 1965. *Les Anciens Royaumes de la Savane*. Léopoldville: Institut de Recherches Economiques et Sociales.

Vebeek, L. "Attitudes Vis-à-vis des Biens Matériels ». *Cahiers des Religions Africaines* Vol. 31, no 61-62, 1997, 177-183.

Verdu, Paul. 2012. «Perspectives de la génétique humaine sur l'origine de la diversité *de populations des pygmées d'Afrique Centrale* ». Journal des africanistes, 82-1/2,2012. Pp.53-71. https://journals.openedition.org/africanistes/4269?lang=en. Retrieved 10-2019.

Visonà, Monica Blackmun et al. 2001. *A History of Art in Africa*. New York: Prentice Hall, Inc., and Harry N. Abrams, INC., Publishers.

Waife, Ronald. 1978. *Traditional Methods of Birth Control in Zaire*. Pathpapers Number 4. The Pathfinder Fund.

Watt, W. Lyne. 1942. "Stall-Feeding of Goats and Sheep by the Kikuyu Tribe, Kenya." *The East African Agricultural Journal*. October 1942.

Webster, Donavan. 1999. ''Journey to the Heart of the Sahara." National Geographic. vol. 195, no 3, March 1999. Pp. 2-33.

Westerlund, David, "Spiritual Beings as Agents of Illness." In Olupona, Jacob K., Editor. 2000, *African Spirituality: Forms, Meanings, and Expressions*. New York: The Crossroad Publishing Company. Pp. 152-175.

Weydert, Jean. 1938. *Les Baluba Chez Eux*. Heffingen: Grand-Duche de Luxembourg.

Wicker, Kathleen O'Brien. 2000. "Mami Water in African Religion and Spirituality." In Olupona, Jacob K. Editor. 2000. Op Cit. Pp. 198-222.

Wilcox, A. R. ND. *The Rock Art of Africa*. Rutledge Library Editions – Archeology.
https://books.google.com/books?id=qilKDwAAQBAJ&pg=PA197&lpg=PA197&dq=Do roth

Bibliography

ea+Bleek+1933+Rock+Painting&source=bl&ots=7EFMK2Xgb5&sig=ACfU3U1z8jNg-NKobKqjitvsXFn6uqtGA&hl=en&sa=X&. Retrieved 3-12-2020.

Williams, Chancellor. "Chapter VIII, The Resurrection and the Life: Case Studies by Stata." In

Williams, Chancellor. 1987. *The Destruction of the Black Civilization: Great Issues of a Race from 4500 B.C. to 2000 A.D.* Chicago: Third Word Press.

Yoka, Lye Mudaba. 1990. "Spiritualité et Créativité Artistique Aujourd'hui." In *Cahiers des Religions Africaines, vol.24., n.47, janvier-juillet 1990.* Pp. 229-237.

Young, Crawford. 1965. *Politics in the Congo.* Princeton, New Jersey: Princeton University Press.

Zahan, Dominique. 2000. "Some Reflections on African Spirituality." In Jacob K. Olupona, Editor, *African Spirituality: Forms, Meanings and Expressions.* New York: The Crossroad Publishing Company. Pp. 3-25.

Index

A

a Bwanga bwa Njiminyi Story 29
a compassionate caretaker 205
addressing moral violations 175
African First Peoples in Asia and Oceania 290
Akan people (The Akan Forest States) 19, 244, 298, 300, 301
akh (intercessor spirit to God on behalf of the living and the dead) 24
Aksum Stela Towers 110
Alliance Pacts: 243
amandhla – lower mind 19
ancestors as God's mediators and family elders 147
Ancestorship and Eldership: 155
ancestor shrines 158
ancestral spirits 27, 39, 78, 96, 106, 150, 151, 155, 156, 158, 159, 165, 169, 174, 175, 188, 189, 200, 236, 257
animal stories 83, 84
ara, ẹgbẹ (body) 19
architectural monuments 110
Asante Model 244
Atum-Re 285
Ay-Situ: in Pre-Islamic Somalia 145

B

babies' returning spirits 44, 56
Balubaale in the religion of Baganda 146
Bantu migrants 302
ba (spirit of the dead, could exit and reenter the body) 24
Behaviors that constitute African religious ethics 165
Belief in mystical powers 24, 28, 48
beliefs about ancestral veneration 148
biological kinship 195
biological systems' and life organs' movements 53
Birth Names 79
Birth Rites for all Newborn Babies: 45
Birth Titles 79
Black First Peoples in Australia 292
Black First Peoples in the Americas 293
body decorations 112, 116
breath of life from divine Creation 17, 69, 128, 130, 182

C

Call and Response Dialogue 86
Call to Priesthood 33
Candomblé 109
care for children 205
care for particular crops grown in Lubaland 271
care for the dying 205
care for the household 205, 207
care for the sick 205
care for the unborn child 215
cares for the departing 227
caring for the baby at birth 216
cattle in Africa 266
Chiefs and Kings as Unity Builders: 247
Chi-Ukwu (Igbo) 41, 43, 123, 133
Circumstances Prompting Community Prayers to the Supreme Being 152
Clan and Totemic Names 80
Commemoratives 89
communication with the ancestors 156
Community-strengthening rituals 201
Consecration of the Achiever of Wealth 36
cradle songs 83, 84
creation by breathing 144, 190
creation by divine speech 69, 127
creation by gesture 69, 127
creation by manual action 127
creation by self-emanation 127
creation in four 128
creation in pairs of seniors and juniors 129
Creation movements 51
creation myths 127, 146, 181
creation processes 131, 182
creative imagination 92, 95, 101
Cult to Great Spirit Lyangombe 155

D

decorative scenes of Pharaohs' tombs 112
Dedication of the Luba Senior Wife 35
Desert Rock Painters 288
Determining the Baby's Spiritual Identity 44
devotion to ancestral spirits 155
devotion to great spirits 154
dikasa dya mu bulaba (footprint) 23, 30
Dinka Priesthood 34
diseases with known treatments 220
diseases with particular cultural interpretations 222
Divination, Prescriptions and Remedies 27
Divine creation and the making of the human community 181

Index

Divine creation of the Luba of the Congo, DRC 61
Divine creation of the Yoruba of Nigeria 284
Divine creation of the Zulu of South Africa 18
Divine creation stories of the Bambara and Fulani of West Africa 17
Divine creation stories of the Dogon of Mali 61, 69, 127, 143
Divine creation stories of the Fon of Benin 61
Divine creation stories of the Gikuyu of Kenya 233, 255
Divine creation stories of the Kongo of the Congo, DRC 20
Diviners 26
domesticated animals in Ancient Egypt 266, 280

E

Egyptian Creation Trinity: Nun, Shu, and Tefnut 127, 285
Egyptian pyramids 59, 110
Egyptian solar Trinity: Osiris (husband), Isis (wife), Horus (son) 127, 145
Elamites (in Elam, Iran) 297
émi (spirit infused by Creator Olódùmarè) 19
endemic diseases 220, 224
epic and lamentation songs 88
Eshu, Ogun, Olókun 144
Ethiopian Coptic churches 59
ethnic pride and appeal to unity 88
examples of prayers to the Supreme Being 153
existential body movements 51
external politics 242

F

Failed Rules of Rotation: 240
family-kinship community builder 181
Faro 181, 182
fauna and flora 133, 134, 233
fetishes 26, 106, 108, 230, 257
figurative monuments 108
fisheries 138, 139, 140, 298, 299
flexible body structure movements 53, 61
food crop plants indigenous to Africa 271
Fortification of the Senior Wife's House. 106

G

Gender Roles 186
Gikuyu Religion 155, 190, 257
Gikuyu's sycamore plant totem 258, 278
goat and sheep in Africa 268
God's attributes as the Omnipotent One 122, 234
God's Superiority to All Created Powers 125
Great Spirit Mindiss of the Sérèer of Senegal's Sine Valley 154
Great Zimbabwe 111

H

Harappants and Dravidians (in the Indus Valley) 297
healers 31, 150
hominids 283, 284, 285, 286
house paintings 112

I

immigrant Woot and Bushong founders (Kingdom of Kuba) 235, 303
Immortality 24, 40
Indirect Rule 241
Inner Divine Spirit and Cognate Life-sustaining Forces 18
inner spirit 48
isitunzi – etheric body 19
itongo – ray 18

J

Journey to Consecration 34

K

Kabale, Benda and Mikombo wa Kalewu (among the Luba) 146
ka (life force spirit) 23
Kalûnga (Kongo) 51, 122, 131
Karanga (The Great Kingdom of Zimbabwe) 63, 111, 302, 310
King Shaka-Zulu (the Zulu Empire) 239, 245
Kings' Rituals of Political Integration 247
kinship-based collective sacred rituals 200
kinship community 195
Kongo Religion 18, 20, 149
Kuba Model 244

L

Lord Spirits 128, 143, 130
Luba Creation Trinity: Maweja Nangila (Creator), Maweja Cyama (First Lady), Maweja wa Cyama (Firstborn Son) 128, 143, 144, 182, 234
Luba incarnate spirit Trinity: Kabale, Benda, and Mikombo wa Kalewu 146
Luba Kasai Model 246
Luba kinship generations 196
Luba self-exiled leader Chibinda Iunga (the Lunda Empire) 242, 303
Lukasa Memory Board of the Luba 103
Lunda Model 245

Index

Lunda twin princess, Kinguri and Cinyama, (Kingdoms of Kasanji and Lwena) 242, 243, 303
Lyangombe among the peoples of the Great Lakes of East Africa 147, 155

M

Maa Ngala (Bambara and Fulani) 17, 61, 122
Makenga: A Sole Seer-Healer 32
Makenga's Acquisition of Supernatural Powers 32
Makenga's Supernatural Gifts and Requirements 32
Malinke (Mali Empire) 88, 298, 299
Manga to Produce Desired Outcomes 30
Marriage Alliance with Potential External Enemies 243
marriage as a divine institution 183
marriage as a kinship alliance between the groom's family and the bride's family 185
mashi (blood, vehicle of life) 21
Maturity Names and Initiation Names 80
Maweja Nangila (Luba) – God as Creator 124, 128, 130, 144, 146, 182, 184, 234
Mawu and Lisa (Fon of Benin) 61
mbôngi: kinship-based community politics 199
Medicine Men (Women) 28
menga (blood, houses and vehicles the breath of life) 20
mfumu kutu (double, resides in the air) 20
Mindiss: Great Spirit of the Sérèer of Senegal's Sine Valley 154, 155, 160
minerals 137, 138, 140, 277, 279
mogya (reason) 19
Mongala (Mande) 234
Mongo Bilima 159
moral foundations for marriage stability 188
moral imprecations 175
moral restraints 171
moral transgressions /violations 172
moyo (heart, organ of life) 21
moyo (principle of life, eternal) 20
moyo (soul, seat of emotions) 22
moyo (the inner voice, conscience) 21
mubidi (physical body) 21
mudidimbi (shadow) 23
Mvelimqanti (Swazi) – The First to Appear 41, 152
Mvidi Mukulu 44, 81, 124, 126, 234
Mystical Agents of Good 26
Mystical, Personal Magical Powers 29, 48

N

nature spirits 48, 149, 159, 160, 291

Ndzundza Ndebele House Painting 115
Ngai (Gikuyu) 122, 123, 124, 152, 190, 233, 250
Ngoyi and Pamba (Luba of the Congo, DRC) 285
Nilote conquerors 304
nitu (sacred body, permeated by the principle of life) 20
Nomadic Kanembu People (Kanem-Borno) 301
Nshima Starchy Meal 96, 100, 173, 193, 210
nsuni (human body as flesh) 20
ntoro (total sum of inherited characteristics) 19
Nubians' building of Upper Egypt and expansion to Lower Egypt 294
Nummo Twins 182, 202
Nzambi, other name of Mvidi Mukulu, God (Luba) 32, 109

O

Odùdúwà and Shango in Yoruba religion 146, 235
offerings and sacrifices to the ancestors 158
okàn (heart as seat of emotions and psychic energy) 19
okra (guiding spirit, bearer of destiny) 19
Olódùmarè (Yoruba) 17, 19, 34, 109, 122, 125, 144, 151, 182, 233, 235, 255, 284
Orèlúéré 132, 182, 233, 251
Original Immortality and the Advent of Death 40
orí-inú (Internal head, controls and guides activities) 20
orí (physical head) 19
Orìshà-nlá 17, 19, 127, 233

P

Parallel Administrations: 249
performance movements 56, 60
personal names 79, 198
Personal Names as Reflection of Social Relations 79
Physical Personification of God 123
Political Organization 237
political power 201, 235, 242, 259
Prayer to God 151
Prayer to God expressing a relationship of dependence 151
preeminence of the senior wife 105
preventive Manga among the Luba 29
procreation as a mission from divine creation 189
Procreation as a Mission from Divine Creation 189
Procreation as Genetic Package Transfer 190
Proper Investiture Rituals 236
Proverbs Fostering Sociability 192

R

reincarnation 17, 40, 43, 189, 223
repartees between rivals 69, 73, 92
riddles and enigmas 69, 70, 92
right of access to public places (freedom of movement) 170
rights to life, physical integrity, and food 168
right to the integrity of one's sexual sacredness 169

S

Sabaians (In Southern Arabia) 296
Sacred Attitudes 257
SACRED MUTUAL STEWARDSHIP OF HUMANS AND NATURAL SPECIES 255
sacred natural rights 166, 167, 168, 171
sanctions for moral transgressions 173
seers 25, 31, 150
Self-Exile 242
Simboumba Tanganagati 234
similar manga between the Luba and the Dagbamba 30
Social Rank Titles 81
Somali aesthetic implements 112
Songye Balopwe under the Leadership of Nkongolo Mwamba 178, 242, 303
Soninke (Ghana Kingdom) 298, 299
Sorko Fishermen's Communities (Songhay Empire) 300
sovereignty rights over one's property 170
special care for millet, teff, and native rice 275, 276, 277, 279
Speech Articulations 88
spiritual care for children 214
spiritualization 30
Spiritualization through Death 40
Spiritualization through Ordination into Priesthood 33
Spiritualization through Trance 30
Spiritual Seers-Healers 31
stewardship 192
stone monument construction 59
Sumerians (in Mesopotamia) 296
sunsum (responsible for character) 19
supernatural sanctions for moral transgressions/violations 174
Symbolic Actions 101
Symbolic Objects 102
Symbolic Representations of Relationships 103

T

Territorial Autonomy 240
the ethical order given to humans by God 165, 171, 173
the family community 183
The First Peoples 287
the Hema cattle care and cow naming system 267, 268
the idea of community in the Luba creation story 182
the individual and the community 181
the individual and the community in African philosophy of life 183
the right to one's juniors' respect and tributes of the first fruits 169
Tiebele Tiny Village's painted houses 116
Tool Making 61
traditional medicine 28, 256, 257
trees of life
  (baobab, palm tree, Sahara and Kalahari Desert trees of life) 135, 137, 140
twelve power-releasing orifices on the human body 24

U

Uhammiri/Ogbuide Anyanwu, Ala, and Amadioha: among the Igbo 43, 103, 125, 145, 154
umzimba – physical body 19
Unkulunkulu (Zulu) 123
use of appropriate kinship terminology 196
utiwetongo – spiritual mind 18
utiwomuntu – human mind 18
utwesilo – animal mind 19

V

violations of seniority rights 179
vuvulu (human body as physical structure) 20

W

Wene, also called Nimi a Lukeni (Kingdom of Kongo) 303
Who God is to the Luba 124
witches among the Luba 25
witches as agents of illness and death - the Badyaranké of Senegal 25
Women's hand-made jewelry 115

Y

Yansi experience with fetishes 26
Yorùbá and Luba Numbering Systems 82
Yorùbá Oba 247

Yorùbá Priest 33

Z

Zulu Model 245